$f\mathbf{P}$

Sam^l Adams

# Samuel Adams

## A Life

## Ira Stoll

*Free Press*

New York London Toronto Sydney

Free Press
A Division of Simon & Schuster, Inc.
1230 Avenue of the Americas
New York, NY 10020

First Free Press hardcover edition November 2008

FREE PRESS and colophon are trademarks of Simon & Schuster, Inc.

For information about special discounts for bulk purchases,
please contact Simon & Schuster Special Sales at 1-800-456-6798 or
business@simonandschuster.com

*Book design by Ellen R. Sasahara*

Manufactured in the United States of America

1   3   5   7   9   10   8   6   4   2

Library of Congress Control Number: 2008015005
ISBN-13: 978-0-7432-9911-4
ISBN-10:      0-7432-9911-6

# Contents

# Contents

"His mind was replete with resources that dissipated fear ... he stood forth early, and continued firm, through the great struggle, and may justly claim a large share of honor, due to that spirit of energy which opposed the measures of administration, and produced the independence of America. Through a long life he exhibited on all occasions, an example of patriotism, religion, and virtue honorary to the human character."

—Mercy Otis Warren, *History of the Rise, Progress, and Termination of the American Revolution*, 1805

*Samuel Adams*

# "Pillar of Fire by Night"

## 1777

*"Let us awaken then, and evince a different spirit,—a spirit that shall inspire the people with confidence in themselves and in us,—a spirit that will encourage them to persevere in this glorious struggle, until their rights and liberties shall be established on a rock."*

—*Samuel Adams, 1777*

O F ALL THE difficult moments in the American Revolution, one of the most desperate for the revolutionaries was late September 1777. British troops controlled New York City. The Americans had lost the strategic stronghold of Fort Ticonderoga, in upstate New York, to the British in July. In Delaware, on September 11, troops led by General George Washington had lost the Battle of Brandywine, in which two hundred Americans were killed, five hundred wounded, and four hundred captured. In Pennsylvania, early in the morning of September 21, another three hundred American soldiers were killed or wounded and one hundred captured in a British surprise attack that became known as the Paoli Massacre.[1]

Washington's troops were suffering from what one delegate to Congress called "fatigue occasioned by the bad rainy weather & long night marches."[2] The rain had soaked the American army's ammunition, making it useless.[3] The American troops would spend the coming winter at Valley Forge, Pennsylvania, subsisting on firecakes made of flour and water, and leaving bloody footprints in the snow for lack of shoes; already one thousand of Washington's roughly nine thousand troops were barefoot.[4] The delegates to Congress doubted their own generals. Charles Carroll of Carrollton, Maryland, wrote to General Washington, "I am sorry to observe that two officers in high command in our army are said to be much addicted to liquor: what trust, what confidence can be reposed in such men?"[5]

The diplomatic situation was similarly unpromising for the revolutionaries. France had not yet agreed to an alliance with America. Some individual French officers volunteered on their own, but even they were suffering, or worse. The *Journals of Congress* for September 17 record that one "Mons. du Coudray, colonel brigadier in the service of his most Christian Majesty, the king of France, and commander in chief of the artillery in the French colonies of America, gallantly offered to join the American army as a volunteer, but, in his way thither, was most unfortunately drowned in attempting to pass the Schuylkill." The Congress resolved that the corpse of the man John Adams said had a reputation as "the most learned and promising officer in France" be buried "at the expence of the United States, and with the honors of war."[6]

Burial with the honors of war was about the best that American political leaders could hope for. The enemy was closing in. Pennsylvanians lowered the 2,080-pound bronze bell from the spire of their State House, with its inscription from Leviticus, "Proclaim Liberty throughout all the land unto all the inhabitants thereof," and carted it to the basement of the Zion Reformed Church in Allentown for safekeeping.[7] And just in time—the British captured Pennsylvania's capital, Philadelphia, America's largest city, on September 26. Congress, which had been meeting there, fled briefly to Lancaster, Pennsylvania, then to York, a hundred miles west of Philadelphia. The departure from Philadelphia was frantic, prompted by an alarm from Washington's aide, Alexander Hamilton, who said the enemy soldiers were so close that one had shot his horse.[8] One delegate to Congress was wakened by a servant at two in the morning and advised to abandon the city.[9] A delegate from Virginia, Richard Henry Lee, evacuated Philadelphia in such a hurry that he left his extra clothes behind.[10]

Another delegate to Congress, John Adams of Massachusetts, wrote in his diary, "The prospect is chilling, on every Side: Gloomy, dark, melancholly, and dispiriting."[11]

The number of delegates present at Congress had dwindled to a mere twenty from the fifty-six members who had signed the Declaration of Independence in 1776. Those remaining gathered for a private meeting in York to question whether there was any hope of success.

One of those present was John Adams's cousin, the patriot leader Samuel Adams, who had already suffered losses that would have shattered an ordinary man. His first wife and four of their children died of natural causes before the war began. At the Battle of Bunker Hill, British officers decapitated Samuel Adams's close friend Joseph Warren and presented his head as a trophy to the British commanding general.[12] Samuel Adams had spent the better part of three years at the Congress in Philadelphia separated from his two surviving children and his second wife. "Matters seem to be drawing to a crisis," he had written her recently.[13] Back in Boston, the British soldiers ripped out the pews of Old South Church, where Samuel Adams's father had once worshipped, covered the floor with dirt, and used the church as a riding academy.[14] Samuel Adams's own house in Boston was vandalized by British troops so badly that it was uninhabitable.[15] If the Revolution failed, Samuel Adams could expect to meet the same fate at the hands of the British as Warren.

Yet on that day in York in late September 1777, Samuel Adams, a slightly heavy, gray-haired fifty-five-year-old with large dark blue eyes, a prominent nose, and a high forehead, gave his fellow members of Congress a talk of encouragement.

"If we despond, public confidence is destroyed, the people will no longer yield their support to a hopeless contest, and American liberty is no more," Samuel Adams said in the voice John Adams described as clear and harmonious.[16] "Through the darkness which shrouds our prospects the ark of safety is visible. Despondency becomes not the dignity of our cause, nor the character of those who are its supporters."

He went on, comparing the American revolutionaries to the Israelites who had left the slavery of Egypt. According to Exodus, chapter 13, God had guided them in the wilderness with a "pillar of cloud by day" and a "pillar of fire by night." Samuel Adams addressed the delegates:

> Let us awaken then, and evince a different spirit,—a spirit that shall inspire the people with confidence in themselves and in us,—a spirit that will encourage them to persevere in this glorious struggle, until their rights and liberties shall be established on a rock. We have proclaimed to the world our determination "to die freemen, rather than to live slaves." We have appealed to Heaven for the justice of our cause, and in Heaven we have placed our trust. Numerous have been the manifestations of God's providence in sustaining us. In the gloomy period of adversity, we have had "our cloud by day and pillar of fire by night." We have been reduced to distress, and the arm of Omnipotence has raised us up. Let us still rely in humble confidence on Him who is mighty to save. Good tidings will soon arrive. We shall never be abandoned by Heaven while we act worthy of its aid and protection.[17]

When Samuel Adams said that the "ark of safety" was visible "through the darkness," he turned out to be prescient. On October 17, at Saratoga, north of Albany, New York, the American general Horatio Gates accepted the surrender of 5,800 British soldiers led by General John Burgoyne. The American troops seized from the British twenty-seven pieces of artillery and thousands of pieces of small arms and ammunition.[18]

Detailed news of the victory at the Battle of Saratoga did not reach Congress at York until October 31, but when it did it was greeted with exuberance. "We had almost began to despair, but at length our joy was full," wrote a congressman from Connecticut, Eliphalet Dyer. The president of the Congress, Henry Laurens of South Carolina, wrote, "the glorious intelligence is now extending from City to City diffusing Joy in the heart of every Loyal American." The victory at Saratoga turned the tide of the war. News of it was decisive in bringing France into a full alliance with America against the British. Samuel Adams joked that Gates's messenger, who had dawdled for a day between Saratoga and York courting a young woman he later married, should be presented with spurs and a horsewhip.[19]

On November 1, just after receiving news of the victory at Saratoga, Congress adopted a report drafted by Samuel Adams, declaring Thursday, December 18, as "a day of thanksgiving" to God, "particularly in that he hath been pleased in so great a measure to prosper the means used for the support of our troops and to crown our arms with most signal success." The resolution went on to say that the day would be set aside so that:

> with one heart and one voice the good people may express the grateful feelings of their hearts, and consecrate themselves to the service of their divine benefactor; and that together with their sincere acknowledgments and offerings, they may join the penitent confession of their manifold sins, whereby they had forfeited every favour, and their humble and earnest supplication that it may please God, through the merits of Jesus Christ, mercifully to forgive and blot them out of remembrance; that it may please him graciously to afford his blessing on the governments of these states respectively, and prosper the public council of the whole; to inspire our commanders both by land and sea, and all under them, with that wisdom and fortitude which may render them fit instruments, under the providence of Almighty God, to secure for these United States the greatest of all human

blessings, independence and peace; that it may please him to prosper the trade and manufactures of the people and the labour of the husbandman, that our land may yet yield its increase; to take schools and seminaries of education, so necessary for cultivating the principles of true liberty, virtue and piety, under his nurturing hand, and to prosper the means of religion for the promotion and enlargement of that kingdom which consisteth "in righteousness, peace and joy in the Holy Ghost."[20]

# Introduction

# "Truly the Man of the Revolution"

*"For depth of purpose, zeal, and sagacity, no man in Congress exceeded, if any equalled, Sam. Adams."*

—*Thomas Jefferson*

S AMUEL ADAMS'S INSPIRING speech at York, delivered at a pivotal moment, when the Congress was losing hope, has been lost in the attic of history. Six of the nine biographies of Samuel Adams do not even mention the address.[1] The congressional declaration of a day of thanksgiving has likewise been widely forgotten, though some credit those words of Adams with starting Thanksgiving as an American national holiday rather than being a New England custom.[2] Samuel Adams today is best known as a brand of beer. But the religious themes he struck in his York speech—that the Americans were like the biblical Israelites of Exodus, and that God was intervening directly on their side—are essential for understanding the American Revolution. So, too, was the association, in the thanksgiving declaration of 1777, of liberty with virtue and piety. These ideas help explain why the Americans fought on in the revolutionary cause in the face of discouraging setbacks and overwhelming obstacles.

Many leaders offered the same religious views. In Kingston, New York, on September 9, 1777, the chief justice of the state of New York, John Jay, said in remarks reprinted in the press, "we should always remember, that the many remarkable and unexpected means and events by which our wants have been supplied, and our enemies repelled or restrained, are such strong and striking proofs of the interposition of Heaven, that our having been delivered from the threatened bondage of Britain, ought, like the emancipation of the Jews from Egyptian servitude, be forever ascribed to its *true cause*, and instead of swelling our breasts with arrogant ideas of our power and importance, kindle in them a flame of gratitude and piety, which may consume all remains of vice and irreligion. Blessed be God."[3] In New Jersey, in early October, the elected patriot governor, William Livingston, spoke of "reliance upon the divine blessing" and of how "conspicuous the finger of Heaven" had been in expelling the British from his state.[4]

Congress's actions also reflected these assumptions. On September 11, 1777, Congress, still in Philadelphia, voted to order the importation of twenty thousand Bibles "from Holland, Scotland, or elsewhere" into America. A committee appointed to consider the matter had concluded that "the use of the Bible is so universal, and its importance so great."[5] Congress's first recorded business in York, on October 1, 1777—likely the morning after Samuel Adams's speech—was to note the appointment of two chaplains. One was an Anglican, William White, and the other a Presbyterian, George Duffield.[6] Less than a week later, on October 6, Congress appointed a third chaplain, the Congregationalist Timothy Dwight, to serve a brigade of Connecticut troops.[7]

But Jay, Livingston, and the other delegates to Congress aside, Samuel Adams was the archetype of the religiously passionate American founder, the founder as biblical prophet, an apostle of liberty. Other types are part of American lore: the plantation-owner–general, George Washington; the plantation-owner–architect, Thomas Jefferson; the plantation-owner–constitutionalist, James Madison; the scientist-inventor-printer-diplomat, Benjamin Franklin; the lawyer, John Adams; the immigrant banker, Alexander Hamilton.

Samuel Adams's achievements were widely recognized in his own time. Thomas Jefferson called him "truly the Man of the Revolution" and said "for depth of purpose, zeal, and sagacity, no man in Con-

gress exceeded, if any equalled, Sam. Adams."[8] When Samuel's cousin
John Adams arrived in Paris in 1779, the French declared that he was
"not the famous Adams."[9] When the top British general in America,
Thomas Gage, offered a general amnesty in June 1775 to all revolutionaries who would lay down their arms, he exempted only two
men—John Hancock and Samuel Adams.[10]

John Adams wrote of his cousin Samuel, "Adams is zealous,
ardent and keen in the Cause. . . . Adams I believe has the most thorough Understanding of Liberty, and her Resources, in the Temper
and Character of the People, tho not in the Law and Constitution, as
well as the most habitual, radical Love of it, of any of them—as well as
the most correct, genteel and artful Pen. He is a Man of refined Policy,
stedfast Integrity, exquisite Humanity, genteel Erudition, obliging,
engaging Manners, real as well as professed Piety."[11]

Samuel Adams was indeed a man of "real as well as professed
piety"—a man of deep religious conviction whose confidence, zeal,
and endurance in the struggle for freedom were grounded in a belief
that an intervening God was on his side. He was the moral conscience
of the American Revolution, a man who never lost sight of the Revolution's political and religious goals, which for him were fundamentally
intertwined. But he did not become a clergyman, and he sometimes
clashed with ministers he viewed as insufficiently supportive of the
revolutionary cause. Passionate, determined, stubborn, thrifty, elo-
quent, idealistic, humble, he was a religious revolutionary—and much
more.

He was a newspaperman who recognized the power of the press in
shaping political events and who wrote frequently, passionately, and
elegantly under a host of pseudonyms about all aspects of public life;
the quality of his prose alone makes him worth reading today.

He was poor compared to many of his fellow patriots, and he was
a critic of extravagant personal spending by the rich and of the influence of money on politics. Yet he was not bitter, and he was an ardent
defender of property rights and opponent of certain taxes.

He was a congressman and a beloved governor of Massachusetts, who, after overthrowing the British, faced the challenge of administering a new democratic government. Though he voted in Massachusetts to ratify the United States Constitution, after independence he allied himself politically with those who emphasized the importance of state and local governments as opposed to the Federalists like Washington and John Adams who wanted a powerful central government.

He was such a radical that modern historians have likened him to black nationalist Malcolm X, anarchist Emma Goldman, and the communist revolutionaries in Russia, China, and Vietnam.[12] Yet he saw himself as a conserver of the New England Puritan tradition of his seventeenth-century forefathers and was motivated more by biblical stories of the liberation of slaves than by Enlightenment ideas of a new man.

He was so progressive for his time that he declined to accept a slave as a gift, appealed to the American Indians for aid in the Revolution, extended public education in Massachusetts to girls, and believed that "Even Savages" could be educated for democracy.[13] Yet he sometimes veered toward anti-Catholic bigotry.

History has not been kind to Samuel Adams. A biography of him in 1885 by James K. Hosmer described him as "to a large extent forgotten." The secular trend in American universities and public schools was to the detriment of the reputation of the revolutionary who hoped America would become a "Christian Sparta." The Cold War caused some Americans to view revolutionary radicals as threats rather than heroes. Much of American history is the story of the triumph of a strong federal government over the state and local governments that were championed by Samuel Adams. And as British-American ties warmed, it became fashionable for American historians to make the eighteenth-century British look less oppressive and more sympathetic than they actually were by depicting Samuel Adams as a hate-filled and cunning conniver.[14]

For all his detractors, though, Samuel Adams has had admirers, too, and not only among his contemporaries. "As far as the genesis of America is concerned, Samuel Adams can more properly be called the 'Father of America' than Washington," wrote Hosmer, a Harvard Divinity School graduate and Unitarian minister who became a history professor and who went on to write an admiring history of the Jews.[15] A great-grandson of Samuel Adams, William V. Wells, published a three-volume biography of the patriot in 1865 that spoke of Adams's "incorruptible integrity and Republican simplicity of character" and his "amazing industry, his courage, ceaseless vigilance, and wise statesmanship, and his cheerfulness and fortitude amid disasters."[16] It is appropriate that the largest and most positive biography of Samuel Adams, by Wells, was published at the end of the Civil War. As Hosmer put it, what William Lloyd Garrison was to the abolition of slavery, "Samuel Adams was to independence,—a man looked on with the greatest dread as an extremist and a fanatic by many of those who afterwards fought for freedom."[17]

In his mixture of religion with politics, his skepticism of a powerful federal government, his warnings about extravagance and the influence of money on elections, his recognition of the power of the press, and his endurance in a war for freedom, Samuel Adams has much to say to modern Americans. If his ideas and his style have not consistently dominated American history, they are undeniably still with us today. In that sense Samuel Adams was not, as he has been called, the "Last of the Puritans" but rather one of the first Americans.

This will be a book about who Samuel Adams was, why he is forgotten, why he should be remembered. As the *Massachusetts Spy* wrote in concluding its obituary of Samuel Adams on October 19, 1803: "This is but a gazette sketch of his character; to give his history at full length, would be to give an history of the American revolution."

# Chapter 1

# "Born a Rebel"

# 1722–1764

*"I pity Mr. Sam. Adams for he was born a Rebel."*

—*John Adams, 1794*

S AMUEL ADAMS WAS born on Sunday, September 16, 1722, in Boston, into a community with a long tradition of standing up for its liberties against the king.

He was British, and so he could—and did—lay claim to the five-hundred-year-old legacy of the Magna Carta. The Great Charter had been signed by King John in 1215 after an armed rebellion of barons took London in a protest over excessive and arbitrary taxation. It included limited guarantees of religious liberty, saying that "the English Church shall be free, and shall have its rights undiminished, and its liberties unimpaired."[1]

He was a resident of the Massachusetts Bay Colony, and so he could—and did—lay claim to the legacy of its founders, Protestant Puritan Christians who had fled England during the reign of King Charles I, which lasted from 1625 to 1649. Charles had earned the suspicion of the Puritans by marrying a French Catholic. The suspicion turned out to be well founded. Charles's right-hand man on religious matters, Bishop William Laud, banned certain Protestant books, constructed churches in the ornate Gothic style rather than the plainer Puritan fashion, and cut off the ears of clergymen who dared oppose him. Parliament did not meet for eleven years during Charles's rule.[2] Tens of thousands of Puritans left England for America; those who stayed behind eventually launched their own revolution against Charles and, led by Oliver Cromwell, established a Puritan common-wealth in England lasting from 1649 to 1659.

Aboard a ship headed for Massachusetts Bay, the man who would serve repeatedly as governor of the colony, John Winthrop, made a speech that foreshadowed Samuel Adams's remarks to the members of Congress at York nearly 150 years later. As Adams in 1777 said, "We shall never be abandoned by Heaven while we act worthy of its aid and protection," so Winthrop in 1630 spoke of a "covenant" between God and the Puritans headed for New England aboard the *Arbella*. Winthrop, too, expressed confidence that if the Puritans kept their end of the bargain, the God of Exodus would do his part. "We shall find that the God of Israel is among us, when ten of us shall be able to resist a thousand of our enemies," Winthrop promised.[3]

John Cotton had preached the farewell sermon to Winthrop's fleet; eventually, Cotton, too, chose to flee King Charles and Bishop Laud. Cotton became the first minister at the first church in Boston, serving from 1633 to 1652. The Harvard historian and expert on the Puritans Perry Miller called him "the dominating figure in the councils of the New England clergy" who "set the model for New England ortho-doxy."[4] Cotton wrote in 1644 of "the People, in whom fundamentally all power lyes," and said it was necessary "that all power that is on earth be limited, Church-power or other."[5] He spoke of the Roman Catholic Church as "the Mother of Harlots and Abominations of the earth."[6]

Such views only heightened the fears in Boston when James II, a Catholic, acceded to the throne of England in 1685, shortly after Charles II had revoked the original charter of the Massachusetts Bay Colony. James II imposed a new ruler, Sir Edmund Andros, "Governor, Captain-General and Vice-Admiral of His Majesty's Dominion of New England." In case the title alone failed to make the point sufficiently to the Bostonians, Andros was accompanied by two companies of red-coated British troops, a seventy-four-gun ship of the line, and the first Anglican clergyman in Massachusetts Bay.[7] The colonists dispatched John Cotton's son-in-law, Increase Mather—the pastor of Boston's Second Congregational Church, the head of Harvard College, the man described as "the most powerful minister in New England"—to England to try to restore the colony's liberties.[8] In the meantime, colonists took matters into their own hands. Armed groups of them gathered in the streets and escorted the "Governor, Captain-General and Vice-Admiral of His Majesty's Dominion of New England" to jail.

Increase Mather's son and co-pastor at the Second Church, Cotton Mather, drafted a declaration that was read from the balcony of Boston's Town House on the day of the rebellion against Governor Andros, April 18, 1689. It began by referring to the discovery of a "horrid Popish plot wherein the bloody Devotoes of Rome had in their Design and Prospect no less than the Extinction of the Protestant Religion; which mighty Work they called the utter subduing of a Pestilent Heresy." It called the Catholic Church "the great Scarlet Whore" and said that until the arrival of Andros, New England had been "a Countrey so remarkable for the true Profession and pure Exercise of the Protestant Religion." It accused Andros of contradicting Magna Carta, "the rights of which we laid claim unto." It made reference to protests about taxation without representation, saying, "Persons who did but peaceably object against raising of taxes without an Assembly, have been for it fined, some twenty, some thirty, and others fifty Pounds." It complained that among the one thousand British troops sent to fight one hundred Indians in New England were "Popish Commanders." And it concluded with a reference to William III of Orange, a Protestant who had taken over the British throne from James II in the Glorious Revolution of 1688: "The almighty has been pleased to prosper the noble undertaking of the Prince of Orange, to preserve the three Kingdoms from the horrible brinks of Popery and Slavery."[9]

Andros twice tried and failed to escape from jail. The first time, on a Friday evening, he dressed in women's clothing and made it past two guards, only to be stopped by a third who noticed that the "woman" was wearing Andros's shoes.[10] The second time, Andros's servant "enticed the centinel to drink" and the governor made it as far as Rhode Island before being returned to captivity. Not even a letter from King William III of England was enough to free Andros immediately; the governor remained jailed for more than two months after the king's order for his release was received in Boston. Andros finally sailed for London in a miserable winter voyage on February 5, 1690, having endured nearly ten months in captivity.[11]

And Samuel Adams was not only British and a resident of the Massachusetts Bay Colony, he was born into a Boston family with its own history. John Cotton's granddaughter, Maria Mather, was married to Samuel Adams's maternal grandfather, Richard Fifield. Maria Mather was Increase Mather's daughter and Cotton Mather's sister.[12] She survived until 1746,[13] long enough for Samuel Adams, as a young adult, to have made her acquaintance.

Samuel Adams was a descendant of Henry Adams, a farmer who had arrived in Boston with his wife, eight sons, and a daughter in 1632 or 1633 as part of the wave of Puritans fleeing King Charles and Bishop Laud.[14] Samuel Adams himself was the fourth of twelve children that were born to his parents, and one of only three of the twelve who survived past age two.

Samuel Adams's mother, Mary, is described by one Adams biographer as a woman "of severe religious principles."[15] Beyond that Mary Adams suffered the loss of nine of her twelve children, little is known of her.

The patriot's father was also named Samuel Adams and is known to history as Samuel the Deacon, or Samuel the Elder, to avoid confusion. It was a prosperous household. Samuel the Elder's father, John, was a sea captain who had moved to Boston from what is now Quincy, Massachusetts, in 1687. Samuel the Elder made his living by selling beer maker's malt, which he made in a little malt house in his backyard—an inspiration for today's Samuel Adams brewery.[16] The

Adams family lived in a house on Purchase Street with a garden, a small orchard, and land running down to Boston Harbor. Samuel the Elder was involved in politics and city life as a selectman, a justice of the peace, and as a deacon of New South Church, which he had helped to found in 1715 when Old South became too crowded. The people of Boston elected him as a member of the legislature of Massachusetts. He served as a director of a land bank company that issued paper money for use by farmers until the company was outlawed by Parliament in 1741, a British decision that dealt a financial setback to the Adams family.[17]

*The New England Primer*, from which young Samuel Adams almost certainly learned to read, included, before even the alphabet, a Bible quote from King David speaking to his son Solomon: "My Son, know thou the God of thy Father & Serve Him with a perfect heart, & with a willing mind, for the Lord searcheth all hearts." The primer included an account of the martyrdom of John Rogers, a Protestant minister in London who was burned at the stake on orders of Catholic Queen Mary in 1555. "His wife, with nine small children, and one at her breast, following him to the stake, with which sorrowful sight he was not in the least daunted, but with wonderful Patience died courageously for the Gospel of Jesus Christ," was how the primer recounted the story of a man motivated by religious principle meeting death at the hands of a British monarch. The primer also included the Ten Commandments, prefaced with the language from Exodus, chapter 20: "God spake all these words, saying, I am the Lord thy God, which have brought thee out of the Land of Egypt, out of the House of Bondage."[18] Even the alphabet was taught with religion, from A—"In Adam's Fall We sinned All"—to Z—"Zaccheus he Did climb the Tree His Lord to See."[19]

Samuel Adams, like five of the fifty-six signers of the Declaration of Independence, attended Boston Latin School. Required reading at Boston Latin School for a student's first four years included Aesop's Fables, one of the first of which is a tale of a wolf who devoured a lamb despite the lamb's refutation of all the wolf's accusations against him. The moral of the story, according to Aesop, is that "The tyrant will always find a pretext for his tyranny."[20]

In years five through seven of the school, students progressed to reading letters, essays, and orations of the Roman politician Marcus Tullius Cicero.[21] Cicero lived 1,800 years before Samuel Adams, but his commentary was relevant for more than just learning to conjugate Latin verbs. The letters contained lessons in picking winners in democratic contests: "Of the candidates for this year's election Caesar is considered certain."[22] And in the trade-offs between politics and personal wealth: "In regard to my political position, I have resumed what I thought there would be the utmost difficulty in recovering," Cicero wrote, speaking of his resurgent popularity and influence. "In regard, however, to my private property—as to which you are well aware to what an extent it has been crippled, scattered, and plundered—I am in great difficulties."[23]

Cicero's essay on moral duties described a "great and brave soul" as one who "should undertake the conduct of affairs great, indeed, and, especially, beneficial, but at the same time arduous in the highest degree, demanding severe toil, and fraught with peril not only of the means of comfortable living, but of life itself."[24]

Samuel Adams's assignments in his final year at Boston Latin School would have also included translating "A psalm or something divine" into Latin.[25] He learned Latin and also Greek under the tutelage of headmaster John Lovell, who was known as "the pride of Boston's parents and the terror of its youth."[26] Lovell was a loyalist, but his son James became a patriot who was imprisoned by the British for almost eighteen months during the Revolution and who would later serve with Samuel Adams representing Massachusetts in Congress.[27]

Samuel Adams entered Harvard in 1736 at age fourteen and became one of eight of the signers of the Declaration of Independence who were Harvard graduates. By one account, he was rebuked for oversleeping and missing morning prayers.[28] By another, he had to pay a fine as punishment after he was caught violating the ban on distilled liquors by drinking rum.[29] At Harvard, of the twenty-three members of the class that entered with Samuel Adams, seven became ministers.[30] But Adams's pious parents notwithstanding, it seemed he was not cut out to follow the path of many Harvard graduates of the day into a career as a Protestant minister.

The Harvard presidents in Adams's time were Congregationalist Christian ministers who had been educated at Harvard themselves. When Samuel Adams entered, the president of the college was Benjamin Wadsworth, who had graduated from Harvard in 1690 and had served for thirty years as minister of First Church in Boston. After Wadsworth died on March 16, 1737, Harvard's governing boards, after much prayer and deliberation, selected as his successor Edward Holyoke, a minister who had been serving a church in Marblehead, Massachusetts, and who had graduated from Harvard in 1705. Yet even within the relatively strict confines of the religion of the day, which still bore a close resemblance to that of the Puritans who had founded the colony, there was room for debate. At commencement in 1739, three candidates for master's degrees were so bold as to argue the negative to the question "Whether Three Persons in the Godhead are revealed by the Old Testament."[31] More religiously liberal than Yale, Harvard at the time was a place where science was starting to challenge religion, and other basic assumptions were increasingly open to question.

George Whitefield, a priest of the Church of England, arrived in Boston, then a town of about 16,000, in September 1740, just months after Samuel Adams graduated from Harvard. Whitefield was twenty-five years old and Adams had just turned eighteen. On Friday, September 19, Whitefield attended services at King's Chapel, the Anglican church in Boston that catered to the king's appointees. Friday afternoon, Whitefield spoke to two or three thousand people at the Brattle Street Church, a Congregationalist church whose minister was Samuel Cooper, who would become an important revolutionary patriot. Saturday morning, Whitefield preached at Old South Church. On Sunday he spoke at the Old Church, another Congregationalist church, then preached to 12,000 or 15,000 people outdoors on Boston Common.[32]

On Monday morning he preached at the New North Church, where, Whitefield recorded in his diary, most of the audience "wept for a considerable time."[33] Monday afternoon Whitefield was to speak at the New South Church, where Samuel Checkley, who had baptized Samuel Adams, was the minister. There the crowd that gathered to hear Whitefield was so large and excited that it panicked and stampeded. Joseph Sewall, the minister of Old South Church, recorded it this way: "There was a vast assembly at Mr. Checkley's, to hear him, but were thrown into great confusion from a groundless imagination that the gallery gave way. Several were trod to death as the crowd press'd out of the House, 3 died almost presently, 2 since of their wounds. I think a lad jump'd out of the window, and was kill'd by the fall. Others were grievously wounded."[34]

Whitefield himself tells of discovering the disaster. "I happened to come in the midst of the Uproar, and saw two or three lying on the Ground on a pitiable Condition." The preacher also tells of his response. Whitefield attempted revenge on Satan by moving the sermon outdoors onto Boston Common, where a crowd listened in the rain: "God was pleased to give some Presence of Mind, so that I gave Notice, I would immediately preach in the Common. The Weather was wet, but above eight Thousand followed into the Fields, to whom, I preached. . . . I endeavor'd, as God enabled me, to improve what had befallen us, and tho Satan in this has bruised our Heels; yet I doubt not but even this will be a Means of bruising his accursed Head."[35]

So it went around the Boston area for nearly a month. Whitefield preached to seven thousand in Harvard Yard in Cambridge, where, he reported, the president treated him "very civilly."[36] He preached to a crowd of blacks in Boston about the apostle Philip's conversion of the Ethiopian eunuch. He prayed with the governor of the colony and with the poor at the almshouse.[37] "Almost every evening the house where he lodged was thronged, to hear his prayer and counsels," reported Thomas Prince, one of the pastors of Old South Church.[38]

He preached in Marblehead, Salem, Ipswich, Portsmouth, and York, two sermons a day, sometimes in churches with aisles so crowded he had to enter through a window. His farewell sermon on Boston Common drew thirty thousand people from all over New England. Whitefield recorded that he "exhorted them steadily to imitate the Piety of their Forefathers."[39] When Whitefield left Boston, the governor of Massachusetts followed him, weeping, forty-five miles west, all the way to Worcester. Joseph Sewall wrote in his diary, "It is wonderful to behold a young man (about 26) preaching thus twice a day, with great earnestness, the Gospel of Christ. Many, particularly among the youth, seem to be affected."[40]

Whitefield at this time was nominally an Anglican, a member of the Church of England, an Episcopalian, while the overwhelming majority of New Englanders, including Adams, were Congregationalists, descendants of the Puritan dissenters from the Church of England. (Many of the Congregationalists would eventually become Unitarians, but not until the early nineteenth century.) Whitefield's strict theology of predestination was controversial, as was even the very idea of itinerant preaching. Adams, while no disciple of Whitefield, seems to have been among those youth "affected" by the visit. Shortly afterward, he joined the Brattle Street Church.[41] While church attendance was widespread at the time, church membership was limited to those who underwent a conversion experience. Though at least one historian has claimed that the Samuel Adams who joined the Brattle Street Church in 1742 was "another man of the same name,"[42] the evidence suggests that the new church member was our Samuel Adams—years later the church's minister sent a letter confirming as much.[43]

Beyond that, it is unquestionable that Whitefield's visit to Boston left a lasting impression on Samuel Adams. Forty years later, in December of 1780, Adams wrote to a friend of how Whitefield "thundered in the pulpit against Assemblies & Balls."[44] That a preacher could draw a crowd of twice the population of Boston and cause a frenzy that killed five underscores the "Great Awakening" of religious fervor that accompanied Whitefield's visit. The Reverends Benjamin

Colman and William Cooper of Boston's Brattle Street Church called Whitefield "the wonder of the age."[45] His visit to New England is perhaps described most dramatically by a Connecticut farmer, Nathaniel Cole, in an account worth repeating for the way it portrays the effect of Whitefield's visit on individual souls:

> I saw before me a Cloud of fogg rising; I first thought it came from the great River, but as I came nearer the Road, I heard a noise something like a low rumbling thunder and presently found it was the noise of Horses feet coming down the Road and this Cloud was a Cloud of dust made by the Horses feet; it arose some Rods into the air over the tops of Hills and trees and when I came within about 20 rods of the Road, I could see men and horses Sliping along in the Cloud like shadows and as I drew nearer it seemed more like a steady Stream of horses and their riders, scarcely a horse more than his length behind another, all of a Lather and foam with sweat, their breath rolling out of their nostrils every Jump; every horse seemed to go with all his might to carry his rider to hear news from heaven for the saving of Souls, it made me tremble to see the Sight. . . .
>
> Mr. Whitfeld . . . looked almost angellical—a young, slim, slender youth before some thousands of people, and with a bold, undaunted countenance. And my hearing how God was with him everywhere . . . it solemnized my mind, and put me in a trembling fear before he began to preach, for he looked as if he was Cloathed with authority from the great God . . . and my hearing him preach gave me a heart wound, by god's blessing.[46]

When Samuel Adams returned to Harvard to receive his master's degree in 1743, at age twenty-one, it was for arguing in the affirmative the question "Whether it be lawful to resist the supreme magistrate, if the commonwealth can not be otherwise preserved?" As it was thirty-three years before the Declaration of Independence, this was an episode that provided support for comments like the one quoted by John

Adams in a letter to his wife, Abigail, in January 1794: "I pitty Mr. Sam. Adams for he was born a Rebel."[47]

Rebel not being a paying profession at the time, Adams became an apprentice in the counting house of a prominent Boston merchant, Thomas Cushing. He opened his own store, but by one account, he was more interested in reading about politics and literature than in paying attention to ledgers, invoices, and bookkeeping.[48] He ended up in his parents' home, subsisting on the income from their malt house.

His father died March 8, 1748,[49] at age fifty-seven. Samuel Adams was twenty-four. His loss must have been salved somewhat by the entrance into his life of Elizabeth Checkley, the daughter of the minister who had baptized him. Increase and Cotton Mather and Benjamin Wadsworth had ordained her father, who was himself a 1715 graduate of Harvard and the son of a deacon of Old South Church. Elizabeth Checkley's mother, Elizabeth Rolfe, was rescued as a little girl by a black slave who hid her in the cellar during an Indian raid that killed Elizabeth Rolfe's father, Rev. Benjamin Rolfe, Harvard class of 1684.[50]

Elizabeth Checkley and Samuel Adams had more than Harvard and Christianity in common. Her family's losses nearly exactly matched his; she was one of only three of the twelve Checkley children to survive to adulthood. Her father, while despondent over the deaths of so many of his children, at least still was alive, and on Tuesday, October 17, 1749, the Reverend Samuel Checkley officiated at the marriage of Samuel Adams, twenty-seven, and Elizabeth Checkley, twenty-four. The union was described in the family as an "extremely happy" one.[51] She was pregnant in 1750 and gave birth to a boy who lived for only eighteen days. A year later, she gave birth to a son, Samuel, who lived to adulthood. In 1753 she gave birth to a third child, a son, who lived only thirty-seven hours. Her first daughter was born in 1754 and died after three months and nine days. Her second daughter, Hannah, was born in 1756 and lived to adulthood. Her sixth delivery, in 1757, was a stillborn son. For nineteen days, she lingered. Then, at 8 A.M. on Sunday, July 25, 1757, she passed away. Samuel Adams wrote in his family Bible, "To her husband she was as sincere a Friend as she was a faithful Wife. . . . She ran her Christian race with remarkable steadiness and finished in triumph. She left two small children. God grant they may inherit her graces."[52]

It may have been the rush of good feelings from the beginning of the relationship with Elizabeth Checkley that emboldened Samuel Adams to try his hand at newspaper writing. His debut was with a weekly called the *Independent Advertiser*, which published from 1748 to 1750. The printers promised "a most welcome reception" to "whatsoever may be adapted to state and defend the rights and liberties of mankind, to advance useful knowledge and the cause of virtue."[53] Samuel Adams took them up on their offer with a pair of essays that, like his master's degree question, foreshadowed the campaign he was to lead in the decades ahead. In "Loyalty and Sedition," Adams wrote that "true loyalty" cannot exist "in an arbitrary government," because true loyalty "is founded in the love and possession of liberty." He wrote that "The true object of loyalty is a good legal constitution, which, as it condemns every instance of oppression and lawless power, derives a certain remedy to the sufferer by allowing him to remonstrate his grievances, and pointing out methods of relief when the gentle arts of persuasion have lost their efficacy."

In another essay, Adams observed, "There is no one thing which mankind are more passionately fond of, which they fight with more zeal for, which they possess with more anxious jealousy and fear of losing, than liberty." He called liberty "the choicest gift that Heaven has lent to man." He said that the charter of the Massachusetts Bay Colony "secures to us all the English liberties, besides which we have some additional privileges which the common people there have not." These additional privileges are thanks to "our fathers"—the Puritans— who "had so severely felt the effects of tyranny and the weight of the bishop's yoke, that they underwent the greatest difficulties and toils to secure to themselves and transmit to their posterity these invaluable blessings." Adams cautioned in this essay that there is a difference between talking about liberty and acting with respect for it. "It is not unfrequent," he wrote, "to hear men declaim loudly upon liberty, who, if we may judge by the whole tenor of their actions, mean nothing else by it than their own liberty,—to oppress without control or the restraint of laws all those who are poorer or weaker than themselves." And he linked the idea of true liberty to that of virtue: "Neither the wisest constitution nor the wisest laws will secure the liberty and happiness of a people whose manners are universally corrupt."[54]

These issues were more than mere abstractions for Samuel Adams and his fellow Bostonians. In May 1747, the pastor of the First Church in Boston, Charles Chauncy, preached an election sermon stressing that rulers "must take all proper care to preserve entire the civil rights of a people" by "appearing in defence of their liberties" and guarding "against the designs of those, who would rule in a despotic manner."[55] Liberty seemed at risk in immediate and tangible ways. In late November 1747, a British naval commodore sent a gang of seamen into Boston and seized fifty of the town's 16,000 residents by force to help man his ships. Fortunately for the fifty, a crowd of Bostonians gathered, attacked the British sailors, and freed the captives. Then the crowd marched to the governor's house and demanded that the British sailors be prosecuted.[56]

Property, too, was at risk of being snatched up by the British or their agents. The sheriff, Stephen Greenleaf, was threatening to auction off the house of Samuel Adams the Elder—the house in which Samuel Adams the son now lived—to settle what he said were the estate's obligations from the closed Land Bank. A notice was placed in the *Boston Evening Post* of March 9, 1752, declaring that the auction would take place at the Royal Exchange Tavern in King Street from 3 P.M. to 5 P.M. That sale was apparently staved off, but not for good, as on October 27, 1755, Samuel Adams took to the pages of the *Boston Gazette* to protest that the sheriff's advertisement for sale of Samuel Adams the Elder's property would "tend to weaken the security of English property." By writing in the newspaper, Samuel Adams was appealing to the people, to the court of popular opinion. "Lest it should be thought I act an unreasonable part, I desire it may be known that there is a dispute whether the estate is indebted to the Land Bank Company, or the Company to the estate, and the Merits of the Cause have never been *fairly* and *legally* heard." Adams said that all he was asking for was to be treated with the privileges of a British subject, protected by its "Constitution and laws." And he warned that anyone who tried to buy the land could count on "its being defended by its present Owners and Possessors, with the whole Strength of Law."[57]

Undeterred, the sheriff kept trying, without success, to sell the estate. A March 1, 1756, advertisement in the *Boston Evening Post* read, "Whereas the Real Estate of Samuel Adams, late of Boston, Esq., deceased, taken by Execution to satisfy his dues to the late Land Bank or Manufactory Company, has divers times been exposed to public sale, but has not yet been sold: notice is herby given, that the said Estate will be sold by the subscriber to such person as will give most for the same."

As Samuel Adams advanced as a writer and as a husband, he was also following in his father's footsteps and beginning a political career, entering political life as an officeholder for the town of Boston. This was not necessarily as glorious an honor as one might think; about 115 individuals were selected for various obscure tasks. There were four hogreeves, officers charged with taking care of stray hogs. Other Bostonians served as fire wardens, "cullers of staves," "fence-viewers," "informers of deer," and "surveyor of hemp." On March 12, 1753, Samuel Adams was chosen by the Town Meeting as one of twelve town scavengers, empowered to keep the streets clean.[58] On March 15, 1756, the *Boston Evening Post* reported that, at the annual meeting of freeholders and other inhabitants of the town, he had been chosen one of four collectors of taxes.[59] He was returned to the office for another year in March of 1757, the *Boston Weekly News-Letter* reported on March 17, 1757, a report confirmed in the *Boston Evening Post* of March 21, 1757. And for another year in March of 1758, the *Boston Evening Post* and the *Boston Post Boy* both reported March 20, 1758.

The tax collector job into which Samuel Adams settled was only slightly more dignified than that of hogreeve or scavenger, as Cicero himself had recognized in a text that Samuel Adams had probably read at Boston Latin School: "Now as to the trades and modes of getting gain that are to be regarded as respectable, and those that are to be deemed mean and vulgar, the general opinion is as follows: In the first place, those callings are held in disesteem that come into collision with the ill will of men, as that of tax gatherers."[60]

Why did Adams do it? He needed the money. Tax collectors were entitled to keep between 3 percent and 12 percent of what they collected, depending on the year.[61] For an up-and-coming politician, the job was also an opportunity to accumulate favors. The collectors enjoyed a certain degree of discretion. "Abatements could win many friends," wrote a historian of Boston, G. B. Warden, who found records from 1761 and 1763 showing that Adams "always waited until after the May elections" to begin collecting taxes.[62] One biographer claimed that Adams "seldom made an outright demand for money and was easily put off for weeks, months, and even years."[63]

The job ended messily for Adams. He eventually sued some delinquent taxpayers, and then was sued himself by the town for failing to collect all the taxes he was supposed to have collected. The debt dragged on for years after he had left the position.[64] The firsthand experience in colonial aversion to paying taxes—even those levied by governments in which the taxpayers participated by elections or town meetings—would nonetheless be useful background for Adams.

The difficulty in collecting taxes came in a Boston whose residents were quite sophisticated about minimizing their own taxes and understanding the effect of a high tax rate on the growth of a city. The June 9, 1755, issue of the weekly *Boston Gazette* featured a front-page letter from a Bostonian complaining about an increased tax burden falling on fewer taxpayers as some Bostonians left the town for lower-tax jurisdictions:

The business of the Town is still decaying, the taxes are not at all lessened, but continue very high—A great many of our industrious inhabitants are gone into the country, the burden now falls on a small number; and they less able to bear it than ever—This number is still decreasing, the rich complain of their rates, and some have moved and others are about moving into the country towns, where they are greatly eased. For my own part, I have a love for my native Town, but as my taxes are so large, I am resolved to move my family into the country.

Boston may have had a need for officials to monitor the deer and hogs in its streets, which smelled of manure, of wood smoke, and of salt air. But it was worldly about taxes, and, increasingly, about other matters as well. The town's newspapers—and there were several of them, published weekly—carried ads for "brown Pomeranian linen," "India ginghams," "ebony bone and ivory stick fans," "looking-glasses of several sizes in mahogany frames," wallpaper, and "womens and mens kidd and lamb white and colour'd gloves and mittens," all imported by way of London.[65] A walk through the colonial gallery at the Museum of Fine Arts in Boston is a reminder that Boston at this time was less a frontier backwater than an elegant provincial capital. In one case gleam silver sugar bowls and creampots, tankards and flagons with hinged lids crafted by Paul Revere. Along the walls stand cabinets, chests, and chairs, their mahogany surfaces polished to a high gloss, gracefully curved wooden legs extending elegantly to carved toes with claws. Oil paintings by John Singleton Copley portray the Boston merchants wearing fine silk and velvet, their wives draped in double-strands of pearls, gem-studded brooches, and lace-trimmed dresses.

Even some of the less wealthy among the Bostonians, such as Samuel Adams, had far-flung real estate holdings. Adams had an interest in land on the west side of the Kennebunk River in what is now Maine, but was then part of the Royal Colony of Massachusetts. (Maine would not become a state of its own until 1820.) A notice he placed in the October 22, 1755, *Boston Gazette* called a meeting in Boston of the proprietors of that tract with the agenda, among other things, "to raise money to assist the inhabitants in building a Meeting House, and settling a minister among them."[66] It is unclear how the venture turned out.

In mid-eighteenth-century Massachusetts, Boston was one of 227 towns in a colony that stretched along the coast from what is now Maine in the north, southward to Nantucket and Martha's Vineyard off Cape Cod, and inland to the Berkshires towns of Lenox and Great Barrington.[67] A 1722 map of the city depicts a harbor crammed with shipyards and twenty-six wharfs, including an Adams wharf and the seven-hundred-yard, appropriately named, Long Wharf. The map records that of the town's three thousand houses, one thousand were of brick and the rest of timber. At least eleven churches coexisted more or less peacefully with nearly one hundred taverns and two dozen distilleries.[68]

Clashes between British and French interests in the West Indies, in Nova Scotia, and in the Ohio River Valley in 1754 meant that Bostonians were beginning to anticipate a full-scale war. The pastor of the West Church in Boston, Jonathan Mayhew, laid some of the theological groundwork for it in a sermon delivered before Governor William Shirley, the Governor's Council, and the House of Representatives on election day, May 29, 1754. Mayhew said that French Catholic missionaries put the Indians "in great danger of apostatizing from their natural paganism and barbarity into that which is worse, the religion of Rome—a religion calculated rather to make men wicked rather than to keep them from being so." He warned, "Do I see Christianity banished for popery! The Bible, for the mass-book!"[69]

Samuel Adams's father-in-law, Rev. Samuel Checkley, followed up the next year with a May 28, 1755, election day sermon delivered to the colony's leaders at the annual ceremony. Titled "A Day of Darkness," Checkley's address bemoaned "the growth of sin" and "the decay of religion among us." As for the oncoming war, Checkley embraced it, rejecting pacifism. "War will sometimes be inevitable," he preached.

"There are those, I am sensible, who doubt the lawfulness of Christians making war on any occasion; but to me it seems plain that there can be no just ground therefor either from reason or revelation."

Addressing Shirley, Checkley said, "Our hearty wish, and earnest prayer for you, is that the Lord, who is a man of war, would *teach your hands to war, and your fingers to fight*, and would do the same to officers and soldiers under you." The sermon concluded with a prayer that "It be said of us, as it was of Israel, 'Who is like unto thee, O people saved by the lord, the shield of thine help, and who is the sword of thine excellency!'"[70]

When King George II indeed declared war on the French king, on May 18, 1756, it was with what a dispatch from the *London Gazette* reprinted in the *Boston Gazette* of August 2 called "the solemnities customary on the like occasion." A party of horse-grenadier guards led the way, followed by the beadles of Westminster with staves, the constables of Westminster followed by the high constable of Westminster with his staff, the officers of the high bailiff of Westminster "on horseback with white wands," drums and a drum major, trumpets and a sergeant-trumpeter bearing a mace, followed by assorted heralds and sergeants at arms. The text of the declaration of war—"relying on the Help of Almighty God, in our just undertaking, and being assured of the hearty concurrence and assistance of our subjects"—was proclaimed four times in various corners of London, "the spectators at each place expressing their satisfaction by loud acclamations."

That acclamation extended to Massachusetts. Samuel Adams's cousin Amos Adams was born in 1728, graduated from Harvard in 1752, and eventually married a daughter of Rev. Charles Chauncy, the minister of the First Church in Boston. Amos Adams, a pastor in Roxbury, on June 4, 1759, delivered a sermon before the governor in Boston that was titled "The Expediency and Utility of War, in the Present State of Things, Considered." It looked to the Israelites as examples of how "God sometimes secretly influences and spirits his people stand up in defense of liberty and religion." Adams said God "gave charge to the Israelites to be the executioners of his vengeance upon the Cannanitish nations; to make no peace with them, 'til they were utterly destroyed from off the Earth; and in a wonderful Manner assisted them to execute the awful commission: a judgment which those nations deserved for their idolatry." Amos Adams went on to use the same text that Samuel Checkley did in his sermon on war: "We likewise find military skill and power ascribed to God; *He teaches*, says David, *my hands to war, and my fingers to fight*: This special Influence, this powerful assistance, has often been experienced in a just cause, in the Defence of his People, in executing the particular commands of Heaven."

Amos Adams preached that "every lawful attempt to revive, improve, and propagate military skill and discipline be regarded as a public Good," and, further, that men of military character be respected as, "under God, the guardians of our lives, liberties, property and religion." Military discipline, he said, could help protect America against "an invading enemy." This was more than a merely theoretical threat, Amos Adams counseled: "We may expect this *New World* will henceforth be the seat of war; we may expect in our turn to be invaded: Some of us may see our plains flow with human blood."[71]

Another Congregationalist minister, Samuel Dunbar of the First Church in Stoughton, Massachusetts, made a similar argument in the election sermon that he delivered in Boston before the governor and the House of Representatives on May 28, 1760. Dunbar took as his text a passage from 2 Chronicles. As Dunbar recounted it, Asa, "a godly and religious prince, sought to God for help and success. He led them into the field of battle to fight; before the battle, he led them to the throne of grace to pray, to obtain mercy, and find grace to help them, in this time of need and danger. He lift up a cry to God, e're he gave the shout for battle. That battle, that work is begun well, and like to succeed well, which is prefaced with holy, humble prayer."

Dunbar drew a parallel between Asa's army defending the land of Israel from the invading Ethiopians and the Americans and British defending North America from the French and Indians. "If God go forth with our armies, they will be prospered," Dunbar preached.

This divine presence was not guaranteed; it had to be earned by good behavior. "If ye be with God, become a praying and religious people, acting up to your covenant relation and engagements to him, walking in all holy obedience to his laws, and attendance upon his worship and ordinances, God will be with you," Dunbar predicted. "This will give you . . . in time of war, valiant soldiers and victorious armies."[72] Similarly themed sermons warning of slavery and citing the Bible as inspiration for war were delivered by Congregationalists in Connecticut and even by Presbyterians as far away as Virginia.[73]

With divine assistance or without it, victorious armies were much in evidence on the British side of the French and Indian War. Victories were won at Lake George in 1755, at Louisbourg and Fort Frontenac in 1758, and at the Plains of Abraham in 1759. Colonists—including Dunbar and a Virginia surveyor named George Washington—fought alongside the British in some of the battles.

If George II's declaration of war against France was marked by elaborate public ritual, then the accession to the throne of George II's grandson, George III, was truly extravagant. First, on October 26, 1760, a herald known as the Garter King of Arms emerged at five sites in London to declare the twenty-two-year-old Prince of Wales, George William Frederick, as "George the Third, by the Grace of God King of Great Britain, France, and Ireland, Defender of the Faith, and so forth."[74] Then on September 8, 1761, in the Royal Chapel, George III married Princess Charlotte of Mecklenburg, a seventeen-year-old on whom he had laid eyes for the first time just hours before in the garden of St. James's Palace. The wedding banquet, which lasted until 3 A.M., was followed the next day by a ball, and a fortnight later, on September 22, 1761, by a coronation procession, ceremony, and banquet.[75]

The preparations were covered in great detail by the Boston newspapers, even though it took two months for news to make its way across the Atlantic. The October 26, 1761, issue of the *Boston Post Boy* reported that the diamond "stomacher"—an ornamental garment worn over the belly—that Charlotte was to wear at the coronation "is the richest thing of the kind ever yet seen. The capital stone is worth fifteen thousand pounds, and the whole piece is valued at one hundred thousand." For context, £200 was nearly a year's salary for Rev. Samuel Cooper, the pastor of Boston's wealthiest congregation, the Brattle Street Church; £533 is what lawyer John Adams spent on a brick house in Boston; and the fortune of Thomas Hancock, one of the richest merchants in Boston and indeed in all of America, was £70,000 upon his death in 1764.[76] No contingency seemed to be left unconsidered in planning for the coronation—from a reservoir of water erected over Westminster Hall in case a fire broke out at the grand event, to, the *Post Boy* reported, an awning "ready to protect the nobility and gentry from the rain."

The *Boston Evening Post* of November 16, 1761, printed the eighty-seven elements of the order of the procession of the coronation, starting with "The King's Herb-Woman, with her six maids, two and two, throwing sweet herbs," followed by, among others, "a fife in livery coat of scarlet richly laced, four drums clothed as the fife, the drum major, eight trumpeters in rich liveries of crimson velvet, kettle-drums with banners of crimson damask, eight trumpeters as before, four abreast," the sergeant trumpeter, the barons, baronesses, bishops, viscountesses, viscounts, countesses, earls, duchesses and dukes, all in their robes, as well as various ceremonial swords, spurs, a scepter, a chalice, and an orb.

The procession made its way to Westminster Abbey, where, after a sermon, the archbishop of Canterbury, Thomas Secker, addressed George III and engaged him in the coronation oath, a colloquy of pledges of allegiance to the Church of England, the church viewed with such suspicion by the Massachusetts Puritans who had fled Bishop Laud. "Sir, are you willing to take the oath usually taken by your predecessors?" the archbishop asked.

"I am willing," the king answered.

"Sir, will you grant and keep, and by your oath confirm to the people of England, the laws and customs to them granted by the Kings of England, your lawful and religious predecessors; and, namely, the laws, customs and franchises granted to the clergy by the glorious king St. Edward, your predecessor, according to the laws of God, the true profession of the Gospel established in this kingdom, and agreeing to the prerogative of the kings thereof, and the ancient customs of this realm?" asked the archbishop.

"I grant and promise to keep them," George III replied.

A bishop beseeched the king to "protect and defend us, as every good king in his kingdom ought to be the protector and defender of the bishops and churches under their government."

The king replied that he would, "with a willing and devout heart."

The oath taken, George III took his seat in the chair that had been used by Edward, a Catholic saint known as "The Confessor" who had built Westminster Abbey and had ruled England from 1046 to 1066. The archbishop took a spoonful of holy oil and anointed the king, first on the king's palms, saying, "Be these hands anointed with holy oil," then on the breast, saying, "Be this breast anointed with holy oil," then on both shoulders, and between the shoulders, saying, "Be these shoulders anointed with holy oil," then on the elbows, and lastly on the top of his head, saying, "Be this head anointed with holy oil, as kings and prophets were anointed, and as Solomon was anointed king."[77]

The honor of placing Saint Edward's crown upon the king's head was also reserved for the archbishop of Canterbury. The moment was met with trumpets, drums, the discharge of muskets and cannon, and cries of "God Save the King," as well as with a prayer by the archbishop that the "eternal God, King of Kings, fountain of all authority and power, bless" the new king, "thy servant, who in lowly devotion boweth his head unto thy divine majesty." At which words the king bowed his head.[78]

The ceremony was a religious event but also a social one. The *Boston Post Boy* of December 7 reported that amid all the festivity, "The great diamond on the top of his majesty's crown dropt off in Westminster Hall on Tuesday, but it was luckily found immediately after dinner." The *Boston Gazette* of January 4, 1762, informed its readers that at the dinner, the hall was lit with nearly four thousand wax candles, which made the gathered jewels and fine clothing glimmer brilliantly. If that were not enough, George III's biographer Christopher Hibbert reports that a few days later, the newly crowned king and queen joined a banquet to mark Lord Mayor's Day, an event in which four gallons each of Jamaican rum and French brandy were required just for the cooking of the feast of "ortolans, quails, duck's tongues, turtles, Westphalia hams . . . and thirty-two dishes of vegetables." Two hundred and forty bottles of champagne and six hundred of port were ordered for drinking.[79]

The ceremonies may have helped in Britain to confer some authority on a young and inexperienced monarch who was assuming power in the midst of a war, but in Boston the events were treated with detachment. Rather than sharing with readers all the details of the coronation ceremony as soon as they were available, the *Boston Evening Post* meted out the news in installments over several weeks beginning February 8, 1762, explaining almost apologetically, to those who wondered why the bother, that there was room in the newspaper and that the account might be "an agreeable amusement to the generality of our readers at this barren season of the year."

Less agreeable or amusing to Bostonians, including Samuel Adams, were the policies adopted by the new king and his advisers. One might not know it from the lavish spending or displays of wealth at the coronation, but Britain was mired in war debt. That fact had been impressed upon George III by his closest adviser, John Stuart, 3rd Earl of Bute. One of George III's biographers, John Brooke, discovered in essays written by George III under Bute's tutelage even before his accession to the throne that "Over and over again with monotonous regularity the Prince dwelt on the increase of the national debt." Brooke found references in the soon-to-be king's writings to "the heavy debt we now labour under," "the enormous debt the nation labours under." The prince said his goal was to see his country "in time free from her present load of debts, and again famous for being the residence of true piety and virtue."[80] The debt was staggering—by 1763 it was £122.6 million, which meant £4.4 million just in annual interest costs, or more than half the total annual budget of £8 million.[81]

It was enough to cause the king and Bute to seek an end to the war with France, a cessation of hostilities formalized in the February 10, 1763, Peace of Paris. It was also enough to provoke resistance to the high taxes imposed to support the debt, and to the invasive methods of enforcing the tax laws. One member of Parliament, John Wilkes, anonymously wrote and published a satirical weekly newspaper, the *North Briton*. As Wilkes's biographer Arthur Cash described it, the *North Briton* opposed a proposed excise tax on cider "because it would legitimate forced entries and searches of houses and barns, putting into the hands of politicians the means to harass and even destroy their opponents." Wilkes's most famous issue, *North Briton* Number 45, was a response to George III's speech to Parliament on April 19, 1763. The newspaper warned that the cider excise tax meant "private houses are now made liable to be entered and searched at pleasure" and asserted that resistance in the name of freedom would be justifiable. The king responded by sending agents to ransack Wilkes's home and lock him up in the Tower of London.[82]

The war debt led George III and his new first minister, George Grenville, to look to America for additional revenues. First was an effort to step up collection of the existing customs duties, enforcement of which was so lax that they brought in only £1,800 a year.[83] Next was the passage, on April 5, 1764, of the Revenue Act, or Sugar Act. That act actually reduced the tax on molasses imported to America to three pennies a gallon from the six pennies a gallon that had been the rate set by the Molasses Act of 1733. But the catch was that this time around, the British authorities actually intended to collect the tax. Molasses was an essential good, used to distill rum. (An effort by Yale students to swear off rum in response to the tax won some praise but was not widely emulated.) The Sugar Act of 1764 also imposed new taxes on Madeira, coffee, foreign indigo, and foreign sugar, banned the import to the colonies of foreign rum, and required all lumber being shipped from America to Europe to pass first through Great Britain.[84]

It was in reacting to the Sugar Act and the customs crackdown that Samuel Adams first burst onto the public scene as an opponent of the government in London. On May 15, 1764, he was appointed to a small committee of the Boston Town Meeting assigned to draft instructions for Boston's representatives in the Massachusetts legislature. The instructions that resulted, in Adams's hand, summarized important aspects of the conflict to come. "As you represent a town which lives by its trade we expect in a very particular manner that you make it the object of your attention to support our commerce in all its just rights, to vindicate it from all unreasonable impositions & promote its prosperity—our trade has for a long time labord under great discouragements; & it is with the deepest concern that we see such further difficultys coming upon it which will reduce it to its lowest ebb, if not totally obstruct and ruin it," the instructions said.

The instructions objected not only to the substance of the new duties and their enforcement but to the process by which the taxes had been formulated and imposed. The voice of Massachusetts had been insufficiently heard and the colony's agent in London had been provided inadequate guidance. "We cannot help expressing our surprise, that when so early notice was given by the agent of the intention to burthen us with new taxes, so little regard was had to this most interesting matter, that the court was not even called together to consult about it till the latter end of ye year; the consequence of which was, that instructions could not be sent to the agent, tho sollicited by him, till the Evil had got beyond an easy remedy."

The instructions proposed an economic argument, that the trade with the colonies benefited Great Britain and that the new taxes and rules would curtail those profits for Britain. It also made the slippery-slope argument: "What still heightens our apprehensions is, that these unexpected proceedings may be preparatory to new taxations upon us:

For if our trade may be taxed why not our lands? Why not the pro-
duce of our lands & every thing we possess or make use of?"

Adams's instructions sketched the beginning of a legal argument,
demanding that the representatives urge the agent in London "to
remonstrate for us all those rights and privileges which justly belong
to us either by charter or by birth." The argument was that the taxes
strike at "our British privileges, which as we have never forfeited
them, we hold in common with our fellow subjects who are natives
of Britain."

The instructions also contained the germ of the moral argument
that for Samuel Adams would become the central point, more important than either the economic or the legal aspects of the struggle. It
came in the form of a rhetorical question, an allusion to Exodus: "If
taxes are laid upon us in any shape without our having a legal representation where they are laid, are we not reduced from the character
of free subjects to the miserable state of tributary slaves?"

Finally, the "Instructions of the town of Boston" contained a recommendation to the town's representatives for action in North America
as well as for advocacy in England: "As His Majestys other Northern
American Colonys are embarked with us in this most important Bottom, we further desire you to use your endeavors, that their weight
may be added to that of this province, that by the united applications
of all who are aggrieved, all may happily obtain redress."[85]

The significance of the instructions drafted by Adams can certainly
be exaggerated. They are not, as some have claimed, the first call to
unify the colonies—Benjamin Franklin's proposal in 1754, the Albany
Plan of Union, came earlier.[86] Nor are they the first protest against
taxation without representation—as we have seen, Cotton Mather's
declaration on the day of the rebellion against Governor Andros in
1689 made reference to protesting "raising of taxes without an Assembly." But the instructions would prove an important roadmap for the
struggles to come, and, unlike either the Albany Plan or the rebellion
against Andros, these ideas, with Adams's leadership, would blossom
into a full-scale revolution and independence. Adams's authorship of

the instructions increased his stature within Massachusetts politics and positioned him for advancement.

Samuel Adams and Elizabeth Wells were married December 6, 1764. He was then forty-two and she was twenty-eight. There must have been, as at many second marriages, a hint of sadness at the ceremony, and at this one more than most, for officiating was the same Rev. Checkley who was the father of Adams's late first wife. The poignancy of the circumstances, though, seems not to have diminished Adams's satisfaction. He wrote to the minister's son, William Checkley, a little more than a year later, "Believe me, my friend—I wish I could persuade all the agreeable bachelors to think so,—there are social joys in honest wedlock which single life is a stranger to. You will allow me to be a tolerably good judge, having had experience of each in double turns."[87]

John Adams's wife, Abigail, after a weekend visit from the couple, called Samuel and Elizabeth "a charming pair." Abigail wrote to her sister, "In them is to be seen the tenderest affection toward each other, without any fulsome fondness, and the greatest complaisance, delicacy, and good breeding that you can imagine, yet separate from any affectation."[88]

Remarried, newly prominent in politics, and steeped in the traditions of Great Britain and the Massachusetts Bay Colony, Samuel Adams was ready to step resolutely to the forefront in the gathering clash with George III. As for the king, he did his own part to advance the cause of independence, overstepping his authority in a way that made Samuel Adams's concern that the Sugar Act was "preparatory" to even more "new taxations upon us" look prophetic.

# Chapter 2

# "Zealous in the Cause"
# *1765–1769*

*"For true patriots to be silent, is dangerous."*

—*Samuel Adams, 1766*

WHEN PARLIAMENT PASSED the Stamp Act, and George III approved it in February and March 1765, they were acting according to elaborate legal traditions and in ornate, tradition-encrusted surroundings. Parliament met in Westminster Palace, adjacent to the marble-floored, 225-foot-tall Westminster Abbey in which George III was anointed and crowned. The palace belonged to the king, and the complex included Westminster Hall, a ninety-two-foot-tall, 240-foot-long by sixty-eight-foot-wide room whose walls were built in 1097.[1] The Stamp Act itself was 13,000 words, consisting of sixty-three sections, each labeled with a Roman numeral. It required a "stamp duty" to be paid on nearly every piece of paper in the colonies, and even on dice and playing cards. Different taxes were specified for deeds or grants of land of less than 100 acres, of 100 to 200 acres, and of 200 to 320 acres. There were taxes on legal papers of every variety, including those for courts "exercising ecclesiastical jurisdiction," raising colonial fears of plans to impose upon America bishops of the Church of England.[2] The act included provisions for taxes on newspapers and almanacs, on bills of lading and liquor licenses. One tax was imposed on someone who had a license for retailing wine but not liquor, another on someone who had a license to sell both liquor and wine. A system for enforcing the act was included within it, subjecting those who counterfeited the stamp to death "without the benefit of clergy."

The legislation was brought before the elected members of the House of Commons on February 6, 1765, where it initially met with some opposition. The colonists had gotten wind of the Stamp Act and tried, with the help of their sympathizers in Parliament, to resist it. When, during the discussion in Parliament, Charles Townshend referred to the Americans as "Children planted by our care," Colonel Isaac Barré, who had fought in the French and Indian War, responded sharply.

"They planted by your care? No! Your oppressions planted em in America. They fled from your tyranny," Barré said. "And believe me, remember I this day told you so, that this same spirit of freedom which actuated that people at first will accompany them still." Barré's motion to adjourn to avoid approving the Stamp Act failed by a vote of 245 to 49. The bill passed three separate readings and was approved by the king on March 22, 1765.[3]

The colonists, dismayed, planned their response to the Stamp Act in more humble surroundings and with less formal ceremony. The resistance began in a small counting room above Chase and Speakman's distillery, where a printer, a ship captain, a distiller, a jeweler, and a cousin of Samuel Adams met as members of a group that would become known as the "Loyall Nine." Instead of responding in writing, they chose action: hanging an effigy of the local stamp master, Andrew Oliver, from a 120-year-old tree in what the *Boston Gazette* described as "the most public part of town."[4]

The distillery and the elm that became known as the Liberty Tree were both in Hanover Square. The square took its name from the British royal dynasty that included George III and its strategic importance from the fact that it stood on Orange Street, which was the only land route out of Boston and thus heavily traveled. More precisely, it was at the intersection of Essex Street, Newbury Street, and Orange Street (the corner of today's Boylston and Washington Streets in downtown Boston), near, but not on, Boston's town common.[5] One newspaper describes the tree as next to a meeting house, apparently the Hollis Street Church led by Mather Byles, a grandson of Increase Mather.[6] Another describes it as opposite a shop selling goods imported from England and India.[7] In the coming months and years, Liberty Trees sprouted or were so labeled in Braintree, Petersham, Great Barrington, and Cambridge, Massachusetts; Newport and Providence, Rhode Island; Norwich, Connecticut; Annapolis, Maryland; and Charleston, South Carolina. But it all began a short walk from Samuel Adams's home in the South End of Boston, at what was described as a "stately elm . . . whose lofty branches seem'd to touch the skies."[8]

The effigy hanging from Boston's Liberty Tree was accompanied by a boot representing the Earl of Bute and by an imp representing the devil, whose work the stamp master and Lord Bute were thought to be up to. After a day—August 14, 1765—in which thousands inspected the effigy (it had a sign warning "He that takes this down is an enemy to his country"), a crowd of Stamp Act opponents carried it through the streets of Boston, beheaded it, and burned it. Oliver's house escaped being burned to the ground, but only barely; the Boston mob pulled down the fence that surrounded the house, broke the rear windows, and proceeded to raid Oliver's wine cellar and destroy some of his furniture, including "a looking glass said to be the largest in North America."[9]

The mob's next target was the lieutenant governor and chief justice of Massachusetts, Thomas Hutchinson, a 1727 graduate of Harvard. Hutchinson had been bold enough to appear as the crowd was attacking Oliver's house and to attempt to disperse them. He had also angered some Bostonians by publishing, in 1764, a history of Massachusetts Bay Colony that frowned on the 1689 revolution against Andros, calling it "precipitate" and "rash."[10] On the evening of August 26, 1765, a mob burst in on Hutchinson's brick mansion in Boston, and, as Hutchinson's biographer, the Harvard historian Bernard Bailyn, memorably described it, "smashed in the doors with axes, swarmed through the rooms, ripped off wainscotting and hangings, splintered the furniture, beat down the inner walls, tore up the garden, and carried off into the night, besides £900 sterling in cash, all the plate, decorations, and clothes that had survived, and destroyed or scattered in the mud all of Hutchinson's books and papers."[11] When the Boston Town Meeting convened the next day to express its "utter detestation" of the attack on Hutchinson's house, it was an informal gathering not in any palace but in Faneuil Hall, a one-hundred-foot long and forty-foot wide wood-floored room above a marketplace with stalls. The room was only twenty-eight feet high even after considerable height was added in a later expansion.[12]

What was Samuel Adams's role in the riots? The question has become a matter of some debate among historians. On the side of Adams's involvement was John C. Miller, a professor of history at Stanford University, whose 1936 biography of Samuel Adams charges that Adams "spirited up the mobs which terrorized Boston during the revolutionary period." Miller writes that Adams "had not intended that the mob should go to such lengths" against Hutchinson, but nonetheless blames Adams for having "inflamed the mob against the lieutenant governor by picturing him as the author of the Stamp Act." Miller also notes that Adams intervened with the sheriff to obtain the release from jail of the leader of the mob that destroyed Hutchinson's house. Also on the side of Adams's involvement is a professor of history at Northeastern University, William Fowler, Jr., who wrote in his 1997 biography of Samuel Adams, "What happened in August 1765 was directed, planned, and had, at the very least, the tacit consent of all who knew about it in advance. Adams was among those who knew."[13]

On the side of Adams's innocence is a professor at the University of Cincinnati, John Alexander. Alexander's 2002 biography of Samuel Adams contends that "neither Adams nor anyone else who followed" John Locke "would sanction the August 26 violence. All legal means of redress had not been exhausted; the August 26 crowd's violent actions smacked of class warfare."[14]

Other historians are more forgiving of the attack on the houses of Hutchinson and Oliver. G. B. Warden's history of Boston stresses that neither Oliver nor Hutchinson were physically harmed, and speculates, "Perhaps the planners of the riot wished to make the officials realize how important protection of property was."[15]

The historical record offers some intriguing clues, but no conclusive answers to the question of Samuel Adams's involvement in the attacks. John Adams's diary includes an account of a Bostonian who said he saw Samuel Adams at the Liberty Tree on August 14: "He says he saw Adams under the Tree of Liberty, when the Effigies hung there and asked him who they were and what. He said he did not know, he could not tell. He wanted to enquire."[16] A genuine denial or the coy answer of someone who knew more than he was telling?

Regardless of whether Adams planned or authorized the August 14 effigy parade and raid on Andrew Oliver's house, he later made clear that he approved of them. In an article in the *Boston Gazette* referring to the anti–Stamp Act agitators as "Sons of Liberty," he wrote,

> We cannot surely have forgot the accursed designs of a most detestable set of men, to destroy the Liberties of America as with one blow, by the Stamp-Act; nor the noble and successful efforts we then made to divert the impending stroke of ruin aimed at ourselves and our posterity. The Sons of Liberty on the 14th of August 1765, a Day which ought to be for ever remembered in America, animated with a zeal for their country then upon the brink of destruction, and resolved, at once to save her, or like Samson, to perish in the ruins, exerted themselves with such distinguished vigor, as made the house of Dogon to shake from its very foundation; and the hopes of the lords of the Philistines even while their hearts were merry, and when they were anticipating the joy of plundering this continent, were at that very time buried in the pit they had digged. The People shouted; and

their shout was heard to the distant end of this Continent. In each Colony they deliberated and resolved, and every Stamp-man trembled; and swore by his Maker, that he would never execute a commission which he had so infamously received.[17]

Certainly there was circumstantial evidence linking Adams to the activities of August 14 in that one of the members of the Loyall Nine, Henry Bass, was his cousin, and another, the printer Benjamin Edes, was to become one of Samuel Adams's closest colleagues and collaborators. A letter from Bass to his father-in-law in December 1765 recounts that he and Edes and Samuel Adams "had a very Genteel Supper" and "spent the Evening in a very agreable manner Drinkg Healths etc." The letter emphasized the importance of keeping this "a profound Secret." Wrote Bass, "We do every thing in order to keep this and the first Affair Private." The "first affair" could well have been the August 14 protest.[18]

It's more difficult to find evidence for Samuel Adams authorizing or inciting the attack on Hutchinson's house. He condemned the attack, not only in the Town Meeting the next day but in a letter to a friend in London, in which he described the August 26 events as "of a truly mobbish nature."

"The cause of this riot is not known publickly—some persons have suggested their private thoughts of it," Adams wrote. "Be it what it will, the town must appear to every candid person to have had no concern in it. An universal consternation appeard in the faces of every one the next morning, & a meeting of the inhabitants was in a few hours had, the largest ever known on any occasion, who unanimously declared their detestation of it. I voted to assist the Majistrate to their utmost in preventing or suppressing any further disorder."

One is left with three possibilities: Adams had no involvement in the August 26 riot; he was involved and immediately felt genuine remorse; or he was involved and he feigned remorse.

Whatever Adams's role in the violence was, it did nothing to impede his political rise. For the second year in a row, he drafted the instructions of the town of Boston to its representatives in the legis-lature. "The freeholders & other inhabitants, being legally assembled in Faneuil Hall, to consider what steps are necessary for us to take at this alarming crisis, think it proper to communicate to you our united sentiments," the instructions said. Adams declared the townsmen "particularly alarmed & astonished at the act, called the Stamp Act, by which a very grievous & we apprehend unconstitutional tax is to be laid upon the colony." Adams was here not yet explicitly comparing the American colonists to the Children of Israel seeking an Exodus from slavery, but the phrase "very grievous" may have resonated with New Englanders steeped in the language of the Bible, for it is used in Exodus to describe the hail, cattle disease, and locust plagues that God inflicted on the Egyptians.

Why was the Stamp Act such a plague? The instructions of 1765 offered Adams's explanation: "By the Royal Charter granted to our ancestors, the power of making laws for our internal government, & of levying taxes, is vested in the General Assembly: And by the same charter the inhabitants of this province are entitled to all the rights and privileges of natural free born subjects of Great Britain. The most essential rights of British Subjects are those of being represented in the same body which exercises the power of levying taxes upon them, & of having their property tried by Jurys: These are the very pillars of the British Constitution founded in the common rights of mankind." The notion that the constitution was not only a contract but derived from something greater, "the common rights of mankind," was to be an important theme in Adams's writing, and it carried with it important consequences for action, as the instructions went on to state.

"We therefore think it our indispensable duty, in justice to our selves & posterity, . . . to declare our greatest dissatisfaction with this law. . . . And we think it incumbent upon you . . . to use your best endeavors in the General Assembly, to have the inherent, unalienable rights of the people of this province, asserted & vindicated & left upon the public records; that posterity may never have reason to charge the present times, with the guilt of tamely giving them away," said the instructions drawn up by Adams and approved by the Town Meeting on September 18, 1765.[19]

Students of the great documents of American history will recognize some phrases there. The "unalienable rights" mentioned by Samuel Adams in 1765 turned up in the Declaration of Independence of July 4, 1776, in which the signers wrote of "certain unalienable rights." The "to our selves & posterity" mentioned by Samuel Adams in 1765 turned up in the United States Constitution of 1787, whose Preamble spoke of securing "the blessings of liberty to ourselves and our posterity."

Rather than shrinking from such assertive language, the Boston Town Meeting embraced it and its author. One of Boston's representatives to the Massachusetts House of Representatives, also known as the General Court, had passed away, and at a Town Meeting on September 27, 1765, Samuel Adams was elected to fill the seat.[20] He immediately emerged in the legislature in a leadership role similar to the one he had begun to occupy at the Town Meeting.

The House of Representatives met in Boston a mere two hundred yards from Faneuil Hall, in a two-story brick building known as the State House. There was no marketplace on the ground floor, but neither were there the high ceilings and vast chambers of Westminster Palace. The first order of business for the House was responding to a speech by the royal governor, Francis Bernard, a British-born, Oxford-educated lawyer who had arrived in Massachusetts in 1760 after having served for two years as governor of New Jersey. The response, widely ascribed to Samuel Adams, directly addressed the issue of the recent violence—disavowing it, yet also downplaying it and refusing Bernard's suggestion to pay for the damages. "That spirit which your Excellency tells us attacks reputations and pulls down houses, will yet be curbed by the law. The estates of the people will remain guarded from theft or open violence," Adams confidently predicted on October 23, 1765. "We highly disapprove of the acts of violence which have been committed."

The response condemned the Stamp Act with the same—perhaps

even stronger—vigor. To Bernard's assertion that Parliament had the right to tax the American colonies, Adams and the Massachusetts House responded, "there are certain original inherent rights belonging to the people, which the Parliament itself cannot divest them of, consistent with their own constitution: among these is the right of representation in the same body which exercises the power of taxation. There is a necessity that the subjects of America should exercise this power within themselves, otherwise they can have no share in that most essential right, for they are not represented in Parliament, and indeed we think it impracticable."

The response called into serious question Parliament's authority over the colonies. But it stopped short of taking the next logical step and questioning the authority of the king. To the contrary, it described "the people of this province" as having "the strongest affection for his Majesty, under whose happy government they have felt all the blessings of liberty."[21]

The same loyalty to the king was professed days later, in a set of resolutions of the Massachusetts House of Representatives that were authored by Samuel Adams and dated October 29. "Resolved, that this House owe the strictest allegiance to his most sacred Majesty George the Third," was the fourteenth and final resolution. But it seemed more an afterthought than the document's logical conclusion, as the bulk of it was devoted to making both a theological and a legal case against the Stamp Act and, for that matter, any other tax imposed by Parliament on the colonists. Going further than he had six days earlier in the response to the governor, Adams this time explicitly invoked an authority higher than the king—God. "Resolved, that there are certain essential rights of the British Constitution of government, which are founded in the law of God and nature, and are the common rights of mankind," the first resolution said. Adams went on to argue that "no law of society, can, consistent with the law of God and nature," take those rights away. The first among those rights that Adams invoked was the right of property: "Resolved, that no man can justly take the property of another without his consent." This, Adams said, was the basis of "the right of representation in the same body which exercises the power of making laws for levying taxes."[22]

These two prongs of the American argument—God and property rights—would be used by Adams and the colonists all the way from 1765 through independence and beyond. They would be elaborated, but they would remain at the core of the colonial case from this point on. They were not yet, however, enough to prevent the Stamp Act from going into effect, which it did as scheduled on November 1. It was greeted in Boston with contempt melded with religious passion. The *Boston Post Boy* of November 11 recounted that the violent Pope's Day pageantry devoted annually on November 5 to marking "abhorrence of POPERY and the horrid plot which was to have been executed on that day in the year 1605" was redirected this year into a peaceful protest. The North and South End gangs paraded together to the Liberty Tree with effigies "representing the Pope, Devil, and several other effigies signifying Tyranny, Oppression, Slavery." Come evening the effigies were burned in a bonfire atop Copp's Hill. The paper said the cooperation between the rival gangs, usually violently at odds with each other, "may be looked upon as the (perhaps the only) happy effects arising from the Stamp Act." The *Boston Gazette* of November 18 asserted, "the ten commandments given to Moses on Mount Sinai, are of greater authority than ten thousand of the dictatorial mandates of John earl of jackboot, or his creature George Greendevil." Neither the *Gazette* nor the *Post Boy* carried the stamp mandated by the act. The stamp's absence was a signal of the limits to British power in Boston. The newspapers did, however, bring news of protests against the Stamp Act in New Hampshire, in South Carolina, in New York, Connecticut, Virginia, Georgia, and Rhode Island. As Adams put it, "The people are in consternation from one end of the continent to the other."[23]

The practical effect of the Stamp Act on Boston was minimal. The tax went unpaid, the stamps themselves sat unused on an island in Boston Harbor, and, after an initial period of uncertainty, the courts and Custom House opened to stamp-free business as usual. But the principle of the dispute nonetheless grated on Adams, who pursued the matter not only in his public activities, but also in private correspondence. On November 11, 1765, he joined another Bostonian in writing to a British clergyman, "Reverend G————W————,"—quite possibly the same George Whitefield who had so electrified Boston when he visited in 1740—to lay out the case of the colonists. Samuel Adams referred back to the founding of the colony by his Puritan forebears. "We are the descendants of ancestors remarkeable for their zeal for true religion & liberty," he wrote. "When they found it was no longer possible for them to bear any part in the support of this glorious cause in their native country England, they transplanted themselves at their own very great expense, into the wilds of America, till that time inhabited only by savage beasts and men: Here they resolved to set up the worship of God, according to their best judgment, upon the plan of the new testament, to maintain it among themselves, and transmit it to their posterity, & to spread the knowledge of Jesus Christ among the ignorant & barbarous natives."[24]

In a November 13 side letter to the same G.W., a message sent along with the November 11 note, Samuel Adams broached in writing, apparently for the first time, the question of independence, that is, a decisive break between the colonies and Great Britain. "There is at present no appearance of . . . a struggle for independence; & I daresay there never will be unless Great Britain, shall exert her power to destroy their libertys. This we hope will never be done," he wrote.[25] Whitefield had visited Boston again in 1764, preaching three times a week to large crowds, and, upon returning to England, allied himself with the colonists, supporting Benjamin Franklin in his opposition to the Stamp Act, and warning against the tyranny that would come with the imposition of an Anglican bishop in America.[26]

Adams pressed on in his anti-stamp activism as the Boston winter approached, writing on December 19 to a friend in England, John Smith, hammering away at the twin themes of God and property rights. "The first settlers of New England, had been prosecuted in England at a Time when the Nation was intoxicated with bigotry and the ideas of ecclesiastical tyranny. This induced them to cross an untried ocean & take shelter in a dreary wilderness," Adams wrote. He went on, later in the letter, "It is an Original Right of Nature. No Man in the State of Nature can justly take anothers Property without his consent."[27]

On December 23, 1765, Samuel Adams's cousin John, a lawyer who lived south of Boston in Braintree, came to visit Samuel, who took him to what John Adams's diary described as "the Monday night clubb." John Adams wrote that he "spent the Evening very agreably, indeed," among the ten or so in attendance, "politicians all." The account is useful because it gives us a flavor of the behind-the-scenes action among the leaders of the fight against the Stamp Act. Part of what they did was to share intelligence, or to gossip about other leading figures: "We had many curious Anecdotes, about Governors, Councillors, Representatives, Demagogues, Merchants &c." Part of it was to discuss strategy and tactics. John Adams says there was discussion that night about whether to reopen the courts that had initially remained closed after the Stamp Act went into effect. And part of it was the sort of social reinforcement and fellowship that occurs whenever men gather, particularly if they are engaged in a common struggle against a powerful foe. "The Behaviour of these Gentlemen is very familiar and agreabl and friendly to each other, and very polite and complaisant to Strangers," John Adams wrote.

John Adams, the visitor, wrote in his diary descriptions of his impressions of the characters in the room. "Cushing is steady and constant, and busy in the Interest of Liberty and the Opposition, is famed for Secrisy, and his Talent at procuring Intelligence," he wrote. It was Thomas Cushing who had co-signed with Samuel Adams the November 11 letter to "Reverend G———W———."

Then John Adams shared his impression of his cousin: "Adams is zealous, ardent and keen in the Cause, is always for Softness, and Deliccacy, and Prudence where they will do, but is stanch and stiff and strict and rigid and inflexible, in the Cause."

The next patriot to be profiled was James Otis, Jr.—a lawyer who, like Samuel Adams, was the son of a politically active father. Otis, John Adams wrote, "is fiery and fev'rous. His Imagination flames, his Passions blaze. He is liable to great Inequalities of Temper—sometimes in Despondency, sometimes in a Rage. The Rashnesses and Imprudences, into which his Excess of Zeal have formerly transported him, have made him Enemies, whose malicious watch over him, occasion more Caution, and more Cunning and more inexplicable Passages in his Conduct than formerly."

Then, as if he realized that he hadn't fully done his cousin justice, John Adams in his diary circled back to the relative who had brought him into the club. Samuel Adams, he wrote,

> I believe has the most thourough Understanding of Liberty, and her Resources, in the Temper and Character of the People, tho not in the Law and Constitution, as well as the most habitual, radical Love of it, of any of them—as well as the most correct, genteel and artful Pen. He is a Man of refined Policy, stedfast Integrity, exquisite Humanity, genteel Erudition, obliging, engaging Manners, real as well as professed Piety, and a universal good Character, unless it should be admitted that he is too attentive to the Public and not enough so, to himself and his family.[28]

The colonists may have lacked the trappings of authority that the king and the Parliament had, but their objections were enough to win a remarkable change of heart in London. On March 18, 1766, the twenty-seven-year-old King George III gave his approval to Parliament's repeal of the Stamp Act, a repeal that had been passed along with the Declaratory Act asserting Parliament's right to make laws governing the colonies.[29] George Whitefield, in England, met the news by praising God, writing in his letter book, "Stamp Act repealed!—*gloria Deo!*"[30] The king was afterward to see the repeal of the Stamp Act as "fatal," increasing the pride of the colonists and encouraging them to rebel to the point of independence.[31] In April the Boston Town Meeting had convened at Faneuil Hall and voted in advance on "the methods to exhibit their joy" when the news officially arrived of the Stamp Act's repeal; they unanimously decided "to prevent any bonfire from being made in any part of the town, also the throwing of any rockets, squibs, and other fireworks in any of the streets of said town, except the time that shall be appointed for general rejoicing."[32] And indeed, when formal notification arrived in May of the Stamp Act's repeal, it was greeted in Boston with church bells ringing, cannons firing, fireworks, a thanksgiving sermon preached by Rev. Mayhew, and a pipe of Madeira wine—about six hundred bottles' worth—provided to the populace by John Hancock, Thomas Hancock's nephew and the heir to his fortune. The Sons of Liberty erected on the common, near the Liberty Tree, an ornate lantern-lit pyramid decorated with a poem that read in part:

> O thou whom next to Heaven we most revere,
> Fair LIBERTY! Thou lovely Goddess hear!
> Have we not woo'd thee, won thee, held thee long,
> Lain in thy lap and melted on thy Tongue: . . .
> GODDESS! We cannot part, thou must not fly
> Be SLAVES; we dare to scorn it—dare to die.[33]

The news of the repeal of the Stamp Act only boosted the political career of Samuel Adams. In the May 1766 Boston town elections, he was reelected to the Massachusetts House of Representatives as the top vote getter among the six candidates for four seats. He won the votes of 691 of the 746 voters, each of whom was allowed to support four candidates. That was more than the 676 won by Thomas Cushing or the 646 won by James Otis, the other patriots that John Adams had assessed as members of the "Monday night clubb," and he won far more than the 437 won by John Hancock, whose fourth-place finish was enough for a place in the Boston delegation to the State House.[34] Adams's new stature was recognized by his fellow representatives throughout the colony. When the House convened for the new session on May 28, 1766, the members elected Samuel Adams as their clerk. The diary of a Boston merchant, John Rowe, notes the election and remarks that Adams "had a great zeal for liberty."[35] The clerkship was an influential position that carried a £90 a year stipend, which helped to support Adams.[36] The Boston newspapers reported that following the choice, "A sermon suitable for the occasion was preached by the Reverend Mr. Edward Barnard of Haverhill, from those words in Nehemiah V. 19. 'Think upon me my God, for good, according to all that I have done for this people.'"[37]

The theme of thankfulness to God was extended a few days later, on June 3, in Adams's "Address of the House of Representatives of Massachusetts to the Governor." Expressing pleasure at the repeal of the Stamp Act, Adams wrote, "when we look back upon the many dangers from which our country hath, even from its first settlement, been delivered, and the policy and power of those, who have to this day sought its ruin, we are sensibly struck with an admiration of Divine goodness, and would religiously regard the arm which has so often shielded us." Yet far from dissipating entirely, the ill will from the Stamp Act episode festered, with Governor Bernard harping on the destruction of Hutchinson's house, and Adams launching an extensive defense of the position of the colonists. "For true patriots to be silent, is dangerous," Adams had insisted in the June 3 speech.[38] On June 5, on behalf of the House, Adams told Governor Bernard: "Provided we observe the directions of our charter, and the laws of the land, both which we have strictly adhered to, we are by no means accountable but to God and our own consciences."[39]

Adams used the lull that followed the repeal of the Stamp Act to cultivate ties with patriots from other colonies and to urge them to be on the lookout for future incursions on their liberties. To Christopher Gadsden of South Carolina, whom Otis had described to Adams as "a zealous assertor" of the colonists' cause, Adams wrote that the Stamp Act, "which was calculated to enslave & ruin us," had actually turned out to be a blessing. "When the colonies saw the common danger they at the same time saw their mutual dependence & naturally called in the assistance of each other, & I dare say such friendships and connections are established between them, as shall for the future deter the most virulent enemy from making another open attempt upon their rights as men & subjects," Adams wrote, suggesting that while such "open" attempts might be deterred, there was still "reason to fear that the libertys of the colonys may be infringed in a less observable manner."[40]

If the Stamp Act had been calculated to "enslave" the colonists, it also heightened consciousness in Boston of the contradiction inherent in protesting such measures in the name of liberty while at the same time possessing their own actual, live, slaves. In May of 1766, the Boston Town Meeting instructed its representatives in the House to try to pass a law banning the importation and sale of slaves.[41] Samuel Adams opposed slavery. His niece recalled that in 1764 or 1766, a female slave named Surry was given to Elizabeth Adams as a gift. When she told her husband about it, Samuel Adams said immediately, "A slave cannot live in my house. If she comes she must be free." Unlike some other American founding fathers who held slaves or who waited until death to free them, Samuel Adams indicated with his action that he understood that freedom must extend also to African-Americans.[42]

While the British backed off from the Stamp Act, it wasn't long before they were seeking to translate the powers declared in the Declaratory Act into actual revenues. The August 31, 1767, *Boston Post Boy* and the *Boston Gazette* of the same day both reported on their front pages that Parliament was considering a law to impose a tax of 3 cents a pound on all tea imported into the colonies, with additional taxes on glass, flint, paper, lead, and "painters colours." The September 14, 1767, *Boston Evening Post* brought news from London that "His Majesty" had given "the royal assent" to the bill "for granting certain duties in the British Colonies and plantations in America . . . and for more effectually preventing the clandestine running of goods in the said colonies & plantations."

The Revenue Act—or Townshend Act, as it was known after its sponsor, Charles Townshend, who had become the chancellor of the exchequer—was initially met in Boston and in the rest of the colonies with a more calm reaction than the one that greeted the Stamp Act. There was no riot this time around, at least not immediately. It would take some work first. The *Boston Gazette*, printed and owned by Adams's friend Benjamin Edes, who was one of the Loyall Nine, did its part. On December 28, 1767, it printed on its front page a letter from "a farmer"—John Dickinson of Pennsylvania—urging, "My countrymen, ROUSE yourselves, and behold the ruin hanging over your heads." If Great Britain "can order us to pay what taxes she pleases," the farmer wrote, "we are as abject slaves."

Perhaps inspired by the farmer's letter, Samuel Adams roused himself and began one of the most productive phases of his career as a revolutionary. David McCullough begins Part I of his magnificent biography of John Adams with John Adams's observation that "The Revolution was effected before the war commenced. The Revolution was in the minds and hearts of the people."[43] Another eminent historian, Arthur M. Schlesinger, begins his history of the role played by newspapers in the American Revolution with a quote from David Ramsay's 1789 history of the American Revolution, in which Ramsay contended, "In establishing American independence, the pen and the press had a merit equal to that of the sword."[44] From 1768 to 1770, Samuel Adams worked furiously on both the political front and the press front to defend the liberty of the colonists from the threat posed by the Townshend Act and the effort to enforce it.

Others served in the Revolution as spies or soldiers or diplomats, but one of Adams's key roles was as a writer. He wrote in a study next to his bedroom. His wife could hear the quill pen scratching against paper nonstop, long into the night. One Adams biographer recounts that a contemporary of Adams had business that required him to pass by the Adams house regularly after midnight. The lamp in Sam Adams's study, which could be seen from the street, was nearly always lit, no matter how late it was: "He knew that Sam Adams was hard at work writing against the Tories."[45]

Boston in January of 1768 was not yet in the midst of an actual war, but it was in the middle of an honest-to-goodness newspaper war, the sort of battle for circulation and advertising revenue and news that occasionally itself erupted into genuine violence. It pitted the Tory publisher of the *Boston Chronicle*, John Mein, against Adams's colleagues at the *Boston Gazette*, Benjamin Edes and Edes's partner, John Gill. When Mein encountered Gill on the street in January 1768, the Tory newspaperman savagely assaulted Gill with a club.[46]

Adams's articles were published nearly weekly under a variety of pen names in the pages of the *Boston Gazette*. He didn't just send them in from a distance; he and other revolutionary patriots would gather in the newspaper office on the weekends to help make up the newspaper, which was so widely read that Hutchinson complained, "The misfortune is that seven eighths of the people read none but this infamous paper."[47]

Adams used many different methods to promote his ideas— speeches, letters, committees, small meetings, large meetings. But one of the most effective was a common printing press, a temperamental, creaking, groaning, six-foot-high, six-foot-wide device of wood and string and iron by which one sheet of paper at a time was pressed up against a form of inked type. The power of the press came from human arm and back and shoulder muscles. The printer would turn a crank attached to a leather belt to slide the bed of type and quoins and tympans and blanket and frisket and paper under the platen. Then he would reach across and pull toward him the iron arm of the press, with its well-worn wooden handle. A squeeze at the end of the motion would force the platen down against the outer tympan and the blanket and the inner tympan and the frisket and finally press the paper itself against the ink-covered lead type. This was how each week, the publishers of the *Boston Gazette*, Benjamin Edes and John Gill, spread the ideas of Adams and of other patriots.

Isaiah Thomas, the publisher of the *Massachusetts Spy*, wrote about the *Boston Gazette* in his classic 1810 history of printing in America. "During the long controversy between Great Britain and her American Colonies, no paper on the continent took a more active part in defence of the country, or more ably supported its rights, than the *Boston Gazette*; its patrons were ever alert and ever at their posts, and they had a primary agency in events which led to our national independence," wrote the rival patriot publisher. Thomas said that "the most distinguished revolutionary patriots in Boston," including Samuel Adams, "frequently convened at this celebrated *Gazette* office," for meetings to concoct "many of the measures of opposition to the British acts of parliament for taxing the colonies—measures which led to, and terminated in the independence of our country."[48]

This was no secret at the time. Lieutenant Governor Hutchinson wrote that "Otis and the two Adams, Cooper & Church go regularly every Saturday to set the Press."[49] "Church" was Benjamin Church, a surgeon and graduate of Harvard and Boston Latin School who was active in the revolutionary cause. John Adams recorded in his diary for Sunday, September 3, 1769, that he spent the evening with Samuel Adams and John Gill "preparing for the next day's newspaper,—a curious employment, cooking up paragraphs, articles, occurences, &c, working the political engine.[50] Governor Bernard described Samuel Adams and the patriot James Otis as "the principal managers of the *Boston Gazette*."[51] The colonial government was sensitive to what appeared in the press and reacted to it. In 1768, Governor Bernard and Liutenant Governor Hutchinson tried unsuccessfully to bring a libel charge against the *Boston Gazette*.[52] Defeat of the effort prompted Samuel Adams, as "Populus," to write in the paper, "There is nothing so fretting and vexatious, nothing so justly TERRIBLE to tyrants, and their tools and abettors, as a FREE PRESS."[53]

Massachusetts, the cradle of liberty, had the most newspapers (ten, at the peak in 1775) and the most places with newspapers (five, the same year) of any of the colonies, and it led in number of printers (thirty-four at the peak in 1774) and the number of items they published during the run-up to the Revolution. "The Boston firm of Edes

& Gill was the leading printer in America" during the revolutionary years, reports G. Thomas Tanselle in a paper on American printing from 1764 to 1783.[54] The historian Kenneth Lockridge has estimated a literacy rate of about 85 percent for adult males in Massachusetts as the Revolution approached, high relative to other colonies.[55] The *Boston Gazette*'s circulation was about two thousand.[56]

Samuel Adams earned his meager living as a tax collector and as a politician. But during one of the crucial periods to the Revolution, one of his primary functions was as a volunteer newspaper columnist who was pressing a relentless campaign. He wrote mainly under the pen name "Vindex"—after the Roman senator first to revolt against the emperor Nero. But he used more than a dozen other monikers, from "Cotton Mather" and "A Puritan" to "Candidus," "Valerius Poplicola," and "Alfred." Each was a window into a different aspect of Adams's personality and role in the Revolution. "A Puritan" was anti-Catholic, consumed with religious rights, conscious of his Puritan forefathers. "Candidus" was satirical, wry, intellectually combative, acid, scathing toward the British and their allies among the colonists. "A Chatterer" was a cool but close observer of the political maneuvers of the local authorities. "Vindex" was a logical defender of the rights of the colonists. "A Bostonian" was a proud guardian of his hometown's reputation. "Determinatus" was defiant and stubborn. "Valerius Poplicola" was concerned with virtue and conscious of his place in history. The historian Douglass Adair, while acknowledging that "in most cases the identity of the man behind the pseudonym was an open secret," has noted that the number of names "created the impression of a host of Massachusetts opinions, all 'patriotic,' of course, and all squinting with suspicion toward England."[57]

While the pen names had different personalities and emphases, it is possible to discern some common arguments in Samuel Adams's newspaper writing during this period, in his private correspondence, and in his official speeches and documents drafted as a Massachusetts and Boston politician.

———————

For Adams, the foremost of these arguments was a religious appeal, urging readers to remember to stay faithful to the spirit that animated their Puritan predecessors. Samuel Adams joined John Hancock—who was himself the son of a clergyman—in writing a March 24, 1766, letter from the town of Boston to the inhabitants of Plymouth. That town's original settlers had arrived on the *Mayflower* in 1620, "Having undertaken for the Glory of God, and Advancement of the Christian Faith, and the Honour of our King and Country, a Voyage to plant the first Colony," as their compact put it. Adams and Hancock wrote that Plymouth's encouragement of Boston's resistance to the Stamp Act was evidence that its residents "still retain the truly noble spirit of our renowned ancestors."

As for those ancestors, Adams and Hancock wrote, "When we recollect the ardent love of religeon and liberty, which inspired the breasts of those worthys; which induced them at the time when tyranny has laid its oppressive hand on church and state in their native country, to forsake their fair possessions and seek a retreat in this distant part of the earth—When we reflect upon their early care to lay a solled foundation for learning, even in a wilderness, as the surest if not the only means of preserving and cherishing the principles of liberty and virtue, and transmitting them to us our posterity, our mind is filled with deep veneration, and we bless and revere their memory." The Bostonians noted that there had been attempts in the past to infringe on their liberty, including that of Andros, whose name had been "handed down to us with infamy." And they wrote that their "fervent wish" was that "the spirit of our venerable forefathers, may revive and be defused through every community in this land: That liberty civil and religious, the grand object of their view, may still be felt enjoy'd & vindicated by the present generation, and the fair inheritance, transmitted to our latest posterity."[58]

The suggestion that Adams's faith descended more or less directly from that of John Winthrop might be greeted with skepticism by modern Americans. There were, after all, nearly 150 years between the voyage of the *Arbella* and the Declaration of Independence, years that in Europe included the lives of the skeptic Voltaire and the scientist Isaac Newton. They were years full of scientific developments that, for many, including some of the founders of the United States, tended to erode the idea of an intervening God. In his 2003 book on the Declaration of Independence, the Harvard Law School professor Alan Dershowitz writes that Thomas Jefferson, the primary drafter of the Declaration, "was neither a man of the Bible nor a person 'of faith.' He was a man of science and reason. . . . His God was most certainly not the intervening Judeo-Christian God of the Bible. It was 'Nature's God'—what the Jefferson scholar Allen Jayne calls the remote 'watchmaker God of deism . . . who established the laws of nature at the time of creation and then left it alone.'"[59]

But Samuel Adams's actual writings demonstrate he was acutely aware of Winthrop's voyage and its cause. He sought to associate his own cause with it, again and again. In a January 15, 1768, letter on behalf of the House of Representatives of Massachusetts to the Earl of Shelburne, Adams wrote, "Your Lordship is not insensible that our forefathers were, in an unhappy reign, driven into this wilderness by the hand of power. At their own expense they crossed an ocean of three thousand miles, and purchased an inheritance for themselves and their posterity, with the view of propagating the Christian religion, and enlarging the English dominion in this part of the earth."[60] In an April 4, 1768, article signed "A Puritan"—one of a series of articles that Adams wrote for the *Boston Gazette* under that pen name— he said, "I confess I am surpriz'd to find, that so little attention is given to the danger we are in, of the utter loss of those *religious Rights*, the enjoyment of which our good forefathers had more especially in their intention, when they explored and settled this new world." He went on, "What we have above everything else to fear is POPERY," calling it "the idolatry of Christians."[61]

Biblical references and talk of God suffused his writing as he argued publicly on behalf of the American cause. In a January 12, 1768, letter on behalf of the Massachusetts House of Representatives to the colony's agent in London, Dennys De Berdt, Adams wrote, "It is the glory of the British constitution, that it hath its foundation in the law of God and nature." These laws were "invariable" and "never made for politicians to alter."[62] He made the same argument in the January 15, 1768, letter to the Earl of Shelburne, writing, "It is the glory of the British constitution, that it has its foundation in the law of God and nature."[63] On behalf of the Massachusetts House of Representatives to Lord Camden on January 29, 1768, Adams wrote, "The proposition, that taxation and representation are inseparable, is founded on the immutable laws of nature: but the Americans had no representation in the parliament, when they were taxed: are they not then unfortunate in these instances, in having that separated, which God and nature have joined?"[64]

As "Vindex" in the *Boston Gazette* of December 19, 1768, Adams wrote that the laws of God and nature are "the only true basis of all government." "For government is an ordinance of Heaven, design'd by the all-benevolent Creator, for the general happiness of his rational creature, man," Adams wrote.[65] In the next week's issue of the *Gazette*, "Vindex"/Adams described the people of Boston as "tenacious of those sacred rights and liberties wherewith God hath made them free."[66]

The British were depicted by Adams to the public as a threat to religious liberty. Mocking an article in a Tory-leaning paper about the supposedly helpful effect of British troops in maintaining order, Adams responded in the *Boston Gazette* of February 13, 1769, by warning of the consequences of that view, predicting "I expect if this opinion should further prevail, very soon to see" British troops guarding "our church doors in time of divine service, to keep the people from mobbing, when the assemblies are dismissed."[67]

The theme of the British troops as a threat to Boston religion was developed extensively in the *Journal of the Times,* a detailed diary of events in the city that was published first in New York and Philadelphia and then reprinted in Boston. The entry for November 6, 1768, reports, "This being Lord's day, the minds of serious people at public worship were greatly disturbed with drums beating and fifes playing, unheard of before in this land—What an unhappy influence must this have upon the minds of children and others, in eradicating the sentiments of morality and religion, which a due regard to that day has a natural tendency to cultivate and keep alive." On December 25 came the complaint that the troops quartered in Boston dishonored the name of God "with horrid oaths and blasphemies," and that the British common soldiers lacked chaplains and Bibles, so that the army "has less appearance of religion among them than there is among any other in Europe." On April 30, 1769, the *Journal* reported that an elderly woman reading the Bible in her home was set upon by a British soldier who attempted to rape her. On June 5, 1769, came another complaint about British military music marring the Lord's day, nothing that "All application for a redress of this grievance, has been ineffectual; disorders upon the Sabbath, are increasing."[68] No evidence has been found directly linking Adams to the *Journal*, though Governor Bernard wrote to the secretary of state for the colonies, the right honorable the Earl of Hillsborough, that it was composed "by Adams and his associates."

Latter-day press critics have faulted Adams, perhaps unfairly given the lack of evidence for his direct involvement, for what the critics say were "fiction" and "slanderous lies" in the *Journal*.[69] But if the editors of the *Journal of the Times* were guilty of sensationalism, they would hardly be the last newspaper editors to be so accused. If the news reports had no basis at all in fact, it would seem likely that they would be quickly discredited, at least in the town where they were supposed to have originated, by readers with firsthand knowledge of events. It stands to reason, then, that the reports tapped into at least a genuine underlying sense of apprehension about the presence of the British troops in town and what it meant for the religion that Bostonians professed to cherish. And in any event, Adams's goal as a journalist was not to deliver a bias-free, strictly factual, balanced, neutral, "objective" account, but to advance his cause. He was an opinion journalist, a pundit, a columnist, an editorial writer, not a modern news reporter.

Adams was not uniformly friendly to all religions. He harbored an animus toward Catholicism, referring in a January 12, 1768, letter to "the conquered province of Canada, where the exercise of the Romish religion, so destructive to civil society, is allowed." Nor was he an admirer of the Church of England, warning in the same letter, to Dennys De Berdt, that "the establishment of a Protestant Episcopate, in America" would be "very alarming to a people, whose fathers, from the hardships they suffered, under such an establishment, were obliged to fly their native country into a wilderness, in order peaceably to enjoy their privileges, civil and religious."[70] (The Church of England reciprocated the scorn; in 1767 an Anglican bishop, John Ewer, had preached a sermon to the Society for the Propagation of the Gospel claiming that the Puritans had left England to live in America "without remembrance or knowledge of God . . . in dissolute wickedness."[71])

In the *Boston Gazette* of April 11, 1768, Adams, writing as "A Puritan," portrayed the threat of Catholicism being imposed on America as worse even than the Stamp Act. He wrote that "much more is to be dreaded from the growth of POPERY in America, than from Stamp-Acts or *any other* Acts destructive of mens *civil* rights: Nay, I could not help fancying that the Stamp-Act itself was contrived only to inure the people to the habit of contemplating themselves as the slaves of men; and the transition from thence to a subjection to Satan, is mighty easy." The article goes on to investigate rumors of advancing papism in various New England towns, exploring as far as York, in what later became the state of Maine. There, Adams reported with evident disapproval, some "have been seen in public company with the *crucifixes* at their breast."[72]

Nor did Adams have much tolerance for those with doubts about God. "A man who WAVERS, is but a step from TOTAL APOSTACY!" he wrote with apparent alarm in the April 18, 1768, *Boston Gazette*, under the pen name "A Puritan."[73]

In more expansive moods, Adams was more patient. He recognized that his forefathers left England to obtain "a liberty to worship God according to the dictates of their conscience," as he wrote the Earl of Shelburne on January 15, 1768.[74]

Adams often likened the Americans to the Israelites or the Jews. Sometimes the comparison was explicit, and unfavorable. In that April 4, 1768, *Gazette* article signed "A Puritan," Adams wrote of the risk that Americans could become Catholics. "I know full well that it is farthest from the imagination of some of our solid men and *pious* Divines, whom I intend particularly to address on the occasion, that ever this *enlightened* continent should become the *worshippers of the Beast*: But who would have thought that the oblig'd and instructed Israelites would so soon after they were delivered from the Egyptian Task-masters, have fallen down before a *golden* Calf!"[75]

Other times the comparisons were more subtle, but would have resonated nonetheless with Bostonians familiar with the words of the Bible. Writing as "Determinatus" in the *Boston Gazette* of August 8, 1768, Adams slipped in a reference to "taskmasters" without invoking those who supervised the Hebrew slaves in Egypt. But it was almost certainly an allusion to them. "I am no friend to 'Riots, Tumults, and unlawful Assemblies,'" Adams wrote. "But when the People are oppress'd, when their Rights are infring'd, when their property is invaded, when taskmasters are set over them, when unconstitutional acts are executed by a naval force before their eyes, and they are daily threatened with military troops, when their legislature is dissolv'd! . . . in such circumstances the people will be discontented, and they are not to be blamed."

The idea spread, with one Boston resident describing a speech from a leader of those aligned against the British in 1768 as concluding, "We will defend our liberties and property by the strength of our arm and the help of God. To your tents, O Israel."[76]

The notion of Massachusetts as Israel was not Adams's invention. Rev. Samuel Cooper of Boston's Brattle Street Church had sermonized of Massachusetts Bay as "This British Israel."[77] Cotton Mather, in his 1726 book *Faithful Account of the Discipline Professed and Practices in the Churches of New England*, cited Jewish practice as a guide, though not law, on everything from how many congregants were required for a new church ("The Jews of old held, That less than

Ten Men of Leisure, could not make a Congregation") to the reading of the scripture aloud on the Lord's day ("The Pentateuch was divided into fifty four Parashoth, or Sections, which they read over in the Synagogue every year.")[78] Part of the required curriculum for Harvard students from 1735 to 1755, which included the time Samuel Adams was a student there, was the study of Hebrew grammar from a textbook written by Judah Monis, who had converted to Christianity from Judaism one month before joining the Harvard faculty.[79] But Adams used this metaphor of the colonists as children of Israel to motivate others, and his belief in it was a source of strength, comfort, and mission for him.

If there is an alternative explanation to religious belief for Adams's motivation in the revolutionary cause, it is economic. Adams stressed property rights almost as much as religious rights in arguing against Britain's treatment of the colonies, and he described taxes imposed by Britain as an infringement upon those rights. And as a tax collector for the town of Boston who had trouble collecting what he was supposed to, Adams had a deep understanding of how much colonial Americans did not like to pay taxes.

In a January 12, 1768, letter on behalf of the Massachusetts House of Representatives to the colony's agent in London, Dennys De Berdt, Adams wrote, "It is an essential, natural right, that a man shall quietly enjoy, and have the sole disposal of his own property." He went on, in the same letter, to argue:

> It is observable, that though many have disregarded life, and contemned liberty, yet there are few men who do not agree that property is a valuable acquisition, which ought to be held sacred. Many have fought, bled, and died for this, who have been insensible to all other obligations. Those who ridicule the ideas of right and justice, faith and truth among men, will put a high value upon money. Property is admitted to have an existence, even in the savage state of nature. The bow, the arrow, and the

tomahawk; the hunting and the fishing ground, are species of property, as important to an American savage, as pearls, rubies, and diamonds are to the Mogul, or a Nabob in the East, or the lands, tenements, hereditaments, messuages, gold and silver of the Europeans. And if property is necessary for the support of savage life, it is by no means less so in civil society. The Utopian schemes of leveling, and a community of goods, are as visionary and impracticable, as those which vest all property in the Crown, are arbitrary, despotic, and in our government unconstitutional. Now, what property can the colonists be conceived to have, if their money may be granted away by others, without their consent?[80]

In the January 15, 1768, letter to the Earl of Shelburne, he wrote, "The security of right and property, is the great end of government."[81]

Writing as "Vindex" in the *Boston Gazette* of December 19, 1768, Adams said "the industrious man is intitled to the fruits of his industry," describing that as "the plain and obvious rule of equity." He called property "the best cement of society."[82] The Yale historian Edmund Morgan has discerned even in this language what he calls "the Puritan Ethic," noting that Adams framed the British taxes as, in Morgan's words, "an attack not merely on property but on industry," that is, on the virtue of hard work.[83]

Adams played a significant role as a writer and thinker, but he was also a practical politician. He understood the importance of Boston reaching out to other towns in the province and of Massachusetts reaching out to other colonies in North America. In February 1768, the Massachusetts House of Representatives, of which Samuel Adams was clerk, sent a letter to the other colonial legislatures about the Townshend Act and the desirability of coordinated action in response. "All possible care should be taken, that the representations of the several Assembly upon so delicate a point, should harmonize with each other," the letter, drafted by Adams, said. It went on to give Adams's core property rights argument: "It is an essential unalterable right in nature ingrafted into the British Constitution, as a fundamental law & ever held sacred & irrevocable within the Realm, that what a man has honestly acquird is absolutely his own, which he may freely give, but cannot be taken from him without his consent."

The editor of the Massachusetts Historical Society's edition of the *Journals of the Massachusetts House of Representatives,* Malcolm Freiberg, has described this "circular letter," as it came to be known, as "a moderate document couched in temperate language that mildly protested."[84] It's an apt description; the Massachusetts House members refer to their "humble opinion, which they express with the greatest deferrence to the Wisdom of the Parliament." The letter concludes by expressing "firm confidence in the king our common head & Father."[85]

The confidence, if genuine rather than strictly rhetorical, was apparently misguided. George III responded sharply, notwithstanding the letter's moderate tone. The colonists heard about it third-hand, in an April 22 message from Hillsborough, that was in turn conveyed on June 21 by the royal governor of Massachusetts, Francis Bernard. "It gives great concern to his majesty," Bernard read from Hillsborough, that the Massachusetts House "should have presumed to . . . resolve upon a measure of so inflammatory a nature as that of writing to the other colonies on the subject of their intended representations against some late acts of Parliament." The king attributed the letter to "attempts made by a desperate faction to disturb the public tranquility," and demanded that the governor "require of the House of Representatives, in his Majesty's name, to rescind the resolution which gave birth to the Circular Letter."[86]

The House appointed a committee, including Adams, Otis, and Hancock, to respond. On June 30, they did, with a letter to the Earl of Hillsborough arguing that their circular letter had been well within the right to petition the king for redress, a right, they noted pointedly, "settled at the revolution, by William the Third."[87] The letter was read with some unusual precautions—the gallery was cleared, and the doorkeeper was instructed to block the door, apparently to prevent Governor Bernard from adjourning the House once he realized what was about to happen. Then the House voted on whether to rescind the circular letter, as the king had demanded. By a vote of 92 to 17, with Adams among the 92, the representatives of Massachusetts refused the king's order to back down.

In explaining their action in a letter to the governor on the day of the vote, Adams and the Massachusetts House of Representatives invoked God: "We have been actuated by a conscientious, and, finally, a clear and determined sense of duty to God, to our King, our country, and our latest posterity."[88] The silversmith Paul Revere commemorated the event by crafting a large "Sons of Liberty Bowl," which Adams and John Hancock saw when it was first unveiled.[89] It had engraved upon it a reference to "No. 45," "Wilkes and Liberty." The bowl weighed forty-five ounces and, according to the Museum of Fine Arts in Boston where it now rests, "held 45 gills of rum punch, the beverage preferred by colonists during the boycott of government-taxed tea."[90] But a new number had now joined Wilkes's No. 45 in the numerology of freedom. "To the Memory of the glorious NINETY-TWO," the bowl was engraved, "Members of the Hon[bl] House of Representatives of the Massachusetts-Bay, who, undaunted by the insolent Menaces of Villains in Power, from a strict regard to Conscience, and the LIBER-TIES of their Constituents, on the 30th of June 1768, voted NOT TO RESCIND."[91]

Adams had a knack for using anniversaries to revive public inter-est and spirit, and the next opportunity was August 14, the anniversary of the first protests against the Stamp Act. The day's festivities began at the Liberty Tree, with the discharge of fourteen cannon at dawn, and escalated at noon with the singing of "The Liberty Song." To the lively, slightly martial and slightly hymnal air of "Heart of Oak," the crowd sang, in what the *Boston Gazette* described as "exquisite har-mony . . . frought with a noble ardour."[92] It is easy to imagine Samuel Adams singing along; even his enemies acknowledged "he had a good voice, & was a Master in vocal Musick"[93]:

Come, join hand in hand, brave Americans all,
And rouse your bold hearts at fair Liberty's call;
No tyrannous acts shall suppress your just claim,
Or stain with dishonor America's name.

*In Freedom we're born and in Freedom we'll live.*
*Our purses are ready. Steady, friends, steady;*
*Not as slaves, but as Freemen our money we'll give.*

Our worthy forefathers, let's give them a cheer,
To climates unknown did courageously steer;
Thro' oceans to deserts for Freedom they came,
And dying, bequeath'd us their freedom and fame.

Their generous bosoms all dangers despised
So highly, so wisely, their Birthrights they priz'd'
We'll keep what they gave—we will piously keep,
Nor frustrate their Toils on the Land or the Deep

The Tree their own Hands to Liberty rear'd;
They liv'd to behold growing strong and rever'd;
With Transport then cry'd, now our Wishes we gain
For our Children shall gather the Fruits of our Pain

Swarms of Placemen & Pensioners soon will appear
Like Locusts deforming the Charms of the Year
Suns vainly will rise, Showers vainly defend,
If we are to drudge for what others shall spend

Then join hand in hand brave American all
By uniting we stand, by dividing we fall
In so righteous a cause let us hope to succeed
For Heaven approves of each generous Deed—

All ages shall speak with amaze and applause
Of the courage we'll shew in support of our laws
To die we can bear—but to serve we disdain—
For shame is to Freemen more dreadful than Pain

This Bumper I crown for our Sovereign's health,
And this for Britannia's Glory and Wealth;
That wealth and that glory immortal may be
If she is but just—and if we are but free—[94]

The song was emblematic, full of references to slavery and heaven and the Puritan forefathers, all in keeping with the religious arguments that Samuel Adams had been making in his writings. It foreshadowed the need for unity among the American colonies and the prospect that "to die we can bear"—that American lives would be lost in the cause of liberty. And it made the loyalty to Britannia, or at least its glory, conditional on Britain behaving justly and allowing the colonists their freedom.

The song neatly summed up what was going on in Samuel Adams's mind at the time. The Boston Town Meeting convened on September 12 at Faneuil Hall. It opened with a prayer by the Reverend Samuel Cooper of Brattle Street Church. Then the meeting appointed Otis, Thomas Cushing, Samuel Adams, and John Hancock as a committee to organize a "convention" of the towns of the province, since the governor had refused to gather the assembly. The same Town Meeting noted an act of Parliament declaring that "the subjects being Protestants may have arms for their Defense," and a "good and wholesome law of the province" requiring that every household "shall be always provided with a well-fix'd Firelock, musket, accoutrements and ammunition." Citing the "prevailing apprehension, in the minds of many, of an approaching war with France," the meeting requested that the law be duly observed, "in order that the inhabitants of this town may be prepared in case of sudden danger."[95] Four hundred muskets were displayed at the meeting, a show of force that, Samuel Adams and his colleagues understood, would have been noted by the British as much as by France, the supposed threat of which was strictly a pretense.[96]

The same Boston Town Meeting that addressed the need for arms also addressed the need for heavenly support. "The Town taking into serious consideration the present aspect of their public affairs, and being of the opinion that it greatly behoves a people professing Godliness, to address the Supreme Ruler of the World, on all important occasions, for that wisdom which is profitable to direct, VOTED unanimously, That the Selectmen be a Committee to wait on the several ministers of the Gospel within this Town, desiring that the next Tuesday be set apart as a day of fasting and prayer."[97]

At this juncture, as at the previous ones, George III was ready to disappoint the colonists with a new provocation. Just more than a week after the day of prayer, fifteen British warships arrived in Boston Harbor, bearing two regiments of British troops, complete with artillery. They marched from Long Wharf to the Boston Common, where most of them encamped; others lodged in Faneuil Hall and even in the chamber of the House of Representatives, without the colonists' consent.[98]

The presence of the troops did little to enhance colonial compliance with the Townshend Act. The colonists made do by not using the imported goods that were subject to the tax. The *Boston Evening Post* of October 10 reported that not only tea was being spurned, but coffee, as well: "Instead of coffee, dried peas are now being used by many polite families in town, and thought to be equal in taste and flavor to any coffee imported from abroad.—some use barley for the same purpose."

In a 1768 sermon, Samuel Adams's cousin Amos Adams denounced the first King Charles, "whose arbitrary measures br't his head to the block," and connected the experience of the Puritans who fled England under Charles I to that of the Americans fighting for freedom under George III: "Our liberties, both civil and sacred, are truly our own; they are what our fathers dearly brought, they descend to us as a patrimony purchased at their expense."[99] At Reverend Adams's home in Roxbury, sixty young women met early in the morning for a spinning bee to make linen cloth, leading the newspaper writer who recorded the event to predict that "our present difficulties" would probably result in "the ruin of the manufactures of great Britain" and "the wealth and increase of the Colonies." Said the writer, "the aversion to British manufactures increases in proportion to the measures taken to impoverish and enslave us."[100]

For Samuel Adams, the arrival of the British troops, even in prospect, was both grating and an opportunity for action. At least one informant, Richard Silvester, swore to Thomas Hutchinson that about a fortnight before the troops arrived in Boston, Adams had vowed, "on lighting the beacon we should be joined with thirty thousand men from the country with their knapsacks and bayonets fixed" and also "We will destroy every soldier that dares put his foot ashore: His majesty has no right to send troops here to invade this country and I look upon them as foreign enemies."[101] While the veracity of that testimony has since been called into question,[102] there is no doubt that Samuel Adams wrote to Massachusetts's agent in London, Dennys De Berdt, soon after the troops arrived, "May God preserve the Nation from being greatly injured if not finally ruin'd by the Vile insinuations of wicked men *in America*."[103]

Samuel Adams soon realized that killing British soldiers was too extreme a goal, at least immediately. So he focused on getting the troops to withdraw from the town of Boston proper to the island in the harbor known as the Castle. "The Barracks at the castle are sufficient to contain MORE THAN THE WHOLE NUMBER of troops now in town, and ARE EMPTY," he wrote in an unsigned article in the October 10, 1768, *Boston Gazette*.[104]

All of Adams's agitation was so successful, and met with such a receptive audience, that resistance to the British taxes and other restrictive measures spread across Massachusetts society. Bailyn reports a country servant afraid to go out to the barn on a dark night because of the Stamp Act, and a rebellion among the Harvard class of '68—1768—who assembled at their own Liberty Tree in Harvard Yard.[105]

All these years the debt Samuel Adams owed dating back to his time as a tax collector had been hanging over him. On March 13, 1769, he petitioned the Town Meeting finally to discharge him of the debt, explaining that the fire of 1760 and the smallpox of 1764 meant that a number of Bostonians were "unable to make payment" because of "poverty and misfortune."[106] The episode seems not to have eroded his political strength or popularity; on Friday, May 5, the voters of Boston assembled at Faneuil Hall to choose their members of the House of Representatives. John Hancock led the balloting with 505 of the 508 votes cast, but Samuel Adams was next, with 503, one more than either James Otis or Thomas Cushing, who were the other two members elected to the Boston delegation.[107] When the legislature convened on Wednesday, May 31, it was under protest that "a military guard with cannon pointing at the very door of this state house, where this Assembly is held, is inconsistent with that Dignity, as well as that Freedom, with which we have a right to deliberate." Among the body's first actions was to elect Samuel Adams clerk of the House of Representatives. Adams's friends Edes and Gill were chosen as the printers of the House records. On the afternoon of July 12, the House read a first, second, and third time, and then passed, a bill to allow a new tax collector, Robert Pierpoint, "to collect the Taxes uncollected by Samuel Adams," who must have been relieved to have that burden lifted.[108]

In the spring of 1769, Adams and his political allies managed for the first time to obtain and publish copies of Governor Bernard's letters back to London. Adams used them to mock Bernard. In one pamphlet printed by Edes and Gill, Adams focused on a letter to the London ministry by Governor Bernard reporting on an action by the Sons

of Liberty. The group of patriots had arrived at the house of a com-
missioner of customs,

> with an Intention to surprise him and prevent his Escape; but he
> being at the Castle, where the commissioners had been driven
> for safety, they did nothing but plunder his fruit trees. This is
> a very solemn Account indeed; but he never laid this "Manoe-
> vre of the Sons of Liberty," *extraordinary* as it was, before the
> Council, which he never failed to do on like Occasions; think-
> ing possibly, that respectable Body might be of Opinion, that a
> Gentleman of any political Party may be suppos'd to have had
> his Orchard or Fruit Gardens robb'd by *liquorish Boys*, without
> making a formal Representation before his Majesty's first Min-
> isters of State.[109]

The same pamphlet went on to poke fun at Bernard's reaction
upon learning his letters had been intercepted. "It is remarkable,"
Adams wrote, "that Governor Bernard, not long before these Letters
were made public, expressed to a certain Gentleman, his earnest wish,
that the people of this Province could have a Sight of all his Letters to
the Ministry, being assured that they would thereby be fully convinced
that he was a Friend to the Province—Indeed he made a Declaration
to the same Purpose, in one of his public Speeches to the House of
Representatives. Upon the arrival of the Letters, however, he discovered, as some say, a certain Paleness, and complained of as an Hardship that his Letters, wrote in Confidence, should be expos'd to the
View of the Public."[110]

The documents emboldened Adams to appeal directly to George
III. In a June 27, 1769, petition to "The King's Most Excellent Majesty," Adams and the rest of the House of Representatives declared
themselves "impressed with the deepest gratitude to ALMIGHTY
God" for calling the king's family to the British throne. They wrote
that their grievances could be addressed by "your majesty alone under
God." The petition documented seventeen complaints against Ber-

nard and asked that he "may be forever removed from the Government of this province."[111]

Remarkably, George III surrendered to this request from Massachusetts, just as he had acceded to the repeal of the Stamp Act, and on August 1, 1769, Bernard set sail back to England.[112] Reflecting there on his experiences for nine years as the royal governor of Massachusetts, he was reported to have muttered, "Damn that Adams, every dip of his pen stung like an horned snake."[113]

To celebrate Bernard's departure, and to mark the fourth anniversary of the Stamp Act protest, the Sons of Liberty gathered on August 14 at the Liberty Tree in Boston where the effigy of Andrew Oliver had hung. They drank toasts to John Wilkes and to "The Glorious Ninety-Two," then proceeded to the Liberty-Tree Tavern in Dorchester, where 350 Sons of Liberty, including Samuel and John Adams, as well as John Hancock, Paul Revere, Benjamin Church, James Otis, and the printers Benjamin Edes and John Gill, dined in a tent that had been pitched for the purpose and drank forty-five toasts, including to "Liberty without Licentiousness to all Mankind," to "A perpetual Constitutional Union and Harmony between Great Britain and the Colonies," and to "the Liberty of the Press."[114] John Adams's diary reports the group sang versions of "The Liberty Song," including one by Benjamin Church. The diary also claims that, to the honor of the Sons of Liberty, despite all the toasts, he saw not one person intoxicated, "or near it." Wrote John Adams of his cousin Samuel and James Otis, "Otis and Adams are politick, in promoting these Festivals, for they tinge the Minds of the People, they impregnate them with the sentiments of Liberty. They render the People fond of their Leaders in the Cause, and averse and bitter against all opposers."[115] Samuel Adams's name appears at the top of the 355 names on "An Alphabetical List of the Sons of Liberty who din'd at Liberty Tree Dorchester, August 14, 1769," notwithstanding that there were other patriots, like John Adams and Samuel Abbot, whose names would appear first in alphabetical order.[116]

While Bernard had departed Boston, the British regiments had not, and tensions ran high. In the *Boston Gazette*, James Otis referred to the local customs commissioners as "superlative blockheads" and wrote of one of them, "I have a natural right if I can get no other satisfaction to break his head."[117] The day after the article appeared, one of the commissioners, John Robinson, confronted Otis at a coffee house and, the *Gazette* reported, "suddenly turned and attempted to take him by the nose, and failing in the attempt, he immediately struck at him with his cane, against which Otis defended himself, and returned the compliment."[118] The *Boston Post-Boy* reported that Otis "received many very heavy blows on his head, and one particularly on his forehead, that instantly produced a copious discharge of blood." Otis was carried off by his friends to attempt to recover.[119] Adams portrayed the affair as a planned attempt to assassinate Otis.[120] Otis's temperament had been erratic already before the blow to his head, and after it, his mental state deteriorated so that it became increasingly clear that Samuel Adams would have to be the one to take the lead in arguing, organizing, and planning against the British.[121]

Adams and his fellow patriots were starting to recognize that they were involved in more than a local tax dispute or even a colonial one but in a struggle with historic, global ramifications. That, at least, was the implication of the title of an October 1769 pamphlet written by Adams, *An Appeal to the World,* which offered a detailed rebuttal of the "many false and malicious aspersions" contained in memos and letters written by Governor Bernard and other British officials and transmitted to the ministry in London. Though Bernard had been gone for two months, Adams railed at him as if he were still hovering nearby, accusing the "wicked" governor of "an aversion to free assemblies," and of spreading libels against Boston's inhabitants, libels of "the most virulent and malicious, as well as dangerous and pernicious tendency."[122] In the appeal, Adams describes Britain as "a power which is daily . . . contemning our religion."[123]

While Bernard had departed, the soldiers, Samuel Adams complained in an article in the *Gazette,* were "stationed in our very bowels." He shuddered at the thought that someone might "wantonly" order "troops to fire on an unarm'd populace," and repeat in Boston the scene at St. George's Fields in London, where British troops had, on May 10, 1768, fired on a crowd clamoring to free John Wilkes from King's Bench Prison, killing five or six of them.[124] To Boston's agent in London, Dennys De Berdt, Adams wrote on November 6, 1769, that the British troops in Boston had "become the object of contempt even of women & children. . . .

"Britain may fall sooner than she is aware," Adams predicted to De Berdt, "while her colonies who are struggling for Liberty may survive her fate & tell the Story to their Childrens Children."[125]

# Chapter 3

# Massacre

# 1769–1773

*"The Streets of our Metropolis, crimsond with the Blood of our fellow subjects."*

—*Samuel Adams, August 3, 1770*

ECEMBER OF 1769 brought sad news for Samuel Adams. Rev. Samuel Checkley, the father of Samuel Adams's first wife and the minister who had officiated at Adams's baptism and both of his weddings, died on the first of the month. Samuel Adams helped conduct an inventory of Checkley's estate for the Suffolk County probate judge. At Checkley's house on South Street, it included, along with a looking glass, a bearskin muff, four featherbeds, and other household items, a gun, suggesting that the seventy-four-year-old clergyman may have taken to heart the Boston Town Meeting's admonishment the year before to "be prepared in case of sudden danger." The inventory Adams conducted also included a series of items belonging to Checkley that were said to be "At Mr. Adams's house." They included sheets, towels, handkerchiefs, teaspoons and other silverware, and gowns, raising the possibility that the ailing Checkley had moved in with Samuel Adams after Checkley's wife, Elizabeth, had died in July. If nothing else, the fact that Adams helped to conduct the inventory, and the fact that so much of the property was at Adams's house, underscored how close was the relationship between the minister and Adams.[1]

Checkley was buried Wednesday, December 6. An obituary that appeared in both the *Boston Evening-Post* and the *Boston Post Boy* on December 11 reported that Checkley had been in the fifty-first year of his ministry. "He was uncommonly gifted in prayer," the obituary said. "His voice was very pleasant, and his delivery without affectation, natural and graceful. His preaching also was serious, affecting, scriptural, plain and useful." The newspapers described him as "in principle and preaching a moderate Calvinist," "not bigotted," and "far from condemning or censuring any good men that diffr'd from him.

"His piety was deep and effectual, his religion hearty, and his devotion unaffected and fervent," the obituary said. It noted that of Checkley's twelve children, only one survived him, and said that those losses and the death of his wife "greatly affected his spirits, and impaired his constitution, tho' he bore up under them all with very exemplary patience and christian resignation."

Some of the qualities ascribed to Checkley sound much like Samuel Adams, and not only the pleasant voice. "We must not forget to mention his warm attachment both to the constitution and to the rights of his Country, both civil and religious: He never spake with greater smartness and resentment than against those men who he apprehended by their measures, had a design to subvert or curtail them," the obituary said. It concluded by summing up Checkley as "steady always," convincing everyone that "he acted himself, and was govern'd by principle." It said that Checkley died "firm and unshaken in the religion he had always professed and preach'd."[2]

The Sunday that followed the burial, the surviving pastor of the New South Church in Boston, Penuel Bowen, preached a sermon in Checkley's honor, which was later published by Edes and Gill. Bowen said that Checkley "really esteemed religion the only support under the sorrows and afflictions of life, (a large share of which he had,) and used it himself in this view; so he was abundant in recommending it to others for the same valuable purpose: his discourses were almost all in good measure filled with savory matter for the consolation of mourners, and the encouragement of those who were afflicted and cast down." Bowen, too, stressed Checkley's patriotism: "He loved his country, her liberties and her laws; always gave the weight of his influence on the side of her rights; and was truly patriotic in sentiment and conduct."[3]

Despite his grief, Samuel Adams threw himself into activity in early 1770. The town merchants and patriot leaders, convening not as the Town Meeting but as "The Body," gathered in January to consider how to enforce a ban on importing British goods. Lieutenant Governor Hutchinson declared the meeting illegal and dispatched Sheriff Greenleaf—the same sheriff who had tried to sell Adams's house out from under him—to order it to disband "without delay." Adams replied that the meeting was legal and that its participants were "determined to keep consciences void of offense towards God and towards man."[4] As for the importers, Adams was of the view that "no atonement could be made this side of the Grave: God perhaps might possibly forgive them, but he and the rest of the people never could."[5]

Enforcing the import ban on merchants who did not wish to abide by it could be a dangerous business for those on either side of the issue. On Thursday, February 22, an informer for the customs service, Ebenezer Richardson, tried to topple a sign pointing out one importer for ostracism. A crowd favoring the import ban followed him to his house and pelted it with sticks, stones, and eggs. Richardson responded by firing at the crowd with a musket, killing an eleven-year-old boy. Samuel Adams's friend and personal physician, Dr. Joseph Warren, performed the autopsy.[6] The funeral that followed on Monday, February 26, was the first among what were to be many elaborate and highly politicized funeral rituals. As the *Boston Gazette* of March 5 described it, first "The little Corpse was set down under the Tree of Liberty, from whence the procession began. About five hundred school boys preceded; and a very numerous Train of Citizens followed, in the estimation of good judges at least two thousand of all Ranks, amidst a crowd of spectators; who discover'd in their countenances and deportment the evident marks of true sorrow." The Sons of Liberty ordered a board affixed to the Liberty Tree with biblical verses about the need to punish the wicked, by which it was clear they meant Richardson.[7]

Or perhaps the definition of the wicked also included the British solders there to impose the customs duties. On March 2, a soldier showed up at a Boston ropewalk to look for work earning extra money twisting rope for use on the harbor's ships. A local ropemaker asked the soldier if he wanted work. When the soldier answered yes, the ropemaker invited the soldier to go clean his outhouse. The soldier took offense, and in the fracas that ensued, ropemakers and soldiers traded blows with sticks and clubs. On March 3, Boston ropemakers and British soldiers clashed again, leaving a British private with a broken skull and arm.[8]

These low-grade scuffles continued into the evening of Monday, March 5, first on Cornhill (now Washington Street), then in Boylston's Alley. A lone sentry, Private Hugh White, stood guard in front of the Custom House, and when a boy insulted White's captain, White hit the boy in the head with his musket. Sometime after 8 P.M., with the light of the first-quarter moon shining on the snow-covered streets of Boston, a tall man in a red cloak addressed a crowd in Dock Square.[9] Samuel Adams, who wore a red cloak but was of average height, later stressed the importance of ascertaining the identity of this still unknown instigator, though he bridled at the suggestion that it was a Boston officeholder.[10]

Church bells began ringing, first those of the Brattle Street Church, then those of the Old Brick Church. Cries of "Fire!" filled the streets, as the Bostonians thought the bells were a fire alarm. Crowds poured into King Street, a wide plaza between the Town House and the Custom House. Private White called for reinforcements, and eight British grenadiers led by Captain Thomas Preston set out down King Street in the chaos to come to White's aid.[11]

The red-coated British troops set up in a semicircle facing the crowd. The people were calling them "Lobsters," taunting the soldiers, goading them to fire, a cry that mixed with the fire alarms still in the air. Then a chunk of ice—a snowball, or perhaps an icicle or hard slab of snow from the roof of the Custom House—or maybe it was a club, or a stick, hit Private Hugh Montgomery. He fell to the ground, and whether by accident or by frustration, discharged his musket into the crowd.[12] The other soldiers fired, too, in a chain reaction. Captain Preston initially did not order them to stop. In a few minutes, five colonists were fatally wounded, and as the Bostonians scattered and rushed to tend to their casualties, the British troops marched back to their quarters.[13]

From then onward, the clash between Boston civilians and redcoats has been shrouded in the fog of war. Were the British shots commanded or spontaneous? Who initiated the aggression? The distance of time makes it harder, not easier, to sort out facts that live, sworn witnesses at the time could not agree on. What is certain is that Adams pressed immediately and aggressively to wring every possible bit of political advantage from the bloodshed. The foremost modern historian of that deadly night, a Massachusetts law professor and state judge named Hiller Zobel, credits Samuel Adams with naming the clash "the Boston Massacre."[14]

In the immediate aftermath, a crowd of thousands gathered at Faneuil Hall. When that became too crowded, they moved to Old South Church, where they met and demanded the removal of the British troops from Boston. The crowd's intent was not only to protect the colonists from further massacres, but also to protect the redcoats from retribution. Lieutenant Governor Thomas Hutchinson whispered with the top British military commander in Boston, Lieutenant Colonel William Dalrymple, and then announced that one regiment of troops would evacuate to an island in Boston Harbor. As John Adams recalled it later, "With a self-recollection, a self-possession, a self-command, a presence of mind that was admired by every man present, Samuel Adams arose with an air of dignity and majesty, of which he was sometimes capable, stretched forth his arm, tho' even then quivering with palsy, and with an harmonious voice and decisive tone, said, 'if the Lieut. Governor or Col. Dalrymple, or both together, have authority to remove one regiment, they have authority to remove two—and nothing short of the total evacuation of the town by all the regular troops, will satisfy the public mind or preserve the peace of the province.'"[15]

Both regiments did leave Boston, at least briefly. Samuel Adams pressed his advantage. He paid the Superior Court a visit to demand an immediate trial of Captain Preston, who had been in charge of the troops that committed the massacre. The court decided the forty-year-old Irishman would get a fairer trial if some time was allowed for tempers to cool. But to placate Samuel Adams, the judges acted on a different case, agreeing to arraign and try Ebenezer Richardson for the murder of the eleven-year-old. He was convicted and jailed until George III eventually granted him a pardon at the request of Hutchinson.[16] The decision of Samuel Adams, joined by John Hancock, Dr. Warren, and Rev. Samuel Cooper, to pay the judges a visit was seen by Hutchinson as heavy-handed. The lieutenant governor described Adams as having "harangued" the judges.[17]

If Adams favored a speedy trial for Preston, he also was concerned that the accused have the benefit of legal representation. The lawyer who, with John Adams, defended Preston, Josiah Quincy, Jr., wrote that he told his client that he refused to act as defense attorney "until advised and urged to undertake it" by Samuel Adams, Hancock, Warren, and Cooper.[18] While John Adams was entirely capable of acting on his own and of differing with Samuel Adams, there is no evidence that Samuel ever faulted John for accepting Preston as a client or for doing his best to defend him, or that the situation strained relations between the cousins. The indictment of Preston and the other soldiers charged the British troops with "not having the Fear of God before their eyes, but being moved and seduced by the instigation of the devil and their own wicked hearts."[19]

The funerals for the massacre victims made the one for the boy slain by Richardson seem modest. The *Boston Gazette* reported, "It is supposed that there must have been a greater number of people from town and country at the funeral of those who were massacred by the soldiers, than were ever together on this continent on any occasion." Most of the shops in town were shut, and church bells rang not only throughout Boston but in neighboring Charlestown and Roxbury.[20]

To Benjamin Franklin in London, Adams expressed satisfaction that a published narrative of the massacre favorable to the colonists "had the desired effect; by establishing truth in the minds of honest men, and in some measure preventing the Odium being cast on the Inhabitants, as the aggressors in it."[21]

Adams spoke out for the victims not only in the press but also in government documents. On August 3 he sent a letter to Lieutenant Governor Hutchinson on behalf of the Massachusetts House of Representatives. The letter, which also appeared in the August 6 *Boston Gazette*, was addressed as much to the people of Massachusetts as to the lieutenant governor. "We are obligd at this time to struggle, with all the Powers with which the Constitution hath furnished us, in Defence of our rights; to prevent the most valuable of our Liberties, from being wrested from us, by the subtle Machinations, and daring Encroachments of wicked ministers," it said in part. It went on to name among these encroachments "A Revenue, not granted by us, but torn from us: Armys stationd here without our consent; and the Streets of our Metropolis, *crimsond* with the Blood of our fellow subjects."[22]

When the trial of the soldiers accused of the massacre finally began in November, Samuel Adams provided the prosecutor, Robert Treat Paine, with what a legal history described as "written comments on the evidence, as well as hints on argument points and trial tactics."[23] To the readers of the *Boston Gazette*, Adams provided opinionated running coverage of the trial, at astonishing length—in December 1770 and January 1771, he published about 26,000 words on the trial, so many that the writer himself conceded to the printers that he had "taken up too much room in your useful paper."[24] The dispatches consisted mainly of a forthright defense of the colonists and a critique of the soldiers: "It is a glaring mistake to say, the Soldiers were in danger from the inhabitants: The reverse is true; the inhabitants were in danger from the Soldiers."[25]

In the massacre essays as almost always in Adams's writings, there were religious overtones and references. In the December 17, 1770, *Boston Gazette*, Adams, writing as "Vindex," commented that there was something pleasing about a court of law. It is, he wrote, "solemn as it brings to our minds the tribunal of GOD himself! before whose judgment-seat the scriptures assure us all must appear."[26] In his account of the massacre in the following week's issue of the *Gazette*, "Vindex"/Adams noted the church bells were ringing during the event.[27] Of the jurors who eventually acquitted six of the soldiers and found two guilty of manslaughter rather than murder, Adams wrote, "they are accountable to God and their own consciences, and in *their* day of trial, may God send them good deliverance."[28]

The massacre victims included members of groups that were widely looked down upon by mainstream Boston society at the time. Patrick Carr was a Roman Catholic. Crispus Attucks was either black or a Natick Indian, or a combination. They were both buried with the other victims at the Granary burial ground a short walk from the massacre site. Their race and religion made their killing no less abhorrent to Samuel Adams. As Zobel, the massacre historian, put it, "Black, red, or white, a martyr was a martyr."[29]

Some historians have made the accusation that in Samuel Adams's zeal to convict the British, he suggested that testimony of Catholic or black *witnesses* to the massacre should be discounted because of their religion or race.[30] But the evidence does not bear that out. Though it is true Adams found the testimony of one African-American witness named Andrew suspect, a careful reading of Adams's extensive writings on the case makes it clear that Adams saw Andrew's character, not merely his skin color. Adams described Andrew as someone with a "lively imagination" who was "remarkable for telling romantick stories in the circles of his acquaintance." Adams said he was more inclined to believe the testimony of "*Newtown Prince*, another Negro, of whom for my own part I conceive a better opinion than of *Andrew*."[31] In other words, he was judging black witnesses as individuals rather than as members of a racial category—the opposite of racism. Adams's trial strategy memo to prosecutor Robert Treat Paine makes no reference to the race or religion of either the witnesses or the victims.[32]

As Adams was making progress portraying the colonists as victims in the Boston Massacre, he and the colonists were making some advances with their cause in London. On April 12, 1770, Parliament repealed nearly all the taxes imposed by the Townshend Act, leaving in place only the tax on tea "as a mark of the supremacy of parliament." Explained George III, "There must always be one tax to keep up the right. And as such I approve of the tea duty."[33]

Adams was also cultivating important relationships in Boston, including one with his fellow member of the House of Representatives, John Hancock. The relationship between Hancock and Adams began as a close partnership. Adams wrote to Hancock May 11, 1770, telling him that Hancock's decision to resign his seat in the House of Representatives caused Adams "great uneasiness." Adams called Hancock "a most valueable Member," and entreated him "as a favor" to change his mind, which Hancock did. The letter was signed, "I am with strict truth Your affectionate friend & Brother."[34] At about this time, at least one historian has suggested, Hancock may have put up money to help Samuel Adams settle Adams's arrearages from his time as tax collector from 1756 to 1764.[35] In January of 1771, Samuel Adams joined with Hancock and Paul Revere to petition the town to build a new gunpowder magazine at a safer remove from the British warships in Boston harbor.[36]

By December 1771, for reasons that are now obscure, the relationship between Adams and Hancock had started to fray, though not necessarily over money. A memo that Adams wrote on December 18 documents a conversation Adams had with Harrison Gray, Jr., the son of the treasurer of the colony. "I had been informd that he had told John Hancock Esqr that he heard me say in a threatening manner that Mr Hancock might think as he pleasd, Mr Otis had friends & his (Mr Hancocks) treatment of Mr Otis would prejudice his (Mr Hancocks) Election." Gray denied hearing that, but rather described Adams discussing the possible causes of Otis's mental deterioration. Gray declared "it did not appear to him that I discovered the least Unfriendliness towards Mr Hancock." Adams wrote of his intention to clarify the matter directly with Hancock.[37]

The contrast between Adams and Hancock in all its paradoxes is reflected by the portraits of the two men by John Singleton Copley that hang next to each other in Boston's Museum of Fine Arts. Adams wears a deep red suit with no ornamentation; Hancock a blue suit with elaborate gold trim and gold buttons and buckles. Adams's hair is his own, thin, limp, natural, gray. Hancock wears a wig. Adams stands before a dark background. Hancock sits on a highly polished and elegantly curved chair. Adams looks firmly, insistently into the viewer's eyes, pointing with his left index finger to the Charter of the province of Massachusetts. Hancock averts his gaze, perhaps absorbed in contemplation of the ledger book sitting on the fabric-draped table before him. It is easy to tell who is the wealthier man, the businessman with twenty ships, and who the politician barely scraping by. The matter is underscored by the fact that Hancock reportedly commissioned the Copley painting of Adams, which Adams could not have afforded on his own.

An art history professor at Yale, Jules David Prown, writes in his book on Copley that the Adams portrait "belonged to the Hancock family and is thought to have been painted along with one of the half-length portraits of Hancock a few days after the election of May 27, 1772, in which Hancock and Adams were reelected to the House of Representatives. The purpose of the commission was to emphasize that the two men were still united politically, despite Governor Hutchinson's hopes that Hancock had become disenchanted with radicalism."[38]

Adams used the period after the massacre to refine and elaborate his religious arguments for the liberties of the colonists. His respectful treatment of Patrick Carr notwithstanding, there was still more than a whiff of anti-Catholicism about his ideas, or at least the way he presented them.

In the August 20, 1770, *Boston Gazette,* writing as "A Chatterer," Adams compares "blind submission" to crown-appointed colonial authorities with the way that "a poor deluded Catholic reverenc'd the decree of Holy Father at Rome."[39]

This served to rile up the colonists but was also invoked as an argument to be used in London, where the Church of England held sway, and where Benjamin Franklin was representing Massachusetts to the British government. Writing to Franklin on June 29, 1771, on behalf of the House of Representatives of Massachusetts, Adams said, "Let our fellow-subjects there recollect, what would have been their fate long ago, if their ancestors had submitted to the unreasonable and uncharitable usurpations, exactions and impositions of the See of Rome, in the reign of Henry the VIII. Soon would they have sunk into a state of abject slavery to that haughty power, which exalteth itself above all that is called God."[40]

Adams's religious references went far beyond anti-Catholicism, however. He seemed to see the colonists as living out a biblical narrative, often likening them, both favorably and unfavorably, to the ancient Israelites. In the June 29 letter to Franklin, Adams said, "should all the other Colonies become weary of their liberties, after the example of the Hebrews, this Province we trust, will never submit to the authority of an absolute government." The same letter said the British government was imposing on North America "a subjugation to as arbitrary a tribute as ever the Romans laid upon the Jews."[41]

These references appeared not only in Adams's public writings but in his private correspondence. One of Adams's closest collaborators outside Massachusetts was a Virginian, Arthur Lee; Arthur's brother, Richard Henry Lee, later described the relationship as being so close that Samuel Adams was "grappled" to Arthur Lee's "soul with hooks of steel."[42] When Arthur Lee was ten years old, his father died, and young Arthur was educated in Britain, at Eton and Edinburgh. Lee was trained as both a physician and a lawyer, and he was also an expert botanist.[43] From London, Lee provided political commentary to Adams, including some harsh assessments of Franklin, who he described as closely allied with the secretary of state for the colonies: "not the dupe but the instrument of Lord Hillsborough's treachery." In a June 10, 1771, letter to Adams, Lee wrote that there was no rational hope that "in an open contest between an oppressive administration and a free people, Dr. F. can be a faithful advocate for the latter; or oppose and expose the former with a spirit and integrity which alone can, in times like these, be of any service."[44]

Writing to Arthur Lee on September 27, 1771, Adams said, "are not the ministry lost to all Sensibility to the peoples complaints, & like the Egyptian tyrant, do they not harden their Hearts against their repeated Demands for a redress of Grievances. Does it not fully appear not only that they neither fear God nor regard Man, but that they are not even to be wearied, as one of their ancient predecessors was, by frequent Applications."[45] The reference to the British as similar to the "Egyptian Taskmasters" of biblical Exodus recurs in a private letter from Adams to Arthur Lee of November 3, 1772.[46] In the September 27 letter, Adams asked Lee what the next step was to be taken by an "abused people," and prayed, "May God afford them that Prudence, Strength, & fortitude by which they may be animated to maintain *their own* Liberties at all Events."[47]

In the same letter to Lee, Adams enclosed a copy of a protest by "patriotick Clergymen in Virginia against an Episcopate in America." Adams said the British claim of authority to place over America a host of "placemen civil and ecclesiastical" was "as terrible as an Army of Soldiers." He wrote that "The Junction of the Cannon & the feudal Law you know has been fatal to the Liberties of Mankind. The design of the first Settlers of New England was to settle a plan of govt upon the true principles of Liberty in which the Clergy should have no Authority. It is no wonder that we should be alarmd at the Designs of establishing such a power. It is a singular pleasure to us that the Colony of Virginia tho Episcopalian should appear against it."[48]

Some have suggested that the issue of bishops in America was an overblown or manufactured threat, paranoid propaganda invented by Adams to bolster the revolutionary cause.[49] One Adams biographer, Stewart Beach, who is generally sympathetic to Adams, claims "there was no actual danger" of Anglican bishops being imposed on the colonies.[50] The concern was not entirely imagined, however. The archbishop of Canterbury from 1758 to 1768, Thomas Secker, the man who had anointed George III, was an open advocate of a bishop for North America, meeting with the secretary of state to recommend it. As Brown University historian Carl Bridenbaugh has noted, Secker influenced the debate on the issue even after his death. In his will he left £2,000 to the Society for the Propagation of the Gospel in Foreign Parts, of which half was to support the establishment of a bishop for the colonies. He also authorized the posthumous publication of a letter he had written in 1750, when he was bishop of Oxford, arguing in favor of bishops in America. Secker's letter used the same language—that of liberty—used by the colonists.[51] "It is not merely from my attachment to the church of England, that I am a favourer of the scheme in question, but from my love of religious liberty; which in this point the members of the church of England, in our colonies, do not enjoy," Secker wrote. As for the "dissenters," of whom Secker himself was one before joining the Church of England, "We have neither power, nor wish, to oppress them or their brethren in any way," Secker insisted. The letter acknowledged that the desire for American bishops was widely shared among the leaders of the Church of England: "I believe there scarce is, or ever was a Bishop of the Church of England, from the Revolution to this day, that hath not desired the establishment of Bishops in our colonies."[52] Even some American loyalists acknowledged that the desire existed, while conceding that the idea was wrongheaded. Peter Oliver, the brother of stamp master Andrew Oliver and, by marriage, a relative of Thomas Hutchinson, fled America to London after the Revolution. He wrote in his 1781 *Origins and Progress of the American Rebellion* that the New England Congregationalists had "inherited from their Ancestors an Aversion to Episcopacy," and that it had been "a great Mistake of the Governors of the *Church of England*, in proposing to the Colonies to have their consent to a *Bishops* residing among them."[53]

If Adams had a hostility to bishops, he also had, for a religious man who had been so close to Rev. Checkley, a surprising readiness to lash out at ministers who differed with him politically. He insisted that those ministers were a minority, but nevertheless it must have stung when the "ministers of the Congregational Churches in Massachusetts in Convention" acted on May 30, 1771, to congratulate Thomas Hutchinson, then fifty-nine years old, on taking office as governor. Hutchinson, who had been acting governor since Bernard's departure in 1769, was the first royal governor of the colony in thirty years to have been born in Massachusetts. He had deep roots in the colony; he was a graduate of Harvard, and a descendant of Anne Hutchinson, who had been banished from Massachusetts Bay by the Puritans in 1638 for her unconventional religious views. She ended up in New York, where she and five of her children were murdered by Indians, and her name endures on a parkway north of the city.

The wound was still apparently a sore one for Thomas Hutchinson; his biographer Bernard Bailyn recounts that in August 1770, when three members of the Governor's Council demanded the removal, from the walls of its chamber, of portraits of Charles I and James II, two kings who had been hostile to the Puritans, Hutchinson wrote to a friend that he was stunned: "The frenzy was not higher when they banished my pious great grandmother."[54] While Hutchinson was a member of a Congregationalist church, the New Brick Church, according to Bailyn he frequently attended an Anglican church. Hutchinson wrote to Francis Bernard in 1771, "had I been born and bred" in the Church of England, "I would never have left it for any other communion."[55]

All the more reason that the congratulatory resolution by the Congregational ministers on Hutchinson's accession must have grated on

Adams, now forty-eight years old. Adams pointed out in an article in the *Boston Gazette* soon afterward that only seventeen of nearly four hundred Massachusetts ministers had approved the motion. Only twenty-four had even attended the meeting, Adams said. Of the clergy overall, Adams expressed confidence. "There is in that venerable order a great majority, who will not go up to the house of Rimmon, or bow the knee to Baal," he said, comparing fealty to the British and their representative in Hutchinson to the worship of false gods mentioned in the Bible.[56] Adams wrote to Arthur Lee that some of the clergy "have ever been ready to sacrifice the rights as well as the honoured religion of their country, to the smiles of the great."[57] He wrote in the *Boston Gazette* of August 5, 1771, again as "Candidus," "though the body of the people of this province, treat the clergy, as I hope they always will, with all due respect, yet they are not priest-ridden as in some other parts of the world, and I hope in God they never will be—They claim a right of private judgment; and they will always venture to express their own sentiments of men or things, of politicks or religion, against the sentiments of the clergy, whenever they think the clergy in the wrong."[58]

In the October 7, 1771, *Boston Gazette*, "Candidus"/Adams derided the "adulating priestlings" who had defended Governor Hutchinson's decision to be paid by the British ministry rather than by the Massachusetts House. "In all ages the *supercilious* part of the clergy have adored the Great Man, and shown a thorough contempt of the understanding of the people," he wrote. "But *the people*, and a great part, I hope, of the clergy of this enlightened country, have understanding enough to know, that a Governor independent of the people for his *support*, as well as his *political Being*, is in fact, a MASTER; and may be, and probably, such is the nature of uncontroulouble power, soon will be a TYRANT."[59]

In the *Boston Gazette* of November 11, 1771, Adams, writing as "Candidus," likened the Massachusetts clergy siding with the governor and the British to the priests who allied with King Jeroboam of Israel to offer sacrifices to golden calves at Bethel rather than sacrifices to God at Jerusalem. "Are we not fallen into an age when some even of the Clergy think it no shame to flatter the Idol; and thereby to lay the people, as in the days of Jeroboam, the son of Nebat, under a temptation to commit great wickedness, and sin against God?" Adams asked. "He who can flatter a despot, or be flattered by him, without feeling the remonstrances of his own mind against it, may be remarkable for the guise and appearance of sanctity, but he has very little if any true religion—If he habitually allows himself in it, he is a hardened impenitent sinner against GOD and COUNTRY."[60]

He wrote to Arthur Lee on November 13, 1771, expressing satisfaction that in only two of Boston's twelve non-Episcopalian churches had clergy read a pro-British thanksgiving declaration drafted by the governor. Adams said he wasn't sure whether the declaration was "more insolent to the people or affrontive to the majesty of Heaven." Of the two clergymen who read it, one was a newcomer who had only been in Boston six weeks; his congregation was "much disgusted." The other minister, "a known Flatterer of the governor," "was deserted by a great number of his Auditory in the midst of his reading."[61] The flatterer was Rev. Ebenezer Pemberton; Governor Hutchinson was a member of his New Brick Church.[62]

If Adams did not hesitate to rebuke Congregationalist ministers who sided against him politically, he was also willing to defend his political allies when they were criticized for unorthodox religious beliefs. When Tories criticized an anti-British activist, Thomas Young, for being a deist, Adams wrote as "Vindex" in the *Boston Gazette* of November 30, 1772, that Dr. Young had "acted vigorously in the cause of American freedom," and wrote of Young's critics, "The cloak of Christianity is the threadbare garb of hypocrisy."[63]

It was garb, however, that Adams wrapped himself and his cause in, and that inspired him to persist at a time when enthusiasm for the fight was waning among some of his fellows. Rev. Samuel Cooper wrote to Benjamin Franklin on January 1, 1771, of a "pause in politics," and Hutchinson wrote to a friend that it was the calmest moment in five years.[64] "Hancock and most of the party are quiet;

and all of them except Adams abate of their virulence," Hutchinson reported to London.[65] Another Bostonian wrote on April 25, 1771, "At Present, things are very quiet."[66]

Part of the reason was that once faithful patriots were falling away from the cause. John Adams recounted in his diary for June 2, 1771, that word reached him in Worcester of James Otis's "conversion to Toryism." Samuel Adams had tried to get the state House of Representatives to protest the governor's removal of the legislature, also known as the General Court, to Cambridge from Boston. But Adams was met by Otis rising to say that Governor Hutchinson was a "good man" who had an "undoubted Right to carry the Court where he pleased."[67] John Hancock, too, as we have seen, was thinking about resigning from the House; Hutchinson later recalled that Hancock "intended to quit all active concern in public affairs, and to attend to his private business."[68] Even John Adams, who in 1770 had joined the House of Representatives as a member from Boston, had returned to his Braintree farm and left the legislature after what David McCullough described as a "physical breakdown."[69] John Adams wrote in his diary for November 21, 1772, that his "retirement" had agreed with him, and vowed, "Above all Things, I must avoid Politicks, Political Clubbs, Town Meetings, General Court &c. &c. &c."[70]

Samuel Adams biographer and descendant William V. Wells poignantly describes this moment in a chapter subheading as "Adams Stands Alone."[71] But on a more exalted level, Adams did not believe he was alone. He had with him the confidence that God was on his side, a feeling that prompted him to press ahead, even as others retired, converted to Toryism, or pondered quitting. He shared his religious reasoning with the public in an insistent, nearly frenetic barrage of newspaper writings and public documents.

Faced with the British ministry and its governor who would "usurp" the liberties of America, it was Americans' "indispensable duty to God and their Country, by all rational means in their power to RESIST THEM," Adams wrote as "Candidus" in the *Boston Gazette* of October 14, 1771.[72]

Writing as "Valerius Poplicola," Adams returned to the *Boston Gazette* of October 5, 1772, and returned also to the theme that Americans had a religious duty to stand up for their liberties:

> Is it not High Time for the People of this Country explicitly to declare, whether they will be Freemen or Slaves? It is an important Question which ought to be decided. It concerns us more than any Thing in this Life. The Salvation of our Souls is interested in the Event: For wherever Tyranny is establish'd, Immorality of every Kind comes in like a Torrent. It is in the interest of Tyrants to reduce the people to Ignorance and Vice. For they cannot live in any Country where Virtue and Knowledge prevail. The Religion and public Liberty of a People are intimately connected; their Interests are interwoven, they cannot subsist separately; and therefore they rise and fall together. For this Reason, it is always observable, that those who are combined to destroy the People's Liberties, practice every Art to poison their Morals. How greatly then does it concern us, at all Events, to put a Stop to the Progress of Tyranny.[73]

His private correspondence echoed the same theme, that the cause of liberty was inextricably joined with the question of salvation. In a December 14, 1772, letter to Rev. Samuel Checkley's son, William Checkley, "the only surviving branch of a Family I loved," Adams described his opponents as "the irreclaimable Enemies of Religion & Liberty."[74]

This was a dark period for Adams in more ways than just politically. On April 13, 1772, he wrote to James Warren, a member of the House of Representatives from Plymouth, "My Dear Mrs. Adams joyns with me in expressing the sincerest thanks to Mrs. Warren for her kind letter of condolence. To mingle sorrows is the part of a friend *only*. Those who are not possessd of the indistinguishable Principle of *real* friendship are strangers to the pleasure of sharing in Affliction. What is Life without Friendship! To partake in the Joys of the rude world is often dangerous but seldom satisfactory. The Tears of sincere friendship are refreshing like gentle Showers after a scorching Drought and always producing the harvest of solid Comfort."[75]

It raises the puzzle: What was Mrs. Warren offering condolences for? Samuel Adams's parents had both already passed. One likelihood is that it was the death of Elizabeth Adams's sister Kitty, who was happily married before being, as Samuel Adams put it, "cutt off without a moments Warning of the fatal stroke of Death!"[76] But the timing of Kitty's death is unclear. Samuel Adams's reference to it is from an October letter, long after Mercy Otis Warren's letter of condolence. Adams writes to Warren as if the loss was his as well as Elizabeth's. Mercy Otis Warren's letter of condolence does not exist in either her papers or Samuel Adams's. Another possibility is that Elizabeth Adams, who would have been thirty-six at the time, had been pregnant and suffered a miscarriage. The marriage is not known to have produced any children. Samuel Adams, as ever, dealt with his sorrow by plunging into his work, work that Elizabeth Adams shared as best she could. In a later letter to James Warren, Samuel Adams wrote, "Mrs Adams who has the Sauciness to overlook me while writing, a trick I cannot break her of, will not suffer me to close without mentioning her particular Regards."[77]

With the Congregationalist clergy generally supportive but not fully reliable and the press being used to its full advantage, Samuel Adams's passion for the cause of liberty still had not spread to the extent that he had hoped. So he tried a new technique for getting out the message. On Monday, November 2, 1772, in the Boston Town Meeting at Faneuil Hall, Adams moved to create a "committee of correspondence" with twenty-one members "to state the rights of the Colonists and of this Province in particular, as men and Christians and as subjects; to communicate and publish the same to the several towns in this province and to the world as the sense of this town, with the infringements and violations thereof that have been, or from time to time may be, made—Also requesting of each town a free communication of their sentiments on this subject." The meeting unanimously approved the motion.[78]

Perhaps skeptical of the project, high-profile patriots such as John Hancock and Thomas Cushing declined to serve on the Committee of Correspondence.[79] Others, such as the Marblehead merchant Elbridge Gerry, a graduate of Harvard's class of 1762, were skeptical of the committee's initial assignment, particularly the aspect relating to the rights of the colonists "as Christians." Adams replied with a letter to Gerry on November 14, 1772, by saying, in essence, that the clergy could not be trusted to make the religious case for revolution, and that the task therefore passed to the town's civic leaders. He wrote, "I cannot but hope, when you consider how indifferent too many of the Clergy are to our just & righteous Cause, that some of them are the Adulators of our Oppressors, and even some of the best of them are extremely cautious of recommending (at least in their publick performances), the Rights of their Country to the protection of Heaven, lest they should give offence to the little Gods on Earth, you will judge it quite necessary that we should assert [and] vindicate our Rights as *Christians* as well as Men & Subjects."[80]

Adams was characteristically undeterred by the skepticism. He stocked the Boston Committee of Correspondence with men he had brought into the cause such as Dr. Joseph Warren, Josiah Quincy, and Benjamin Church.[81] When the committee finally came out with its statement, "Rights of the Colonists," of which Adams is credited with being the primary draftsman, the document caused a sensation. Approved by the Boston Town Meeting on Friday, November 20, 1772, it was reprinted by Benjamin Franklin in England, and provided a framework for the Declaration of Independence and, in some ways, the First Amendment to the Constitution that eventually followed.

The document began with reference to the rights of the Colonists "as Men." Among those rights were "First. a Right to *Life*; Secondly to *Liberty*; thirdly to *Property*." All men have a right, Adams wrote, "in case of intollerable Oppression, Civil or Religious, to leave the

Society they belong to, and enter into another." The religious references began in this section; Adams did not reserve them for the section on the Rights of the Colonists as Christians. Rather, this portion of the document said that "every Man living in or out of a state of civil society, has a right peaceably and quietly to worship God according to the dictates of his conscience." It cited the Scottish philosopher John Locke's 1689 "Letter Concerning Toleration" in arguing that "In regard to Religeon, mutual tolleration in the different professions thereof, is what all good and candid minds in all ages have ever practiced." But it recommended that that tolerance not be extended to Roman Catholics, whose allegiance to the pope rather than their local government leads "directly to the worst anarchy and confusion, civil discord, war and blood shed."[82] It called the right to freedom "the gift of God Almighty."[83]

With respect to the rights of the colonists as Christians, the statement cited the Massachusetts charter granted by William III and Mary in 1691 and the Toleration Act passed by the British Parliament in 1689. Both guaranteed freedom of conscience to all Christians except for Roman Catholics.[84] The statement went on to enumerate as part of the "list of infringements & violations of rights" the "various attempts, which have been made and are now making, to establish an American Episcopate." Adams noted, "our ancestors came over to this Country that they might not only enjoy their civil but also their religious rights, and particularly desired to be free from the Prelates, who in those times cruelly persecuted all who differed in sentiment from the established Church." He accused those who wanted to impose an American episcopacy with threatening to infringe "that liberty wherewith Christ has made us free."[85]

In a transmittal letter circulating the statement to the other towns of Massachusetts, Adams and his colleagues on the Committee of Correspondence again invoked the founders of the colony. If the other towns failed to stand up against the British, the Bostonians, he wrote, would "forever lament the extinction of that generous ardor for Civil and Religeous liberty, which in the face of every danger, and even death itself, induced our fathers to forsake the bosom of their Native Country, and begin a settlement on bare Creation."[86]

The committee, and similar ones in other towns, played a crucial role in uniting the colonists in sympathy with the Bostonians. The statement "The Rights of the Colonists" itself echoed through New England and beyond. In Gorham, near what is now Portland, Maine, the Town Meeting on January 7, 1773, adopted a report of a committee of correspondence that had been appointed in that town, finding:

> *Resolved*, That it is clearly the opinion of this town, that the rights of the colonists, and the several infringements of those rights, are fairly and justly stated by the inhabitants of Boston, in their printed pamphlet sent to the several towns.
>
> *Resolved*, That the thanks of the town of Gorham be given to the town of Boston, for their vigilance and patriotic zeal shewn in the defence of our constitutional and charter rights.
>
> *Resolved*, That it is the opinion of this town, that it is better to risk our lives and fortunes in the defence of our rights civil and religious, than to die by piece-meals in slavery.[87]

The Gorham statement, in turn, was reprinted in the *Pennsylvania Packet* of March 1, 1773, so that the Boston statement of the rights of the colonists was reverberating more than three months after it was issued, from Gorham a hundred miles north of Boston to Philadelphia three hundred miles south.

Adams followed up "The Rights of the Colonists" with additional letters directed to specific towns. In a December 27, 1772, letter, Adams, on behalf of the Committee of Correspondence of Boston, wrote to the Committee of Correspondence of Cambridge, "We trust in God, & in the Smiles of Heaven on the Justice of our Cause, that a Day is hastening, when the Efforts of the Colonists will be crownd with Success; and the present Generation furnish an Example of publick Virtue, worthy the Imitation of all Posterity. In this we are greatly encouraged, from the thorough Understanding of our civil & Religious Rights Liberties & Privileges, throughout this province."[88] Two days later, Adams wrote to the Committee of Correspondence of Plymouth congratulating them on their readiness "to assert the natural religious & civil rights of the Colonists."[89]

Adams later credited the Committees of Correspondence with having "raisd the spirits of the people, drawn off their attention from *picking up pins*, and directed their Views to great objects."[90]

Through this lonely period of political agitation, Adams remained engaged as a newspaper columnist with a sharp wit. That wit was regularly directed at writers for other newspapers. Replying to an article by "Chronus" that had appeared in the *Massachusetts Gazette*, Samuel Adams's "Candidus" of the *Boston Gazette* wrote on December 16, 1771, "He tells us that 'he seldom examines political struggles that make their weekly appearances in the papers.' If by this mode of expression he means to inform us, that he seldom reads the papers with impartiality and attention, as every one ought, who designs to make his own observations on them, I can easily believe him; for it is evident in the piece now before me."[91]

Adams, writing as "Candidus" in the *Boston Gazette* of December 14, 1772, ridiculed Richard Draper's *Massachusetts Gazette* as "the Court Gazette." He accused it of "the gross Misrepresentation of well known Facts." Wrote Adams, "If Mr. Draper has had the least Inclination to have ascertained the falsehood of the Paragraph inserted in his Paper of the 26th of November, it was so notorious, that without giving the Selectmen the Trouble of it, he might have done it himself, by enquiring of perhaps the first *honest* Man he had met in the Street.: But it was calculated to mislead the reader."

The experience seemed to have ingrained on Adams some insights from the perspective of both a news source and a publisher. For potential sources, "It should make one cautious not too suddenly to communicate any Piece of Intelligence, especially of Importance, and still more especially of political importance, to one whose Business it is to publish what he hears." And for publishers, the challenge of credibility. "It is sometimes not an easy thing, to perswade a Man to believe that to be true, which he wishes may not be true.: It must needs be difficult to establish in the minds of impartial Men, the reputation of a Paper, the Publisher of which . . . 'has suffered,' it may be said *repeatedly*, 'what was so *different from the fact* to be inserted' before he 'had Opportunity to be very particular in his Inquiries about it.'"[92]

Newspapers were the forum for Adams's ideas about religion and liberty. They spread news of foreign events and summarized the thoughts of European writers such as Emer de Vattel and Baron de Montesquieu. They also kept Bostonians informed of local news. Adams's March 23, 1773, "Report to the Town of Boston" was printed in the *Massachusetts Spy* of March 25, 1773, and the *Boston Gazette* of March 29, 1773. The version that was printed in the *Boston Gazette* concluded, "It was also Voted, That said Report be printed in the several News-Papers."[93]

Property rights was a theme in Adams's writings in this period second only to the religious one. As "Candidus" in the September 9, 1771, *Boston Gazette*, Adams cited John Locke in asserting "The supreme power cannot take from any man any part of his property without his own consent." He said that "the preservation of property" is "the end of government, and that for which men enter into society."[94] It was an accurate citation of Locke, who had written in his *Second Treatise on Government*, published in 1689, that "The great and chief end, therefore, of men's uniting into commonwealths, and putting themselves under government, is the preservation of their property."[95] Again as "Candidus," Adams returned to citing Locke in the December 23, 1771, *Boston Gazette*. Adams renders the quote from Locke's *Second Treatise on Government* almost exactly: "Government cannot be supported without great charge; and tis fit that every one who enjoys a share in the protection should pay his proportion for the maintenance of it. But still it must be with their own consent, given by themselves or their representatives."[96]

The statement of the rights of the colonists drafted by Adams and approved by the town of Boston on November 20, 1772, spoke of the right of property and asserted "a private man has a right to say, what wages he will give in his private affairs."[97]

Still, religion was the primary theme. Adams as "Candidus" in the *Boston Gazette* of December 14, 1772, asserted, "Our religious Rights are threatned."[98]

The drumbeat of criticism, and particularly the enthusiastic response of so many Massachusetts towns to Boston's "The Rights of the Colonists," forced Hutchinson to respond. On January 6, 1773, the governor delivered a speech to an emergency session of the legislature in which he warned of the road that Adams's arguments would lead down. "I know of no line that can be drawn between the supreme authority of Parliament and the total independence of the colonies," he said, asking, "Is there anything which we have more reason to dread than independence?"[99]

If Hutchinson expected that to scare off Adams and his allies, he was to be sorely disappointed. In a January 26, 1773, answer on behalf of the Massachusetts House of Representatives to Hutchinson's address, Adams wrote, "the great design of our ancestors in leaving the kingdom of England, was to be freed from a subjection to its spiritual laws and courts, and to worship God according to the dictates of their consciences."[100]

The religious references kept coming, in nearly every document touched by Adams's quill. In a March 23, 1773, report to the town of Boston, Adams referred to "the Law of the Creator," which he said no human law could be of force against.[101] To the town clerk of Weymouth, he wrote of "civil & religious liberty."[102] To the clerk of Gardnerstown, he wrote of "a sense of liberty civil & religious."[103] Both letters were sent April 13, 1773, on behalf of the Committee of Correspondence of Boston. In an April 13, 1773, letter on behalf of the

Boston Committee of Correspondence to the town clerk of Duxbury, Massachusetts, Adams wrote, "may God inspire us with that ardent Zeal for the support of religious and civil Liberty which animated the Breasts of the first Settlers."[104] Such zeal would be necessary for the Bostonians to endure the new hardships that would befall them as the conflict with the British escalated in the years ahead.

# Chapter 4

# Tea Party

## *1773–1774*

*"We shall be respected in England exactly in proportion to the firmness and strength of our opposition."*

*—Samuel Adams, 1774*

As useful as Adams's appeals in the press had been for the cause of liberty, in early 1773 Adams was fending off reports that such leaders as John Hancock had stopped participating. Writing to Arthur Lee on April 9, 1773, Adams assured him, "Mr. Wilkes was certainly misinformd when he was told that Mr. H. had deserted the Cause of Liberty. Great pains had been taken to have it thought to be so; and by a scurvy Trick of lying the Adversaries effected a Coolness between that Gentn & some others who were zealous in that Cause. But it was of short Continuance, for their falshood was soon detected." As evidence of Hancock's staunchness, Adams cited to Lee the fact that Hancock had declined an offer of a seat on the Governor's Council and instead chose to continue as a member of the Massachusetts House of Representatives, "where he has in every Instance joyned with the friends of the Constitution in Opposition to the Measures of a Corrupt Administration."[1]

Hancock and Samuel Adams were both reelected by Boston to the House of Representatives on May 5, 1773, with Hancock winning the support of 417 of 419 voters and Adams winning the support of 413.[2] Meanwhile, Parliament had been debating a bailout of the East India Company, which, despite its charter as a legal monopoly, had seen its business so eroded by smugglers that it was sitting on 18 million pounds of surplus tea and debts of £1.3 million. On May 10, Parliament approved the Tea Act of 1773, allowing the East India Company to sell its surplus tea to America, provided that the Townshend Act duty be collected. During the discussion of the matter in Parliament, one member, William Dowdeswell, was prophetically skeptical. Addressing himself to Lord North, the prime minister who had proposed the plan, Dowdeswell predicted, "I tell the Noble Lord now, if he don't take off the duty, they won't take the tea."[3]

If Parliament was doing its part to strain relations between Britain and Massachusetts, the Massachusetts House of Representatives—that is, Samuel Adams and his allies—would do its part, as well. On Wednesday, May 26, the House convened in Boston for a new legislative session. Adams was elected clerk, as he had been every year since 1766, and was sworn in with an oath that ended, "So help you God." The same day, Charles Turner, pastor of the church in Duxbury, opened the legislative session with an emphatic sermon on the duties of civil leaders and the rights and responsibilities of citizens. "The perpetual nourishment of godliness in the heart, is the indispensable duty of the civil governor—for the honor of God, for his own sake, and for the sake of the people," Turner preached, not only before the House and Samuel Adams but also Governor Hutchinson, who was in attendance to mark the start of the session.

For the royally appointed Hutchinson, Turner had a pointed warning: "The People may, by a constitution, make an office hereditary in a Family, or leave it to particular persons to appoint rulers, agreeably to a constitution established by the whole society, when, so far and so long as they think it best; but still they have an unalienable right to alter such constitution at pleasure, and to interpose *immediately* in the election of their officers, whenever they judge it proper."

Turner left little doubt that he felt such an alteration, if not immediately warranted, certainly was approaching the point at which it should be seriously considered. "Unlimited power has generally been destructive of human happiness," he preached. "Whether this people and all they enjoy shall be at the *absolute* disposal of a distant legislature, is soon to be determined." He referred to England unfavorably, citing "the known prevalence of bribery and venality in the land from which our Ancestors fled," and picking up a favorite theme of Adams in complaining of "how dormant and unexecuted, the laws of England against popery, are known to remain—a roman-catholick bishop at Canada—a popish priest at Nova-Scotia, as we suppose publickly supported, and counselors in a British American Island, of the same religious complexion—together with the late zealous application, for an English-American Episcopate."

The last was a key point, because for Turner, "religious liberty is so blended with civil, that if one falls it is not to be expected that the other will continue." Correcting and defending against this was the responsibility of the people, according to Turner's sermon. "It is not only their privilege, but it is also their duty, properly to assert their freedom and take all rational and necessary methods for public security and happiness, when constitutional boundaries are broken over, and so their rights are invaded." While the people had a duty to obey good rulers, "it must be as much their duty" to oppose destructive ones, Turner said, stressing, "It concerns men of every order, station and employment, to be advocates for their country's rights."

He laid out the choice facing Adams and the other members of the House: "How distressing the thought of being slaves, how charming that of being free! While liberty is fruitful, in trade, industry, wealth, learning, religion and noblest virtue, all that is great and good and happy; slavery clogs every sublimer movement of the soul, prevents everything excellent, and introduces poverty, ignorance, vice and universal misery among people."[4]

Hutchinson winced and changed color during the sermon, and

once made a move for the door. He pointedly did not invite Turner to the festive meal that followed the preaching. Adams, for his part, thought highly enough of the sermon to send a copy along to Arthur Lee in London.[5]

Adams also did his best, in the ensuing legislative session, to live up to Turner's charge. The first opportunity came quickly. On Friday, May 28, Adams moved in the House a proposal to respond to a letter received from the House of Burgesses of Virginia. The letter included a copy of a March 12, 1773, resolution by the Virginia House appointing Arthur Lee's brother, Richard Henry Lee, a lawyer named Patrick Henry, and a twenty-nine-year-old slaveholding plantation owner named Thomas Jefferson to "a standing committee of correspondence and inquiry."[6] Adams's motion found that "this House is fully sensible of the necessity and importance of a union of the several colonies in America, at a time when it clearly appears that the rights and liberties of all are systematically invaded; in order that the joint wisdom of the whole may be employed in consulting their common safety." Massachusetts praised the Virginians for "the vigilance, firmness and wisdom, which they have discovered at all Times in support of the rights and liberties of the American colonies," and voted to "heartily concur with them in their said judicious and spirited resolves." Adams's motion was adopted by a vote of 109 to 4, and Massachusetts appointed its own fifteen-member Committee of Correspondence, a group that included Samuel Adams, John Hancock, James Warren, and Elbridge Gerry.[7]

The next key move against the British in the Massachusetts House took place on Wednesday, June 2, and it also was led by Adams. It was what later generations of newspapermen would call a scoop, and one of the most undeniable varieties of scoop—the document-based scoop. First the galleries of the House were cleared. Then, as the *Journal of the House* recorded it, "Mr. Adams acquainted the House, that he had perceived the Minds of the People to be greatly agitated with a prevailing report that letters of an extraordinary nature has been written and sent to England, greatly to the prejudice of this province." Adams reported that he had obtained copies of the letters on the basis that they could be read aloud in the House but that they could not be printed or copied "in whole or in part."[8] Read aloud they were, and they turned out to be signed by Governor Hutchinson and his allies such as the lieutenant governor and former stamp master Andrew Oliver. In one, Hutchinson had said "there must be an abridgment of what are called English liberties," language that to him was stating the obvious practical problems of the colonial lack of representation in Parliament but that Adams and his sympathizers saw as a plot against their interests and rights.[9] The House voted 101 to 5 that the "tendency and design" of the letters was "to overthrow the Constitution of this government, to introduce arbitrary power into the province." It also took the step of appointing a committee, including Adams, Hancock, and Cushing, to further consider the letters and what to do about them.[10]

By the next day, Hutchinson was heatedly denying he wrote letters with the intention he was charged with by the House. He reiterated that the letters were "expressly confidential." Not for long, though, if Adams was to have anything to do with it. On the afternoon of Thursday, June 10, the House was informed that Adams had "convers'd with the gentleman from whom he received the letters" and that the gentleman, realizing that the news of the contents of the letters was already starting to seep out, had now authorized "that the House should be fully possessed of them to print, copy, or make what other use of them they please."[11]

Make use of them Adams and his allies did, praising God for having "wonderfully interposed to bring to light the plot that has been laid for us by our malicious and invidious enemies."[12] Less than a week later, on the afternoon of Wednesday, June 16, the House approved a lengthy and strong resolution describing Hutchinson's and Oliver's letters as "insidious," saying they seemed designed "to suppress the very spirit of freedom." The House accused Hutchinson and Oliver of supporting British tax plans so that their salaries could be paid by the crown rather than by the colonists. The resolution said the two men had made a plan to "advance themselves to posts of honor and profit . . . at the expense of the rights and liberties of the American colonies." One element of the plan, "introducing a fleet and an army" into Massachusetts Bay, was designed not only to enforce the taxes but also "to intimidate the minds" of the colonists, the resolution charged. The House blamed the introduction of troops for "great corruption of morals and all that confusion, misery and bloodshed." The resolution concluded by praying that the king would forever remove Hutchinson and Oliver from the government of the province. Samuel Adams, Cushing, and Hancock were appointed a committee to prepare a petition to the king.[13]

The committee worked quickly, and by June 23 had developed a draft petition to the king that drew heavily on the resolution the House had adopted the week before. A draft that exists in Samuel Adams's handwriting describes Hutchinson and Oliver as "evil men" and accuses them of "annihilating" the "rights & liberties of the English colonies." It finishes with a fawning flourish toward the king: "And as the said Tho$^s$ Hutchinson Esq$^r$ and Andrew Oliver Esq$^r$ have by their above mentioned conduct and otherwise rendered themselves justly obnoxious to your Majestys loving Subjects, we pray that your Majesty will be graciously pleased to remove them from their posts in this government, and place such good and faithful men in their stead as, your Majesty in your great wisdom shall think fit."[14] The House approved the resolution by a vote of 80 to 11, rejecting 73 to 13 a suggestion that the decision be delayed until the next session to allow the representatives a chance to consult with their constituents. The *Journal of the House* records an order that the petition be transmitted to Benjamin Franklin and Arthur Lee in London "to be presented to his Majesty as soon as may be."[15]

While Samuel Adams was publicly paying tribute to the king's "great wisdom," he was also acting publicly and privately to make sure that the colonists would have options if the king chose not to act wisely. The day before the House had approved Adams's petition to the king, the representatives asked the governor to return gunpowder to them from the magazines where it was being kept. The representatives said they were concerned that their stock of powder was "deficient," but left unsaid what they would need it for, aside from a vague reference to "the safety of this province."[16] In a June 21 letter to Arthur Lee in London, Samuel Adams suggested that to restore peace and liberty in Massachusetts, the removal of Hutchinson and Oliver alone might not suffice. "Perhaps however you may think it necessary that some on your side of the water should be impeached & brot to condign punishment. In this I shall not differ with you," Adams wrote.[17]

The British had made some adjustments on their side of the water, appointing a minister for the colonies, Lord Dartmouth, who, Adams acknowledged, "is famed in America for his piety." Wrote Adams to a friend, a patriot leader from Western Massachusetts, Joseph Hawley, on October 13, 1773, "However illy we may deserve it, the great men in England have an opinion of us as being a mightily religious people."[18] Dartmouth, as a Methodist, was not a member of the Church of England, and he joined so enthusiastically in the colonists' effort to Christianize the native American Indians that a school for that purpose at Hanover, New Hampshire, was named for him.[19] When Hutchinson eventually met him face-to-face, the New Englander thought the lord had "too much religion."[20] But Dartmouth was circumscribed by the laws passed by Parliament, by the king, and by other ministers, including the head of the ministry, Lord North, who was Dartmouth's step-brother.[21] Samuel Adams was under no illusions about where things were headed. His letter to Hawley said, "If we persevere in asserting our rights, the time must come, probably a time of war, when our just claims must be attended to & our complaints regarded."[22]

Dartmouth relied on the information he was fed from Hutchinson, who, rightly or wrongly, blamed Samuel Adams for most of his troubles. "He has obtained such an ascendancy as to direct the town of Boston and the House of Representatives, and consequently the Council, just as he pleases," Hutchinson wrote about Adams in an October 9, 1773, letter to Dartmouth.[23]

Meanwhile, word of the Tea Act had begun to seep into Boston. The August 23, 1773, *Boston Evening Post* carried an extract from a May 26 letter from London, reporting that "in a short time, perhaps a month, a cargo will be sent to Boston" of tea "subject to the duty payable in America." On October 4, 1773, the *Boston Post Boy* carried a letter from New York dated September 27, warning that three hundred chests of tea were headed for Boston as part of a scheme by Lord North to establish the Tea Act "as a precedent for every imposition that the Parliament of Great-Britain shall think proper to saddle us with." By October 18, the *Post Boy* was likening the Tea Act to the hated Stamp Act—"both designed to raise a revenue, and to establish *parliamentary despotism* in America"—and accusing the Americans who had accepted commissions to sell the tea for the East India Company of proving themselves to be men who "would impiously sheath the dagger of oppression in the bowels of your country."

Samuel Adams was only too glad to swing into action. The tea crisis offered an opportunity, in the abstract, for advancing the cause of liberty. On top of that, as the authoritative historian of the tea episode, Benjamin Woods Labaree, notes, two of the East India Company's agents in Boston were Governor Hutchinson's sons, Elisha and Thomas, and another, Richard Clarke, was related to the Hutchinson family by the marriage of his daughter.[24] On October 21, the Massachusetts Committee of Correspondence sent a letter signed by Adams and Cushing to the other colonies, stressing that it was of "the utmost importance" that the colonies "be united" in opposing British actions such as allowing the East India Company to ship its tea to America.[25]

On November 3, Adams and Hancock renewed both their political alliance and the rituals of the Stamp Act and the Boston Massacre funerals. They showed up at the Liberty Tree with a crowd of Bostonians hoping to confront the tea "consignees," as those receiving the tea were known. Clarke and the Hutchinson sons wisely stayed away, though some members of the crowd visited Clarke's house. There, Jonathan Clarke, one of Richard's sons, fired a pistol at the crowd, which responded by throwing rocks to break the house's windows.[26]

November 5, Pope's Day and a traditional moment for anti-British agitation in Boston, the Town Meeting met at Faneuil Hall. A resolution drafted by Adams embraced positions that had already been taken by Philadelphia—affirming the right of freemen to their own property, denying Parliament's right to impose taxes on Americans without their consent, and asserting that the tax was intended "to introduce arbitrary government and slavery."

"It is the duty of every American to oppose" what the resolution called "a violent attack upon the liberties of America." Further, anyone who in any way aids or abets the "unloading receiving or vending the tea" is "an enemy to America," the Town Meeting decided.[27] The town named Adams to a committee to inform the Hutchinson sons of its demand that they resign their appointments as receivers of the tea.[28]

The press conveyed the feelings of the Bostonians about the issue; the *Massachusetts Spy* printed a warning that tea, "by being kept a considerable time, will breed a kind of insect, somewhat resembling a flea," that is "pernicious to the health," and that "as the East India Company are so anxious to force their rotten tea into this country, it is most probable that it is greatly damaged by those insects, so that they cannot sell it at home, for which reason it behoves the Americans to be very cautious in buying tea of any kind, more especially what comes from England; but the surest way to be safe is to drink none." Another writer claimed, "I would be less alarmed at the landing of the bedding of those unhappy persons who died at Baghdat of the plague, than one chest of the slave making tea."[29] Women got involved—more than five hundred in Boston pledged publicly to abstain from drinking tea.[30]

By Sunday, November 28, the matter was no longer hypothetical. The *Dartmouth*, loaded with 114 chests of East India Company tea, arrived in Boston Harbor. That set a deadline for the events that followed—customs rules dictated that the Townshend Act duty had to be paid within twenty days of when the goods landed, or by December 17. Otherwise, the tea could be seized by customs officers. The next morning, church bells rang and the town was plastered with posters calling residents to a meeting with the message, "Friends! Brethren! Countrymen! The Hour of Destruction or Manly Opposition to the Machinations of Tyranny stares you in the Face."[31] A crowd of thousands again gathered at Faneuil Hall, and then, when that overflowed, in Old South Church. Samuel Adams made a motion, unanimously adopted by the meeting, "that the tea should not be landed; that it should be sent back in the same bottom to the place whence it came, at all events, and that no duty should be paid on it."[32] And Samuel Adams, acting for the town of Boston, instructed the ship's captain to land the other goods the vessel carried, but to leave the tea aboard the *Dartmouth*.[33]

The next morning, November 30, the Body reconvened and received, from Sheriff Greenleaf, an order from Governor Hutchinson to disband. Samuel Adams rose and, according to the notes of a witness present, gave a fifteen- or twenty-minute speech "in the most vehement tone." To Hutchinson's description of himself as "his *Majesty's Representative* in this province," Adams replied, "He? He? Is he that Shadow of a Man, scarce able to support his withered Carcase or his hoary Head? Is he a *Representation of Majesty?*" Adams added, according to this account, that "a free and sensible People when they felt themselves injured would always and had a Right to meet together to consult for their own Safety—that he thought that Meeting so far from being riotous, that they were as regular and orderly as any People whatsoever, as the House of Representatives themselves and by what he could learn as the House of Commons." Lest the meeting or the watch on the tea ship be forcibly broken up, Samuel Adams observed that he kept a firearm "in order and at his bedside, as every good citizen ought," and "should not hesitate" to use it.[34]

As the December 17 deadline drew nearer, two more ships laden with East India Company tea arrived from London. The *Eleanor* arrived on December 2, and by December 15, the *Beaver* had joined the other two tea-bearing ships at Griffin's Wharf.[35] Samuel Adams played the leading role in interacting with the ship owners and their captains during the standoff. On December 3, Adams, on behalf of the town, commanded the captain of the *Eleanor*, James Bruce, not to land any of the tea, but to proceed to Griffin's Wharf and discharge the rest of his cargo.[36] On December 11, the owner of the *Dartmouth*, Francis Rotch, was summoned before the Boston Committee of Correspondence, which the town had charged with managing the crisis, and asked why the ship had not yet left to return to England. "The ship must go," Adams told Rotch. "The people of Boston and the neighboring towns absolutely require and expect it."[37] On December 14, Adams accompanied Rotch to ask the customs collector for permission for the *Dartmouth* to leave Boston and return to London with the tea. When that request was rejected, Rotch appeared again before the crowd of thousands in Old South Church on December 16, the day before the deadline, and was told to appeal directly to Governor Hutchinson, who was at his country house in Milton, seven miles away.[38] When Rotch returned to the church early in the evening, he announced that the royal governor would not allow the vessel to leave Boston without unloading the tea. Samuel Adams stood up and announced, "This meeting can do nothing more to save the country!"[39]

It was the signal for the commencement of the Boston Tea Party. In a matter of hours, patriots disguised as Indians had swarmed aboard the ships and emptied 342 chests of tea into the cold seawater of Massachusetts Bay.[40] Some of the "Mohawks" had changed into their costumes in the parlor of Benjamin Edes, publisher of the *Boston Gazette*.[41] The identities of the participants in the Tea Party were a closely held secret at the time, but by virtually all accounts Samuel Adams was not among those wielding hatchets to crack open the tea crates. There were plenty of willing hands, and Adams was already turning his mind to how to frame the episode in a way that was consistent with his principles and that would attract the most sympathy for his cause.

No sooner had the tea splashed into the harbor than Adams was communicating the news, through the Committee of Correspondence network, to other towns in Massachusetts, to Philadelphia, and to New York. In letters dated December 17, 1773, Adams reported the destruction of the tea while emphasizing that it took place "without the least Injury to the Vessels or any other property."[42] Property rights, after all, were one of Adams's main arguments against taxation by the British, so it was important to put this point in sharp relief. In a December 31 letter to Arthur Lee in London, Adams repeated the point that no property besides the tea had been destroyed, and he refined the argument further by laying the blame for the destruction of the tea on "the consignees, together with the collector of the customs, and the governor of the province," who had refused to allow the cargo to be returned safely to London. Along with property rights, as nearly always for Adams, came the religious references. In the same letter to Arthur Lee, Adams noted with apparent satisfaction that the meetings that led to the Tea Party took place "at the Old South church." As for a fourth ship that had been headed for Boston laden with tea, he wrote that it had been wrecked: "The only remaining vessel which was expected with this detested article, is by the act of righteous heaven cast on shore on the back of Cape Cod, which has often been the sad fate of many a more valuable cargo."[43]

British efforts to extract compensation from Boston for the destroyed tea, and to punish the town for its actions, would not be so easily disposed of.

As tensions and spirits were running high in the effort of the colonists to secure liberty from Britain, Samuel Adams found time to intervene in another struggle for liberty that was further from fruition. On June 25, 1773, the House had appointed Adams and Hancock to a committee to consider what its journal records as "A petition of Felix Holbrook, and others, Negroes, praying that they may be liberated from a state of bondage, and made freemen of this community; and that this Court would give and grant to them some part of the unimproved lands belonging to the province, for a settlement, or relieve them in such other such way as shall seem good and wise upon the whole."[44]

As a new legislative session approached, Adams wrote to another member of the committee, John Pickering, Jr., of Salem, reporting that "the Negroes whose petition lies on file and is referrd for consideration . . . earnestly wish that you would compleat a plan for their reliefe. And in the mean time, if it be not too much trouble, they ask it as a favor that you would by a letter enable me to communicate to them the general outlines of your design."[45] While the fact that the slaves chose to approach Samuel Adams to mediate the matter speaks well of his reputation, when the petition came up again before the House on January 26, 1774, the lawmakers did not dispose of it, but again referred it to a committee of Adams, Hancock, Cushing, and a few others.[46] Later in the winter, the House did approve "An Act to prevent the importation of Negroes or other Persons as slaves into this Province; and the purchasing them within the same." But Governor Hutchinson refused to sign the bill into law.[47]

In appealing to Adams and other Massachusetts government officials for their freedom, the slaves used arguments that echoed Adams's appeals against the British. It is hard to say whether Adams's spirit of liberty had spread even to the slaves, or whether the slaves were just using rhetoric designed to resonate with their audience. Either way, the language is striking. In one petition for freedom to the House of Representatives and the governor in the spring of 1774, "a grate number of Blackes of this province" wrote that they had been "held in a state of Slavery within the bowels of a free and Christian Country." They said, "we have in common with all other men a naturel right to our freedoms." And they said, "By our deplorable situation we are rendered incapable of shewing our obedience to Almighty God . . . we cannot searve our god as we ought whilst in this situation."[48] The resolution of their situation, however, at least in Massachusetts, would have to await the fate of the broader, simmering conflict between Great Britain and the colonists.

The people of Boston, and some from surrounding towns, gathered at Old South Church again on March 5, 1774, to mark the anniversary of the Boston Massacre. John Hancock delivered the oration, and while some credit Hancock's pastor, Rev. Samuel Cooper, with helping to craft the language, the religious references could just as easily have belonged to Samuel Adams. Adams's daughter, Hannah, his nephew Joseph Allen, and some loyalists credited (or, in the case of the loyalists, blamed) Adams for assisting Hancock with writing the speech. Hannah Adams and Joseph Allen said they even remembered the times and places at which the two patriot leaders met to polish the words.[49] Adams was pleased enough with the final product that he sent a copy of the text to Arthur Lee in London.[50]

The British troops in Boston, Hancock complained in his speech, "endeavored to deprive us of the enjoyment of our religious privileges, to vitiate our morals, and thereby render us deserving of destruction. Hence, the rude din of arms which broke in upon your solemn devotions in your temples, on that day hallowed by heaven, and set apart by God himself for his peculiar worship. Hence, impious oaths and blasphemies so often tortured your unaccustomed ear." The massacre, Hancock said, was a moment when "heaven in anger, for a dreadful moment, suffered hell to take the reins; when Satan, with his chosen band, opened the sluices of New England's blood, and sacrilegiously polluted our land with the dead bodies of her guiltless sons! . . .

"'Tis immortality to sacrifice ourselves for the salvation of our country. We fear not death," Hancock said, speaking for the colonists, "We dread nothing but slavery." He contrasted the British troops with "a well-regulated militia," from which Hancock said the colonists had nothing to fear. "When a country is invaded, the militia are ready to appear in its defense . . . they fight for their houses, their lands, for their wives, their children . . . for their liberty, and for themselves, and for their God."

The address neared its conclusion with a direct plea to the colonists, likening Boston to biblical Jerusalem, and the British to the Philistines who oppressed the children of Israel, i.e., the colonists. Hancock urged his audience, "not only that ye pray, but that ye act; that, if necessary, ye fight, and even die, for the prosperity of our Jerusalem. Break in sunder, with noble disdain, the bonds with which the Philistines have bound you."

And lest the reference to the "prosperity of our Jerusalem" be misunderstood, Hancock quickly noted that "an honest, upright man in poverty" was better than a "wealthy villain," and thanked God "that America abounds in men who are superior to all temptation, whom nothing can divert from a steady pursuit of the interest of their country, who are at once its ornament and safeguard." He offered only the example of "an Adams"—presumably Samuel. "From them," Hancock said, "let us catch the divine enthusiasm; and feel, each for himself, the godlike pleasure of diffusing happiness on all around us; of delivering the oppressed from the iron grasp of tyranny; of changing the hoarse complaints and bitter moans of wretched slaves into those cheerful songs, which freedom and contentment must inspire."

Hancock's conclusion, delivered in the church, sounded almost like a sermon, building up to a quote from the Hebrew prophet Habbakkuk:

I have the most animating confidence that the present noble struggle for liberty will terminate gloriously for America. And let us play the man for our God, and for the cities of our God; while we are using the means in our power, let us humbly commit our righteous cause to the great Lord of the Universe, who loveth righteousness and hateth iniquity. And having secured the approbation of our hearts, by a faithful and unwearied discharge of our duty to our country, let us joyfully leave our concerns in the hands of him who raiseth up and pulleth down the empires and kingdoms of the world as he pleases; and with cheerful submission to his sovereign will, devoutly say: "Although the fig tree shall not blossom, neither shall fruit be in the vines; the labor of the olive shall fail, and the field shall yield no meat; the flock shall be cut off from the fold, and there shall be no herd in the stalls; yet we will rejoice in the Lord, we will joy in the God of our salvation."[51]

In his encouragement of faith in hard times, Hancock—or Adams, helping to craft his remarks, which were widely reprinted[52]—anticipated the determination of the British to punish Boston harshly for the destruction of the tea. George III had been influenced by a conversation with General Thomas Gage, who had recently come back from America and told the king that the colonists "will be Lyons whilst we are Lambs, but if we take the resolute part they will undoubtedly prove very meek."[53] Lord North, the king, and Parliament decided to close the port of Boston, cutting off the lifeblood of trade to the city's economy.

The idea of collective punishment bothered at least some British lawmakers, who warned it would be counterproductive. During the debate on the Boston Port Bill at Westminster Palace on March 25, 1774, Edmund Burke, one of the members of the House of Commons who tended to be more sympathetic to the colonists, recommended targeting the ringleaders rather than retaliating against the entire town. He listed Samuel Adams prominently among those who he thought should be punished. "The persons guilty [were] Mr. Hancock, and Mr. Samuel Adams," he said. "You have these men who were delinquent. Punish them. Do not punish the town, when you know a delinquent." Calling the Port Act "the most dangerous unjust" bill "that ever was," Burke insisted again, "Punish Hancock, Adams, and others you know, but not all."[54]

Over Burke's objection, the law closing the port passed.[55]

Adams was, characteristically, secure in his faith and undaunted by either the British action or the threat of an action aimed specifically at him. To James Warren, on March 31, 1774, Adams wrote, "It is our Duty at all Hazards to preserve the publick Liberty. Righteous Heaven will graciously smile on every manly and rational Attempt to secure that best of all of his Gifts to Man, from the ravishing Hand of lawless & brutal Power."[56]

The British kept up their efforts to crack down on the colonists, restricting not only trade, but also freedom of the press. Reported Adams in an April 4, 1774, letter to Arthur Lee, "a lawyer of great eminence in the province, and a member of the house of representatives, was thrown over the bar a few days ago, because he explained in a public newspaper the sentiments he had advanced in the house when he had been misrepresented."[57]

The Boston Port Act was but one in a series of measures approved by the king and Parliament in the spring of 1774 to punish Boston for the Tea Party. The Massachusetts Government Act, or Massachusetts Regulatory Act, made the members of the Governor's Council appointed by the king rather than by the House of Representatives, and it restricted Town Meetings to once a year. The Impartial Administration of Justice Act allowed the Massachusetts governor to send government officials accused of capital crimes to England for trial, removing loyalist officials from the jeopardy of patriot juries. The Quartering Act allowed British troops to use the colonists' buildings as barracks.[58] Together, the laws became known as the Coercive Acts or Intolerable Acts.

If the British intent was to intimidate or deter Samuel Adams, the acts were a total failure. Adams was dismissive, in part because of the low regard in which he held his foes. He saw the British as overly indulgent in their displays of wealth. He wrote to Arthur Lee that future historians would record that the British were "at last absorbed in luxury and dissipation; and to support themselves in their vanity and extravagance they coveted and seized the honest earnings of those industrious emigrants." He predicted that the British would sink into obscurity, while "providence will erect a mighty empire in America." And he counseled a hard line, suggesting much the same approach toward Britain that George III was adopting toward America: "We shall be respected in England exactly in proportion to the firmness and strength of our opposition."[59]

If the British intent in passing the Coercive Acts was to intimidate the people of Boston or deter them from supporting Samuel Adams, that, too, was a total failure. On Tuesday, May 3, the inhabitants of Boston gathered for the annual ritual of electing representatives to the Massachusetts House; Samuel Adams won the support of 535 of the

536 votes cast and was also named moderator of the Town Meeting.

On Friday, May 6, the town met again. After opening with a prayer by the Reverend Samuel Cooper, the session, moderated by Samuel Adams, proceeded to adopt a resolution calling for unity with the other colonies in a boycott and embargo of Britain as a protest of the Boston Port Act. "VOTED, That it is the opinion of this Town, that if the other Colonies come into a JOINT resolution to stop all importations from Great-Britain, and Exportations to Great Britain, and every part of the West-Indies, till the Act for blocking up this Harbour be repealed, the same will prove the salvation of North-America and her liberties: On the other Hand, if they continue their Exports and Imports, there is high reason to fear that Fraud, Power, and the most odious Opression will rise triumphant over Rights, Justice, social Happiness and Freedom. And ordered, that this Vote be forthwith transmitted by the Moderator to all our Sister Colonies in the Name and behalf of this Town." The *Boston Post Boy* reported that one observer said he never saw such unanimity as there was at Faneuil Hall that Friday. It also reported that "our worthy fellow citizen, Mr. Paul Revere," had been dispatched with important letters to the southern colonies.[60]

The *Boston Evening Post* of May 16 brought a report from London, dated March 31, that a ship had sailed for Boston "with orders to bring to England, in irons" Samuel Adams and John Hancock. The prospect of returning to the country his forefathers had fled turned Adams's mind to the precedent of their struggles. He wrote to the Connecticut patriot Silas Deane on May 18, 1774, suggesting that the colonists go for a year without importing British goods: "What would this be in Comparison with the Sacrifice our renowned Ancestors made that they might quietly enjoy their Liberties civil and religious? They left, many of them, affluence in their Native Country, crossd an untryed Ocean, encounterd the Difficulties of cultivating a howling wilderness, defended their Infant Settlements against a most barbarous Enemy with their richest Blood."[61]

It was easy for Adams to contemplate giving up goods imported from Britain, because material possessions never mattered much to him. His attitude toward property, like that toward other liberties, was informed and influenced by his religious views and his related ideas about virtue and the Puritan founders of Boston. "The Virtue of our Ancestors inspires us—they were contented with Clams & Muscles," Adams wrote to William Checkley on June 1, 1774. "For my own part, I have been wont to converse with poverty; and however disagreeable a Companion she may thought to be by the affluent and luxurious who never were acquainted with her, I can live happily with her the remainder of my days, if I can thereby contribute to the Redemption of my Country."[62]

As Adams was recalling the Puritans' journey to America from England, the man who had been his adversary, Thomas Hutchinson, was reenacting the voyage, in the opposite direction. His trip was not in irons, but a voluntary mission aimed at advancing his family's financial interests. Having been relieved of his duties by a new governor sent from England, Thomas Gage, Hutchinson sailed, on June 1, 1774, from Boston with his son Elisha and daughter Peggy aboard the *Minerva*.[63] It was a twenty-eight-day passage through wet and foggy weather during which the outgoing governor spent much of his time lying in bed in his cabin, seasick. When the *Minerva* finally landed off Dover, three horse-drawn carriages brought the Hutchinsons to London, where, upon arriving, the former governor immediately notified Lord Dartmouth. On July 1, Dartmouth called for Hutchinson's presence at his house, and after almost an hour of conversation, the two set off to see King George III at St. James's Palace. Hutchinson, still queasy from the seasickness, was not dressed for a royal audience, and had plenty of time to worry about it as Dartmouth primped. When Hutchinson finally got before the king, the new arrival from Massachusetts kissed the monarch's hand. George III wasted no time in grilling Hutchinson on how the governor's letters came to be published in New England. Hutchinson blamed Franklin and "the two Mr. Adamses."

Replied the king: "I have heard of one Mr. Adams, but who is the other?" Hutchinson explained that John Adams was a lawyer, assuming that word of *Samuel* Adams had preceded him to England.

King: "Brother to the other?"

Hutchinson: "No sir, a relation."

The king inquired by name about several of the revolutionary activists, including Hancock and Cushing. George III asked about Cushing, "is he not a great man of the party?" Hutchinson replied, "he has been for many years Speaker, but a Speaker, Sir, is not always the person of the greatest influence. A Mr. Adams is rather considered as the opposer of Government, and a sort of Wilkes in New England."

The king asked what gave Adams his importance, and Hutchinson replied, "A great pretended zeal for liberty, and a most inflexible natural temper. He was the first that publickly asserted the Independency of the colonies upon the Kingdom."

The answer seemed to have satisfied the king, as the conversation turned to religion. Hutchinson had already told the king he had depended "on the protection of Heaven" to guard him in Boston. The king asked about the message preached from the pulpits: "I have heard, Mr. H., that your ministers preach that, for the sake of promoting liberty or the publick good, any immorality or less evil may be tolerated?"

Hutchinson demurred, but the king pressed on with questions about religion in New England. "Why do your ministers generally join with the people in their opposition to Government?" the king asked.

Hutchinson replied by describing the way Congregational ministers were employed. "They are, Sir, dependent upon the people," he said. "They are elected by the people, and when they are dissatisfied with them, they seldom leave till they get rid of them."

The king asked Hutchinson about his own ancestors, and Hutchinson said they were, in general, dissenters from the Church of England. Hutchinson also said that he himself sometimes attended prayers at "your Majesty's chapel," the Anglican church in Boston, but more commonly attended "a Congregational church, which has a very worthy minister, a friend to Government, who constantly prays for your Majesty, and all in authority under you."

"What is his name?" asked the king.

"Doctor Pemberton," Hutchinson replied.

"I have heard of Doctor Pemberton that he is a very good man," the king replied of the minister that Samuel Adams had described as a "known flatterer" whose audience walked out in the middle of his sermon.

Hutchinson did his best to describe to the king the way in which the Boston population was motivated by religious concerns. Advising the king on choosing new members of a Massachusetts Governor's Council, Hutchinson said, "The body of the people are Dissenters from the Church of England; what are called Congregationalists. If the Council shall have been generally selected from the Episcopalians, it will make the change more disagreeable."

The meeting between George III and Hutchinson had lasted nearly two hours, with Hutchinson standing the entire time. Lord Dartmouth was worried that Hutchinson, still weary from his ocean passage, would become exhausted, but Hutchinson told Dartmouth that the king had received him so graciously that he had not felt at all uncomfortable. The Massachusetts governor retired from the palace to his lodgings on Parliament Street, where he spent his days receiving British officials. On July 5, Dartmouth's undersecretary, John Pownall, visited, and said his plan was to bring over Samuel Adams "and the other principal incendiaries; try them, and if found guilty, put them to death." This, according to an account by a Hutchinson descendant, "seemed to be at one time the determination of the Cabinet; and the Lords of the Privy Council actually had their pens in their hands, in order to sign the Warrant to apprehend them."[64] As much as Thomas Hutchinson differed with Samuel Adams, Pownall's story made the Coercive Acts seem a mild and preferable option by comparison.[65]

As if all that were insufficient to indicate the mood in London toward the colonies, George III and Parliament took one more step—

the Quebec Act. Ostensibly directed toward Canada rather than the American provinces, the act awarded some disputed inland territories to Quebec, established an appointed council instead of an elected assembly to govern the province, and allowed the 65,000 Catholics of Quebec "the free Exercise of the Religion of the Church of Rome," and their clergy "their accustomed Dues and Rights."[66]

Meanwhile, back in Boston, on May 25, the House of Representatives had convened at the State House for a new session. Samuel Adams was unanimously elected clerk. Afterward, the representatives were joined by Hutchinson's replacement as governor, General Thomas Gage, and the group proceeded to the Old Brick Meeting House for a sermon by Rev. Gad Hitchcock of Pembroke. The minister preached on a text from Proverbs: "When the righteous are in authority, the people rejoice: but when the wicked beareth rule, the people mourn."[67] Rulers, Hitchcock said, should "frame such laws" as "may be best calculated to encourage piety and virtue, industry and frugality, and prevent immorality and vice, and every species of oppression and misery." He referred to God as "the great patron of liberty," and said, "It is better to trust in the Lord than to put confidence in princes."[68]

Events thereafter moved in rapid succession. On Saturday, May 28, General Gage ordered the House adjourned until June 7, and its meeting place moved to Salem. The new governor hoped that it would be less of a revolutionary hotbed than Boston, but the forced move served only to provide Samuel Adams and his allies another grievance. Adams, with Hancock and Cushing, had been named to a committee of the House to respond to Gage's remarks opening the session, and when the committee did report, on June 9, it devoted much of its message to complaints about the move. "The removal of the Assembly from the Court-House in *Boston*, its ancient and only convenient seat, has lately given great discontent to the good people of this province," the committee said. The House responded by appointing another committee, also with Adams and Cushing as members, "to consider the State of the Province and the Act of Parliament for shutting up the Harbor of Boston, and report."[69]

The committee took less than ten days to make its report, the only obstacle being one member unwilling to go as far as Adams. That member was gulled into thinking the committee had nothing dramatic in mind, and left for home, giving Adams and his allies an opening.[70] On Friday, June 17, the galleries of the Salem Court House were cleared, and the doors shut and locked, the key safely in Samuel Adams's own pocket.[71] Then Cushing reported the committee's opinion that it was "highly expedient and necessary" that a meeting be held of representatives from all the American colonies, "to deliberate and determine upon wise and proper measures to be by them recommended to all the colonies, for the recovery and establishment of their just rights and liberties, civil and religious."[72]

The House greeted the committee's recommendation by suggesting a time and place—September 1 at Philadelphia—for what would be the first Continental Congress. The House also chose five men to represent Massachusetts Bay at the Congress: Samuel Adams, his cousin John Adams, Thomas Cushing, James Bowdoin, and Robert Treat Paine. They voted the group the sum of £500 for expenses. Racing to complete a flurry of measures before General Gage caught wind of their actions and dissolved the meeting, the members of the House "strongly recommended" that the inhabitants of Massachusetts "renounce altogether the consumption of India Teas," encourage domestic manufactures, and discontinue the use of imported goods. Finally, the House expressed irritation that the governor had failed to act on its request to declare "a day of publick fasting and prayer." Gage explained in a letter home that he "saw no cause for an extraordinary day of humiliation, which was only to give an opportunity for sedition to flow from the pulpits."[73] The House advised parish ministers that, in the absence of an action by the governor, they should go ahead and set apart "some convenient day" for that purpose.[74]

———————

Meanwhile, Boston was bracing for the closure of its port. Not everyone was as steadfast as Adams. On June 27, a group of Bostonians, led by wealthy merchants John Rowe and John Amory, moved in the Town Meeting to censure and disband the Boston Committee of Correspondence. Samuel Adams managed to defeat the motion.[75]

General Gage, observing the pressure, made a last-ditch effort to win over Adams, sending a colonel to convey assurances that "by changing his course, he would not only receive great personal advantages, but would thereby make his peace with the King." Adams's daughter recounted that her father replied indignantly, "Sir, I trust I have long since made my peace with the King of kings. No personal consideration shall induce me to abandon the righteous cause of my country. Tell Governor Gage it is the advice of Samuel Adams to him no longer to insult the feelings of an exasperated people."[76]

Adams and the other town leaders were faced not only with clumsy British overtures but with the practical difficulties of feeding a town with a closed port. They relied on the generosity of surrounding towns and colonies, who sent donations from as far away as South Carolina. Adams used even routine thank-you notes to express his faith in God and his determination to live up to the precedent set by his Puritan predecessors. He wrote on August 4, 1774, to a Farmington, Connecticut man, Fisher Gay, who had sent to Boston 116 and a half bushels of rye and 190 bushels of corn as a donation, "We are in hopes to keep our poor from murmuring, and that, by the blessing of Heaven, we shall shortly be confirmed in that freedom for which our ancestors entered the wilds of America."[77]

Among those supported by donations was none other than Samuel Adams himself. Before Adams departed for Philadelphia, some Bostonians pitched in and bought their congressman, "wont to converse with poverty," a new suit and pair of shoes.[78] So equipped, on August 10 Adams said goodbye to his thirty-eight-year-old wife and his eighteen-year-old daughter, leaving them in the care of his twenty-two-year-old son. He also left behind his Newfoundland dog, Queue, who had a reputation for disliking the presence of British troops in Boston with the same intensity that his master did.[79] At fifty-one, Adams was leaving Massachusetts for what was perhaps the first time in his life. One of the five delegates from Massachusetts, James Bowdoin, had dropped out, leaving Samuel and his cousin John, along with Thomas Cushing and Robert Treat Paine, to share a coach drawn by four horses, accompanied by six servants, four on horseback and two on foot. At least two of the servants were well armed, though they would have been little match for a regiment of British regulars determined to seize Samuel Adams. John Adams described the farewell scene as "affecting, beyond all description affecting."[80] He also recalled, "The anxiety and expectation of the Country was very great."[81]

# Chapter 5

# Congressman

## *1774–1775*

*"It was this man, who by his superior application managed at once the faction in Congress at Philadelphia, and the factions in New England."*

—Joseph Galloway, delegate to Congress
from Pennsylvania, *1774*

F OR MUCH OF the three-hundred-mile journey from Boston to Philadelphia, Samuel Adams and his fellow delegates from Massachusetts were greeted as heroes. At Wethersfield, Connecticut, more than thirty of the town's gentlemen invited the Massachusetts delegation to a dinner in their honor at the local tavern. Afterward, the group from Massachusetts climbed the steeple of the Wethersfield church and surveyed the countryside. Seven miles from New Haven, they were received by what John Adams described in his diary as "a great Number of Carriages and of Horse Men who had come out to meet us." Among the greeting party were "the Sherriff of the County and Constable of the Town and the Justices of Peace." When the group finally arrived in New Haven proper "all the Bells in Town were sett to ringing, and the People Men, Women and Children, were crouding at the Doors as if it was to see a Coronation. At

Nine O Clock the Cannon were fired, about a Dozen Guns I think."
The visiting Harvard men had a tour of the library and chapel at Yale.
They made their way through Stratford, Fairfield, and Norwalk,
Connecticut, and then to Rye, New York, where they were shocked
at the lack of religion and education in New York as compared to the
ardently Congregationalist Massachusetts and Connecticut. Wrote
John Adams, "Religion dont flourish in this Town. The congregational Society have no Minister. . . . There is no Law of this Province
that requires a Minister or school Master."

On August 20, the travelers arrived in New York City, where they
"walked up the broad Way, a fine Street, very wide," and saw King's
College, as Columbia was then known. It was unimpressive: "there
is but one Building at this Colledge and that is very far from full of
Schollars." John Adams found the streets of New York vastly more
"elegant than those in Boston, and the Houses are more grand." Still,
he said, "With all the Opulence and Splendor of this City, there is very
little good Breeding to be found. . . . There is no Modesty—No Attention to one another. They talk very loud, very fast, and Altogether. If
they ask you a Question, before you can utter 3 Words of your Answer,
they will break out upon you, again—and talk away." Allies warned
them that there was considerable opposition in New York to their
cause, some of its based on concern that "the levelling Spirit of the
New England Colonies should propagate itself into N. York," others
"prompted by Episcopalian Prejudices, against New England."

By August 27, the travelers had crossed the Hudson into New
Jersey and made their way to Princeton, where they continued their
tour of American colleges. A professor of mathematics and natural
philosophy was kind enough to show them the library. John Adams's
judgment: "It is not large, but has some good Books." The delegation
from Massachusetts also joined the prayers at the Princeton chapel
and drank a glass of wine with the college's president, the Presbyterian minister John Witherspoon, whom John Adams described as
"as high a Son of Liberty, as any Man in America." When the group
John Adams described as "dirty, dusty, and fatigued" finally crossed

into Pennsylvania on August 29, they were greeted five miles outside Philadelphia and ushered to a welcome dinner.

John Adams viewed the adulation his traveling party was met with along the way as "Demonstrations of the Sympathy of this People with the Massachusetts Bay and its Capital."[1] But both Adamses in Philadelphia, along with the other Massachusetts delegates, also had to confront a newly pressing problem—fear by the other colonies of the rashness or extremism of Massachusetts, and of its potential ambitions for either separatism or dominance. Samuel Adams wrote to Joseph Warren that there was "a certain degree of jealousy in the minds of some, that we aim at a total independency, not only of the mother-country, but of the colonies, too; and that, as we are a hardy and brave people, we shall in time overrun them all."[2]

Those feelings were not imaginary. Samuel Adams was further down the road to independence at this juncture than many of the other delegates to Congress and than many others who later became known as founding fathers. Benjamin Franklin was in London, drafting a plan for a reconciliation between Britain and the colonies that was predicated on Massachusetts paying restitution for the destroyed tea.[3] Alexander Hamilton was a nineteen-year-old student at King's College in New York, inspired by the Boston Tea Party to begin speaking out against British taxation of the colonies.[4] James Madison was a county activist in Virginia. George Washington wrote to a fellow Virginian who suggested that the Bostonians sought independence, "I am as well satisfied as I can be of my existence that no such thing is desired by any thinking man in all North America; on the contrary, that it is the ardent wish of the warmest advocates for liberty, that peace and tranquility, upon constitutional grounds, may be restored, and the horrors of civil discord prevented."[5] Thomas Jefferson was a Virginia politician promoting a plan for America to be governed by King George III but with an independent legislature, like Scotland. The author of the *Letters from a Farmer*, John Dickinson, a Quaker and a delegate from Pennsylvania, placed his priority on reaching a peaceful reconciliation.

The delegates gathered at Philadelphia did include some who shared Samuel Adams's vision. Silas Deane of Connecticut wrote home to his wife that Christopher Gadsden of South Carolina, in addition to being "one of the most regularly religious men I ever met with," "leaves all New England sons of liberty far behind, for he is for taking up his firelock and marching direct to Boston."[6] Gadsden proposed that Congress approve a preemptive attack on General Gage at Boston before more troops arrived from England.[7]

But Samuel Adams was correct to perceive that other delegates viewed him with some suspicion. Joseph Galloway, a delegate from Pennsylvania, described Samuel Adams as among the "congregational and Presbyterian Republicans" who used "fiction, falsehood, and fraud" to "incite the ignorant and vulgar to arms." As Galloway described it:

> Continual expresses were employed between Philadelphia and Boston. These were under the management of Samuel Adams—a man who though by no means remarkable for brilliant abilities, yet is equal to most men in popular intrigue, and the management of a faction. He eats little, drinks little, sleeps little, thinks much, and is most decisive and indefatigable in the pursuit of his objects. It was this man, who by his superior application managed at once the faction in Congress at Philadelphia, and the factions in New England. Whatever these patriots in Congress wished to have done by their colleagues without, to induce General Gage, then at the head of his Majesty's army at Boston, to give them a pretext for violent opposition, or to promote their measures in Congress, Mr. Adams advised and directed to be done; and when done, it was dispatched by express to Congress.[8]

Samuel Adams went to considerable lengths to keep a low profile, so as to allay that "jealousy" from representatives of the other colonies. Meeting at newly completed Carpenter's Hall rather than the larger and fancier Pennsylvania State House, which had also been offered, the delegates elected a Virginian, Peyton Randolph, as chairman of the Congress.[9] It was a recognition of Virginia's pivotal role. On one hand, it was among the colonies most spirited in its defense of Massachusetts, which everyone realized was the hot point of the struggle. On the other hand, it sometimes seemed to have other priorities. Both aspects of Virginia's role were on display in a letter Richard Henry Lee sent to Samuel Adams shortly before the commencement of Congress, reporting that he had prepared a set of resolves for the Virginia Assembly declaring "that the blocking up, or attempting to block up, the Harbour of Boston, until the people there shall submit to the payment of taxes imposed on them without the consent of their Representatives, is a most violent and dangerous attempt to destroy the constitutional liberty of and rights of all North America." The same letter reported, however, that Lee had been prevented from offering the resolves for a vote "by many worthy Members who wished to have the public business first finished."[10]

Among the first issues to arise as a point of contention at the Congress was whether to include an official prayer.

One of the Massachusetts delegates, Thomas Cushing, moved that the first Continental Congress be opened with a prayer. John Jay of New York and one of the Rutledges of South Carolina, either Edward or John, objected, as John Adams recalled it in a letter to his wife, Abigail, that "because we were so divided in religious Sentiments, some Episcopalians, some Quakers, some Aanabaptists, some Presbyterians and some Congregationalists, so that We could not join in the same Act of Worship." Then Samuel Adams rose "and said he was no Bigot, and could hear a Prayer from a Gentleman of Piety and Virtue, who was at the same Time a Friend to his Country." Samuel Adams said he was a stranger in Philadelphia, but had heard that Jacob Duché, an Episcopal clergyman, fit that description. On Samuel Adams's motion, Congress invited Duché to lead prayers the next morning. Duché indeed appeared and read to the delegates, among other passages, the 35th Psalm, in which David asks the Lord to take up his shield, spear, and battle-axe and "fight against them that fight against me."[11] Samuel Adams wrote to Joseph Warren soon thereafter, in a letter published almost immediately in the *Boston Gazette,* that Duché had been chosen in part because "many of our warmest Friends are Members of the Church of England." Samuel Adams said he had found Duché's prayer to be "most excellent," and an indication that the clergyman was "a warm Advocate for the religious and civil Rights of America."[12]

In Philadelphia, Adams was making new friends, and mixing with men who would later join him in leading the Revolution. Arthur Lee's brother, Richard Henry Lee, was a delegate from Virginia, as were Patrick Henry and George Washington. John Jay was there representing New York.[13] Adams tried to stay in touch with old friends, too. From Philadelphia, he wrote to the Committee of Correspondence of Boston on September 14, 1774, asking God to inspire the group "with wisdom and fortitude," urging it to keep up its work he had once led, and concluding "with my warmest Prayers to the Supreme Being for the Salvation of our Country."[14]

The Bostonians, at least, did not let Samuel Adams down. On Saturday, September 17, the Suffolk Resolves, having been drafted by Adams's close friend Dr. Joseph Warren and carried express by Paul Revere on horseback to Philadelphia in the record time of five days,[15] were laid before Congress. In their call to the Puritan past and insistence on religious liberty, the resolves could have flowed from the pen of Samuel Adams himself. "Great-Britain, which of old persecuted, scourged, and exiled our fugitive parents from their native shores, now pursues us, their guiltless children, with unrelenting severity," the resolves said. "It is an indispensable duty which we owe to God, our country, ourselves and posterity, by all lawful ways and means in our power to maintain, defend and preserve those civil and religious rights and liberties, for which many of our fathers fought, bled and died, and to hand them down entire to future generations."

The resolves made reference to the Quebec Act, finding, "the late act of parliament for establishing the Roman Catholic religion and the

French laws in that extensive country, now called Canada, is dangerous in an extreme degree to the Protestant religion and to the civil rights and liberties of all America; and, therefore, as men and Protestant Christians, we are indispensubly obliged to take all proper measures for our security."[16]

Congress greeted the resolves by agreeing unanimously to publish them in the newspapers and to "thoroughly approve the wisdom and fortitude" of those who wrote them.[17] In a letter home to Rev. Charles Chauncy, Samuel Adams described the Suffolk Resolves as "spirited and patriotick" and seemed heartened, writing, "I think I may assure you that America will make a point of supporting Boston to the utmost."[18] To Joseph Warren, Adams wrote that Congress "give you a full pledge of their united efforts in your behalf," but cautioned, too, "They have not yet come to final resolutions. It becomes them to be deliberate."[19]

Adams certainly had not been forgotten in his hometown. Although he was in Philadelphia, he and Cushing, along with John Hancock, were reelected on September 21 to the Massachusetts House of Representatives.[20]

In Boston, the winds of war were gusting. The *Massachusetts Spy* printed a new patriotic song, "The Glorious Seventy Four," to be sung to the same "Hearts of Oak" tune that Samuel Adams joined in with back during the fight against the Stamp Act. The new lyrics concluded:

> With sons whom I foster'd and cheris'd of yore
> Fair freedom shall flourish till time is no more;
> No tyrant shall rule them,—'tis Heaven's decree,
> They shall never be slaves, while they dare to be free.
>
> Hearts of oak were our sires,
> Hearts of oak are their sons
> Like them we are ready, as firm and as steady,
> To fight for our freedom with swords and with guns.[21]

On October 6, Paul Revere arrived in Philadelphia from Boston with the latest from the Committee of Correspondence, which reported that Samuel Adams's hometown was bristling with British battlements. "Cannon are mounted at the entrance of the town," the letter said, and "fortifications are to be erected on Corpse-Hill, Beacon-Hill, & Fort-Hill, &c. so that the fortifications with the ships in the harbour, may absolutely command every avenue to the town both by sea & land." The Bostonians warned "that from all they can hear from Britain, Administration is resolved to do all in their power to force them to a submission—that when the town is enclosed, it is apprehended the inhabitants will be held as hostages for the submission of the country." They asked Congress for advice on whether to flee or stay: "if the Congress advise to quit the town—they obey—if it is judged that by maintaining their ground they can better serve the public cause, they will not shrink from hardship & danger."[22]

Dr. Thomas Young wrote to Adams reporting that, upon the news that the British had seized a supply of colonial gunpowder from Charlestown, tens of thousands of colonists had taken up arms and marched in that direction, from as far away as Connecticut. Samuel Adams replied to him, "I have written to our friends to provide themselves without delay with Arms & Ammunition, get well instructed in the military Art, embody themselves & prepare a complete set of rules that they may be ready in Case they are called to defend themselves against the violent attacks of Despotism."[23]

Congress responded more mildly, by appointing a three-person committee, including Samuel Adams, to write a letter to General Gage expressing concern, and by resolving that anyone collaborating with Gage in changing Massachusetts's form of government "ought to be held in detestation and abhorrence by all good men, and considered as the wicked tools of that despotism, which is preparing to destroy those rights, which God, nature, and compact, have given to America."[24]

On Friday, October 14, the committee that had been appointed to enumerate the violations of the rights of the colonies issued its draft report to the Congress. Samuel Adams was a member of the group, and his influence could be detected in the draft by those familiar with his thinking. Among the grievances listed was the Quebec Act, which, the report said, was "not only unjust to the people in that Province, but dangerous to the interests of the Protestant religion and of these Colonies, and ought to be repealed."[25]

The first Continental Congress concluded with an "association," signed by the delegates, "avowing our allegiance to his majesty," but nevertheless pledging not to import or export goods from America to Great Britain. There were several Samuel Adams–like notes, from the pledge to "wholly discontinue the slave trade" to a promise to "encourage frugality, economy, and industry, and promote agriculture, arts and the manufactures of this country, especially that of wool" and to "discountenance and discourage every species of extravagance and dissipation, especially all horse-racing, and all kinds of gaming, cock-fighting, exhibitions of shews, plays, and other expensive diversions and entertainments." The Quebec Act was assailed as encouraging Canadians "to act with hostility against the free Protestant colonies."[26]

The next day, Congress approved an "address to the people of Great-Britain," warning them that if the Canadians, "their numbers daily swelling with Catholic emigrants from Europe," succeeded in reducing "the ancient free Protestant Colonies to the same state of slavery with themselves," the British Protestants might be next. "Admit that the Ministry, by the powers of Britain, and the aid of our Roman Catholic neighbors, should be able to carry the point of taxation, and reduce us to a state of perfect humiliation and slavery," Congress hypothesized. "Suppose you should prove victorious—in what condition will you then be? What advantages or what laurels will you reap from such a conquest? May not a Ministry with the same armies inslave you—It may be said, you will cease to pay them—but remember the taxes from America, the wealth, and we may add, the men, and particularly the Roman Catholics of this vast continent will then be in the power of your enemies—nor will you have any reason to expect, that after making slaves of us, many among us should refuse to assist in reducing you to the same abject state."[27]

Finishing up its business in a final productive rush, the Congress on October 26 approved a petition for Benjamin Franklin to convey to George III, which Samuel Adams also signed. Adams's name would be known in London—the Massachusetts lawyer Josiah Quincy, Jr., traveling there at this time, wrote home to his wife, "The character of your Mr. Samuel Adams stands very high here. I find many who consider him the first politician in the world."[28] Full of florid language directed at the king, the petition was addressed, "To the Kings most excellent majesty Most gracious Sovereign" from "We your majestys faithful subjects." It concluded, "That your majesty may enjoy every felicity through a long and glorious reign over loyal and happy subjects, and that your descendants may inherit your prosperity and dominions 'til time shall be no more, is and always will be our sincere and fervent prayer." But in paragraphs sandwiched between the flattery, the petition complained of the Quebec Act's "establishing an absolute government and the Roman Catholick religion throughout those vast regions, that border on the westerly and northerly boundaries of the free protestant English settlements." It said, "Had our creator been pleased to give us existence in a land of slavery, the sense of our condition might have been mitigated by ignorance and habit. But thanks be to his adoreable goodness, we were born the heirs of freedom, and ever enjoyed our right under the auspices of your royal ancestors, whose family was seated on the British throne, to rescue and secure a pious and gallant nation from the popery and despotism of a superstitious and inexorable tyrant."[29]

While inveighing against popery in one letter, Congress was at the same time appealing to the inhabitants of Quebec to ally against England, trying to make the Canadians understand that their freedoms were being violated. The appeal to the inhabitants of Quebec downplayed the religious differences between the colonists. "We are too well acquainted with the liberality of sentiment distinguishing your nation, to imagine, that difference of religion will prejudice you against a hearty amity with us. You know, that the transcendent nature of freedom elevates those, who unite in her cause, above all such low-minded infirmities," the appeal said. "The Swiss Cantons furnish a memorable proof of this truth. Their union is composed of Roman Catholic and Protestant States, living in the utmost concord and peace with one another, and thereby enabled, ever since they bravely vindicated their freedom, to defy and defeat every tyrant that has invaded them."[30] (The Canadian Catholics, who found out about the anti-Catholic letters to England at the same time they received the more tolerant letter addressed to them, were unmoved, repelled by what one historian has since called "the stupid action of the Congress in needlessly insulting the Canadian Catholics whose friendship and cooperation were now solicited."[31])

If the letter to the inhabitants of Quebec, like the invitation to Rev. Duché to deliver the opening prayer at the Congress, indicated a new openness to religious pluralism by Samuel Adams, that attitude may have been imbibed from the atmosphere in Philadelphia. John Adams's diary indicates he visited a Presbyterian meeting one Sunday, dined with a young Quaker lawyer later that week, and was introduced to Charles Carroll, a Roman Catholic from Carrollton, Maryland, "a very sensible Gentleman." There was no Congregationalist meeting house in Philadelphia,[32] so John Adams attended services at the Moravian, Quaker, Baptist, Methodist, Anglican, and even the Roman Catholic meeting houses or churches. His account of the Catholic service was that he "heard a good discourse upon the Duty of Parents to their Children, founded in justice and Charity. The Scenery and the Musick is so callculated to take in Mankind that I wonder, the Reformation ever succeeded. The Paintings, the Bells, the Candles, the Gold and Silver. Our Saviour on the Cross, over the Altar, at full Length, and all his Wounds a bleeding. The Chanting is exquisitely soft and sweet."[33]

Whether Samuel Adams came along on these adventures in comparative religion is unknown, though the cousins lived in the same Philadelphia rooming house and often collaborated, dined, and traveled together. And even John Adams, while impressed, was not entirely won over, noting in his diary, "Phyladelphia with all its Trade, and Wealth, and Regularity is not Boston. . . . our Religion is superiour."[34]

Boston was nowhere close to Philadelphia's diversity of religious practices. The Massachusetts House of Representatives had voted in 1774 to approve a bill exempting Quakers and Antipaedobaptists—those who opposed baptizing infants—from paying taxes to support the Congregational churches and clergymen.[35] But that fell short of the fuller separation of church and state that was desired by the leader of the Antipaedobaptists, Isaac Backus.

Backus had been born in Connecticut in 1724, was moved by the Great Awakening, and became a Congregationalist minister. In 1756, he moved to Middleborough, Massachusetts, which is to the south of Boston, near Plymouth, where he took up the job of pastor of the Middleborough First Baptist Church (the Baptists baptized adults rather than newborns). Though he never attended or graduated college, he served from 1765 to 1799 as a trustee of Brown University.[36] In 1773, he issued "An Appeal to the Public for Religious Liberty, Against the Oppressions of the Present Day." The appeal, printed in Boston, echoed Samuel Adams in referring to what Backus called "our fathers and brethren, who inhabit the land to which our ancestors fled for religious liberty."[37] But he was more critical of the Puritan forefathers than was Adams, who tended to view them in heroic terms. In Backus's "Appeal," he went so far to accuse the founders of Massachusetts Bay of adopting popish tendencies, quoting a "learned author" who "never delivered a plainer truth, than when he said, 'The reforming churches flying from Rome, carried some of them more, some of them less, all of them something of Rome with them, especially that spirit of imposition and persecution which too much cleaved to them.'"[38] Into that category he put the use of tax dollars to support the Congregational clergy, a practice he argued "implies an acknowledgement, that the civil power has a right to set one religious sect up above another," which, in turn, he said, "tends to destroy the purity and life of religion."[39]

Backus and his sympathizers saw a parallel between the way the colonists were being taxed by Parliament and the way Massachusetts Baptists, or Antipaedobaptists, were being taxed by the Massachusetts authorities. So Backus decided to take his case to Philadelphia, where the colonial representatives were gathered to make the case against taxation without representation and against infringements on religious liberties. He issued a letter to the delegates gathered there, explaining that "the elders and brethren of twenty Baptist churches met in Association at Medfield, twenty miles from Boston, September 14, 1774, have unanimously chosen and sent unto you the reverend and beloved Mr. Isaac Backus as our agent, to lay our case, in these respects, before you." The petition went on, "we claim and expect the liberty of worshipping God according to our consciences, not being obliged to support a ministry we cannot attend. . . . These we have an undoubted right to, as men, as Christians, and by charter as inhabitants of Massachusetts Bay."[40]

As Backus recalled it in his diary and his history of New England, John Adams and Samuel Adams both responded with long speeches asserting that "There is, indeed, an ecclesiastical establishment in our province; but a very slender one, hardly to be called an establishment." When Backus disputed that claim, Samuel Adams shifted the argument, telling Backus that it was the royal governor, not the House of Representatives, that was to blame. Samuel Adams, according to Backus's account, "tried to represent" that ordinary Baptists had an easy time of it in Massachusetts Bay; "and more than once insinuated that these complaints came from enthusiasts who made it a merit to suffer persecution; and also that enemies had a hand therein." Backus responded that it may strike Adams as a matter of enthusiasm but that to him it was "absolutely a point of conscience." It had been four hours of discussion in Carpenter's Hall, lasting till eleven at night, but by the end the delegates from Massachusetts, while discouraging Backus from raising his hopes too high, were nonetheless promising that they would see what they could do to provide him with some relief.[41]

---

As Adams packed up his belongings and prepared to return to Boston, it must have been with mixed feelings. Congress had expressed the solidarity of all the colonies with Boston, which was an achievement in its own right. And it had agreed to joint economic action, with non-importation and nonexportation, even though those actions had some loopholes and delays in implementation. Still, there was no decisive break between America and Britain. The struggle for liberty, while it had escalated, was not yet fully joined, as the colonists declared themselves "faithful subjects" of George III, language that must have rankled Adams. He could stomach it, however, for the reason that, as he had written to Joseph Warren on September 25, "It is of the greatest importance, that the American opposition should be united."[42] There was not yet a consensus in favor of more extreme actions, such as setting up a new government. He also knew that by resolving to meet again on May 10, 1775, if the colonial grievances remained unresolved, the First Continental Congress had laid the groundwork for more conclusive action ahead. He would be glad to return to his family and his hometown. Finally, Adams, as he departed Philadelphia for Boston in a heavy rain on Friday, October 28,[43] could have the satisfaction of knowing that if it came time for the Hearts of Oak of Boston to fight for their freedom "with swords and with guns," he would be at the scene rather than far away in Philadelphia.

Such feelings might have accounted for the haste with which Samuel Adams, his cousin John, and Thomas Cushing returned home (Robert Treat Paine parted ways with them in New York, where he took a boat to Newport). From Boston to Philadelphia in August had taken nineteen days. They made it back in thirteen days, explaining to those who wanted them to stay and dine with them along the road that "We had been so long from home and our affairs were so critical, We hoped they would excuse us if we passed thro the Town as fast as possible."[44] Not that all entertainments were refused. In Worcester, Massachusetts, "two young Ladies" sang their returning delegates "The New Liberty Song,"[45] whose lyrics had been printed the week earlier in the *Massachusetts Spy,* and which were indicative of the resolute stance with which the people of the colony were meeting the British incursion. It went:

Boston be not dismay'd
Tho tyrants now oppress
Tho fleets and troops invade
You soon will have redress
The resolutions of the brave
Will injur'd Massachusetts save

The delegates have met
For wisdom all renown'd
Freedom we may expect
From politicks profound
Illustrious Congress, may each name
Be crowned with immortal Fame!

Tho troops upon our ground
Have strong entrenchments made
Tho ships the town surround
With all their guns display'd
'Twill not the free-born spirit tame
Or force us to renounce our claim

Our charter-rights we claim
Granted in ancient times
Since our Forefathers came
First to these Western Climes
Nor will their sons degenerate
They freedom love—oppression hate

If Gage should strike the blow
We must for freedom fight
Undaunted courage show

While we defend our right
In spite of the oppressive band
Maintain the freedom of the land.[46]

When the delegates arrived in Boston on the evening of November 9, the town's church bells rang in their honor and in celebration of their safe return.[47]

If Samuel Adams planned to resume his seat in the House of Representatives of Massachusetts, he was to be disappointed, for that body was no more, at least in official title. Though General Gage had called the House to convene at Salem, he soon changed his mind, citing "the many Tumults and Disorders which have since taken place, the extraordinary resolves which have been passed in many of the Counties," and "the present disorder'd, and unhappy state of the Province."[48] The House reconstituted itself as a "provincial Congress" and met anyway, with Samuel Adams a member. One of its first items of business was to reelect the four delegates who had represented Massachusetts at the First Continental Congress to represent Massachusetts again at the second, and to add to the delegation another heavyweight, John Hancock.[49] The appointment was made in a way that underscored the representative nature of the work of the delegates to the Continental Congress; the Provincial Congress allowed them to serve until December 31, "and no longer," a term limit that made clear at the outset the difference between kings and congressmen.[50] Adams also returned to Faneuil Hall and the Boston Town Meeting, where he was appointed chairman of a committee to implement the non-importation agreement that had been passed at the Continental Congress.[51]

The newspapers were full of the same issues discussed in Philadelphia, including the threat of Catholicism in Canada. "Was it not enough to have given the Romish religion in Canada a free toleration? Why must it be established?" asked a letter from Holland printed in the November 21, 1774, *Boston Post Boy*. "The act for establishing popery in Canada is all the more disagreeable, as at this very time, the present King of France is oppressing the protestants in his dominions."

All around, the colonists were making military preparations. In Roxbury, Samuel Adams's cousin Amos Adams, pastor of the First Church, opened a meeting with a prayer and then was appointed moderator of the group that proceeded to choose military officers for the parish, selecting captains, lieutenants, and ensigns for two companies.[52] James Warren wrote to John Adams, "If these matters continue, I may as well beat my plow shares into swords, and pruning hooks into spears."[53]

Patriot militias and British troops were already starting to engage. On December 14, 1774, four hundred New Hampshire militiamen seized Fort William and Mary, at Portsmouth, subduing six British troops and capturing more than one hundred barrels of gunpowder.[54] Throughout New England, the colonists trained for action. To the Virginia patriot and critic of Benjamin Franklin, Arthur Lee, on January 29, 1775, Samuel Adams wrote, "I am well informd that in every Part of the Province there are selected Numbers of Men, called Minute Men—that they are well disciplined & well provided—and that upon a very short Notice they will be able to assemble a formidable Army." Adams continued, portraying the military buildup as a throwback to the Puritan settlers of New England, who had to fight for their survival against hostile Indians: "The People are recollecting the Achievements of their Ancestors and whenever it shall be necessary for them to draw their Swords in the Defence of their Liberties, they will shew themselves to be worthy of such Ancestors."[55]

Even intelligence networks were mobilized. Paul Revere recalled that he spent the fall of 1774 and the winter of 1775 as a leader of a committee of about thirty that met at Boston's Green Dragon Tavern, on Union Street near Faneuil Hall, "for the purpose of watching the movements of the British soldiers, and gaining every intelligence of the movements of the Tories." He said, "We were so careful that our meetings should be kept secret, that every time we met, every person swore upon the Bible that he would not discover any of our transactions but to Messrs Hancock, Adams, Doctors Warren, Church, and one or two more."[56]

Wild rumors coursed through the colonies. A Philadelphia merchant, Stephen Collins, wrote to Robert Treat Paine about a report that the Massachusetts Provincial Congress had been dissolved on account of "an attempt being made to raise 20,000 men immediately and attack the King's Troops." Wrote Collins, "The report is, that S. Adams Esqr. made the motion & urged it strongly." The account was false, but it was nonetheless illuminating about Adams's reputation at the time.[57]

Perhaps with Backus's complaint still lingering in his mind, Samuel Adams made a point of insisting in his correspondence that his hometown was a model of religious comity. He wrote to Stephen Collins on January 31, 1775, that in Boston, "The Different denominations of Christians here (excepting those amongst them who Espouse the cause of our Enemies) are in perfect peace and Harmony, as I trust they always will be."[58]

Such was the case in Salem, where, as the Pulitzer Prize–winning historian David Hackett Fischer records in his book *Paul Revere's Ride*, when British troops marched on Salem on Sunday, February 26, 1775, Baptists, Quakers, and Congregationalists joined to thwart them. The British troops were met by a Salem minister, Thomas Bernard, at a drawbridge between the troops and the cannon they had been sent to seize, and on their way out of town, a local woman yelled at them for having "broken the peace of our Sabbath."[59]

Adams was a keen observer of how religious dynamics affected the involvement of other colonies and of individual colonists in the struggle against Britain. It would be hard to miss. Fischer notes several ways in which the New England Congregationalists recoiled at the British. They were revolted by the cruelty with which misbehaving British troops were beaten by their superiors, in a manner that far exceeded the injunction of Deuteronomy, chapter 25, verse 3, "He may be given up to forty lashes, but not more, lest being flogged further, to excess, your brother be degraded before your eyes." They were upset that soldiers interrupted a fast day and partied to excess on St. Patrick's Day. They accused Gage of being a papist, as some of his ancestors were long after it was fashionable in England. A January 1775 cartoon by Paul Revere showed Lord North presenting George III with a "Bill for the total abolition of civil and religious liberty in America," while America, looking skyward, prayed, "Lord thou didst drive out the heathen before, our hope is in thee." God replied, from behind a cloud, "I have delivered and I WILL deliver."[60]

The invoking of God in civil affairs extended beyond Massachusetts. In a February 4, 1775, letter to Adams, Richard Henry Lee recounted with pleasure that a ship from London owned by a Virginia merchant had been turned away "without being suffered to take a single hogshead of Tobacco, because she had brought a few chests of tea." Lee went on to assert, "The cause of Liberty must be under the protection of Heaven, because the Creator surely wills the happiness of his Creatures; & having joined the faculty of reasoning with our natures, he has made us capable of discerning that the true dignity and happiness of human nature are only to be found in a state of freedom."[61]

In a March 4, 1775, letter to Arthur Lee, Adams attributed New York's delay in appointing delegates to the Second Continental Congress to the combination of "high Church Clergymen and great Landholders." The clergymen, according to Adams, did not want to interfere with Britain's plans to establish "an American Episcopate," while the landholders "are Lords over many Slaves; and are afraid of the Consequences that would follow, if a Spirit of Liberty should prevail among them."[62]

In the same letter to Lee, Adams wrote of how the mood of Bostonians had been emboldened by religious faith. "The publick Liberty must be preservd though at the Expense of many Lives!" he wrote. "The Language of the people is, 'In the Name of the Lord we will tread down our Enemies.'"[63]

Such language, boldness, and faith were all on display in abundance the next day, March 5, in Old South Meeting House, during the annual commemoration of the Boston Massacre. The meeting was moderated by Samuel Adams, and the previous year's orator, John Hancock, was also in attendance. So, too, were a smattering of British officers. Adams invited them from the back of the church to front-row seats so that, as he put it later in a letter to Richard Henry Lee, "they might have no pretence to behave ill for it is a good maxim in politicks as well as war to put & keep the enemy in the wrong."[64]

This year's orator was Dr. Joseph Warren, joining in the line of speakers that had included not only Hancock but also Benjamin Church and James Lovell. He dressed the classical part, wearing a white toga that contrasted with the black with which the pulpit was draped in memory of the massacre victims.[65] His speech began with a reprise of the history of settlement in North America, likening the Puritans leaving Europe to Noah leaving a destroyed and sinful world. "Our fathers having nobly resolved never to wear the yoke of despotism, and seeing the European world, at the time, through indolence and cowardice, falling a prey to tyranny, bravely threw themselves upon the bosom of the ocean, determined to find a place in which they might enjoy their freedom, or perish in the glorious attempt," Warren said. "Approving heaven beheld the favourite ark dancing upon the waves, and graciously preserved it until the chosen families were brought in safety to these western regions."

The British ministry clung to its claim to the right to tax the colonies, Warren said, as if it were hugging a "darling idol; and every rolling year affords fresh instances of the absurd devotion with which they worship it." As for the massacre victims, Warren was unflinching in invoking their memory, and in accusing their killers.

Take heed, ye orphan babes, lest, whilst your streaming eyes are fixed upon the ghastly corpse, your feet glide on the stones bespattered with your father's brains. . . . We wildly stare about, and with amazement, ask, who spread this ruin round us? what wretch has dared deface the image of his God? has haughty France, or cruel Spain, sent forth her myrmidons? has the grim savage rused again from the far distant wilderness? or does some fiend, fierce from the depth of hell, with all the rancorous malice, which the apostate damned can feel, twang her destructive bow, and hurl her deadly arrows at our breast? no, none of these; but, how astonishing! It is the hand of Britain that inflicts the wound.

The speech did more than dwell on the wounds of the past, however. It inspired Bostonians for the fight ahead. "The man who meanly will submit to wear a shackle, contemns the noblest gift of heaven, and impiously affronts the God that made him free," Warren said. "Where justice is the standard, heaven is the warrior's shield."[66]

As Warren's speech ended, Adams rose and, as G. B. Warden describes it in his history of Boston, reminded the audience to come again next year to commemorate the "bloody massacre." At the word "bloody," the officers—who, by at least one account, were on a mission to assassinate Adams—cried "Fie, oh fie!" The Bostonians, used to dropping "r"s, interpreted it as a cry of "Fire,"[67] at which point, as Adams put it, "confusion ensued."[68] Another account has one of the British officers challenging Samuel Adams to a duel, and proposing a place to meet. Adams reportedly responded by offering to meet the officer's general.[69]

It was an ominously close call, and could easily have produced another massacre, or a flash point that started the war. In the days that followed, Samuel Adams, probably happy to have escaped unharmed, expressed confidence that happier days awaited, thanks to God. To a southern friend on March 12, 1775, he wrote, "I cannot help thinking that this Union among the Colonies and Warmth of Affection, can be attributed to Nothing less than the Agency of the supreme Being. If we believe that he superintends and directs the great Affairs of

Empires, we have reason to expect the restoration and Establishment of the publick Liberties, unless by our own Misconduct we have ren- derd ourselves unworthy of it; for he certainly wills the Happiness of those of his Creatures who deserve it, & without publick Liberty, we cannot be happy."[70]

# Chapter 6

# Lexington and Concord

## 1775

*"O! What a glorious morning is this!"*

—*Samuel Adams, April 19, 1775*

As the Boston winter drew to a close, and spring of 1775 approached, Adams faced the prospect of leaving for Congress in Philadelphia with his hometown teetering on the brink of war. The might of the British was apparent in the masts of Royal Navy warships bristling in Boston Harbor, visible from Adams's home on Purchase Street. There was His Majesty's Ship the *Preston*, with fifty cannon aboard; the *Somerset*, with sixty-eight guns; the *Boyne*, with seventy; the *Asia*, with sixty-four; the *Mercury* and the *Glasgow*, with twenty guns each; the *Diana*, a six-gun schooner—all told, nearly three hundred cannon available to flatten Boston at an admiral's order.[1]

Adams expressed optimism that his colonial colleagues would prevail, even against such formidable firepower. To a Virginian named Washington (not George, but perhaps his brother) Adams wrote of his fellow Bostonians, "When they are pushed by clear necessity for the defence of their liberties to the trial of arms, I trust in God, they will convince their friends and their enemies, of their military skill and valor. Their constant prayer to God is to prevent such necessity;

but they are daily preparing for it."[2] On March 23, the Provincial Congress appointed Adams, Elbridge Gerry, and Robert Treat Paine to a committee "to bring in a resolve, expressing the sense of this Congress, that for this people to relax in their preparations to defend themselves, &c., would be attended with the most dangerous consequences."[3]

Adams did his best to make sure they had all the allies possible, drafting an appeal to the Mohawk Indians. "Brother,—They have made a law to establish the religion of the Pope in Canada, which lies so near you. We much fear some of your children may be induced, instead of worshipping the only true God, to pay *his* dues to images made with their own hands," the appeal warned. "We humbly beseech that God who lives above, and does what is right here below, to enlighten your minds to see that you ought to endeavor to prevent our fathers from bringing those miseries upon us; and to his good providence we commend you."

Adams advised the Indians to get ready for war: "We therefore earnestly desire you to whet your hatchet and be prepared with us to defend our liberties and lives."[4]

The Mohawks never really came through, but the spirit of the appeal was contagious, and a few months later, the patriot leaders of Massachusetts heard from two heads of the St. John's tribe. The chiefs said that they were joining with their brethren the Penobscot Indians in what is now Maine "and are resolved to stand together, and oppose the People of Old-England, that are endeavouring to take your, and our Lands and Liberties from us."

The St. John's chiefs told the Massachusetts legislators, "We are Brothers of one Father, and one God made us all, and we will stand by you, as long as the Almighty will give us strength, and we hope you will do the same to us."[5]

In addition to reaching out to the Indians, Adams and his fellow representatives of Massachusetts reached out to the neighboring colonies. On April 8, the Provincial Congress voted to raise and equip an army with the other New England colonies.[6] Adams was appointed to a committee to draft a letter to Connecticut, Rhode Island, and New

Hampshire (Vermont was not yet separate from New York). The letter, dated April 10, said that the Provincial Congress had concluded that "very little, if any, expectation of the redress of our common and intolerable grievances is to be had from the humble and dutiful petition and other wise measures of the late honorable Continental Congress." The time had come for more practical measures, such as raising an army. The letter was to be signed "Wishing that the American colonies may, at this important crisis, be under the direction of Heaven."[7]

The next week, the Provincial Congress, meeting at Concord, designated a day of fasting and prayer to be held Thursday, May 11, to implore that "the union of the American colonies in defence of their rights, for which, hitherto, we desire to thank Almighty God, may be preserved and confirmed; that the Provincial, and especially the Continental Congress, may be directed to such measures as God will countenance . . . and that America may soon behold a gracious interposition of Heaven, for the redress of her many grievances, the restoration of all her invaded liberties, and their security to the latest generations." With that prayer, on Saturday, April 15, the Provincial Congress adjourned.[8]

Samuel Adams and John Hancock, rather than risking another confrontation with the British troops in Boston, planned to leave directly for Philadelphia, where the Continental Congress was scheduled to meet on May 10. Before that, they would spend the weekend in Lexington at the house of Rev. Jonas Clarke, a cousin of Hancock.[9]

They were more vulnerable there than they could have imagined. On April 14, a letter from Lord Dartmouth to General Gage authorizing the arrest of the leaders of the Provincial Congress arrived in Boston: "It is the opinion of the King's servants, in which His Majesty concurs, that the first and essential step to be taken towards reestablishing Government, would be to arrest and imprison the principal actors and abettors of the Provincial Congress whose proceedings appear in every light to be acts of treason and rebellion."[10] The letter was a copy; the original arrived on another ship that landed on April

16 and that also brought news that seven regiments of reinforcements were on the way.[11]

The 16th of April was a Sunday, but the level of British troop activity and readiness was so high that Paul Revere rode out to Lexington to give a first warning to Adams and Hancock. Rather than leaving for Philadelphia immediately, they hung back as mounted British patrols scoured the countryside outside Boston, demanding that travelers tell them where Adams and Hancock were. By the evening of April 18, two more warnings reached Adams. As Rev. Clarke later recalled it, the group gathered in the house suspecting "that under cover of darkness, sudden arrest, if not assassination, might be attempted." The Lexington militia deployed an armed guard of eight men at Clarke's home to protect the patriot leaders, and thirty more militiamen readied at a nearby tavern.[12]

That same evening, a high-level informant in the British camp confirmed to Dr. John Warren that the British regular troops were planning "to seize Samuel Adams and John Hancock, who were known to be at Lexington, and burn the stores at Concord." Warren called immediately for Paul Revere, and, as Revere remembered, "begged that I would immediately set off for Lexington, where Messrs Hancock and Adams were, and acquaint them of the movement, and that it was thought they were the objects." As the historian of Paul Revere's famous midnight ride, David Hackett Fischer, put it, "Paul Revere's primary mission was not to alarm the countryside. His specific purpose was to warn Samuel Adams and John Hancock, who were thought to be the objects of the expedition."[13]

Revere traveled from Boston to Charlestown in a small rowboat with muffled oars, making his way around the British warships in the harbor in violation of a curfew. At Charlestown, at about 11 P.M., he borrowed a horse, Brown Beauty, from a deacon of the Congregational church, John Larkin. By midnight, after a close call with a British patrol, Revere and his horse clattered up to the Clarke parsonage in Lexington, where Samuel Adams and John Hancock were asleep in a downstairs bedroom. A sergeant from the Lexington militia greeted Revere by warning him to keep the noise down. Revere replied, "Noise! You'll have noise enough before long! The Regulars are coming out!"[14]

He proceeded to bang on the door of the parsonage, loud enough to wake Adams and Hancock, who said, "Come on in, Revere, we're not afraid of *you*."

A half-hour later, another messenger from Boston, William Dawes, appeared with the same warning, of thousands of red-coated British troops marching inland from Boston. Rather than going back to bed or fleeing, Adams, Hancock, and Clarke set out for the tavern where the Lexington militiamen were gathered. There, after some discussion, they decided that the neighboring town of Concord, where considerable colonial military supplies were stored, might also be a target of the British mission, and must be warned. Revere and Dawes, on horseback, headed for Concord. This time, the British patrol was less easily evaded, and Revere, along with other patriot messengers, was captured. "They particularly inquired where Hancock and Adams were," one such messenger, Elijah Sanderson, recalled. Revere was interrogated by a British major who held a pistol to his head and threatened, as Revere recalled, "he would blow my brains out." As Fischer writes of Revere, "Everything, without exception, that he said and did to his captors was consistent with a single goal. He was trying to move these men away from Lexington—away from Hancock and Adams."[15]

The two patriot leaders were gathered on the town common at 1 A.M. with the captain of the Lexington militia, John Parker, and with the Congregational minister who was host to Adams and Hancock, Jonas Clarke. Barrels of gunpowder were stored below the pulpit of Clarke's church.[16] Such combination of ministry and matériel was not uncommon; thirteen patriot cannon were reportedly deployed in front of the Congregational church in Worcester.[17] The Lexington militia loaded their muskets with powder and ball in the presence of Adams and Hancock.[18] The two patriot leaders then returned to Clarke's house, where they spent hours arguing over what to do. Hancock frantically cleaned his gun and sharpened his sword, itching to get to the front and face down the redcoats. Adams put his hand on Hancock's shoulder and said, "That is not our business. We belong to the cabinet." Revere, having finally escaped the British, burst in and urged Adams and Hancock to leave immediately. Finally, they did, setting out in Hancock's coach toward a parsonage northwest of Lexington, in Woburn. After arriving there, they were about to sit down to a meal when yet another panting messenger from Lexington arrived warning that the regulars were coming. This time there was no debating. Hancock's coach was hidden behind a pile of brush. Adams and Hancock scrambled into the woods to hide, then fled further northwest, to the house of Amos Wyman. On the way, hearing the exchange of gunfire in the distance, Adams and Hancock must have realized that their struggle was entering a new phase.

And it was. The shots heard 'round the world, at Lexington and Concord, and as the British troops retreated to Boston under fire from colonists hiding alongside the road, left fifty colonists killed or dead from their wounds, thirty-nine wounded, and five missing. The British lost sixty-five killed, 180 wounded, and twenty-seven missing, according to General Gage.[19] Before the battle, the minister at Concord, William Emerson, had preached a sermon on Chronicles, chapter 13, verse 12, "And behold God himself is our captain, and his priests with sounding trumpets to cry alarm." On the battlefield itself, Emerson encouraged one eighteen-year-old militiaman, "Stand your ground, Harry! Your cause is just and God will bless you."[20] Like the clergyman, Adams met the event not with trepidation or panic but with confidence, saying to Hancock, "O! What a glorious morning is this!" Historians have interpreted his joy as relating not to the bloodshed but to the acceleration of progress toward American independence.[21]

As John Adams put it, "the Battle of Lexington on the 19th of April, changed the Instruments of Warfare from the Penn to the Sword." John Adams set off from his home in Braintree to interview witnesses to the clash at Lexington, and came away convinced that "the Die was cast, the Rubicon passed, and as Lord Mansfield expressed it in Parliament, if We did not defend ourselves they would kill Us." Soon thereafter, he set out for Philadelphia.[22] Hancock and Samuel Adams had lingered from April 24 to 27 in Worcester, where, to judge by a letter Hancock sent to the Committee of Safety, they felt a bit like castaways. "Mr. S. Adams and myself, just arrived here, find no intelligence from you and no guard," Hancock wrote. "How are we to proceed?" The patriot leaders, progressing toward Philadelphia, then stopped at Hartford, where, on April 29, they had a secret meeting with Connecticut leaders to plan a brazen effort to seize Fort Ticonderoga.[23]

John Adams overtook them just before they reached New York. The news of the clashes at Lexington and Concord preceded the delegates from Massachusetts and served to rally public opinion around them. Some of the news was even true, though much was not. A letter "To the Inhabitants of New York" dated April 28, 1775, reported that when the British troops at Lexington "came to the house where said Hancock and Adams lodged, (who luckily escaped them;) they searched the house, and when they could not find them, these barbarians killed the woman of the house and all the children in cool blood, and then set the house on fire." The letter, signed, "An American," concluded, "Therefore it seems there is nothing for us to do, but to appeal unto God in the use of what force and strength we have in defence of our liberties and properties, and rely on his Almighty aid for help to repel the tyrant's rage."[24]

As John Adams recorded it, as the travelers from Massachusetts approached New York, "we were met by a great Number of Gentlemen in Carriages and on horseback, and all the Way their Numbers increased till I thought the whole City was come out to meet Us. The same Ardour was continued all the Way to Philadelphia."[25]

Samuel Adams made quite a sight as he arrived in Philadelphia. In the vanguard were the city's newly chosen military officers, marching two-by-two, with drawn swords, followed by two or three hundred gentlemen on horseback. Then Samuel Adams and John Hancock

arrived in a phaeton and pair, trailed by John Adams and Thomas
Cushing in a single-horse chaise, followed in turn by Robert Treat
Paine and by the congressional delegations from New York and Connecticut. An observer recorded that the streets were "crowded with
people of all ages, sexes, and ranks," and that "the procession marched
with a slow, solemn pace. On its entrance into the city, all the bells
were set to ringing and chiming, and every mark of respect that could
be was expressed."[26]

Samuel Adams's discomfort with the pomp must have been allayed
by the ample reminders that he was still both a war refugee and a
hunted man. In an expense filing he submitted later, he explained he
had to pay for new clothes, as "When I sat off from Lexington after
the memorable Battle there, I had with me only the Cloaths on my
back, which were very much worn, those which I had provided for
my self being then in Boston, and it was out of my Power at that time
to Recover them."[27]

Boston was, as he put it in a letter home, a "prison." Though
reports reached him that his wife had made it safely out of the city
to Dedham, or Cambridge, he had no good information on what had
happened to his son or daughter. "Our Boston friends are some of
them confined in a Garrison, others dispersed I know not where," he
wrote.[28] Adams's friend John Gill of the *Boston Gazette* was jailed for
twenty-nine days for printing "treason," while Benjamin Edes put his
press and some type in a boat and rowed his way up the Charles River
to patriot-controlled Watertown, where he resumed publication of the
newspaper.[29] Those residents of Boston who were not literally jailed
might as well have been, or worse. As one British soldier put it in a
letter home dated April 30 that was intercepted and passed to the Provincial Congress of Massachusetts, "There is no market in Boston: the
inhabitants are all starving." He predicted, "we shall surely burn the
whole country before us if they do not submit, which I do not imagine
they will do, for they are an obstinate set of people."[30] The British
and their allies, including the rector of the Anglican King's Chapel in
Boston, made plans to seize the Green Dragon Tavern where Samuel

Adams and his associates had gathered and convert it into a military hospital for their own use.[31]

Even Samuel Adams's wife's own fate was less than certain: "My great concern is for your health and safety," he wrote to "My Dear Betsy," urging her to "take the advice of friends with respect to removing further into the country," and urging her to send letters to him via William Checkley in Providence.

As for Samuel Adams himself, the risk to his safety was considerable. Intelligence from London spoke of two sets of orders from the king to Gage, one to send Adams and Hancock to England for trial, another to hang them in Boston.[32] Adams wrote to his wife that as he and Hancock approached Philadelphia, "we have each of us two Centinels at our respective lodgings." He pronounced himself in good health and spirits.[33]

# Chapter 7

# Congressman, II

## *1775–1779*

*"Is not America already independent? Why then not declare it?"*

—*Samuel Adams, 1776*

THE GATHERING OF the Congress must have felt in some ways as familiar to Adams as his return to a second year at college. Many of the delegates from the meeting that had adjourned in October of 1774 had returned in May 1775. Adams was reunited with Christopher Gadsden of South Carolina, with John Jay of New York, and with George Washington, Patrick Henry, and Richard Henry Lee of Virginia. Even the opening prayer, at the First Congress a matter of such symbolic weight and contention, had now settled into a pattern—Rev. Mr. Duché was called on for a repeat performance.[1] (Back in Massachusetts, the provincial Massachusetts legislature convened in Watertown for an election sermon from Samuel Adams's Harvard and Boston Latin School classmate, the president of Harvard, Samuel Langdon, who spoke of the British officials as "wicked men" bent on "establishing Popery." He offered by way of contrast "the Jewish government," established divinely, according to the Bible, as "a perfect Republic."[2])

In other ways, though, things in Philadelphia were different. There was a new venue—instead of Carpenter's Hall, the delegates met in the Pennsylvania State House (later known as Independence Hall), a handsome red-brick and gray-granite building that rose to a wood-shingled roof with white balustrades and a soaring wooden churchlike steeple. Outside, birds chirped in the heavy mid-Atlantic air. Delegates entered through a sun-drenched central hallway and met in a drafty, wood-paneled first-floor room with thirty-foot coffered ceilings and two fireplaces flanked by Ionic pilasters. The pilasters, together with the triangular pediments capping the doors, evoked the classical architecture of the ancient Greeks whose republican form of government many of the delegates so admired.

There were some new faces. Samuel Adams finally met face-to-face with Benjamin Franklin, the oldest of the delegates, who had returned from London. Congress's first order of business was receiving a report signed by Franklin and by Samuel Adams's friend Arthur Lee, Franklin's longtime rival in London, disclosing that "three regiments of foot, one of dragoons, seven hundred marines, six sloops of war, and two frigates, are now under orders for America."[3]

That report underscored the biggest difference of them all between this Congress and the first. The outbreak of clashes between British troops and colonial militia lent a new urgency to this meeting, and as Congress convened, much of the work ahead related to managing what, it became increasingly clear, was a war.

The delegates were initially buoyed by good news from the north. On May 17, word reached Congress that Ticonderoga had been seized by a group of colonial volunteers led by Ethan Allen and Benedict Arnold, and with it a supply of cannon and military stores. The plan Adams had helped set in motion at the meeting at Hartford had paid off.

One early problem for Congress to solve was the defense of New York. Samuel Adams and George Washington were named to a committee with the New York delegates to consider how many American troops would be needed and where they should be posted.[4] Another task was to prepare a letter to the people of Canada. The committee assigned by Congress to draft the letter consisted of Samuel Adams, John Jay, and Silas Deane.[5] Samuel Adams also joined Washington on a committee "to consider of ways and means to supply these colonies with Ammunition and military stores and to report immediately."[6] And he joined Franklin and Richard Henry Lee on a committee "to consider the best means of establishing posts for conveying letters and intelligence through this continent."[7]

The committees worked quickly. The letter to Canada presented the choice as between freedom or enslavement to British tyranny, and announced to the north, "We, for our parts, are determined to live free, or not at all; and are resolved, that posterity shall never reproach us with having brought slaves into the world."[8] The committee on defending New York decided that the number of troops "be left to the provincial congress of New York to determine," in what may have been the first instance of America's central government devolving responsibility. But it also imposed standardizing regulations on what was even then a tendency of New York to lead the way in wages, recommending that the New York troops' "pay shall not exceed" what was being offered to soldiers in New England.[9] Keeping military pay differentials at egalitarian New England levels rather than at southern plantation–style extremes was a cause that Samuel Adams worked hard on without much success; John Adams reported home that despite the "utmost endeavors" of himself and his cousin, "Those ideas of equality, which are so agreeable to us natives of New England, are very disagreeable to many gentlemen in the other colonies," who thought Massachusetts paid its private soldiers too much and its officers too little.[10]

It was a remarkable first month of Congress for Samuel Adams, whose role as a leader of the group was clear at the outset. During May, Congress had named a total of six committees. Samuel Adams sat on four of the six, far more than any other of the about fifty delegates gathered. No other delegate sat on more than two committees.

When, on May 24, Peyton Randolph returned to Virginia for a

meeting of the Assembly, of which he was speaker, John Hancock was unanimously chosen president of the Congress.[11] (Thomas Jefferson arrived in Philadelphia June 21 to replace Randolph as a delegate for Virginia.)[12] For Adams, Hancock's accession was another political victory, as it installed a fellow delegate from Massachusetts in an important post. Samuel Adams was much poorer than Hancock and differed with him on various issues. Their relations would go through periods of warmth and coolness. But the traveling companions who had shared a bedroom at Rev. Clarke's parsonage that fateful night in Lexington knew each other well, and Adams could be sure that he would have access to Hancock if he needed it.

The business in Congress was not all high statesmanship. Adams was called on to deal with more practical and mundane matters as well, everything from refereeing squabbles between generals to figuring out the best way to deal with outbreaks of smallpox among soldiers and even among delegates to Congress.[13] Delegates from the New England states, of whom Adams was one, were assigned to "have at least 10,000 pairs of shoes, and 10,000 pair of stockings, purchased in those states, and sent forward to General Washington's head quarters, with all possible expedition, for the use of the soldiers under his command." Adams was appointed to a three-person committee "to procure a translation into the German language of the Treaty between the courts of London and Hesse, for troops to be employed in America."[14] Samuel Adams sometimes chafed at the cumbersome elements of having Congress manage the war effort. He wrote to James Warren, "The Spirit of Patriotism prevails among the Members of this Congress but from the Necessity of things Business must go on slower than one could wish. It is difficult to possess upwards of Sixty Gentlemen, at once with the same Feelings upon Questions of Importance that are continually arising."[15]

The delegates made time, amid the practical preparations for war, for spiritual preparations as well. A three-person committee that included two of Samuel Adams's Massachusetts colleagues, John Adams and Robert Treat Paine, brought in a motion declaring Thursday, July 20, a day of fasting and prayer. Perhaps because of Samuel Adams's absence from the committee that drafted it, perhaps as a compromise to win the approval of the whole Congress, the resolution left open, at least rhetorically, the opportunity, short of independence, for peaceful reconciliation with Britain:

> This Congress, therefore, considering the present critical, alarming and calamitous state of these colonies, do earnestly recommend that Thursday, the 20th day of July next, be observed, by the inhabitants of all the English colonies on this continent, as a day of public humiliation, fasting and prayer; that we may, with united hearts and voices, unfeignedly confess and deplore our many sins; and offer up our joint supplications to the all-wise, omnipotent, and merciful Disposer of all events; humbly beseeching him to forgive our iniquities, to remove our present calamities, to avert those desolating judgments, with which we are threatned, and to bless our rightful sovereign, King George the third, and inspire him with wisdom to discern and pursue the true interest of all his subjects, that a speedy end may be put to the civil discord between Great Britain and the American colonies, without farther effusion of blood: And that the British nation may be influenced to regard the things that belong to her peace, before they are hid from her eyes: That these colonies may be ever under the care and protection of a kind Providence, and be prospered in all their interests; That the divine blessing may descend and rest upon all our civil rulers, and upon the representatives of the people, in their several assemblies and conventions, that they may be directed to wise and effectual measures for preserving the union, and securing the just rights and priviledges of the colonies; That virtue and true religion may revive and flourish throughout our land; And that all America may soon behold a gracious interposition of Heaven, for the redress of her many grievances, the restoration of her invaded rights, a reconcilation with the parent state, on terms constitutional and

honorable to both; And that her civil and religious priviledges may be secured to the latest posterity.

And it is recommended to Christians, of all denominations, to assemble for public worship, and to abstain from servile labour and recreations on said day.

Ordered, That a copy of the above be signed by the president and attested by the Secy and published in the newspapers, and in hand bills.[16]

The results produced by the resolution were noted by James Warren in a letter to Samuel Adams: "Three millions of people on their knees at once, supplicating the aid of Heaven, is a striking circumstance, and a very singular one in America. May the blessings of Heaven follow in answer to our prayers."[17]

Samuel Adams's faith in God was tried and tested by the events of war. Not all the news was as good as that from Ticonderoga. From Boston came the sad word that Dr. Joseph Warren had been killed by the British in the Battle of Bunker Hill on June 17, 1775. John Adams wrote to James Warren that when initial news of the clash arrived at Philadelphia, it was 11 P.M. on Saturday night, June 24. The two Adamses and Hancock went out into the streets of Philadelphia to rouse the city's leading men, "in order to beg some powder." Before morning, ninety quarter-casks of gunpowder were on their way from Philadelphia to Boston.[18] Samuel Adams's letter to his wife, Elizabeth, offers a window into how he reacted, and evidence that for him, faith was not only a matter for congressional proclamations, but a personal source of strength. Samuel Adams wrote his "dearest Betsy" from Philadelphia late at night. "I pray God to cover the heads of our Countrymen in every day of Battle, and ever to protect you from Injury in these distracted Times. The Death of our truly amiable and worthy Friend Dr Warren is greatly afflicting," he wrote. "But it is our Duty to submit to the Dispensations of Heaven, 'Whose Ways are ever gracious, ever just.' He fell in the glorious Struggle for the publick Liberty."[19] Warren's wife had died in 1773, and Adams did what he could to help take care of the four children, all younger than thirteen, who had been left orphaned by the death of their father on the battlefield.[20]

The prospect that Samuel Adams would meet a fate similar to that of Warren was heightened by a proclamation issued June 12 by "His Excellency, The Hon. Thomas Gage, Esq., Governor and Commander in Chief in and over his Majesty's Province of Massachusetts-Bay, and Vice Admiral of the Same." Like Governor Andros before him, Gage was quickly learning that a gaudy title did not necessarily translate into good treatment from the Boston locals. He made a last-ditch attempt at reconciliation, offering and promising His Majesty's "most gracious pardon to all persons who shall forthwith lay down their arms, and return to the duties of peaceable subjects, excepting only from the benefit of such pardon, Samuel Adams and John Hancock, whose offenses are of too flagitious a nature to admit of any other consideration other than that of condign punishment." Gage also made his own effort to appeal to the colonists by putting his offer and argument in a religious context, blaming the "well known incendiaries and traitors" for introducing "the name of God . . . in the pulpits to excite and justify devastation and massacre." Gage concluded by expressing the hope that "God in his mercy shall restore to his creatures in this distracted land, that system of happiness from which they have been seduced, the religion of peace, and liberty founded upon law." The document was issued by Gage in the name of "his Majesty George the third, by the Grace of GOD of Great Britain, France, and Ireland, KING, Defender of the Faith, &c," and ended with the phrase, "GOD SAVE THE KING."[21]

In the same letter to his wife in which he spoke of his grief at the death of Warren, Adams reacted to the news of Gage's order not with dread or panic but with humor and his typical firm resolve. "Gage has made me respectable by naming me first among those who are to receive no favor from him," he wrote. "I thoroughly despise him and his proclamation."[22]

Perhaps he was putting on a brave front so his wife did not worry. But it is also possible that Adams in Philadelphia, though distant from his immediate family, was nonetheless among friends and busy with work, and felt secure enough to laugh in all honesty about the threat he was under. Cousin John was also representing Massachusetts in Congress, and he and Samuel were frequent social and political companions. They both roomed at Sarah Yard's lodging house across Second Street from City Tavern,[23] and John Adams's financial records show Samuel Adams first reimbursing John for shared expenses, then providing a £25 loan.[24] On June 15 of 1775, John and Samuel Adams took an early-morning walk in the State House yard for some exercise and fresh air before Congress met for the day, and John Adams spoke of his plan to suggest Washington as the American general. "Mr. Adams seemed to think very seriously of it, but said Nothing," John Adams recalled in his autobiography. Later that day in Congress, Samuel Adams seconded John Adams's motion to appoint George Washington as general-in-chief of the American army.[25]

The close relationship between the cousins sometimes left other Massachusetts delegates to Congress feeling left out. Robert Treat Paine complained of "the Cold haughty disrespectful behaviour of the two Adams toward me."[26] Hancock seemed to resent both Adamses supporting Washington rather than himself. It was typical of Hancock's vanity; the wealthy merchant once threatened to quit the Brattle Street Church because Samuel Adams's name was listed before his own in its first bill of incorporation. The matter had to be resolved by drawing up a second bill listing the names in alphabetical order.[27] Samuel Adams, for his part, seemed to resent Hancock's conspicuous consumption and the effect that his riches had in influencing voters in Massachusetts. John Adams reports that his cousin "had become very bitter against Mr. Hancock, and spoke of him with great asperity in private circles."[28]

Adams himself, age fifty-two and with no military experience to speak of save for the war of ideas, gave signs of enjoying directing the generals. Shortly after Washington was named general, the Virginian submitted to Patrick Henry a series of questions for Congress. Samuel Adams was named with Patrick Henry and Adams allies Richard Henry Lee and Silas Deane to a small committee "to take into their consideration the sd. queries and report their opinion with regard to the answers proper to be given."[29] In a June 22 letter to Elbridge Gerry, Samuel Adams wrote, "Our patriotic general Washington will deliver this letter to you. . . . I regret his leaving this city; but have the satisfaction of believing that he will add great spirit to our army."[30]

He and Richard Henry Lee were also on a committee "to revise the Journal of the Congress, and prepare it for the press," work that must have reminded Samuel Adams of his longtime service as the clerk of the Massachusetts House of Representatives, or of his time helping to edit the *Boston Gazette*.[31]

If Adams was feeling any homesickness for such work, he was able to allay it with a brief visit to Massachusetts—though not to his hometown of Boston, still under British military occupation—after Congress adjourned on August 1, 1775. He passed through Worcester on August 10 and arrived in Cambridge August 11. In Worcester, to judge by an account in the *Massachusetts Spy*, he would have gotten word of an attempted British attack on Salem by a Captain Linzee, who, according to a letter from Gloucester, "stood himself with diabolical pleasure to see what havock his cannon might make, 'Now (said he) my boys, we will aim at the damned Presbyterian church—Well, my brave fellows, one shot more and the house of God will fall before you.'" The patriotic letter writer reported that while Captain Linzee "was thus venting his hellish rage, and setting himself as it were against heaven, the Almighty was on our side, not a ball struck or wounded an individual person."[32]

The visit to Massachusetts was a chance for Samuel Adams to reunite with his wife and children, but it was also a business trip. Congress had sent Washington $500,000 in the care of the Massachusetts delegates,[33] and Adams inspected the beginnings of the Continental Army and visited its general at Cambridge, getting an update on the progress of the war.[34] Adams later reported to a friend, "Until I visited head quarters at Cambridge, I had never heard of the valour of Prescott at Bunker's Hill, nor the ingenuity of Knox and Waters in planning the celebrated works at Roxbury."[35] While meeting Washington, Adams may have also discussed the balance between anti-Catholicism and the American cause in Canada; shortly afterward, in time for Pope's Day, Washington issued a general order warning the troops against "the observance of that ridiculous and childish custom of burning the Effigy of the pope," and expressing his surprise "that there should be Officers and Soldiers in this army so void of common sense, as not to see the impropriety of such a step at this Juncture; at a Time when we are solliciting, and have really obtain'd, the friendship and alliance of the people of Canada, whom we ought to consider as Brethren embarked in the same Cause. The defence of the general Liberty of America: At such a juncture, and in such Circumstances, to be insulting their Religion, is so monstrous, as not to be suffered or excused."[36] Given Samuel Adams's hostility to Catholicism, it is possible that Washington's comment was aimed partly at him.

Samuel Adams also plunged back into the government of Massachusetts, which was in a bit of an unsettled state, since Governor Gage did not recognize the authority of the House of Representatives and the House did not recognize the authority of Gage. The Provincial Congress that had served as an interim government had dissolved in favor of a House of Representatives, which, exiled from Boston, had convened at the Congregationalist Meeting House in Watertown. The House, in turn, had named a twenty-eight-person Council to exercise executive authority in place of the governor, and it had chosen Samuel Adams, while he was still away in Philadelphia, as one of the Council members.[37] Upon his return, on August 16, the Council appointed Adams to a committee to receive and distribute donations for the dispersed residents of the town of Boston.[38] The *Massachusetts Spy* of August 30, 1775, reported, "The honorable Council of this colony have been pleased to appoint the hon. Samuel Adams, Esq., Secretary."

It was just in time, as the Continental Congress was scheduled to reconvene. In September 1775, John Adams encouraged Samuel to make the journey from Massachusetts to Philadelphia, all three hundred miles of it, on horseback, which was, as Samuel Adams wrote a friend upon dismounting, "an exercise which I have not used for many years past."[39]

Upon arrival in Philadelphia not only was Samuel Adams saddlesore but his heart ached. With the First Continental Congress had begun a period of seven years during which Adams was, with the exception of brief congressional recesses, separated from his family. He received news of them only from other travelers or by the unreliable postal traffic, which was at risk of being seized by the British. "My Dear, I have so often wrote to you, without having a single Line in Answer to one of my Letters, that I have doubted whether you have received any of them," Adams had written to his wife on June 16, 1775. "It is painful to me to be absent from you."[40] Amos Adams updated him that Elizabeth had "hold out with so much steadiness and calmness under tryals so grievous," a contrast to the late Dr. Warren's mother, who was "almost inconsolable."[41] On October 20, 1775, Samuel Adams wrote to Elizabeth, "My dear Betsy, I have not yet received a letter from you, altho' it is more than seven Weeks since I left you. . . . Pray, my dear, let me hear from you soon. I am greatly concerned for your Security & happiness, and that of my Family. I wrote to my Daughter yesterday."[42]

Samuel Adams's faith helped him cope with the separation and isolation. In the October 20 letter to his wife, Adams wrote from Philadelphia with an almost fatalistic attitude as the British occupied Boston. "I am so fully satisfied in the Justice of our Cause, that I can confidently as well as devoutly pray, that the righteous Disposer of all things would succeed our Enterprises. If he suffers us to be defeated in any or all of them I shall believe it to be for the most wise and gracious Purposes and shall heartily acquiesce in the Divine Disposal."[43]

He wrote her again on November 7, 1775, with a similar, but slightly more upbeat message. "Righteous Heaven will surely smile on a Cause so righteous as ours is, and our Country, if it does its Duty will see an End to its Oppressions. Whether I shall live to rejoyce with the

Friends of Liberty and Virtue, my fellow Laborers in the Common Cause, is a Matter of no Consequence. I will endeavor by Gods Assistance, to act my little part well—to approve my self to Him, and trust every thing which concerns me to his all-gracious Providence."[44]

Adams saw a connection between private virtue and public actions. It helped him make sense of betrayal. George Washington had intercepted a secret letter to the British general, Thomas Gage, from Benjamin Church, the Massachusetts doctor who had helped with the *Boston Gazette*, served on the Boston Committee of Correspondence, composed a liberty song for the Stamp Act protest anniversary celebration, and been a confidant for intelligence gathered by Paul Revere.[45] Samuel Adams wrote to James Warren shortly after the discovery of Church's treason, "He who is void of virtuous Attachments in private Life, is, or very soon will be void of all Regard for his Country. There is seldom an Instance of a Man guilty of betraying his Country, who had not before lost the Feeling of moral Obligations in his private Connections." Before Church "was detected of holding a criminal Correspondence with the Enemies of his Country, his Infidelity to his Wife had been notorious," Adams wrote. So it was necessary, in Adams's view, "to have the Principles of Virtue early inculcated on the Minds even of Children, and the moral sense kept alive." A reason, he wrote to Warren, is that "no People will tamely surrender their Liberties, nor can any be easily subdued, when Knowledge is diffusd and Virtue is preservd. On the Contrary, when People are universally ignorant, and debauched in their Manners, they will sink under their own Weight without the Aid of foreign Invaders."[46]

In America's case, the foreign invaders were on the way. If the Congress had not formally declared war, the king all but did so. On August 23, 1775, George III proclaimed the colonists "in open and avowed rebellion."[47]

In England, there were starting to be some recriminations. One motion in Parliament in November of 1775 sought to identify who should be blamed for the disaster that was Britain's policy toward America. It requested that George III tell Parliament "who were the original Authors and Advisers to His Majesty of the following measures, before they were proposed in Parliament—for taxing *America*, without the consent of its Assemblies, for the Purpose of a Revenue—for extending the Jurisdiction of the Courts of Admiralty and Vice Admiralty—for taking away the Charter of the Province of *Massachuset's Bay*—for restraining the American fishery—for exempting Murderers from trial in America—for transporting accused colonists to England for Trial—and most especially for establishing Popery and Despotism in Canada."[48]

John Wilkes, who had just concluded a term as lord mayor of London and who kept in close touch with Samuel Adams's correspondent and ally in London, Arthur Lee, spoke at length in favor of the motion, warning, in language slurred by his deteriorating teeth,[49] "the Americans, sir, are a pious and religious people." He rebutted a claim by the ministry that the patriots had ended the freedom of the press by pointing out that "General Gage's foolish and contemptible proclamation against Samuel Adams and John Hancock, two worthy gentlemen, and, I dare to add, true patriots, declaring them rebels and traitors . . . was reprinted in all the American papers."[50]

But a harsher approach carried the day against Wilkes and his minority of forward thinkers. The next month, December, Parliament debated an act that would allow American ships, even those in harbors or at docks, to be confiscated. To Lord Mansfield's qualms about the measure, Lord Townshend, the father of the hated tea tax, replied, according to one account of the debate, "By severity alone the deluded Americans could be recalled to their duty. It was high time that their factious partisans should feel the rod of correction, and the noble Viscount sincerely hoped, that the day was near at hand, when Messrs. Hancock and Adams would take refuge in Switzerland, to spare the executioner the trouble of giving an account of their departure."[51]

Adams, not in Switzerland but at Congress in Philadelphia, seemed almost to chafe at his new role as a full-time politician rather than a journalist. "You will possibly think I have set myself down to furnish a few Paragraphs for Edes & Gills News Paper," he wrote to James Warren. Instead he emphasized that he was mentioning the things "in Confidence that you will not publish them." He acknowledged, "it is painful to me, you know, to keep secrets."[52]

Still, his activities in Congress included sensitive military matters that needed to remain secret. In December 1775, for example, he was appointed to a committee consisting of one member from each colony "to devise ways and means for furnishing these colonies with a naval armament, and report with all convenient speed."[53] It was the beginning of the American navy.

The comparison of the American struggle for freedom to the Jews' exodus from the slavery of Egypt was never far from Adams's mind. In a private letter to James Warren on December 26, 1775, Adams says of the people of Massachusetts, "Certainly the People do not already hanker after the Onions & the Garlick!"[54] It was a reference to the restless Israelites in the desert, in Numbers 11:5, complaining to Moses about the manna, and recalling wistfully the food back in Egypt: fish, cucumbers, melons, leeks, onions, and garlic.

The diary of Christopher Marshall, a Dublin-born Philadelphia pharmacist active in the patriot cause, offers a glimpse of what day-to-day life was like for Samuel Adams in this period. On September 18, 1775, Marshall reports that he "spent some time with Samuel and John Adams." On September 20, he writes, "Past three went to the place, where Samuel Adams, Governor Ward, John Adams and Christopher Gadsden and son came, drank coffee, and spent the afternoon in free conversation."[55] On October 28, Christopher Marshall reports that he spent the afternoon drinking coffee "in company with John Hancock and lady, Samuel and John Adams, Cushing, Dyer, Treat Paine, [John] Langdon, Silas Deane, and another delegate not known to me."[56] Much of what went on in Congress, in other words, was not the formal sessions, but the after-hours caucusing and conversation that Samuel Adams excelled in dating to his days dominating the Boston Town Meeting.

On November 24, 1775, Marshall got wind of a ball being planned for that night. It struck him as "very disagreeable at this melancholy time." So he set off for Hancock's house. Not finding him home, he headed for the State House to look for Hancock, hoping to meet him in the street on the way from Congress. Failing that, he asked the door-keeper at Congress to call Samuel Adams, who appeared at the door. "I then informed him of the account received of a ball, that was to be held this evening, and where, and that Mrs. Washington and Col. Hancock's wife were to be present, and as such meetings appeared to be contrary to the Eighth Resolve of Congress, I therefore requested he would give my respects to Col. Hancock, desire him to wait on Lady Washington to request her not to attend or go this evening. This he promised." Later that evening, Marshall recalls, "I went down to Samuel Adams's lodgings, where was Col. Dyer. Spent some time pleasantly, until Col. Harrison came to rebuke Samuel Adams for using his influence for the stopping of this entertainment, which he declared was legal, just and laudable. Many arguments were used by all present to convince him of the impropriety at this time, but all to no effect."[57]

The flap over the ball—a reminder that Hancock, unlike Adams, had his wife with him at Philadelphia, in part because his wealth allowed him to make that possible—may have contributed to the hint of resentment toward Hancock in Samuel Adams's letter to Elbridge Gerry on January 2, 1776. Or maybe Adams was just in a sour mood. The winter had set in, and his cousin John had left for a brief visit to Massachusetts. Samuel Adams wrote to Gerry, "I hope our country will never see the time, when either riches or the want of them will be the leading considerations in the choice of public officers." He explained, "The giving such a preference to riches is both dishonourable and dangerous to government. It is indeed equally dangerous to promote a man to a place of public trust only because he wants bread, but I think it is not so dishonourable; for men may be influenced to the latter from the feelings of humanity, but the other argues from a base, degenerate, servile temper of mind."[58]

In Philadelphia, Adams would have met Thomas Paine. They

might have discussed their experiences as tax collectors; Paine had worked as one in the British country town of Lewes before making his way to America.[59] By the account of Dr. Benjamin Rush, a Philadelphia physician who was a delegate to the Congress, after Paine finished writing his pamphlet *Common Sense,* Rush advised Paine to "show it to Dr. Franklin, Mr. Rittenhouse, and Mr. Samuel Adams, all of whom I knew were decided friends to American independence." Rush writes that he mentions this to refute claims that any of the three men had actually had a hand in drafting the pamphlet.[60] It is easy to see why someone would think Samuel Adams had been involved. Paine later acquired a reputation as a skeptic of organized religion and clashed with Samuel Adams on that point. But the pages of *Common Sense,* as issued on January 10, 1776, were full of the sort of religious rhetoric and invocation of biblical, even divine, authority that Samuel Adams was well known for using, and its publication must have lifted Adams's spirits.

"Government by kings," the pamphlet said, "was the most preposterous invention the Devil ever set on foot for the promotion of idolatry." It quotes passages of the Bible arguing against monarchy, including "And all the people said unto Samuel, Pray for thy servants unto the Lord thy God that we die not, for WE HAVE ADDED UNTO OUR SINS THIS EVIL, TO ASK A KING." Paine wrote, "These portions of scripture are direct and positive. They admit of no equivocal construction. That the Almighty hath entered his protest against monarchial government is true, or the scripture is false."

In addition to citing the Bible, Paine appealed to Protestant anti-Catholicism. "Monarchy in every instance is the Popery of government," he wrote.

These were not just passing references or a rhetorical gloss. They were arguments repeated and references made again and again by Paine throughout the entire lengthy pamphlet. Monarchy was likened to man's original sin, and called "a form of government which the word of God bears testimony against." George III was likened to "the hardened, sullen tempered Pharaoh" who kept the children of Israel in bondage in Egypt. The "king of America," Paine wrote, "reigns above," and his law is "the divine law, the word of God." Of colonial anger toward the British, he wrote, "The Almighty hath implanted in us these unextinguishable feelings for good and wise purposes."

Weighing reconciliation with the British against independence, Paine and *Common Sense* came down on the side of independence, arguing that taking up arms for a cause short of independence seemed "unwarrantable by the divine law." Independence, on the other hand, offered an opportunity that had not been known since biblical times. "We have it in our power to begin the world over again," he wrote. "A situation, similar to the present, hath not happened since the days of Noah until now."

Paine ended *Common Sense* with a section addressed to the Quakers, who were numerous in Philadelphia and whose religious pacifism made many of them tend toward loyalism, or at least a coolness toward the cause of independence. He chided them for "mingling religion with politics," quite a turnabout for a writer who in most of the preceding work had done just that.

Franklin said *Common Sense* had "great effect on the minds of people at the beginning of the revolution."[61] "Common Sense is all the vogue here," William Checkley wrote to Samuel Adams from Providence, Rhode Island, on February 26, 1776.[62] James Warren reported to Samuel Adams from Watertown, Massachusetts, that "the sentiments, the principles, and the whole book are prodigiously admired here by the best judges."[63] The historian Bernard Bailyn has written that the pamphlet had "unique power."[64] By the end of the year, according to Paine biographer Thomas Nelson, more than 150,000 copies of the pamphlet had been sold.[65]

Adams reacted favorably. He had not given up his role as a newspaperman entirely. Perhaps goaded into action by the threat of being outdone by Paine, on February 3, 1776, Samuel Adams returned to the pages of the *Boston Gazette* as "Candidus," arguing for an actual declaration of independence. "When the little pamphlet, entitled 'Common Sense,' first made its appearance in favor of that so often abjured idea of independence upon great Britain, I was informed that no less than three gentlemen of respectable abilities were engaged to answer it. As yet, I have seen nothing which directly pretends to dispute a single position of the author," he wrote.[66] Adams added arguments of his own. "By declaring independence we put ourselves on a footing for an equal negotiation" he argued, as opposed to the current situation, in which "we are called a pack of villainous rebels."[67]

Adams's "Candidus" essay devoted special attention to the Quakers, as Paine had done in *Common Sense*. The denomination was not as widely reviled in America as the Catholics were, but their neutrality or, worse, tendency to side with the British grated on Adams, especially during his residence in Philadelphia, where Quakers were common. He wrote as "Candidus," "I heartily wish too many of the Quakers did not give cause of complaint, by endeavoring to counteract the measures of their fellow-citizens for the common safety. If they profess themselves only pilgrims here, let them walk through the men of this world without interfering with their actions on either side. If they would not pull down kings, let them not support tyrants; for, whether they understand it or not, there is, and ever has been, an essential difference in the characters."[68]

The work of the Congress did not allow Adams many spare moments for newspaper writing, however. General Washington had written to the president of Congress from Cambridge on December 31, asking for guidance on whether to allow the enlistment of "free Negroes" in the Continental Army, and also inquiring about pay for chaplains, whose service Washington thought would have "great utility."[69] Adams was named on January 15 to a three-member congressional committee to answer the letter. The committee reported the next day, and Congress acted by approving wages for chaplains of $33.33 a month, and by ruling "That the free negroes who have served faithfully in the army at Cambridge, may be re-inlisted therein, but no others." The exclusion of new recruits on the basis of race fell short of Samuel Adams's ideal of freedom for all, but it was a setback to some southern delegates who had wanted black soldiers totally banned from the Continental Army.[70] As for the chaplains' pay, by June 1778 it had been raised to $50 a month, equal to that of a colonel.[71]

Meanwhile, Cousin John had returned from Massachusetts; on February 26, 1776, Christopher Marshall's diary reports, "Past seven, went to Samuel and John Adams's lodgings; stayed till past nine."[72] Samuel Adams was so often engaged on the congressional committees charged with answering Washington's frequent letters to Philadelphia that, in at least one instance, the general cut out the middleman, and rather than addressing himself to the president of the Continental Congress—that is, John Hancock—wrote a back-channel letter to Samuel Adams, with an almost apologetic preface.

Dear Sir: Amidst a multiplicity of Business Smaller matters are apt to be overlook'd, this I conceive to be the case with respect to the proposition of a Colo. Baillie for opening a Road, and which I laid before Congress for their direction some months ago. . . . If a safe and easy communication can be opened with Canada through the channel above spoken of many advantages undoubtedly will result from it; but as I am unacquainted with the Country through which this road is to pass; as I know nothing of the Gentlemen advising and can form no other opinion of the matter than from the Maps, the only design of my giving you the trouble of this letter is just to reach the attention of Congress to the subject matter so far as to say yea or nay.[73]

Amid the rush of work, faith and family were two constants for Samuel Adams. To a fellow revolutionary in Massachusetts, Adams wrote from Philadelphia on April 15, 1776, that the heart of the British king, George III, "is more obdurate, and his Disposition towards the People of America is more unrelenting and malignant than was that of Pharaoh towards the Israelites in Egypt."[74] On the evacuation of the British from Boston, Adams wrote a friend in April 1776, "We owe our grateful Acknowledgements to him who is, as he is frequently stiled in sacred Writ, 'The Lord of Hosts' 'The God of Armies.'"[75] To

James Warren he wrote, "it becomes us to rejoice and religiously to acknowledge the Goodness of the Supreme Being who in this Instance hath signally appeard for us."[76]

Writing to a friend in Boston on April 30, 1776, Adams said, "I have long been convincd that our enemies have made it an Object, to eradicate from the Minds of the People in general a Sense of true Religion & Virtue, in hopes thereby the more easily to carry their Point of enslaving them. Indeed my Friend, this is a Subject so important in my Mind, that I know not how to leave it. Revelation assures us that 'Righteousness exalteth a Nation'—Communities are dealt with in this World by the wise and just Ruler of the Universe. He rewards or punishes them according to their general Character. The diminution of publick Virtue is usually attended with that of publick Happiness, and the publick Liberty will not long survive the total Extinction of Morals."[77]

As for family, Adams wrote from Philadelphia in June 1776 to Perez Morton,[78] deputy secretary of the Massachusetts House, "I am apprehensive that Mrs. A———will soon be in Want of Money for her Support, if that is not already the case. I shall therefore be much obligd to you if you will let her have such a part of the Fees you may have receivd as you can conveniently spare."[79] Washington had won a victory in Massachusetts in March, ridding Boston of the British siege by surrounding the city with the guns seized at Ticonderoga. After the British had left Boston, Betsy Adams had returned to the family home on Purchase Street, but found it so thoroughly vandalized by British troops as to be uninhabitable, and returned to Dedham until 1778.[80] On her way out of Boston, she would have passed the stump of the Liberty Tree. The great elm had been felled during the British occupation, producing fourteen cords of firewood and killing a British soldier in an accident while he tried to remove its limbs.[81]

In Philadelphia, Samuel Adams kept pressing for a formal declaration of independence, not only in the "Candidus" newspaper article, but in his private correspondence with other leaders of the Revolution, including Rev. Samuel Cooper in newly liberated Boston. "Is not America already independent? Why then not declare it?" Adams asked impatiently in a letter to Cooper on April 3, 1776. "Can Nations at War be said to be dependent either upon the other? I ask again, why not declare for Independence? Because say some, it will forever shut the Door of Reconciliation. Upon what terms will Britain be reconciled with America? . . . Upon our abjectly submitting to tyranny."[82]

Finally, on June 7, Richard Henry Lee offered a resolution: "Resolved, That these United Colonies are, and of right ought to be, free and independent States, that they are absolved from all allegiance to the British Crown, and that all political connection between them and the State of Great Britain is, and ought to be, totally dissolved."[83] Congress was not yet ready to approve the motion, but, not wanting to waste more time, they took the step of appointing a committee to draft a declaration of independence in the event that one was needed. Much of its work was done by Thomas Jefferson. A second committee, of one member from each colony, was named to develop a plan of confederation—a formal document, eventually approved as the Articles of Confederation, setting out the bylaws of national government for an independent America. Samuel Adams was chosen to represent Massachusetts on that committee. If he regretted that it was two Virginians rather than himself who both moved for independence and drafted the resolution, he made no indication of it. Better to show that the move for independence was continent-wide rather than confined to Massachusetts or to Congregationalists. Close observers would know of Samuel Adams's long correspondence and collaboration with Richard Henry Lee's brother Arthur and draw their own conclusions; 202 years later, Garry Wills, in his book *Inventing America: Jefferson's Declaration of Independence*, would write that Samuel Adams "became the most influential man at the first two Congresses."[84]

Certainly Samuel Adams must have been pleased by the stirring language that so characterized the Declaration of Independence. It closely followed the arguments and phrases that he had been using in Massachusetts and Boston documents and in his newspaper columns for more than a decade. The Declaration included four separate references to God, from the first sentence's invocation to "the laws of nature and of nature's God" to the famous second sentence, "We hold these truths to be self-evident: That all men are created equal: that they are endowed by their creator with certain unalienable rights; that among these are life, liberty, and the pursuit of happiness," and on through an appeal to "the Supreme Judge of the world." On the Declaration of Independence, beneath the words, "for the support of this Declaration, with a firm reliance on the protection of divine Providence, we mutually pledge to each other our Lives, our Fortunes and our sacred Honor," Samuel Adams signed his name at the top of the list of delegates from Massachusetts, with John Adams's signature right beneath it.

Samuel Adams's only regret was that it had taken so long. He wrote a friend on July 9, 1776, "Much I am affraid has been lost by delaying to take this decisive step. If it had been done nine months ago we might have been justified in the sight of God and Man three months ago."[85]

The Declaration echoed throughout the land. In a general order issue July 9, Washington announced the news to the troops in the same breath as he emphasized the importance of their religious duties:

> The Colonels or commanding officers of each regiment are directed to procure Chaplains accordingly; persons of good Characters and exemplary lives—To see that all inferior officers and soldiers pay them a suitable respect and attend carefully upon religious exercises. The blessing and protection of Heaven are at all times necessary but especially so in times of public distress and danger—The General hopes and trusts, that every officer and man, will endeavour so to live, and act, as becomes a Christian Soldier defending the dearest Rights and Liberties of his country.
>
> The Hon. The Continental Congress, impelled by the dictates of duty, policy and necessity, having been pleased to dissolve the Connection which subsisted between this Country,

Thomas Hutchinson, lieutenant governor, then governor of Massachusetts, fled to England, where he told King George III that Samuel Adams "was the first that publickly asserted the Independency of the colonies upon the Kingdom." This painting by Edward Truman is from 1741.

Arthur Lee, a Virginia-born physician, lawyer, and botanist, kept Samuel Adams informed with frequent letters from Europe. A contemporary described the relationship as so close that Adams was "grappled" to Arthur Lee's "soul with hooks of steel." This miniature portrait by William Russell Birch is from 1795.

Arthur Lee's brother Richard Henry Lee, a delegate to the Continental Congress from Virginia and a political ally of Samuel Adams, made the motion for independence. This painting by Charles Willson Peale is in the National Portrait Gallery of the Smithsonian Institution in Washington, D.C.

*The Granger Collection, New York*

John Hancock, one of the wealthiest merchants in Boston, was with Samuel Adams in Lexington—on the way to Congress at Philadelphia—on the morning the Revolutionary War began. Adams disliked what he saw as Hancock's extravagance, but the two men reconciled and helped Massachusetts ratify the federal Constitution. After the Revolution, Hancock became governor of Massachusetts and Adams served as his lieutenant governor. This 1765 painting by John Singleton Copley, owned by the City of Boston, is on deposit at the Museum of Fine Arts, Boston.

*The Granger Collection, New York*

Samuel Adams's cousin John Adams was his regular traveling companion when they both served as delegates to the Continental Congress at Philadelphia. The two worked together in winning independence and on drafting the Massachusetts constitution of 1780. This 1793 painting by John Trumbull is in the National Portrait Gallery of the Smithsonian Institution in Washington, D.C.

*The Granger Collection, New York*

THE GREEN DRAGON TAVERN

The Green Dragon Tavern, on Union Street near Faneuil Hall, was where silversmith Paul Revere assembled a committee to watch the movements of British soldiers and report to Samuel Adams. After the war, craftsmen assembled there to urge Adams to vote to ratify the federal Constitution. *Woodcut, collection of the author*

The Liberty Tree, a stately elm at a busy Boston intersection, was the gathering place for Stamp Act protests that included Samuel Adams. Other towns throughout the colonies established their own liberty trees. When the British occupied Boston, they felled the elm for firewood. *Woodcut, collection of the author*

The interior of Old South Meeting House, a Congregationalist church where Bostonians met when the crowds were too big for Faneuil Hall, is elegant in the spare, Puritan manner. Samuel Adams agitated against the British from its pews and also sang hymns there. *Collection of the author*

The exterior of the Old South Meeting House. It was inside that Samuel Adams gave the order to begin the Boston Tea Party. During the war, British soldiers covered the floor of the church with dirt and used it as a riding academy. *Collection of the author*

The Old State House/Town House, Boston, where the Massachusetts Senate and House of Representatives sat; Samuel Adams served as clerk of the House, president of the Senate, and, finally, governor. *Collection of the author*

This bronze statue of Samuel Adams by Anne Whitney was erected in 1880 in front of Faneuil Hall in Boston, where Adams was often elected as the moderator of the Town Meeting. Its base reads, "Samuel Adams, 1722-1803 / A patriot who organized the revolution and signed the Declaration of Independence / A statesman incorruptible and fearless / Governor true leader of the people." *Collection of the author*

Painted by Johnston      Vol. 72.      Eng. by H. B. Hall

This engraving of Samuel Adams by H. B. Hall is styled after a painting
by John Johnston that was lost in a fire. It was included in a three-volume
biography of Adams by his great-grandson William V. Wells that was
published in 1865. Adams gazes out from the portrait resolute yet serene.
*Collection of the author*

Samuel Adams signed the Declaration of Independence at the top
of the list of delegates from Massachusetts, with John Adams's
signature right beneath it. Samuel Adams's handwriting became
shakier as he aged and his palsy worsened, and he eventually relied
on a secretary to write for him.

Samuel Adams is buried in Boston alongside the Boston Massacre victims at the Granary Burying Ground, a few blocks away from the Old State House and the Old South Meeting House. *Collection of the author*

and Great Britain, and to declare the United Colonies of North America, free and independent States: The several brigades are to be drawn up this evening on their respective Parades, at Six OClock, when the declaration of Congress, shewing the grounds and reasons of this measure, is to be read with an audible voice.

The General hopes this important Event will serve as a fresh incentive to every officer, and soldier, to act with Fidelity and Courage, as knowing that now the peace and safety of his Country depends (under God) solely on the success of our arms: And that he is now in the service of a State, possessed of sufficient power to reward his merit, and advance him to the highest Honors of a free Country.[86]

Captain Samuel Hovey wrote from New York to his father, the Reverend Ivory Hovey of Plymouth, Massachusetts, on July 10,

yestarday was Read in the presants of our Bragad the Declaration of the Independent State of the Collanes after a long Spech from our Brigiderr Gennaral Heath Which had the Hope of all that heard it and after the Declaration was read We gave three Hosanas which made the Woods Ring in after that we Sang a Salm and one Chaplin pray with and made an excellent prair. Sir I can assure you that wee have got one of the finest Gennaral that is in the army—to our Brigad he is so pleasant and free with all officers and soders that there is not Wone but Whch loves him. I have Dined with him a grate may tims and he took great care of his Soliders and is Very Strict for all of them to attend metens. . . . But you have heard of the plot that was laid by the toris to Distroy our powder House and kill our head man But thro' the goodness of God they were found out.[87]

Having spent nearly a year away from home and having achieved his goal of a declaration of independence, Samuel Adams allowed himself to think of a brief visit to Massachusetts. Adams's wife had begged him to try to come home, even "if the visit is ever so short." She wrote to Samuel that she had spent three days dining at Cambridge and "was treated by General Washington and his wife with great friendship—I was in hopes I should have the opportunity of returning the compliment by inviting them to dine with you at our house."

She closed the letter with a postscript: "I am low in cash."[88]

James Warren had also urged Adams to return home, citing health concerns. "Such long and intense application in a place so unhealthy must be too much for a firmer constitution that yours," he wrote. "Your health must be attended to. . . . You must therefore take a ride and relax your mind and breath[e] some of our Northern Elastic Air."[89] It was not that Adams thought his work was over. He was concerned about the challenges ahead. Declaring independence, he knew, was in some ways the easy part; winning and keeping it would more difficult. He wrote, "May God give us wisdom, fortitude, and perseverance, and every other virtue necessary for us to maintain that independence which we have asserted!"[90]

The first challenge, in his Puritan's mind, was making sure that Americans behaved in a manner worthy of the free men that they were. On July 27, 1776, Adams wrote to a friend, "I conjure you and every Man of Influence by Example and by all Means to stem the Torrent of Vice."[91] Adams tended not to give detailed examples of this torrent himself, but ministers of the time, including Samuel's cousin Amos Adams, were more than willing. In a sermon preached at Roxbury in 1769, Amos Adams spoke of "the great increase of profane cursing and swearing in the land." He also denounced "the excessive use of spirituous liquors." "Little use was, for a long time, made of spirituous liquors unless for medicine—for common refreshment they were seldom or never taken," Amos Adams said. "But our trade with the West India Islands, has abundantly furnished us with the means of intemperance. The great plenty of spirituous liquors hath proved a temptation too hard for many to withstand, and truly threatens the destruction of thousands of our inhabitants. That which once only served for peculiar occasions, is now become the common drink of

a great part of our labouring people. Many have so habituated themselves to strong drink, that they will perform no service without the
liberal use of it." The excessive use of rum, Amos Adams had warned,
was leading men to become "stupid, idle, poor husbands."[92] Samuel
Adams's own reputation in regard to alcohol is less sober; one biographer claims he "was a familiar figure in Boston taverns," though his
nickname of "Sam the Publican" probably derives from the definition
of "publican" as a tax collector rather than a tavern keeper.[93]

The second challenge was the military one. "We now look towards
N. York. May Heaven prosper our arms there," Adams wrote to the
president of the Massachusetts Board of War, Samuel Phillips Savage.[94] On August 12, 1776, Adams set off from Philadelphia for Boston,
accompanied by Colonel William Tudor.[95] He stopped on the way in
New York to visit with General Washington at the front and inquire
directly after that city's defenses, much as he had visited Washington
at Cambridge a year before, when Boston was the city in the shadow
of the British fleet. He reported to his cousin John in Philadelphia, "I
found the general and his family in health and spirits; indeed, every
officer and soldier appears to be determined."[96]

The British kept a close watch on his activities. The American
journal of Ambrose Serle, who was secretary to the British military
commander in America, Admiral Richard Lord Howe, notes in an
entry for August 15, 1776, "When Saml. Adams traveled lately (i.e.
before the Congress's Resoln. Of Independence) from Mass. Bay to
Philadelphia, he maintained openly in all the Towns & Villages, that
independence must be avowed as the Principle of Resistance; that
indeed he had not conceived till lately, it would be necessary so soon
to avow it."[97]

When he arrived in Massachusetts in August, Samuel Adams
must have gotten a talking to from his wife about the need for him
to write her regularly. Or perhaps seeing her made him think of her
more often. Upon returning to Congress in Philadelphia in October, he wrote to her frequently, sharing his religious confidence. On
November 7, 1776, Adams wrote his wife that he'd been told that Lord

Howe had offered a general pardon with the exception of only four persons—Benjamin Franklin, Richard Henry Lee, John Adams, and "my self." Wrote Adams, "I am animated with the full Perswasion that righteous Heaven will support the Americans if they persevere in their manly Struggles for their Liberty."[98]

"I am still in good Health and Spirits, although the enemy is within Forty Miles of this City," he wrote to her again on December 9, from Philadelphia. He expressed chagrin that the people of Pennsylvania and New Jersey were less staunch in the revolutionary cause than those of New England. He told her that if Philadelphia were to be surrendered, he still wouldn't despair. "It is a righteous cause and I am fully perswaded righteous Heaven will succeed it," he wrote, then briefed her on Congress's plans to retreat—"adjourn," was how he put it—to Baltimore. "It is agreed to appoint a day of prayer," he said, adding that a committee of Congress would bring in a resolution to that effect. "I wish we were a more religious People," he wrote.[99]

In a letter to his wife on December 19, he said, "If Heaven punishes Communities for their Vices, how sore must be the Punishment of that Community who think the Rights of human Nature not worth struggling for and patiently submit to Tyranny. I will rely upon it that New England will never incur the Curse of Heaven for neglecting to defend her Liberties."[100]

If it had crossed Betsy Adams's mind that New England had incurred the curse of heaven, she might be forgiven, for, to judge by the results of the American forces on the battlefield recently, they certainly had not been blessed. After the victory in March 1776 lifting the siege of Boston, Washington and his generals ran into a series of defeats around New York. More than a thousand American soldiers surrendered in the Battle of Brooklyn in August, and 2,837 Americans surrendered at Fort Washington, now upper Manhattan, on November 16.[101] Washington himself, like Congress, kept retreating. On December 19, Thomas Paine published the first installment of his *Crisis,* which began:

These are the times that try men's souls. The summer soldier and the sunshine patriot will, in this crisis, shrink from the service of their country; but he that stands it now, deserves the love and thanks of man and woman. Tyranny, like hell, is not easily conquered; yet we have this consolation with us, that the harder the conflict, the more glorious the triumph. What we obtain too cheap, we esteem too lightly: it is dearness only that gives every thing its value. Heaven knows how to put a proper price upon its goods; and it would be strange indeed if so celestial an article as FREEDOM should not be highly rated. Britain, with an army to enforce her tyranny, has declared that she has a right (not only to TAX) but "to BIND us in ALL CASES WHATSOEVER," and if being bound in that manner, is not slavery, then is there not such a thing as slavery upon earth. Even the expression is impious; for so unlimited a power can belong only to God. . . . I have as little superstition in me as any man living, but my secret opinion has ever been, and still is, that God Almighty will not give up a people to military destruction, or leave them unsupportedly to perish, who have so earnestly and so repeatedly sought to avoid the calamities of war, by every decent method which wisdom could invent. Neither have I so much of the infidel in me, as to suppose that He has relinquished the government of the world, and given us up to the care of devils.[102]

Having "adjourned" with Congress to Baltimore from Philadelphia, Adams continued the correspondence with his wife on December 26, "I pray God to continue your Health and protect you in these perilous times from every kind of Evil. The Name of the Lord, says the Scripture, is a strong Tower, thither the Righteous flee and are safe. Let us secure his Favor, and he will lead us through the Journey of this Life and at length receive us to a better. . . . We have a righteous Cause, and if we defend it as it becomes us, we may expect the Blessing of Heaven."[103]

The blessing materialized, as it had a way of doing when Samuel Adams predicted it. After a Christmas Night crossing of the icy Delaware River, Washington and his troops defeated the British in a surprise attack on Trenton, capturing nine hundred Hessian soldiers. The Americans pressed their advantage with an attack at Princeton on January 3, 1777, winning another victory and taking another three hundred British soldiers prisoner.[104]

The victories vindicated the extraordinary confidence that had been placed in Washington by Samuel Adams, who on December 26 had been named to a three-person committee "to take into consideration the state of the army," and returned the next day with a report after which Congress voted to expand the general's authority by vesting him

> with full, ample, and complete powers to raise and collect together, in the most speedy and effectual manner, from any or all of these United States, 16 batallions of infantry, in addition to those already voted by Congress; to appoint officers for the said batallions; to raise, officer, and equip three thousand light horse; three regiments of artillery, and a corps of engineers, and to establish their pay; to apply to any of the states for such aid of the militia as he shall judge necessary; to form such magazines of provisions, and in such places, as he shall think proper; to displace and appoint all officers under the rank of brigadier general, and to fill up all vacancies in every other department in the American armies; to take, wherever he may be, whatever he may want for the use of the army, if the inhabitants will not sell it, allowing a reasonable price for the same; to arrest and confine persons who refuse to take the continental currency, or are otherwise disaffected to the American cause; and return to the states of which they are citizens, their names, and the nature of their offences, together with the witnesses to prove them.[105]

Samuel Adams explained to James Warren that the large powers vested in Washington were "for a *limitted* time" but, "in my opinion necessary."[106] For all the new powers it had given to Washington,
Congress was still in some ways subservient to the states. On December 31, 1776, from Baltimore, Samuel Adams and a committee of congressional delegates wrote to his old colleagues in Massachusetts with
a "most urgent request" that they forward to General Philip Schuyler
of the Northern Army "certain ordinance and other stores" as well as
"such moneys as he may have need of for the purpose."[107]

As 1776 turned to 1777, Samuel Adams was buoyed not only by news
of Washington's victories but by the dawning reality of independence.
On Thursday, January 2, 1777, Ambrose Serle, Lord Howe's secretary,
breakfasted with two Philadelphia loyalists, Andrew and William
Allen (their father, a Philadelphia merchant, had fled to England) and
noted in his diary, "Saml. Adams has often publicly boasted in Philadelphia of late, that for 20 years past he has been inculcating his republican Opinions among all the young gentlemen in & about Boston, and
that he now saw the happy Fruit of it. Mr. And. Allen says, that of all
the men he ever knew, this Adams is the most capable of leading or
inflaming a Mob. He has vast Insinuation, & infinite art, by wch he has
been able to impose on most Men."[108]

But the realities of the risk to his life and the separation from
his family were never far from his mind. From Baltimore, Samuel
Adams wrote to his wife again on January 29, 1777, expressing confidence and trying to reassure her in her "anxiety" for his safety. "The
Man who is conscientiously doing his Duty will ever be protected by
that Righteous and all powerful Being, and when he has finished his
Work he will receive an ample Reward. I am not more convincd of
any thing than that it is my Duty, to oppose to the utmost of my Ability the Designs of those who would enslave my Country; and with
Gods Assistance I am resolvd to oppose them till their Designs are
defeated or I am called to quit the Stage of Life."[109]

Samuel Adams was a member of Congress's standing committee on accounts or claims, but, as he himself realized, it was not his strong suit. To James Warren on February 1, he wrote from Baltimore, "I get out of my line when I touch upon Commerce, it is a Subject I never understood."[110]

Adams did have to manage his own financial affairs. On February 10, 1777, he finally got around to submitting to James Warren, in Warren's capacity as speaker of the Massachusetts House of Representatives, his expense account from April 26, 1775, to August 27, 1776. He included a charge for hiring a horse, as the two horses provided him from the public stable "were very poor when I took them and both tired on the Road." He reported that one of the horses died in Philadelphia, and that he had purchased a replacement. "His being my own Property, having purchased him without Charge to my Constituents, I think gives me a just Right to make a Charge of Horse Hire." The letter went on to give the dates Adams had been gone serving in Congress—April 26, 1775, to August 14, 1775, then again September 1, 1775, to August 27, 1776, "if an allowance for my services is considered." Adams's negotiating position couldn't have been weaker—he was seeking a salary retroactively for work already performed a year or six months earlier.[111] But both requests were approved.[112]

If he had neglected his own finances, it might have been not only from his lack of aptitude for the subject but because of the crush of business in Congress. On January 13, 1777, he was added to the Board of War, an influential committee that functioned as a Department of Defense. There, among other agendas, he pursued a campaign to root out "the abominable practice of prophane swearing in our Army."[113] On January 14, he was named to a three-person committee to prepare instructions for a newly named "agent for the Indians, in Nova Scotia, and the tribes to the northward and eastward thereof." On January 18, he was appointed a member of a three-person committee to consider an appeal from a quartermaster who had been hauled before a court-martial. On January 22, he was assigned to a three-person committee to consider a letter from General Washington, and, on January 31, to another three-person committee to consider how to honor the memory of Joseph Warren.[114] He was a member of the Medical Committee, the Committee on the Northern War, the Committee on Foreign Alliances, and the Committee on Procuring Cannon.[115] Part of the reason he was chosen was doubtless his ability, his judgment, and his reputation as an ardent patriot. But some of it, too, may have been sheer stamina. Adams was one of the few congressmen who remained. Some of the others had essentially given up and gone home, electing not to follow the group to Baltimore. Delaware had not a single representative in Congress, and New York had but one, who was not authorized to represent the state. On January 24, Congress resolved to write to the states of Delaware and New York, "requesting them immediately to send to Congress representations of their respective states, and to provide, that for the future, applications of this kind may be rendered unnecessary."[116] Even John Adams had made his departure, having left Congress in October 1776, when it was still at Philadelphia, and resuming his seat in Baltimore only on February 4, 1777.[117] There he was a frequent dinner companion of his cousin Samuel; on February 15 they were guests at the house of someone whose dining room featured a portrait of George III hung upside down, a practice explained to them with the words, "See his Head Plac'd where the meanest of his Subjects tread Like Lucifer the giddy Tyrant fell. He lifts his Heel to Heaven but points his Head to Hell."[118]

By March, it was safe to return to Philadelphia, but even there, only eight states were represented.[119] In July came the news that Ticonderoga, conquered by the Americans early in the war, had fallen back into the hands of the British. Samuel Adams again sought solace in faith and family. To a member of the Continental Congress from New Hampshire, John Langdon, Adams wrote on August 7, "We shall succeed if we are virtuous. I am infinitely more apprehensive of the Contagion of Vice than the Power of all other Enemies. It is the Disgrace of human Nature that in most Countries the People are so debauchd, as to be utterly unable to defend or enjoy their Liberty."[120]

On August 19, he wrote his wife, "I earnestly hope with you, my

Dear, that our . . . Life is not always to live at this distance."[121] On September 17, he wrote her that he was "pleased" to hear that a New England colonel had invited a Rev. Thacher "to preach a Sermon to his Regiment." Said Adams, "Religion has been & I hope will continue to be the ornament of N. England. While they place their confidence in Go[d] they will not fail to be a happy People."[122]

Meanwhile, the American military effort took some turns for the worse. Not only did Washington's troops suffer the defeats at Brandywine and the Paoli Massacre described in the opening pages of this book, but the newly formed American navy ran aground, literally. On September 27, the frigate *Delaware* scraped bottom in the Delaware River while trying to stop the British from fortifying Philadelphia. The American ship surrendered, and its commander, Charles Alexander, the top patriot naval officer in the region, was taken prisoner by the British.[123] Even Jacob Duché, the preacher who had given the opening prayers at the first two Continental Congresses, was ready to abandon the cause, writing a letter to Washington about the need for "an immediate cessation of hostilities," and asking Washington to "represent to Congress the indispensible necessity of rescinding the hasty and ill-advised declaration of Independency."[124] After the letter was leaked to the press, Duché left for England.[125] This was the moment that Congress fled to York, Pennsylvania. There, Samuel Adams gave his inspiring speech about "the ark of safety" visible through the darkness. His confidence that "we shall never be abandoned by heaven" was borne out by Gates's victory at Saratoga on October 17, 1777.

Samuel Adams was elated by the news. He wrote to Samuel Savage in Massachusetts, "Our sincere Acknowledgements of gratitude are due to the Supreme Disposer of All Events. I suppose Congress will recommend that a Day be set apart through out the United States for solemn Thanksgiving."[126] After drafting the resolution declaring a day of thanksgiving and prayer, Adams felt able to leave Congress for a trip home. The *Journals of Congress* for Friday November 7, 1777, record both that "a duplicate of the recommendation of Congress to the several states to set apart a day of thanksgiving, signed by the president, be sent to the respective states, and to General Washington and General Gates" and also, "Ordered, That Mr. Samuel Adams, and Mr. J[ohn] Adams, have leave of absence to visit their families."

On the way home, the two Adamses heard complaints about a fellow delegate from Massachusetts, John Hancock, who had preceded them on the way home. John Adams wrote in his diary, "The Taverners all along are complaining of the Guard of Light Horse which attended Mr. H. They did not pay, and the Taverners were obliged to go after them, to demand their Dues." At Fishkill, north of British-occupied New York City, Samuel Adams had a reunion with his son, who was serving as a doctor in the army. John Adams recorded that the meal for the long-awaited event "was a feast—Salt Pork and Cabbage, roast Beef and Potatoes, and a noble suit Pudding, Grog and a Glass of Port."[127]

No sooner had Samuel Adams arrived home to see Betsy after a thirteen-month absence than he found himself back at work. For once, he actually voiced his regret at the press of politics, writing to James Lovell, representing Massachusetts back in York, "Unluckily for me, on my Arrival here, I found the general assembly sitting, and consequently I am plunged in public business sooner than I could wish to have been." The same letter also expressed amusement at Hancock's escort. "I have not seen nor heard of any Dangers on the Road that should require Guards to protect one. It is pretty enough in the eyes of some men, to see the honest Country Folks gapeing & staring at a Troop of Light Horse. But is well if it is not some times attended with such Effects as one would not so much wish for, to excite the Contempt of the Multitude, when the Fit of gazing is over, instead of the much longd for Hosannas."[128] In December, the Massachusetts Assembly reelected Samuel Adams as a delegate to Congress, along with John Hancock, John Adams, Robert Treat Paine, and Elbridge Gerry.[129]

As Washington and his troops spent the winter at Valley Forge, the talk of national politics in America was of the so-called Conway

Cabal, the idea that General Thomas Conway had joined with some congressmen to suggest Horatio Gates as a replacement for Washington as the top American general. This was fueled, in part, by forged letters of Washington in the Tory press, such as one in the March 7, 1778, *Royal Gazette* of New York. Knowledgeable observers saw the allegations as a fabrication. Ezra Stiles, a Congregational minister in New Hampshire who was weighing an offer he would soon accept to become president of Yale College, noted in his diary for March 6, 1778, that he had dinner with Judge Matthew Thornton, a delegate in Congress at the Declaration of Independence.

> Mr. Sam^l Adams now at Boston having made some speeches in Congress respecting the danger of making any man too great or investing him with too much power least he should like Ceasar endanger the public Liberties, and that he would not trust even Gen. Wash. too far: and a faction in the Army thinking G. Wash not eno' pf a Fighter & endeavoring to blow up a breeze and get Gen. Wash. superseded by G. Gates—the tories have for several days propagated that Mr. Adams had made a motion in Mass. Assembly to have them & other States apply to Congress to supersede Washington. But Mr. Adams means no such Thing. Neither would he or Congress or the Army or the Continent be easy to have Gates at the head of the Army.[130]

Adams himself later sought to dispel the idea by writing his wife, in a letter he authorized her to share with Rev. Samuel Cooper's brother, the Boston town clerk, William Cooper, "I never wishd for the Removal of General Washington, but if I had even attempted to effect it, it might have been evidence of my Deficiency in Judgment, or Rashness, but it could be no evidence that I was his Enemy."[131] He was, however, a stickler for civilian control over the military. When word reached Adams that the French Count D'Estaing, visiting Boston, had fired a thirteen-cannon salute in response to a toast to General Washington and the American army, but declined to order the salute in response to a toast to Congress, he wrote home, "Men are prone to idolatry; and some who seem to scorn the worshiping Gods of other Nations, will bow down to graven images of Gold and Silver, and strange Infatuation! of Wood in the form of an Ass and Ape or a Calf, no matter what, if it be the Work of their own Hands."[132]

Meanwhile, in Boston, the work of state government ground on. Adams resumed his post as secretary of the Council, which took a hard line against the possibility that some of the loyalists who had evacuated Boston along with the British troops might return. "The return of such persons into this state may be highly dangerous to the public safety," the Council warned on January 28, 1778.[133] From December 1777 through February 1778, the House of Representatives worked on crafting a new constitution for Massachusetts to formalize its own authority and replace the colonial charter. The town of Boston opposed the effort on the grounds that the constitution should be drafted by a group selected specially for that purpose, rather than by the House.[134] Samuel Adams took Boston's instructions to heart and stood away from the effort; the constitution that resulted was eventually voted down. John Adams, who would be instrumental in drafting the Massachusetts constitution that eventually was approved, also avoided this effort, and left in February for a diplomatic mission in France, risking a dangerous winter voyage across an Atlantic dominated by the British fleet.[135]

Samuel Adams used his time at home to dream of possibilities. In a letter to his schoolmaster's son, James Lovell, now representing Massachusetts in Congress, Adams spoke of his desire to establish a military academy in Boston, or "at least," a "publick school for military Mathematicks."[136] Adams also returned to his seat as moderator of the Boston Town Meeting, presiding on March 14 over a session that decided to allow those in the town who had not had smallpox to inoculate themselves against the disease.[137] At word that the British had sent commissioners aiming to treat with Congress, Samuel Adams set out for York, stopping on the way to dine with a minister in Brookfield, Massachusetts, and meeting up with his son on the road west.[138]

When Adams returned to Congress at York on May 21, it was to crowded quarters—the delegates barely had a room apiece.[139] James Warren kept Adams informed of the news from Boston, reporting, "The Tories are very active in Instilling prejudices into the minds of the people against our Connections with France. The danger of Popery is held up to them."[140]

In York, one of the first orders of business was an investigation of how America was treating British prisoners of war. Congress found that in fact the prisoners were being kept in "airy rooms" that were "frequently swept," and that the captives were attended to by a surgeon and nurses if they became ill. "It appears probable that attempts are making to misrepresent the conduct of these United States towards the prisoners in their possession, in some degree to wipe off or counterbalance the just reproach that has fallen upon our enemies for their barbarity," Congress resolved.[141] Adams was appointed to a three-person committee to consider a letter from American field officers "on parole on Long Island," and he was also added to the Marine Committee, and named to a committee to "enquire into and rectify abuses in the general post office."[142]

The main business of Congress at this time, though, was foreign affairs, or diplomacy, a category into which relations with Great Britain had fallen since independence. On June 6, Congress received letters from the top British military officers in America, General Henry Clinton and Lord Howe, accompanied by three acts of Parliament. The documents were referred to a committee of five that included Samuel Adams and Richard Henry Lee, which promptly brought back a firm response: "Your lordship may be assured, that when the king of Great Britain shall be seriously disposed to put an end to the unprovoked and cruel war waged against these United States, Congress will readily attend to such terms of peace, as may consist with the honor of independent nations, the interest of their constituents, and the sacred regard they mean to pay to treaties."[143] Until that condition was met, Adams had no desire to correspond with the enemy. On June 16, Congress appointed Samuel Adams and Richard Henry Lee to a three-person committee "to prepare a resolution for preventing any correspondence with the enemy."[144]

At least one delegate to Congress allowed himself an exception to the ban, to write an open letter that seems aimed as much at the American public as at the enemy. Writing as "An American" to the Earl of Carlisle, Lord Viscount Howe, Sir William Howe, and other British military and government officials in a letter published in the *Massachusetts Spy* of July 16, 1778, the delegate invoked religious reasoning in rebuffing the British approach. "Your excellencies will, I hope, excuse me when I differ from you as to our having a religion in common with you; the religion of America is the religion of all mankind. Any person may worship in the manner he thinks most agreeable to the Deity; and if he behaves as a good citizen, no one concerns himself as to his faith or adorations, neither have we the least solicitude to exalt any one sect or profession above another," the member of Congress claimed. He went on to rebuke the British for calling on God to blame the Americans for prolonging what the British called "the horrors and devastations of war." "Matters of this kind may appear to you in a trivial light, as mere ornamental flowers of rhetoric, but they are serious things, registered in the high chancery of Heaven," the congressman wrote. "There is One above us who will take exemplary vengeance for every insult upon His majesty. . . . We again make our solemn appeal to the God of heaven to decide between you and us." The letter has been attributed by some historians to Samuel Adams but by others to Gouverneur Morris, who was then representing New York.[145]

On June 20, Congress got word that the British had evacuated Philadelphia, withdrawing some troops to New York and dispatching others to clash with the French in the West Indies.[146] That made it possible for delegates to return to Philadelphia from York, and for the second anniversary of American independence to be celebrated in the city where it was declared. The delegates resolved, "That Congress will, in a body, attend divine worship on Sunday, the 5th day of July next, to return thanks for the divine mercy in supporting the independence of these states, and that the chaplains be requested to officiate and to preach sermons suited to the occasion."[147]

In Philadelphia, attention turned from rebuffing the British toward welcoming the new European ally, France, which made its presence known with the arrival off the coast of a sixteen-ship fleet with four thousand troops aboard.[148] Samuel Adams and Richard Henry Lee were appointed to a three-person committee to "report to Congress on the time and manner of the public reception of Mons. Gérard, minister plenipotentiary of his most Christian Majesty, the King of France."[149] After several days of debate, an elaborate ritual was developed that involved the French diplomat first delivering his credentials to the president of Congress, then awaiting a formal appointment to an audience, to which he would be escorted by two members of Congress in a coach belonging to the United States. One member of Congress

> shall return with the minister plenipotentiary or envoy in the coach, giving the minister the right hand, and placing himself on his left, with the other member on the front seat. When the minister plenipotentiary or envoy is arrived at the door of the Congress hall, he shall be introduced to his chair by the two members, who shall stand at his left hand. Then the member first named shall present and announce him to the President and the house; whereupon he shall bow to the President and Congress, and they to him. He and the President shall then again bow unto each other, and be seated; after which the house shall sit down. Having spoken and being answered, the minister and the President shall bow to each other, at which time the house shall bow, and then he shall be conducted home in the manner in which he was brought to the house. Those who shall wait upon the minister shall inform him, that, if in any audience he shall choose to speak on matters of business, it will be necessary previously to deliver in writing, to the President, what he intends to say at the audience; and if he shall not incline thereto, it will,

from the constitution of Congress, be impracticable for him to receive an immediate answer.[150]

It was the sort of elaborate performance that, if it had taken place in the court of George III, Adams would have been prone to mock. But while Adams was averse to pomposity and extravagance, he understood the use of political theater and ritual, from the Liberty Tree to the funerals of the Boston Massacre victims. In this case, the purpose was to establish the new government of America as peer, not a subordinate, of the long-standing European power that was France. The willingness to recognize the Catholic French monarch as "his Most Christian Majesty" also showed a remarkably pragmatic attitude by Adams to the denomination he was prone to mocking as "popery."

For Adams, these points were hardly an abstraction. He and Richard Henry Lee were chosen by Congress as the two members to "wait upon the Hon. Sieur Gérard, and conduct him to the audience."[151] Their coach—with Adams riding in the front seat[152]—was escorted by a sufficient number of Pennsylvania peace officers to prevent any disruption of their travel.[153] The doors of Congress, usually shut to protect the confidentiality of the wartime proceedings, were to be opened for the occasion, with each member of Congress issued two tickets for use by invited guests.[154] The guests would have seen Adams and Lee introduce the French minister, who gave a brief, warm speech, and was met by equally warm remarks from the president of Congress, Henry Laurens of South Carolina, who said that "the treaties between his most Christian majesty and the United States of America, so fully demonstrate his wisdom and magnanimity as to command the reverence of all nations. The virtuous citizens of America, in particular, can never forget his beneficent attention to their violated rights, nor cease to acknowledge the hand of a gracious Providence in raising them up so powerful and illustrious a friend."[155]

Adams's warmth toward the French was not lost on the Tories, who used it to claim that the price of the alliance would be Roman

Catholicism imposed on America. One article in a loyalist newspaper raised the specter of Samuel Cooper as "Bishop of Boston," and of Benjamin Franklin and Samuel Adams being elevated by the pope as "St. Benjamin" and "St. Samuel" as a reward for their services.[156]

If Adams was warming slightly to Catholics because of the alliance with France, the pacifist Quakers still grated on him. To a Congregationalist clergyman in Massachusetts, Adams wrote from Philadelphia on August 11, 1778, complaining of "the barefaced Falshood of the Quakers & Tories in this City." He went on, "These Quakers are in general a sly artful People, not altogether destitute, as I conceive, of worldly Views in their religious Profession. They carefully educate their Children in their own contracted Opinions and Manners, and I dare say they have in their Hearts as perfect a System of Uniformity of Worship in their Way, and are busily employd about spiritual Domination as ever Laud himself was."[157]

The French intervention was not yet enough to bring the Americans a decisive military victory. British and American troops clashed indecisively at Monmouth Court House, New Jersey, on June 28, and at Newport, Rhode Island, in August. Adams's writing from this period suggests he felt that the conflict really would be decided by God. The newspapers had reported that Hancock had arrived in Boston for a visit on Sunday. Adams wrote a friend that it had been a mistake to injure the feelings of the people by violating the prohibitions against traveling on the Sabbath.[158] To his daughter, Hannah, who had written to him with news of her stepmother's illness, Adams replied from Philadelphia on September 8, 1778, "I commend you dear, to the Care and Protection of the Almighty."[159] When Adams then heard from Betsy herself, he wrote her back that her letter was "like cool water to a thirsty soul."

"I earnestly pray God to restore you to perfect health," he wrote her, going on to rue the death of two Bostonians of "exemplary piety and virtue." He wrote, "I hope the Depravity of Manners is not so great as to exclude all Hopes of Childrens rising up and serving God and their Country in the Room of their Fathers. May Heaven grant us a Time of Reformation!"[160]

Rather than confining such thoughts to his private correspondence, Adams turned them into acts of Congress. On Monday, October 12, Congress took time out from its work sorting out problems with clothing the troops and judging disputes among American diplomats in Europe to pass a resolution on religion and morals. It said:

> Whereas true religion and good morals are the only solid foundations of public liberty and happiness:
>
> Resolved, That it be, and it is hereby earnestly recommended to the several states, to take the most effectual measures for the encouragement thereof, and for the suppressing of theatrical entertainments, horse racing, gaming, and such other diversions as are productive of idleness, dissipation, and a general depravity of principles and manners.
>
> Resolved, That all officers in the army of the United States, be, and hereby are strictly enjoined to see that the good and wholesome rules provided for the discountenancing of prophaneness and vice, and the preservation of morals among the soldiers, are duly and punctually observed.[161]

It was almost certainly this resolution to which Adams was referring approvingly when he wrote Jonathan Trumbull on October 16, 1778, that the Congress had passed a resolution "by a great Majority expressing their Sense that true Religion and good Morals are the only solid Foundations of publick Liberty and Happiness."[162] Some in Congress wanted to go even further and pass a resolution banning theatergoers from federal office. "Whereas frequenting play houses and theatrical entertainments has a fatal tendency to divert the minds of the people from a due attention to the means necessary for the defence of their country, and the preservation of their liberties: Resolved, That any person holding an office under the United States, who shall act, promote, encourage or attend such plays, shall be deemed unworthy to hold such office, and shall be accordingly dismissed," said that resolution, which, however, failed to garner enough support to pass.[163] Samuel Adams's position on it has been lost to history.

Congress did conclude its instructions to Benjamin Franklin, minister to France, with the words, "We pray God to further you with his goodness in the several objects hereby recommended; and that he will have you in his holy keeping."[164] And it did issue a "Manifesto" on October 30, 1778, credited by some sources to Adams, asserting that the British "have made a mock of religion by impious appeals to God, whilst in the violation of His sacred command." The Manifesto claimed that the British were failing to comply "with the dictates of a religion which they pretend, in common with us, to believe and revere." The Manifesto, unanimously approved by Congress, concluded with a threat to take vengeance on the British to deter barbarities on their part: "We appeal to the God who searcheth the hearts of men for the rectitude of our intentions."[165]

A thanksgiving resolution drafted by Adams was adopted by Congress on November 3, 1778, recommending Wednesday, December 30, as a day of public thanksgiving and praise, "It having pleased Almighty God through the Course of the present year, to bestow great and manifold Mercies on the People of these United States." The 1778 resolution omitted the previous year's references to the "Holy Ghost" and "Jesus Christ." Instead, it referred to "our Savior."[166]

Samuel Adams conceived of God above as willing to intervene for the American cause, but only if the Americans themselves did their share by acting with virtue. He wrote from Philadelphia on December 21, 1778, "Our Independence, I think, is secured. Whether America shall long preserve her Freedom or not, will depend on her Virtue."[167]

Writing to James Warren on February 12, 1779, Adams warned of "that Inundation of Levity Vanity Luxury Dissipation & indeed Vice of every kind which I am informd threatens that Country which has heretofore stood with unexampled Firmness in the Cause of Liberty and Virtue." Insisted Adams, "This Torrent must be stemmed. . . . A general Dissolution of Principles & Manners will more surely overthrow the Liberties of America than the whole Force of the Common Enemy. While the People are virtuous they cannot be subdued; but when once they lose their Virtue they will be ready to surrender their Liberties to the first external or *internal* Invader." He wrote to Warren, "I do verily believe, and I may say it inter Nos, that the Principles and Manners of N Engd, produced that spirit which finally has established the Independence of America."[168]

Adams did not want the British taking away property from Americans. But he was not terribly concerned, it seemed, if he did not end up with much property himself. He thought excessive consumption could be harmful. "Luxury & Extravagance are in my opinion totally destructive of those Virtues which are necessary for the Preservation of the Liberty and Happiness of the People," he wrote from Philadelphia to a correspondent in Boston. He prayed for heaven to speedily grant the restoration of "that Sobriety of Manners, that Temperance, Frugality, Fortitude and other manly Virtues which were once the Glory and Strength of my much lov'd native town."[169]

Arguing against allowing wealthy Tories who had fled to return to Massachusetts, Adams wrote from Philadelphia to James Warren, "Gracious Heaven! Defend us from Vanity Folly & the inordinate Love of Money."[170]

In another letter from Philadelphia to Boston, Adams wrote, "I am greatly concerned for my dear native Town, lest after having stood foremost in the Cause of Religion and Liberty she should lose her Glory. We may say *inter Nos*, her Principles and Manners have had great influence in securing the Liberties of America." He worried that Boston may have "exchanged her manly Virtue, for Levity and Luxury and a Train of ridiculous vices, which will speedily sink her in Contempt.

"I am afraid the cry of too many," Adams went on, is, "Get Money, Money still. And then let Virtue follow it if she will!" He warned, "The inordinate Love of Gain, will make a shameful alteration in the character of those who have heretofore sacrificed every Enjoyment to the Love of their Country. He is the best Patriot who stems the Torrent of Vice, because that is the most destructive enemy of his Country."[171]

Meanwhile, as his fond descriptions of the "Principles and Manners of N Engd" hinted, Adams was looking forward to returning home. As early as July 1778 he had expressed his "earnest wish to be released from all publick cares, and sit down with my Family and a little circle of faithful friends in the Cottage of obscurity."[172] After getting the news that the Massachusetts Assembly had reappointed him to Congress for 1779, he wrote to the president of the Massachusetts Council that he was flattered. "I will never decline the Service of our Country," he wrote on December 1, 1778, "But my Health Requires Relaxation, and at this Period of my Life my Inclination would lead me to wish to be employd in a more limited Sphere." He expressed the hope that he would be relieved in April, after being in Pennsylvania for a full year, "and permitted to return to my family."[173]

Among them he included not only his wife and children but his extended relations, the Checkley family. Adams took time amid the rush of congressional business to write a job recommendation letter for Richard Checkley, "a young kinsman of mine." Wrote Adams: "If you can employ him it will be doing him a singular benefit and I shall acknowledge it as a great favor."[174]

On March 23, 1779, he wrote to "My Dear Betsy," "I am still determind to return to Boston in April or May—there to resign the place I hold as secretary and to get myself excusd from any further service here." He wrote, "after nearly five years absense from my family, and in a Climate unfriendly to my Health I have reason to expect I may be permitted to spend the Remainder of my Days in my native Place and enjoy the Pleasures of domestick Life." He concluded, "I hope to see you shortly."[175] He made the same point in a letter of the same date to James Warren: "I find my health declining, and the Air of this County is unfriendly to it. I am therefore steadfastly determind to get my self excusd in April or May at farthest."[176] Expecting his return, the people of Boston reelected him in May to the Massachusetts House of Representatives.[177]

Adams's steadfast determination notwithstanding, when June rolled around, he was still in Philadelphia, serving on congressional committees dealing with mundane but nevertheless crucial issues such as supplies for the American troops and the fine points of relations with France. The *Journals of Congress* for June 9 record an order that Samuel Adams "have leave of absence" but the records for the days that follow show him participating in congressional business, including a discussion of the fate of his friend Arthur Lee, who was embroiled in a feud with another representative of America in France, Silas Deane. It is possible, given Adams's precarious personal finances and the inflation rampant at the time, that he was delaying his trip home until he received an advance on his travel expenses. The records of Congress for June 15 report, "Ordered, That a warrant issue on the treasurer, in favour of Mr. S Adams, one of the delegates of Massachusetts bay, on his application, for fifteen hundred dollars, for which the said State is to be accountable."[178] The politician who more than a year before had seen the consequences of Hancock's guard failing to pay tavern keepers along the road to Boston was determined not to make *that* mistake.

# Chapter 8

# Back to Massachusetts

## *1779–1793*

*"It is essential that the people should be united in the Federal government, to withstand the common enemy, and to preserve their valuable rights and liberties."*

—*Samuel Adams, 1788*

I F SAMUEL ADAMS had decided, upon returning to Massachusetts in late June 1779, to limit his public activities and enjoy the pleasures of "domestick life," no one could have faulted him. He was approaching fifty-seven years old, the age at which his father had died.[1] He had been in public service twenty-three years, since he was first elected a tax collector for the town of Boston in 1756, and he had been battling against British taxation of the colonies for fifteen years, since he drafted the instructions of the representatives of the town of Boston in reaction to the Sugar Act of 1764. He had helped to found a new nation, the United States of America, independent and free.

Adams may have had a full biography already, but even in 1779 he still had a full career ahead of him, almost two decades more of ardent work establishing the young new nation and his home state on their new courses. His influence, though, would from now on emanate mainly from Boston, not the nation's capital.

On July 9, Adams returned to the Boston Town Meeting at Faneuil

Hall, resuming his role as moderator in a sign that while he may have been distant physically from Boston, he retained the confidence of its residents.[2] He also served as the moderator at an August 16 Town Meeting that attempted to fight wartime inflation by mandating price reductions and controls, dictating, for example, that fishmongers "shall not take more" than twelve pennies a pound for cod and nine pennies for haddock. The Boston Town Meeting moderated by Samuel Adams also specified a price for "halybut, without entrails."[3]

The political body that absorbed even more of Samuel Adams's energy than the Boston Town Meeting, though, was the Massachusetts Constitutional Convention. It convened Wednesday morning, September 1, 1779, in the Congregationalist meeting house in Cambridge, steps from Harvard Yard. The role given to religion in the convention was clear at the outset, and not only from the meeting place. Even the term "convention," as the Harvard historians Oscar and Mary Handlin have noted, was familiar from the annual gatherings of Massachusetts ministers.[4] On Friday morning, September 3, when the convention gathered at 8 A.M., as it did regularly, "a motion was then made and seconded, that those gentlemen of the Clergy, who have seats in this Convention, be requested to open the Convention with Prayer, every morning, in rotation, which passed in the affirmative."[5] Nearly three hundred delegates from across the state had gathered to draft a new constitution to replace the colonial charter. Eleven of them were clergymen, including, representing Lexington in the county of Middlesex, Rev. Jonas Clarke.[6] The Boston delegation, which included Samuel Adams, James Bowdoin, and John Hancock, totaled twelve members, and was the largest.

Samuel Adams dominated the convention. He was one of two members named to a committee to receive credentials and declare the delegates.[7] On Saturday morning, September 4, the convention named a committee to prepare a declaration of rights and a constitution of a new government. Twenty-six members were named to represent the state's counties, including John Adams representing Suffolk County and Robert Treat Paine representing Bristol County. Then balloting was held for an additional four at-large members of the committee. Samuel Adams was the top vote getter, with 209 votes of the 237 cast, and he was added to the group.[8] He enjoyed mingling with the representatives from around the state. "We are engaged in the arduous business of forming a new constitution, and I have the pleasure of finding, in the convention met for that purpose, a number of young gentlemen who I think will support the virtue and liberty of our country," he wrote to Richard Henry Lee, keeping in touch with the Virginian even while away from Congress.[9]

Most importantly, the thirty-person committee appointed a three-person subcommittee consisting of Samuel Adams, John Adams, and James Bowdoin to write a draft of a new constitution. The convention adjourned for nearly two months to allow the committee to do its job. Historians have credited John Adams with the bulk of the work, largely on the basis of a letter he wrote twenty-four years later, while an old man, to a Maine lawyer, William Durkee Williamson, who later briefly served as governor of Maine and who wrote a two-volume history of Maine. There is little reason to doubt John Adams's recollection; as a lawyer, John Adams would have been a natural to draw up the legal framework for the government. But John Adams himself conceded he left the most controversial portion of the draft, that concerning relations between the church and the state, to "older and graver persons than myself" who "would be more likely to hit the taste of the public."[10] It was a fine description of his cousin Samuel. The church-state section, known as Article 3, was the subject of "very extensive" debate, and, to accommodate the discussion, the convention voted to suspend its usual rule barring any one member from speaking more than twice on one question. Finally, the section was referred on November 3 to a seven-member committee that included Samuel Adams and three clergymen but not John Adams.[11]

It does nothing to diminish John Adams's contribution to the Massachusetts constitution to observe that the future president left the Constitutional Convention November 11 and sailed for Europe on a diplomatic mission a few days later,[12] while Samuel Adams stayed in Massachusetts and for months patiently navigated the constitution through revision after revision, and then to ratification. The number of delegates present at the Constitutional Convention dwindled as the winter road conditions made travel difficult and a smallpox outbreak deterred some from visiting Boston, where the convention had moved.[13] But Adams sat through session after session, and on committee after committee. The religious issues were among the most contentious. On February 4, 1780, the convention appointed Adams to a five-person committee to draft a declaration "wherein every person, before he takes his seat as a Representative, Senator or Governor, or enters upon the execution of any important office or trust in the Commonwealth, shall renounce every principle (whether it be Roman Catholic, Mahometan, Deistical, or Infidel,) which has any the least tendency to subvert the civil or religious rights established by this Constitution."[14]

Given the intolerance of the underlying assignment, the oath approved by the convention at the suggestion of Adams's committee was surprisingly mild. A test whose purpose was to bar from office adherents to certain religions had an express provision that Quakers, in accordance with their practices, could "affirm" rather than swear, and omit the words "so help me God." The most explicit reference to Catholics was a provision requiring would-be officeholders to swear "that no foreign Prince, Person, Prelate, State, or Potentate hath, or ought to have, any jurisdiction, superiority, preeminence, authority, dispensing, or other power, in any matter civil, ecclesiastical, or spiritual, within this Commonwealth." That line could be interpreted as including the pope. But beyond that, there were no specific disavowals of Catholicism required by the oath, and no denial of infidelity other than the phrase "so help me God" for non-Quakers. Certain elected officials were required to declare, however, "that I believe the christian religion, and have a firm persuasion of its truth." An effort to insert the word "protestant" before "christian" was voted down.[15] Less progressive or inclusive was the vote of the convention against deleting the word "male" before the word "inhabitant" in the section of the constitution setting out who could vote. That there was a vote at all on the topic indicates it was a matter of debate, and one not immediately resolved, as the delegates voted on it repeatedly, once on February 9, and again on February 24. History did not record where Samuel Adams came down on the question.[16]

The same day, February 9, that the vote on women's suffrage was first taken, the convention voted "that the President, Professors, and Tutors of Harvard College be excluded from a seat" in either the Massachusetts House or the new upper chamber, the Senate. A similar motion to exclude "ordained or settled Ministers of the Gospel" from serving in state office was defeated "after a very full debate."[17]

By February 23, the end was in sight. The tinkering with the wording was almost over, and it was time to start winning support for it with the public. Samuel Adams was appointed to a committee "to prepare an address to the people" about the constitution.[18] On February 28, the convention voted to have 1,800 copies of the constitution printed and distributed to the various towns for consideration. On March 2, the convention adjourned until the first Wednesday in June.[19]

In the interval from March to June 1780, 174 towns considered the "Constitution of Frame of Government" that had been so labored over by Samuel Adams and the convention. The largest and most influential of those towns, Boston, took up the question at Faneuil Hall on Wednesday, May 3, at 10 A.M. The meeting opened with a prayer by Rev. Samuel Cooper and proceeded quickly to an election of Samuel Adams as moderator. Next Samuel Adams read the "address to the people" that he had been on the committee to draft. "Your Delegates did not conceive themselves to be vested with Power to set up one Denomination of Christians above another; for Religion must at all Times be a matter between GOD and individuals: But we have nevertheless, found ourselves obliged by a Solemn Test, to provide for the exclusion of those from Offices who will not disclaim those Principles of Spiritual Jurisdiction which Roman Catholicks *in some countries* have held, and which are subversive of a free Government established by the People," the address said. It concluded, "we do most humbly beseech the Great Disposer of all Events, that we and our Posterity may be established in, and long enjoy the Blessings of a well-ordered and free Government."[20]

Samuel Adams proceeded to read aloud to the Bostonians the text of the proposed constitution. It began with a Preamble: "We," it said, "the people of Massachusetts, acknowledging, with grateful hearts, the goodness of the Great Legislator of the Universe, in affording us, in the course of His providence, an opportunity, deliberately and peaceably, without fraud, violence or surprise, of entering into an original, explicit, and solemn compact with each other; and of forming a new Constitution of Civil Government, for ourselves and posterity; and devoutly imploring His direction in so interesting a design, Do agree upon, ordain and establish, the following *Declaration of Rights, and Frame of Government*, as the CONSTITUTION of the COMMONWEALTH of MASSACHUSETTS."

Next came a "Declaration of Rights." The first article was a general statement that echoed both the Declaration of Independence and the instructions that Samuel Adams had drafted for this same body, the Boston Town Meeting, to issue its representatives back in 1765: "ALL men are born free and equal, and have certain natural, essential, and unalienable rights; among which may be reckoned the right of enjoying and defending their lives and liberties; that of acquiring, possessing, and protecting property; in fine, that of seeking and obtaining their safety and happiness."

Next, in Article 2, came a reference to religious liberty. "It is the right as well as the duty of all men in society, publicly and at stated seasons, to worship the SUPREME BEING, the great creator and preserver of the universe. And no subject shall be hurt, molested, or restrained, in his person, liberty, or estate, for worshipping GOD in the manner and season most agreeable to the dictates of his own conscience; or his religious profession or sentiments, provided he doth not disturb the public peace, or obstruct others in their religious worship."

The third article was the one about government funding for religion that had been the topic of such extensive debate in the convention. It spoke of not placing any denomination of Christians above another. "Every denomination of christians, demeaning themselves peaceably, and as good subjects of the Commonwealth, shall be equally under the protection of the law: And no subordination of any one sect or denomination to another shall ever be established by law," the constitution said. But at the same time it functionally required those whose denominations were too small to support their own minister to fund the local Congregationalist clergyman. By way of explanation, the article offered:

> As the happiness of a people, and the good order and preservation of civil government, essentially depend upon piety, religion and morality; and as these cannot be generally diffused through a community, but by the institution of the public worship of GOD, and of public instructions in piety, religion and morality: Therefore, to promote their happiness and to secure the good order and preservation of their government, the people of this Commonwealth have a right to invest their legislature with power to authorize and require, and the legislature shall, from time to time, authorize and require, the several towns, parishes, precincts, and other bodies-politic, or religious societies, to make suitable provision, at their own expense, for the institution of public worship of GOD, and for the support and maintenance of public protestant teachers of piety, religion and morality, in all cases where such provision shall not be made voluntarily.

The Declaration of Rights section of the Massachusetts constitution went on to enumerate, in thirty articles, some similar to the Virginia Bill of Rights, which had been approved there in 1776, a series of rights. If an individual's property was to be appropriated for public uses, "he shall receive a reasonable compensation" for it. No one should be required to furnish evidence against himself in a criminal investigation or trial, and every person accused of a crime has the right "to meet the witnesses against him face to face." Everyone "has a right to be secure from all unreasonable searches, and seizures of his person, his houses, his papers, and all his possessions." No court shall "inflict cruel or unusual punishments." The people have a right "to keep and to bear arms for the common defence." Samuel Adams would have been pleased to protect his old friends at the *Boston Gazette*: "The liberty of the press is essential to the security of freedom in a state: it ought not, therefore, to be restrained in this commonwealth," the Constitution said.

The final right enumerated served as a logical transition to the next section, the "frame of government." That last right guaranteed the separation of powers, saying, "In the government of this Commonwealth, the legislative department shall never exercise the executive and judicial powers, or either of them: The executive shall never exercise the legislative and judicial powers, or either of them: The judicial shall never exercise the legislative and executive powers, or either of them: to the end it may be a government of laws and not of men."

The constitution proceeded to describe the legislative power, the executive power, and the judiciary power. The governor, who in order to be eligible for the office had to "declare himself to be of the christian religion," would be "commander-in-chief of the army and navy, and of all the military forces of the state." He would also have the power to grant pardons. A section of the constitution confirmed the rights and privileges of Harvard College, explaining that "the encouragement of Arts and Sciences, and all good literature, tends to the honor of God, the advantage of the christian religion, and the great benefit of this, and the other United States of America." A section that followed spoke of how wisdom, knowledge, and virtue are necessary to preserve rights and liberties, and of how education should be encouraged in "the principles of humanity and general benevolence, public and private charity, industry and frugality, honesty and punctuality." The legislature was forbidden to suspend the privilege of the writ of habeas corpus, "except upon the most urgent and pressing occasions, and for a limited time not exceeding twelve months." The constitution concluded with a mechanism to revise itself with such amendments "as from experience will be found necessary."[21]

The Massachusetts constitution contained more checks and balances than other state constitutions that had been adopted earlier. The Pennsylvania constitution of 1776 had a one-house legislature, while the Massachusetts frame of government provided for both a House and a Senate. The Virginia constitution of 1776 did not give the state's governor the power to veto legislation, did not provide for popular ratification of the document, and did not contain, as the Massachusetts document did, language leading to the end of slavery in that state.[22]

The Boston Town Meeting considered the constitution all through the day on Wednesday and Thursday, and then—having moved the meeting from Faneuil Hall to the Old Brick Meeting House—voted "that the Ministers of the Gospel be requested to remind their respective Congregations the next Lords day" of "the importance of universally withdrawing them selves for a few hours from their ordinary Engagements, and devoting their Attention to a Matter so deeply interesting to themselves and their Posterity." The appeal drew more than four hundred Bostonians to participate in the meetings, which stretched on through the next week. They suggested adding freedom of speech to the freedom of the press, and strengthening the right of habeas corpus by allowing its suspension only "in time of War, Invasion, or a Time of Rebellion declared by the Legislature to exist, nor for a longer Time than six months." They suggested that the long-debated article three be changed slightly to allow those whose conscience objected to supporting ministers to opt to support the poor instead. Finally, having met from May 3 to May 12, they voted, "almost unanimously," to approve the constitution.[23]

When the Constitutional Convention reconvened on June 7 in Boston's Brattle Street Meeting House, the delegates found that the responses from the other towns were supportive enough to approve the document they had drafted. On Friday, June 16, 1780, after a prayer from Rev. Peter Thacher, the delegates moved to dissolve, their work concluded.[24] It had been nine and a half months since they had first convened in Cambridge, and while some of that time had been spent in adjournment, most of it had been spent crafting the constitution. Samuel Adams had been named by his fellow delegates to twelve different committees and had served as moderator of the crucial Boston Town Meeting, and on June 16, he must have been filled with relief and a sense of accomplishment. "The People of Massachusetts have at length agreed to the Form of a civil Constitution," he wrote to John Adams in Paris. "Never was a good Constitution more wanted than at this juncture."[25]

It was quite a feat. David McCullough has called the Massachusetts constitution "one of the great, enduring documents of the American Revolution" and "the oldest functioning written constitution in the world."[26] Massachusetts judges cited its guarantees of liberty and equality in 1781 when they outlawed slavery in the state, and in 2003 when they ordered the legalization of same sex marriage.[27] Justices of the United States Supreme Court look to it even to this day when deciding on questions of great national importance. When the high court in 1988 ruled in favor of the legality of the independent counsel statute, Justice Antonin Scalia began his dissent in the case of *Morrison v. Olson* by quoting the Massachusetts constitution of 1780 on the separation of powers. When the court, in 2004, ruled in the case of *Hamdi v. Rumsfeld* on whether a member of the Taliban could be detained indefinitely in an American naval brig as an enemy combatant, Justice Scalia again turned to the Massachusetts constitution of 1780, this time to its clause on habeas corpus.

Though it had been years since Samuel Adams had written a regular newspaper column, some of his colleagues still thought of him as a journalist as well as a fellow politician. A letter to Adams from James Lowell, who was representing Massachusetts in Congress at Philadelphia, passed along some diplomatic communications from France with the admonition, "I give it to you as a secret . . . I only say it is not a News Paper Business."[28] Adams wrote to Lowell on March 5, 1780,

"Our Newspapers are remarkeable lately for more groundless Paragraphs than most others."[29]

Yet it was hard to stay away. Under his old pen name "Vindex," Adams returned to the *Boston Gazette* of June 12, 1780, identifying himself as "An old Correspondent," and writing, "May Heaven inspire that Army yet more and more with Military Virtues, and teach their hands to war and their fingers to fight! May every citizen in the army and in the country, have a proper sense of the DEITY upon his mind."[30]

He contributed the rare article when he thought it was warranted. In the *Boston Gazette* of April 16, 1781, Adams described the act of voting in an election as one in which the voter should act in a way that does not trifle "with the sacred trust reposed in him by GOD and his country."[31]

Rather than dwelling on his achievement of shepherding to passage a remarkable constitution for Massachusetts, Samuel Adams rushed on to the next task. He told the Boston Town Meeting, which had just elected him to represent Boston in the Massachusetts House of Representatives, of his intention to return to Congress at Philadelphia, warning that "it was probable" that he would be absent from the state for most of the year.[32] By June 20, 1780, traveling with Elbridge Gerry, he was in Hartford, on his way to Philadelphia, where he arrived in time to take his seat in Congress as a delegate on June 29.[33] The delegates there put him right to work, appointing him on Saturday, July 1, to a three-man committee "to take proper measures for a public celebration of the anniversary of Independence on Tuesday next," and adding him as a member of a committee to consider a response to a letter submitted by General Nathanael Greene. The same day, Adams seconded a motion in which Congress agreed to help pay for the education of the children of Dr. Warren, who had been killed at Bunker Hill.[34] On July 3, Adams made a motion stressing the importance of naval intelligence, particularly concerning "the arrival of any ships of war in or near the port of New York."[35] On Friday, July 21, Adams raised the complaint that officers and soldiers in Massachusetts were going unpaid, and moved to resolve the situation by involving the new Massachusetts government he had helped create.[36] On August 2, a committee issued a secret report written by Adams recommending removing the restriction that had been placed on Washington limiting his ability to operate outside the boundaries of the United States. Congress approved the recommendation.[37]

The next few months were a difficult stretch for Adams. In September came the news of an American general, Benedict Arnold, defecting to the British, or, as Adams put it in a letter home to "My Dear Betsy," "having committed the blackest Treason against his country." Adams did point out with some apparent satisfaction in the same letter that Arnold had been "anathematizd by the Clergy in the Pulpit."[38] Washington's army was having another season of scarcity. Samuel Adams wrote with concern to a friend that General Washington "has written several letters, acquainting Congress of the distressed circumstances of the army for want of provisions, and particularly meat. They have several times lately been without provisions for three or four days."[39] The palsy or tremor that had afflicted Adams's hand even back in the days when he rose to challenge Thomas Hutchinson following the Boston Massacre had gotten worse. Adams wrote to Elbridge Gerry in November, 1780, "Shall I tell you of my trembling Hand, & how unfit an instrument it is to guide a Pen? I do assure you that writing is on that Account become painful to me."[40] A professor of neurology at Columbia University's medical school, Dr. Elan Louis, has studied Adams's handwriting and other historical evidence and concluded that Adams likely suffered from what is today diagnosed as essential tremor, a nerve disorder that afflicts those who have it with uncontrollable shaking.[41] (It may have run in the family; John Adams had a similar ailment.)[42] Adams managed to keep committing his forceful words to paper, though eventually, as the condition worsened, he resorted to dictating his letters to an aide.

In addition, Congress was reorganizing in a way that gave less power to the committees on which Adams was influential, and more power to what we know today as cabinet secretaries. The French ambassador at Philadelphia, the Chevalier de la Luzerne, wrote home to Paris, "Divisions prevail in Congress about the new mode of transacting business by secretaries of different departments. Samuel Adams, whose obstinate and resolute character was so useful to the revolution in its origin, but who shows himself very ill suited to the conduct of affairs in an organized government, has placed himself at the head of the advocates for the old system of committees of Congress, instead of relying on ministers, or secretaries, according to the new arrangement."[43]

Finally, there was the news that the voters of Massachusetts had elected John Hancock their first governor under the new constitution. Samuel Adams had not campaigned for the job himself, yet he confessed in a letter of October 6, 1780, to James Warren that he was "chagrined" and "disappointed" at the result.[44] Adams discussed it further in an October 17, 1780, letter to his wife from Philadelphia: "I am far from being an Enemy to that Gentleman, tho' he has been prevailed upon to mark me as such. I have so much Friendship for him, as to wish with all my Heart, that in the most critical circumstances, he may distinguish between his real Friends & his flattering Enemies."[45]

Friends of both Adams and Hancock had pleaded for a renewal of the partnership. "The Friends of their country cannot stand by idle spectators; they see the encreasing contest with weeping eyes and aching hearts, & wish a reconciliation. Permit me my friend to attempt (however inadequate to the task) a Restoration of friendship between two who once were dear to each other, and who now perhaps from mistakes and misapprehensions seem so distant," Samuel Savage wrote to Adams, invoking the Protestant leaders in Europe: "It was an excellent Observation of Luther, between whom he and Calvin a breach once happened, Calvin, says he, was first in the Transgression, but I glory in being first in the Reconciliation."[46]

Such a reconciliation would have to wait. As word spread from Boston of the ostentatious manner in which Hancock took office as governor, Adams expressed more concern. Hancock was ushered into office with a parade of militia, the discharge of thirteen cannon, and a stop at the Old Brick Meeting House, where Rev. Samuel Cooper preached on Jeremiah chapter 30, verses 20 and 21, "And their congregation shall be established; and their nobles shall be of themselves; and their governor shall proceed out of the midst of them." The congregation then adjourned to Fanueil Hall, where, the *Massachusetts Spy* reported, "an elegant entertainment was provided," in what appeared to be blithe indifference to the provision-less troops of General Washington, and thirteen toasts were drunk, including one to "His Most Catholic Majesty" and another to "His Excellency John Hancock, Esq., Governor of the Commonwealth of Massachusetts."[47]

"I am affraid there is more Pomp & Parade than is consistent with those sober Republican Principles," Adams wrote to John Scollay from Philadelphia on December 30, 1780. "Why should this new Era be introducd with Entertainments expensive & tending to dissipate the Minds of the People? Does it become us to lead the People to such publick Diversions as promote Superfluity of Dress & Ornament, when it is as much as they can bear to support the Expense of cloathing a naked Army?" He added, "It was asked in the Reign of Charles the 2d of England, How shall we turn the Minds of the People from an Attention to their Liberties? The Answer was, by making them extravagant, luxurious, effeminate." The letter went on to refer to the Puritan founders of Boston: "Our Bradfords, Winslows & Winthrops would have revolted at the Idea of opening Scenes of Dissipation & Folly." He said of his hometown: "I once thought that City would be the *Christian* Sparta. But Alas!"[48]

Adams consoled himself, as he always did in dark periods, with faith and family. He wrote to his daughter, Hannah, from Philadelphia on August 17, 1780, "If you carefully fulfill the various Duties of Life, from a Principle of Obedience to your heavenly Father, you shall enjoy that Peace which the World cannot give nor take away." He said he was persuaded that pleasing "an Earthly parent" was not her "principal motive to be religious." Still, he said, "you cannot gratify me so much, as by seeking most earnestly, the Favor of Him who made &

supports you—who will supply you with whatever his infinite Wisdom sees best for you in this World, and above all, who has given us his Son to purchase for us the Reward of Eternal Life."[49]

Adams wrote Hannah's new husband, Thomas Wells, a letter of marital advice from Philadelphia on November 22, 1780. "Piety" he advised, is "indispensable" to the well-being of a family. "Religion in a Family is at once its brightest Ornament & its best Security," Adams wrote.[50]

To Elbridge Gerry on November 27, 1780, Adams urged from Philadelphia that men "of Zeal for the Honor of the Supreme Being" be chosen to fill the seats of government.[51]

To John Adams on December 17, 1780, Samuel Adams wrote from Philadelphia that "gracious Heaven" had defeated Benedict Arnold's traitorous conspiracy. "We have so often seen in the Course of this Conflict, the remarkeable Interposition of divine Providence in our favor," Samuel Adams wrote.[52]

Friendship was a solace, too. Adams had the pleasure in Philadelphia in 1780 of finally meeting Arthur Lee, with whom he had been corresponding regularly for nine years.[53] Most comforting of all, though, must have been the thought of making a final return— for good—to his hometown of Boston. He wrote to his wife, "having spent the greatest Part of my Life in Publick Cares, like the weary Traveller, fatigued with the Journey of the Day, I can rest with you in a Cottage. If I live till the Spring, I will take my final Leave of Congress and return to Boston."[54]

Months after telling her, he formally notified the president of the Massachusetts Senate of his plans, explaining, "I am apprehensive my health will not admit of my spending another summer in this city."[55]

In April 1781, Samuel Adams finally left the Continental Congress for good, after seven years of service—not to retire, but to return to public life in Massachusetts under its new constitution as an elected state senator and president of the state Senate. (The people of Boston had elected him to the state House of Representatives as well as to the Senate, but Adams apparently understood that taking both jobs would defeat the checks and balances contained in the constitution he had crafted.)[56] These were years of triumph but also of challenge. The triumph came with the news of General Charles Cornwallis's surrender to Washington at Yorktown, Virginia, on October 19, 1781. Saratoga had been the American victory that changed the tide of the war, but Yorktown was the victory that, with the help of the French fleet, ended it. Samuel Adams, characteristically, described it as a "Divine Blessing afforded to the Allied forces under the Direction of his Excy Gen$^l$ Washington."[57] The diplomats dragged out negotiations on a final peace treaty until 1783, which was fully eight years after Lexington and Concord. Adams did his best to shape the treaty from the distance of Massachusetts. The state legislature sent Congress at Philadelphia a resolution stressing the importance of maintaining in the peace treaty its rights to "the fisheries" for whales and cod off the Atlantic Coast.[58]

Against the satisfaction of victory was laid the anxiety that the independence and liberty could be lost. Adams saw two main threats: violent insurrections in Western Massachusetts and more subtle decay in the character of the citizens of the commonwealth.

The first troublemaker to arise, in January and February of 1782, was a forty-one-year-old Yale graduate who had served brief stints as both a Congregationalist minister and a Revolutionary War soldier, Samuel Ely. Ely seized on discontent in Western Massachusetts at the power of the government in Boston and the taxes it had imposed, and he organized a convention to overturn the Massachusetts constitution that Samuel Adams had so painstakingly shepherded to approval less than two years before. Ely claimed to have a replacement constitution in his pocket "that even the Angel Gabriel could not find fault with." In April, at Northampton, Ely incited a mob against the local judges, threatening, "we'll go to the woodpile and get clubs enough and knock their Grey Wiggs off and send them out of the World in an Instant." It was enough to get him arrested and sentenced to prison in Springfield, where, on the morning of June 13, a crowd of about 130 men sympathetic to him broke him out of jail. Ely fled to Vermont.

Joseph Hawley, a revolutionary leader from Western Massachusetts who had worked closely with Samuel Adams, attributed the riot and jailbreak to "the Devil" and perhaps, too, "British Emissaries, with British money, among the people." Hawley suggested the legislature in Boston send a committee "to go into the Towns and learn the facts on the Spot, by seeing and hearing," warning, "a neglect of this may deceive and ruin the government."[59]

The committee consisted of Samuel Adams and Artemas Ward, who together traveled to Hampshire County in July and on August 7 met at Hatfield with delegates from forty-four towns. The delegates complained about high taxes, and Adams returned to Boston and moved to reduce the taxes by deferring into the future some debt repayment. None of those who helped Ely break out of prison was punished, and while Ely himself was eventually returned to Massachusetts, he served only six months in jail before being set free by act of the legislature.[60]

Such leniency emboldened Daniel Shays, a farmer, debtor, and Revolutionary War veteran, and other leaders of what came to be known as Shays's Rebellion. On August 22, 1786, delegates from fifty towns in Hampshire County in Western Massachusetts gathered in a convention similar to the one Ely had organized four years earlier. The first of the written complaints they raised was the existence of the Senate in which Samuel Adams sat; they thought it unnecessary.[61] They also complained about taxes, about "the scarcity of money," and about the situation of the legislature in Boston as opposed to some more central location that would be easier for delegates from Western Massachusetts to travel to. They called for the issuance of paper money and an immediate revision of the Massachusetts constitution of 1780.[62] Their supporters proceeded to use violence or the threat of force to stop courts from convening in Northampton, Worcester, Concord, Springfield, Taunton, and Great Barrington.[63]

Samuel Adams had been stepping back a bit from the public spotlight—declining to serve in the United States Congress or on the Massachusetts Governor's Council.[64] He had lost elections for secretary of state in 1780, for governor in 1782, and for lieutenant governor in 1783.[65] But now that the commonwealth and the constitution he had worked so hard to establish were being challenged in a crisis, he once again assumed a central role. Adams was the first senator that Governor James Bowdoin consulted with after the courts were closed.[66] On Friday, September 8, the Boston Town Meeting convened at Faneuil Hall. The meeting chose Samuel Adams both as moderator of the session and as a member of a committee to draft an address to the governor expressing disapproval of the Shays riots and offering assistance to the government.[67]

The committee also drafted a circular letter urging calm: "If grievances have arisen in the government, surely the voice of the people can be taken without flying to arms." The letter contrasted the situation under British rule with that under the new commonwealth. "The obvious intention of reducing to absolute slavery, to a Prince on an island at three thousand miles distance, the people of an whole continent, demanded an opposition worthy of the blood and treasure expended in it," the committee wrote. "How reverse of this is our now happy situation? Subjected to no laws, but such as are made by a Legislature of our own election, agreeably to the form of government established by *our own consent*, taxed by *our own* representatives only, and controled by no authority but what is *derived from ourselves*."

The committee blamed what economic difficulties existed on "the habits of luxury contracted in the late war, from the vast quantity of goods imported," along with "receiving and giving unlimited credit." As a solution, it advised, "let us lay aside the destructive fashions and expensive superfluities of the day; be sober, temperate, and industrious, and, by the blessing of propitious heaven, we shall soon retrieve our circumstances." The group attributed the disturbances to "British emissaries," "wicked and unprincipled men," or "a combination of both."[68]

In February 1787, Adams chaired the committee to draft the proclamation in which the governor and the legislature solemnly declared "That a horrid and unnatural REBELLION and WAR has been openly and traitorously raised and levied against this Commonwealth."[69]

As Shays's Rebellion wore on and developed into open warfare between the Shaysites and militias loyal to the government in Boston, Adams urged a hard line, arguing, "In monarchies, the crime of treason and rebellion may admit of being pardoned or lightly punished, but the man who dares to rebel against the laws of a republic ought to suffer death."[70] As a Massachusetts lawyer, Fisher Ames, said of Adams, "When he was in power, and when Shays's insurrection was to be quelled, he was as ready to use force, and to shed blood, as any body. This is not said by way of reproach, for we confess it is right and lawful to resort to force in defence of our Constitution and laws."[71]

The appearance of Samuel Adams, of all people, on the side of those using force to quash a tax rebellion was seen by some as an ironical turnabout: James Warren wrote to John Adams that their old friend "seems to have forsaken all his old principles and professions and to have become the most arbitrary and despotic Man in the Commonwealth."[72]

That was an overstatement of an exaggeration of an inaccuracy. The principles of civic behavior professed by Samuel Adams in the early and mid-1780s were consistent with those he had expressed before and during the Revolution.

In 1783, he wrote to Congress as president of the Massachusetts Senate, opposing Congress's decision to grant half-pay for life to officers in the Continental Army. He called the pension "inconsistent with that equality which ought to subsist among citizens of free and republican states," and warned, "such a measure appears to be calculated to raise and exalt some citizens in wealth and grandeur, to the injury and oppression of others." He told Congress that it was "irritating to the principles and feelings which the people of some Eastern States, and of this in particular, inherit from their ancestry."[73] Such attitudes grated on some of the officers; at about the time the half-pay for life issue was originally raised, one American general, Alexander McDougall, wrote to another, Nathanael Greene, "I have explicitly told Mr. Adams that our Army no longer consider themselves as fighting the Battles of *Republics in Principle*, but for Empire and Liberty to a people whose Object is Property, and that the Army expect some of that property, which the Citizen seeks, and which the Army protects for him."[74] The argument failed to win over Samuel Adams.

Also in 1783, Adams served on Boston's committee to draft instructions for its representatives, just as he had in 1764. "We find it to be the express sentiment of this Body of this People, that the preservation of Good Government, essentially depends on Piety, Religion, and Morality, and that these cannot be generally diffused among a community but by the Institution of the Public Worship of God," the instructions said. "Piety, Justice, Moderation, Temperance, Industry and Frugality, are absolutely necessary to preserve the advantages of liberty. . . . We cannot too warmly express our gratitude to Almighty God, who hath smiled on the virtuous struggles of the United States, and crowned the conflict with so happy a conclusion, Our Independence is confirmed."[75]

To Elbridge Gerry on April 19, 1784, Samuel Adams said he disapproved of the idea of the Cincinnati, an association of families of Revolutionary War officers. He called the hereditary distinction of families "odious," but said he could understand what motivated it. "The human mind is so captivated with the Thought of being elevated above the ignoble Vulgar," Adams wrote.[76] His feelings failed to stop the society from meeting, but he might have been somewhat consoled if he knew what they were up to; at a meeting of the society on July 4, 1793, at Princeton, New Jersey, the members heard an address from the first president of the American Bible Society, a Presbyterian, Elias Boudinot, who spoke of how the Children of Israel marked their deliverance from bondage with an annual festival, as the Bible said, "remember this day, in which ye came out of Egypt, out of the house of bondage." So, too, Boudinot said, Americans should unite on the Fourth of July to "remember with reverential gratitude to our supreme Benefactor, all the wonderful things He has done for us, in our miraculous deliverance from a second Egypt—another house of bondage."[77]

Adams saw a connection between virtue, religion, and the foreign relations of the newly independent United States. He wrote to Richard Henry Lee on December 23, 1784, "If, my honord Friend, the leading Men in the United States would by Precept & Example disseminate thro' the lower Classes of People the Principles of Piety to God, Love to our Country & universal Benevolence, should we not secure the Favor of Heaven & the Honor & Esteem of the wise and virtuous Part of the World."[78]

In an April 14, 1785, letter to Richard Henry Lee, Adams went so far as to suggest the spread of democracy was a prerequisite to a messianic age of world peace. "I firmly believe that the benevolent Creator designd the republican Form of Government for Man. Will you venture so far as to say that all other Institutions that we know of are unnatural & tend more or less to distress human Societies? Will the Lion ever associate with the Lamb or the Leopard with the Kid till our favorite principles shall be universally establishd?"[79]

Adams's concerns and professions along these lines went beyond private musings to friends. He drafted a June 8, 1785, "Proclamation for the Encouragement of Piety, Virtue, Education and Manners and for the Suppression of Vice":

> Whereas it is essential to the safety and welfare of civil society and the good order and preservation of government, that the duties of piety, religion and morality should be observd and practicd by the People of all orders in a community. I have therefore thought fit, by and with the advice of the Council to make and issue this proclamation, signifying my own sense of the importance of the subject, and earnestly calling upon the citizens of this commonwealth, at large, and more especially persons of authority and influence, ministers of the Gospel and publick instructors of youth . . . to inculcate on the minds of all, the Fear and Reverence of the Supreme Governor of the World—to awaken in them a just sense of his Superintending Providence.

The proclamation called on these same leaders to focus popular attention on "that excellent system of morals" contained "in the sacred scriptures as the rule of human conduct." The observance of these rules, Adams said, was necessary for the support of the constitution. The proclamation went on to stress

> the great Importance of early education of children to our common Happiness, and to legislators and magistrates that they liberally provide for the more publick education of youth, always bearing in their Memories the Duty injoined on them in the Constitution, which, I am persuaded, will afford them pleasure and do Honor to our country. . . . Thus by building on the firm foundation which our pious ancestors laid, education being supported under the auspices of a government elected by the suffrages of the people, the sons of the poor and the rich will joyously partake . . . and those principles of Equality which are essential to the Republican form of our government will thereby be effectually and perpetually preservd.

The proclamation went on to urge judges, sheriffs, constables, and grand jurors to enforce the laws against blasphemy, "profane cursing and swearing," profanation of the Lord's day, gaming, drunkenness, "and every other species of vice," so that "a stop may be put to the progress of impiety and immorality, which, prevailing, will destroy the liberty and Happiness of all societies." With that threat came an incentive, as well:

> I do by this proclamation make it known to all, and every person within this Commonwealth, that those who shall distinguish themselves, by examples of Industry, or Frugality, temperance, sobriety and decency of Manners, the love of our country and true zeal for its welfare, the fear of the Diety and a due regard to the Institutions of His publick worship will at all times be

welcomed by this government, and that it is my Determination to give the preference to such characters in all appointments to places of honor and public trust.[80]

Samuel Adams wrote to John Adams, who was in France, on July 2, 1785, complaining of "too many of the citizens" in Massachusetts "who are imitating the Britons in every idle Amusement & expensive Foppery which it is in their power to invent for the Destruction of a young Country." Asked Samuel Adams, "Can our People expect to indulge themselves in the unbounded Uses of every unmeaning & fantastick Extravagance because they would follow the Lead of Europeans, & not spend all their Money? You would be surprizd the see the Equipage, the Furniture & expensive Living of too many, the Pride and Vanity of Dress which pervades thro every Class, confounding every Distinction between the Poor & the Rich and evincing the Want both of Example and Economy." He offered hope that the replacement of Hancock with Bowdoin as governor "may *perhaps* restore our Virtue."[81] Also in 1785, Samuel Adams was popularly identified with the opposition to the Sans Souci Club, a new group that gathered in Boston for card playing and dancing.[82]

To cousin John, on July 21, 1786, he wrote, "There are two great Objects which I think should engage the Attention of Patriots here, & which appear to me to involve every thing else—to preserve entire our political Liberties, & to support our National Faith."

The case that Samuel Adams sought to preserve political liberties rather than trammel or forsake them, as James Warren would have it, is further made by the outcome of Shays's Rebellion. Only two of the hundreds of rebels were put to death, and Daniel Shays himself, like Samuel Ely before him, fled to Vermont. Unlike Ely, Shays was never returned to Massachusetts for punishment.[83]

Doubts that Samuel Adams remained committed to preserving political liberties are also dispelled by his behavior when it came to the new federal Constitution that delegates meeting at Philadelphia had drafted in the summer of 1787. The gathering had been motivated in part by a perceived need for a stronger central government to handle insurrections such as Shays's Rebellion.[84] The Massachusetts delegate to the Constitutional Convention who was closest to Samuel Adams, Elbridge Gerry, did not sign the Constitution because it lacked a bill of rights.[85] Samuel Adams himself did not attend, a sign of his initial skepticism of the need for a revised and more powerful central government to replace the weaker framework set up by the Articles of Confederation he had helped to craft.

The framers meeting at the Philadelphia convention had drafted a structure of government strikingly similar to the one that Samuel Adams had helped draft for Massachusetts more than seven years earlier. The preamble of the Massachusetts constitution began with a reference to "we," "the people" acting "for ourselves and posterity" to "ordain and establish" the constitution. The federal Constitution began with a Preamble, as well: "We, the people of the United States, in order to form a more perfect union, establish justice, insure domestic tranquility, provide for the common defense, promote the general welfare, and secure the blessings of liberty to ourselves and our posterity, do ordain and establish this Constitution for the United States of America." Just as the Massachusetts frame of government set out separate legislative, executive, and judicial powers, in that order, so, too, did the federal Constitution set forth the legislative powers in Article I, the executive powers in Article II, and the judicial in Article III. Just as the Massachusetts governor was to be "commander-in-chief of the army and navy" of Massachusetts, so the president of the United States was to be "commander in chief of the army and navy of the United States." Just as the Massachusetts governor had pardon power, so did the president of the United States. And just as the Massachusetts constitution provided for its own improvement and revision through amendments, so, too, did the federal Constitution.

For all the familiar echoes, Samuel Adams was initially skeptical, viewing a strong central government as redundant to the state governments, a danger to liberty, and unlikely to be able to meet the needs of far-flung states with regional differences. He wrote Richard Henry Lee on December 3, 1787, expressing doubts about the Constitution drafted at Philadelphia:

> I confess, as I enter the Building I stumble at the Threshold. I meet with a National Government, instead of a Federal Union of Sovereign States. I am not able to conceive why the Wisdom of the Convention led them to give the Preference to the former before the latter. If the several States in the Union are to become one entire Nation, under one Legislature, the Powers of which shall extend to every Subject of Legislation, and its Laws be supreme & controul the whole, the Idea of Sovereignty in these States must be lost. Indeed I think, upon such a Supposition, those Sovereignties ought to be eradicated from the Mind; for they would be Imperia in Imperio justly deemd a Solecism in Politicks, & they would be highly dangerous, and destructive of the Peace Union and Safety of the Nation. And can this National Legislature be competent to make Laws for the free internal Government of one People, living in Climates so remote and whose "Habits & particular Interests" are and probably always will be so different. Is it to be expected that General Laws can be adapted to the Feelings of the more Eastern and the more Southern Parts of so extensive a Nation? It appears to me difficult if practicable. Hence then may we not look for Discontent, Mistrust, Disaffection to Government and frequent Insurrections, which will require standing Armies to suppress them in one Place & another where they may happen to arise. Or if Laws could be made, adapted to the local Habits, Feelings, Views & Interests of those distant Parts, would they not cause Jealousies of Partiality in Government which would excite Envy and other malignant Passions productive of Wars and fighting. But should we continue distinct sovereign States, confederated for the Purposes of mutual Safety and Happiness, each contributing to the federal Head such a Part of its Sovereignty as would render the

Government fully adequate to those Purposes and no more, the People would govern themselves more easily, the Laws of each State being well adapted to its own Genius & Circumstances, and the Liberties of the United States would be more secure than they can be, as I humbly conceive, under the proposed new Constitution. You are sensible, Sir, that the Seeds of Aristocracy began to spring even before the Conclusion of our Struggle for the natural Rights of Men, Seeds which like a Canker Worm lie at the Root of free Governments.

When 364 delegates chosen by the Massachusetts towns convened at Boston on January 9, 1788, for a convention to weigh ratification of the constitution that had been drafted at Philadelphia, approval was by no means assured. In the months since the Philadelphia convention finished its work, Delaware, Pennsylvania, New Jersey, Georgia, and Connecticut had ratified the Constitution, but two of the crucial states, New York and Virginia, had yet to take a position. If Massachusetts, New York, and Virginia rejected the new Constitution, it would have been, for all practical purposes, stillborn. Alexander Hamilton, John Jay, and James Madison, sensing the work at Philadelphia hung in the balance, turned to the press and wrote a series of newspaper articles that came to be known as the Federalist Papers, urging ratification.

The Federalists, as those favoring ratification were known, viewed Adams at the outset as a formidable foe. "S. Adams is full out against it," a twenty-nine-year-old Harvard-educated Boston lawyer, Christopher Gore, wrote to Rufus King, another young lawyer who had represented Massachusetts at the Constitutional Convention at Philadelphia. Gore suspected Adams of inviting the two lawyers to a dinner to measure the strength of the Constitution's backers and get a preview of their arguments. "Being forewarned, I think we shall not be entrapped by the craft of A.," he wrote of the ploy.[86] When the dinner happened, Adams, by Gore's account, was "open and decided" against the Constitution, and remarked to Gore that he thought it was "strange" that people said they could not find out Adams's sentiments on the Constitution, because "he had always been explicit as he then was." Gore warned that unless Adams was swayed by a meeting of the tradesmen of Boston, he "will be indefatigable and constant in all ways and means to defeat the adoption of the proposed frame of government."[87]

The Massachusetts convention of 1788 proceeded in some sense along the lines of the ratification of the Massachusetts constitution of 1780, just as the federal Constitution followed the Massachusetts document in certain respects. Samuel Adams, in attendance as a delegate representing Boston, moved on Wednesday, January 9, that "The Convention will attend morning prayers daily, and that the gentlemen of the clergy of Boston, of every denomination, be requested to officiate in turn."[88] On Monday morning, January 14, Adams moved that the proposed federal Constitution be read aloud in full, just as he had read the Massachusetts constitution in full to the Boston Town Meeting as they considered whether to ratify it.[89] Just as the earlier convention did, this one met in churches—first the Brattle Street Meeting House, then the meeting house in Long Lane. There was one significant difference in that while John Adams had attended the beginning of the convention that resulted in the Massachusetts constitution of 1780 and then left for Europe, this time, Samuel's cousin was in London as the American minister to the Court of St. James.

Samuel Adams's constitutional deliberations were interrupted by a personal tragedy, the death of his only son, Samuel, at age thirty-seven. The *Massachusetts Gazette* reported on January 18: "DIED— yesterday morning, in this town, doctor Samuel Adams. His funeral will proceed from his father's house, in Winter-street, to-morrow, precisely at 4 o'clock, when his relations and friends are requested to attend." At Samuel Adams's urging, the convention voted to adjourn for the purpose of attending the funeral.[90] Family lore had it that after serving as a surgeon in the Revolutionary War, the young doctor "returned to Boston with a shattered constitution and unable to resume his practice."[91]

As he had after the loss of Rev. Checkley, Adams attempted to salve his grief as best he could by throwing himself back into his work. On January 24, he told the convention that he was "one of those who had difficulties and doubts respecting some parts of the proposed constitution," but that he had chosen to be a listener rather than an objector. He wanted, he said, "to have a full investigation of the subject."[92] Henry Knox wrote to a friend in New York that among the Massachusetts delegates there were "150 decidedly for the constitution, about 120 decidedly against it—and about 50 or 60 who appear to determine to hear all that can be said on both sides and then vote as they shall think right, Mr S Adams is in this class."[93]

He was determined to let all the delegates participate. On January 25, Jonathan Smith, of Lanesborough in Berkshire County, rose and addressed the convention. "I am a plain man and get my living by the plough," he said. "I am not used to speak in public, but I beg your leave to say a few words to my brother plough-joggers in this house. I have lived in a part of the country where I have known the worth of good government by the want of it." He recalled Shays's Rebellion. "People that used to live peaceably, and were before good neighbors, got distracted, and took up arms against government," he said. At this point Major Martin Kinsley, a delegate from Worcester County, tried to cut the farmer off, asking what the history of last winter had to do with the Constitution. But Adams intervened and insisted that Smith was in order. "Let him go on in his own way," Adams said, and the man from Western Massachusetts was allowed to continue.[94]

Adams, meanwhile, went on in his own way, inquiring why the framers of the new Constitution had changed the election of congressmen to every two years from the annual elections that had been the law. Fisher Ames, the twenty-nine-year-old lawyer and Harvard graduate representing the town of Dedham at the convention, turned the question back at Adams. "As it has been demanded, why annual elections were not preferred to biennial, permit me to retort the question, and to enquire in my turn, what reason can be given why, if annual elections are good, biennial elections are not better?"

Adams replied that he had only asked the question "for information." and that he had heard enough to satisfy himself of the plan's
propriety.[95] Ames would go on to defeat Adams in a 1788 election to
serve in the Congress established by the new Constitution.

On January 26, the convention discussed section nine of Article I of
the Constitution, which prohibited Congress from banning the slave
trade until 1808. In response to those who lamented that the importation of slaves would continue for twenty years, Adams took a more
hopeful view. According to the records of the debates, he "rejoiced
that a door was now to be opened, for the annihilation of this odious,
abhorrent practice, in a certain time."[96]

The decisive moment in the convention came with the decision
of Adams and Hancock to support ratification. Adams's biographer
Wells quotes a witness, Joseph Vinal, to the effect that the critical
moments came not in the formal session of the convention but in Hancock's home, where Hancock, who had been elected president of the
convention, was laid up nursing a case of gout. A group of delegates
who favored ratification came to see Hancock and found Adams at his
bedside. The visitors asked the two revolutionary leaders of Boston
what their objections were, and Adams and Hancock listed issues that,
if handled with amendments, would win their support for the Constitution. If Adams had any further doubts, they were allayed when Paul
Revere hand-delivered a set of resolutions in favor of the Constitution that had been approved by the skilled workingmen of Boston, or
mechanics, at the Green Dragon Tavern. Daniel Webster recorded the
interaction as follows: "How many mechanics," Adams asked, "were
at the Green Dragon when the resolutions were passed?"

"More, sir," Revere replied, "than the Green Dragon could hold."

"And where were the rest, Mr. Revere?" Adams inquired.

"In the streets, sir," said Revere.

"And how many were in the streets?" Adams asked.

Answered Revere: "More, sir, than there are stars in the sky."[97]

Christopher Gore, who was a delegate from Boston, assessed the dynamic by observing that Adams "is too old not to know that his dependence is more on the people than theirs on him."[98]

Hancock dragged himself out of bed and turned up at the convention on January 31, where he was carried into the hall, "wrapped in his flannels." He recommended nine amendments to the Constitution, among them measures guaranteeing the right to a jury trial in civil actions, restricting Congress's direct taxation power, barring Congress from creating companies that have exclusive advantages, and explicitly declaring "that all powers not expressly delegated to Congress, are reserved to the several states."[99]

Here Adams spoke at length for the first time in the convention. He declared himself "happy" in contemplating the benefits of Hancock's "conciliatory proposition."

"A proposal of this sort, coming from Massachusetts, from her importance, will have its weight," Adams said, predicting that Hancock's suggested amendments would help carry the Constitution to ratification in states such as Virginia, where conventions had not yet met.

"It is of the greatest importance that America should still be united in sentiment," Adams said. "It is essential that the people should be united in the Federal government, to withstand the common enemy, and to preserve their valuable rights and liberties."[100]

Rufus King, elated, wrote to James Madison that Samuel Adams had given "his public and explicit approbation" of Hancock's compromise plan. "We flatter ourselves that the weight of these two characters will assure our success," he wrote. Madison, upon receiving the letter, thought the news so significant that he sent a messenger to show it to Alexander Hamilton—"Read the above immediately," Madison wrote on the letter—with orders to return it to his own hands for safekeeping.[101]

On February 6, Adams submitted another amendment, foreshadowing some of the measures that were soon added to the Constitution as the Bill of Rights. It said, "And that the said Constitution be never construed to authorize Congress to infringe the just liberty of the press or the rights of conscience; or to prevent the people of the United States, who are peaceable citizens, from keeping their own arms; or to raise standing armies, unless when necessary for the defense of the United States, or of some one or more of them; or to prevent the people from petitioning, in a peaceable and orderly manner, the Federal Legislature for a redress of grievances; or to subject the people to unreasonable searches and seizures of their persons, papers, or possessions."[102] Adams's one-sentence amendment contained elements of what became the First, Second, and Fourth Amendments to the Constitution. After discussion, however, Adams withdrew his proposed amendment, paving the way for a final speech by Hancock in which the governor concluded, "As the Supreme Ruler of the Universe has seen fit to bestow upon us this glorious opportunity, let us decide upon it, appealing to him for the rectitude of our intentions, and in humble confidence that he will yet continue to bless and save our country."[103] Then, on February 6, 1788, the Massachusetts convention voted by the narrow margin of 187 to 168 to ratify the Constitution, with Adams among the yea-sayers.

The people of Boston celebrated the vote by ringing bells, firing cannon, and organizing a parade of mechanics and artisans, led by sixteen foresters with axes, and including seventy-three blacksmiths, forty-three shipwrights, seventy-five ropemakers, thirty mast makers, thirty sailmakers, thirty-four ship joiners, six mathematical instrument makers, forty bakers, fifty shoemakers, the federal ship *Constitution* on runners drawn by thirteen horses, and fifteen printers. The procession marched by the houses of those who had represented Boston at the convention, including Samuel Adams, and at each stop, the *Massachusetts Centinel* of February 9, 1788, reported, "testified their approbation of their conduct by three huzzas from the whole line."

The ceremony must have helped lift Adams's spirits. So, too, did the reconciliation between Adams and Hancock that had been effected by the convention. The relationship, long a complex one, had been thought by some informed observers to be beyond repair. On

September 2, 1783, Ezra Stiles had written in his diary, "The difference between M$^r$ Samuel Adams and Gov. Hancock is incurable. M$^r$ Adams exerts his utmost influence to bring M$^r$ Bowdoin into the Governors Chair in Massach."[104] But by after the convention, it had been cured; a French traveler in America, J. P. Brissot de Warville, visited Boston in July of 1788 and found Adams "the best supporter of the party of Governor Hancock."[105]

One of the points of tension in the relationship had been the financial gulf that separated the two men. Writing to Elbridge Gerry on September 9, 1783, Adams observed ruefully, "So fascinating are riches in the eyes of mankind!"[106] Hancock at times affected European hereditary practices, to the point of ordering a punch bowl and jug from China decorated with a family crest of a hand and three cocks.[107] This was not as exceptional as it may sound, or as Samuel Adams probably found it. Benjamin Franklin, too, had sealed his letters with a Franklin coat of arms.[108]

The exceptional one was Samuel Adams, who had nothing but contempt for what he considered pretense. The congressman and Harvard professor Edward Everett in 1825 spoke of the "incorruptible poverty" of Samuel Adams. "His family, at times, suffered almost for the comforts of life, when he might have sold his influence over the counsels of America for uncounted gold, when he might have emptied the royal treasury if he would have betrayed his country."[109] Indeed, another Boston patriot contemporary of Adams, Rev. Samuel Cooper of the Brattle Street Church, secretly accepted a salary from the French.[110] There is no evidence Adams succumbed to any such temptation.

To his wife on November 24, 1780, Adams had written from Philadelphia, "You are Witness that I have not raisd a Fortune in the Service of my Country. I glory in being what the World calls, a poor Man. If my Mind has ever been tinctured with Envy, the Rich and the Great have not been its objects."[111]

These egalitarian, nonmaterialist attitudes were echoed in at least some of Adams's family and educational religious influences. "Better is a little with the fear of the Lord, than great treasure and trouble therewith," said *The New England Primer.* Adams's father-in-law and minister, Samuel Checkley, said in a May 28, 1755, sermon, "Religion is an honour both to particular persons, and also to a people; it is so to persons of all orders and ages, high and low, rich and poor, old and young, yea, to kings and princes, rulers, and judges of the earth."[112] Adams's cousin Zabdiel Adams said in a 1782 sermon, "The supreme ruler of heaven and earth has required this. He will not allow one rule of administration for the poor man, and another for the rich. . . . As on the one hand, they should not take bribes and favour the rich; so on the other, an idle compassion should not lead them to befriend the poor, and indulge them in measures iniquitous, to the exclusion of a worthy part of the community from their just demands."[113]

The poverty of Samuel Adams was relieved only by the death in 1788 of his son. Dr. Samuel Adams was owed payment by the federal government for his services during the Revolutionary War, and the government made good on the debt.[114] That may have eased the resumption of the friendship between Adams and Hancock by narrowing the financial gulf between the two men, a gulf that was narrowed additionally by the marked diminution of Hancock's fortune by war, inattention, and mismanagement.[115] The death of Dr. Samuel Adams may have contributed to the reconciliation of the two Massachusetts patriots in another way, as well, reminding Samuel Adams that the bedridden Hancock, with whom he had worked so closely in the days before the Revolution, was not going to be around forever.

Whatever the motivation, the difference that Stiles had reckoned was "incurable" was cured sufficiently that when Hancock ran for reelection as governor in 1789, Adams ran for lieutenant governor and was elected. In his inaugural speech on May 27, 1789, Adams credited the citizens of the commonwealth for having "given the world another lesson, drawn from experience, *that all countries may be free,* since it has pleased the righteous Governor of the universe to smile upon their virtuous exertions, and crown them with independence and liberty." He made reference to the new national government led by George Washington that had been inaugurated in New York weeks earlier, expressing "a devout and fervent wish that gracious Heaven may guide the public councils of the great federated commonwealth, and the several free and independent republics which compose it." Adams concluded his speech by saying that he was "relying on the aid of Divine grace."[116]

Upon being reelected as lieutenant governor a year later, Adams struck a similarly pious tone: "May the administration of the Federal government, and those of the several states in the Union, be guided by the unerring finger of Heaven!"[117]

The lieutenant governor job, then as now, allowed plenty of free time. Adams used it to engage in his favorite pastime, writing about liberty and what he believed was its universal appeal. He engaged in a correspondence with his cousin John, then vice president of the United States under Washington, which was widely reprinted. The letters are framed in warm language that illustrates the long-standing friendship and collaboration between the two patriot cousins. That friendship was underscored in 1789, when Washington made a presidential visit from New York to Boston. John and Samuel Adams appeared together in the streets of Boston with the president, who was held in such popular esteem that the *Boston Gazette* marked his visit by publishing a poem describing him as "Godlike." Hancock was ill and sent Samuel Adams to Cambridge to escort Washington into Boston.[118] John Adams wrote to Abigail that seeing the president, the vice president, and Samuel Adams riding alongside each other on horseback "to be sure was a spectacle for the town of Boston."

John Adams commented that the remarks of the townspeople on the event "were very shrewd. Behold three Men, Said one, who can make a Revolution when they please. There Said another are the three genuine Pivots of the Revolution." John Adams remarked that he hoped the first of the observations was not so true as the last. The vice president wrote his wife that he hoped a painting would be made of the scene: "Of all the Pictures that ever were or will ever be taken this ought to be done with the greatest Care, and preserved in the best place."[119] If such a canvas was made, it is not known to have survived.

But the letters also contain evidence of growing substantive disagreements between Samuel Adams, a Republican, and John Adams, a Federalist who had returned from his long stay in Europe enthusiastic about adding an element of hereditary nobility to the American system of government. "The love of liberty is interwoven in the soul of man, and can never be totally extinguished," Samuel Adams wrote to John Adams on October 4, 1790. "However irrational, ungenerous, and unsocial the love of liberty may be in a rude savage, he is capable of being enlightened by experience, reflection, education, and civil and political institutions."

Samuel Adams spoke of the importance

> of inculcating in the Minds of youth the fear, and Love of the Deity, and universal Phylanthropy; and in subordination to these great principles, the Love of their Country—of instructing them in the Art of *self* government, without which they never can act a wise part in the Government of Societys great, or small—in short of leading them in the Study, and Practice of the exalted Virtues of the Christian system, which will happily tend to subdue the turbulent passions of Men, and introduce that Golden Age beautifully described in figurative language; when the Wolf shall dwell with the Lamb, and the Leopard lie down with the Kid—the Cow, and the bear shall feed; their young ones shall down together, and the Lyon shall eat straw like the Ox—none shall then hurt, or destroy; for the Earth shall be full of the Knowledge of the Lord.[120]

Samuel Adams believed in the existence of a natural aristocracy among men, but, he wrote John Adams on November 25, 1790, this aristocracy is to be found "Among Men of all Ranks and Conditions. The Cottager may beget a wise Son; the Noble, a Fool." He saw education as an engine of egalitarianism, able to "draw together the Sons of the rich, and the poor, among whom it makes no distinction." Education, he said, shows men "the moral and religious duties they owe to God, their Country, and to all Mankind." He said that "Even Savages might, by the means of Education, be instructed to frame the best civil, and political Institutions with as much skill and ingenuity, as they now shape their Arrows."[121]

If "even savages" could be educated, so, too, certainly then, could women. As lieutenant governor, Samuel Adams participated on a committee appointed by the town of Boston to develop a "New System of Public Education." In addition to reorganizing the Boston school system, the proposal, as a historian of education in Massachusetts, Pauline Holmes, has documented, "made the first provision for the education of girls in the public reading and writing schools." Not that they had achieved full equality; girls were to go to school only from April 20 to October 20, while the boys went to school year-round.[122] But it was a start. We can only speculate about Samuel Adams's motivation, but it may have had something to do with his daughter, Hannah, his only surviving offspring. There is other evidence, too, that Adams believed women could make useful contributions as writers; Mercy Otis Warren wrote him after the Revolution to thank him for spurring her to action. "When the balance of oppression hung heavily over this land, it was the indispensable duty of everyone to cast if but a single mite into the opposite scale. At the request of yourself and some others of your patriotic associates, I then hazarded to the public eye several political pieces which at that time were thought to have some merit," she wrote.[123]

The "New System of Public Education" included both religious instruction and the opportunity to opt out of it. It provided that schoolmasters teach the Westminster Assembly's Catechism that had been contained in *The New England Primer* of the era in which Samuel Adams was a schoolboy, "unless the parents request that they may be taught any particular catechism of the religious society to which they belong; and the masters are directed to teach such children accordingly."[124] This was consistent with the approach advised by Samuel's cousin Zabdiel Adams in that 1782 election sermon: "The *young* should not only be instructed at schools in matters of science, but also in the principles of morality; and *they* together with the *adult* should attend those places where they may hear the sacred obligations of religion pointed out and inculcated. To compel them to attend any *particular society* in preference to *any*, or *all others*, would be an infringement on the rights of conscience. But to oblige them to attend somewhere, is what the authority have an undoubted right to, and it is moreover a most benevolent exercise of power."[125] The new tone of religious pluralism afoot in Massachusetts was also on view when, in 1791, the first Catholic bishop in America, John Carroll of Baltimore, visited Boston and celebrated Mass. Governor Hancock is said to have watched, and there is no record of any objection by his lieutenant governor.[126]

While serving as lieutenant governor, Adams also participated in the debate over the posture Massachusetts should take in the brewing war between Great Britain and France, which had undergone a revolution of its own. When a ship in Boston Harbor, the *Roland*, was equipped with the aid of France as a privateer targeting British vessels, Governor Hancock's attorney general advised seizing the ship, but Samuel Adams, sympathetic to the French in the conflict, prevailed on Hancock to let it sail.[127]

# Chapter 9

# Governor

## *1793–1797*

*"We owe our unceasing gratitude to the Supreme Ruler of the Universe, who safely carried us through our arduous struggle for freedom."*

—*Samuel Adams, 1795*

WITH THE DEATH of John Hancock in office on October 8, 1793, Samuel Adams acceded as governor. Hancock had been one of the richest men in Massachusetts. To keep Adams operating in appropriate gubernatorial style, some men of means presented him with a personal gift of a carriage and "a pair of as handsome horses as there were in the city." But the gift did not fit Adams's humble style of political leadership. He had the coachman drive his wife and a friend of hers around town, and the seventy-one-year-old governor made the trip to deliver his inaugural address the same way he had always gotten around Boston, on foot.[1]

Adams's first address to the legislature as governor of Massachusetts, on January 17, 1794, reflected his religious passion. It began with a reference to "the Supreme Being" who, "in his Holy providence" had removed "our late excellent Governour Hancock" from life "as a sovereign act of God."

It was to that God, Adams said, that he looked for wisdom in performing his duties. He spoke to the elected representatives about "the laws of the Creator," which he said, "are imprinted by the finger of God on the heart of man."[2] He concluded with a plea for the importance of "a virtuous education," "calculated to reach and influence the heart, and to prevent crimes." Such an education, he said, will impress young minds with "a profound reverence for the Deity" and "will excite in them a just regard to Divine Revelation, which informs them of the original character and dignity of Man."[3]

If Adams was looking to education as a form of crime prevention, it was to counter a growing problem. Burglary and desecration of the Sabbath were apparently so common that in 1795 a pastor suggested hiring a guard to protect the homes and property of churchgoers on Sundays.[4]

Adams was elected governor in his own right in 1794, 1795, and 1796. He used the office to promote religion and liberty in speeches and proclamations. On February 19, 1794, he issued a proclamation designating April 17 "as a day of Public Fasting, Humiliation and Prayer, earnestly exhorting the Ministers of Religion to assemble with their respective Congregations on the same day." The gatherings were so that the people could seek God's pardon "thro' Jesus Christ, supplicating His Divine aid," and moving "to cause the Religion of Jesus Christ, in its true spirit, to spread far and wide, till the whole earth shall be filled with His glory." The proclamation also offered an insight into Adams's view of the French Revolution, which overthrew both the monarchy and the Catholic Church and was both more violent and more hostile to religion than the American Revolution. Adams prayed that God would "inspire our friends and allies, the Republic of France, with a spirit of wisdom and true religion, that relying on the strength of His Almighty Arm, they may still go on prosperously till their arduous conflict for a government of their own, founded on the just and equal rights of men, shall be finally crowned with success."[5]

In an address as governor, on May 31, 1794, he spoke of "the God of Armies, who favors the brave in a righteous cause."[6] In a speech on

June 3, 1795, he said, "we owe our unceasing gratitude to the Supreme Ruler of the Universe, who safely carried us through our arduous struggle for freedom."[7] Even toward the end of his career, when the memory of the Puritans was fading even deeper into the past, Adams invoked their legacy. In that same June 3, 1795, address to the legislature, he said, "Our ancestors, when under the greatest hardships and perils, they opened to us the wilderness, they took possession of, and left us for an inheritance, one of the best countries under the sun." He credited them with providing "the institutions of Public Worship, and the support of teachers in Piety, Religion and Morality." Those measures, he said, were wise, as demonstrated by "the great increase of our numbers & happiness."[8]

Adams had mundane duties as governor as well as symbolic ones. He wrote a letter to the governor of Rhode Island requesting the extradition of men charged with theft by a grand jury in Worcester County.[9] But he seemed most confident stressing religious duties and making broad statements of principle. On October 14, 1795, Adams, as he had after the victory at Saratoga in 1777, proclaimed "a day of Public Thanksgiving to God," recommending that on Thursday, November 19, prayer be offered that God "would graciously be pleased to put an end to all Tyranny and Usurpation, that the People who are under the Yoke of Oppression, may be made free; and that the Nations who are contending for freedom may still be secured by His Almighty Aid." And further, "that the Peaceful and Glorious Reign of our Divine Redeemer may be known and enjoyed throughout the whole Family of Mankind."[10]

A year later, Governor Adams offered a similar thanksgiving proclamation, declaring Thursday, December 15, 1796, as "a Day of Public Thanksgiving and Praise to Our Divine Benefactor." Adams noted that "we still enjoy the inestimable Blessings of the Gospel and right of worshipping God according to His own institutions and the honest dictates of our Consciences." He recommended "earnest Supplication to God. . . . That every Nation and Society of Men may be inspired with the knowledge and feeling of their natural and just rights" and "That Tyranny and Usurpation may everywhere come to an end." The proclamation concluded "God save the Commonwealth of Massachusetts!"[11]

On January 19, 1796, Governor Adams ventured, a bit cautiously, into foreign affairs, framing even that in moral terms. "I hope, my fellow citizens, that what I am now about to say will not been deemed improper," he said in a speech to the legislature. He went on to address the treaty John Jay had reached with Great Britain and that had recently been ratified by the United States Senate by a narrow margin. He declared that Jay's Treaty was "pregnant with evil," because "it may restore to Great Britain such an influence over the Government and people of this country as may not be consistent with the general welfare."[12] The treaty's first article was that "There shall be a firm, inviolable and universal peace, and a true and sincere friendship, between his Britannic Majesty, his heirs and successors, and the United States of America, and between their respective countries, territories, cities, towns, and people of every degree, without exception of persons or places."[13] Since the Britannic Majesty in question was none other than Adams's old foe George III, one can see how Adams might have been motivated to speak out. His opinion was shared by the faction that included Thomas Jefferson, who called the treaty "infamous" and "execrable" and "nothing more than a treaty of alliance between England & the Anglomen of this country against the legislature & people of the United States."[14] Washington defended it as preferable to another war with Britain, and Washington's allies, the Federalists, belittled Adams's objections. One, Christopher Gore, wrote to Rufus King that the speech of Adams, whom he described as "one of the loudest bawlers against the treaty," was received "with almost universal disgust."[15]

Washington's Farewell Address of September 19, 1796, was intended both to confront and dismiss such objections as Adams's. "Why, by interweaving our destiny with that of any part of Europe, entangle our peace and prosperity in the toils of European ambition, rivalship, interest, humor or caprice?" Washington asked. "It is our true policy to steer clear of permanent alliances with any portion of the foreign world." While the speech is known for its warning against entangling alliances, it was replete with Adams-style references to the importance of religion. Said Washington:

> Of all the dispositions and habits which lead to political pros-
> perity, religion and morality are indispensable supports. In vain
> would that man claim the tribute of patriotism, who should
> labor to subvert these great pillars of human happiness, these
> firmest props of the duties of men and citizens. The mere politi-
> cian, equally with the pious man, ought to respect and to cherish
> them. A volume could not trace all their connections with private
> and public felicity. Let it simply be asked: Where is the security
> for property, for reputation, for life, if the sense of religious obli-
> gation desert the oaths which are the instruments of investiga-
> tion in courts of justice? And let us with caution indulge the
> supposition that morality can be maintained without religion.
> Whatever may be conceded to the influence of refined education
> on minds of peculiar structure, reason and experience both for-
> bid us to expect that national morality can prevail in exclusion
> of religious principle.[16]

Washington would be succeeded in the presidency by his vice president, John Adams, who won the election of 1796. Samuel Adams received fifteen electoral votes from Virginia, an attempt by that state to make him vice president under Jefferson.[17] The political differ- ence between the cousins pained John Adams, who wrote to Abigail, "Nothing affects me so much as to see McKean, Whitehill, Osgood and even Sam Adams and such Men sett up in opposition to me. It gives Such a Specimen of Party Spirit as is very disgusting, very shock- ing."[18] The United States had recently signed a treaty with Tripoli declaring "the Government of the United States of America is not, in any sense, founded on the Christian religion," but when John Adams made his inaugural address at Philadelphia, where the national capital was for the moment, he stressed his own "veneration for the religion of a people, who profess and call themselves Christians."[19]

Perhaps inspired by Washington, or by his failure to win office in the national election, Samuel Adams made his own farewell address as governor of Massachusetts on January 27, 1797. He spoke of Washington but might have also been thinking of himself: "When a citizen so distinguished by his country withdraws himself from the Councils of the Nation, and retires to peaceful repose, it must afford very pleasurable feelings in his own mind, to be conscious of the good will of the people towards him." He spoke of how "piety, religion, and morality have a happy influence on the minds of men, in their public as well as private transactions" and made a plea for moral education, expressing hope that "our children and youth, while they are engaged in the pursuit of useful science, may have their minds impressed with a strong sense of the duties they owe to their God, their instructors, and each other."[20] Then, as he stepped down from the speaker's desk, his weakened, aged legs collapsed beneath him. He was saved from a crash to the floor only by being caught by the hands of his colleagues.[21]

In his final term as governor, Adams set a day of public fasting and prayer for Thursday, May 4, 1797, "beseeching" God "to endue us with all the Christian Spirit of Piety." The declaration went on to ask God "that the rod of tyrants may be broken into pieces, and the oppressed made Free," and to express hope of "speedily bringing on that holy and happy period, when the Kingdom of our Lord and Saviour Jesus Christ may be everywhere established, and all the people willingly bow to the Sceptre of Him who is the Prince of Peace."[22]

Adams's political opponents wearied of all the praying. Christopher Gore wrote a friend that it would be an occasion for a real day of thanksgiving when Adams finally retired: "After beseeching the Almighty to prosper our husbandry, and our fisheries . . . I will most devoutly pray, that his Servant Samuel may be relieved from the burthens of government."[23] It was typical of the scorn the Federalists had for Adams. Henry Van Schaack, a New Yorker who was living in the

Berkshires, described the governor as "an old debilitated antifederal wretch."[24]

Adams's religious acts as governor were hardly limited to proclamations. When the French wanted to have a celebration, Samuel Adams asked for it to be rescheduled for a day other than Sunday.[25] He refused to sign into law a bill that would have lifted Massachusetts's Puritan ban on theatrical performances.[26] Proponents of drama had argued that a theater in Boston would provide jobs for artisans and attract individuals who, looking for entertainment, "leave us for New-York or Philadelphia." Adams was not persuaded, though the technical illegality does not seem to have prevented performances from being staged at the Boston Theater, which opened in February 1794.[27]

As governor, Adams was also able to extend freedom to those who in other states would still be deprived of it. In the collections of the Historical Society of Pennsylvania is a "certificate of freedom" bearing the signature and seal of "His Excellency Samuel Adams Esq. Governor and Commander in chief." It said, "Be it known to all whom it may concern That William Newton, the Bearer hereof, a Black Man, has resided in the state of Massachusetts, for many years, & acquired legal inhabitancy, & had been taxed for the support of government, & is intitled to the Rights of Citizenship in the United States of America, having supported a good . . . character."[28]

And Adams carried on the tradition of inviting ministers to deliver sermons to the governor and other politicians gathered on election day. These sermons lasted for more than an hour each and were subsequently published as books at public expense.

On May 28, 1794, Samuel Deane, pastor of the First Church in Portland (now in Maine), delivered an election day sermon before Adams that compared the Americans to the Children of Israel. "Moses affords such an example to human governors. He was wont to apply for God to direction, in guiding his refractory people," Deane preached. He spoke of the "practical acknowledgment of God" as "the unquestionable duty of all men." He noted that "the subordinate officers which Moses was advised to constitute, were not only to be able men, capable of performing the duties of their station, but such as feared God." Civil rulers, Deane argued, "ought to be nursing fathers to the church of Christ." How so? "They may secure to Christians the enjoyment of the rights of conscience; prevent their being interrupted in the exercise of their religion; and enable Christian societies to raise contributions among themselves, to serve religious purposes." He prayed that the elected patriots "act in the fear of God, as they are accountable to him for their conduct. . . .

"Nothing," Deane said, "can do more towards the support of government, than the practice of religion and virtue." He prayed, "May persons of all denominations be induced, from evangelical motives, to the religious acknowledgement of the Deity, and the practice of universal holiness."[29]

On May 27, 1795, the election sermon was preached by Peres Fobes, pastor of the church in Raynham. He bemoaned the "numbers of my fellow-citizens who neglect public worship, perform journeys, and unnecessary business on the LORD's Day." The strength and glory of a free republic, Fobes said, depends on the virtue of the people. "Hence a republican form was the choice and fabric of God himself for his own people. Moses with a senate of seventy shared the government of Israel. . . .

"Virtue and religion above all are the strongest pillars of government," he said. "May heaven save us from the vortex of deism—that old harlot, lately re-baptized by the name of reason." He cited the case of William Beadle of Wethersfield, Connecticut, who in December of 1782 committed suicide "after he had murdered an amiable wife and four children." Claimed Fobes, "This appears to have been done in cold blood, and from the genuine principles of his bloated, benevolent deism!"

Of Adams, Fobes said, "Venerable with age, more venerable for his piety and unconquerable love of liberty, we behold him again placed in the first seat of government, by the United voice of his grateful country," and prayed, "May the fostering hand of heaven guard him, at this critical period of life, from every adverse event which might shake the few remaining sands, that now measure his important life."[30]

The election sermon in May of 1796 was delivered by Jonathan French, pastor of a church in Andover. "No form of government yet constructed ever was so congenial to Christianity, as a well regulated Republic," he said. "No religion, ever known, is so conformable to the genius of a free government, as Christianity." He warned that "a foe to GOD is not a friend to man," and complained of how it would be hard to integrate nonreligious people into the justice system. "What is the oath of an infidel, or of a man void of religion?" he asked. He called them "no better than solemn mockery."

He spoke of "the importance of intrusting the instruction of youth to those only, who are persons of religion and good morals; who will teach by example as well as precept."

He said that "no man, who is unfriendly to religion in profession or practice, ought to be intrusted with any important concerns in government." This was a stricter standard than that outlined in the federal Constitution, which Samuel Adams had voted to ratify, and which said that "no religious test shall ever be required as a qualification to any office or public trust under the United States."

French made reference to "our pious ancestors," who, "for the sake of purity of worship, and liberty of conscience, and from a hope of laying a foundation for the propagation of the Kingdom of CHRIST, left all that was dear in their native country, and planted themselves in this then barbarous land."[31]

Several of the election sermons preached before Governor Adams seemed to cater to the governor's humble economic circumstances in a way that might have been insulting had the remarks been made while Hancock was still in office. Deane, in 1794, spoke of "frugality" as a virtue and suggested, "Possibly our political guardians, without the enaction of sumptuary laws, may devise some means to check the rage for foreign superfluities, which is complained of by many as too prevalent, and of a pernicious tendency."[32]

Fobes, in 1795, said that widespread wealth led to moral decay. "Hardly can we find one period of prosperity, in the whole history of the Israelites, or of any other nation on earth, which has not been followed with a decay of piety, and a corruption of morals." He denounced what he called the "pernicious" influence of money on civil elections. "Money is frequently the most forcible logic, and he that carries the longest purse, will often carry the most votes," he said. He suggested there was "wisdom of God" in "the Jewish policy" of a jubilee every fifty years in which land reverted to its original owners, calling that policy "the great palladium of liberty to that people."[33]

Adams himself reminded lawmakers that education had an egalitarian purpose as well as a moral one. In his June 3, 1795, address to the legislature as governor, he spoke of the formation of private academies, which, while they had their advantages, were not without their drawbacks. Lawrence Academy in Groton had been founded in 1793, and Phillips Academy in Andover in 1778. The academies may, Adams said, "have a tendency to injure the ancient and beneficial mode of Education in Town Grammar Schools." "The peculiar advantage" of the grammar schools, he said, "is that the poor and the rich may derive equal benefit from them; but none excepting the more wealthy, generally speaking, can avail themselves of the benefits of the Academies. Should these institutions detach the attention and influence of the wealthy, from the generous support of town Schools, is it not to be feared that useful learning, instruction and social feelings in the early part of life, may cease to be so equally and universally disseminated, as it has heretofore been."[34]

As Adams aged, he sometimes had to use the carriage that he had declined when he walked to his inauguration. It prompted some political criticism from Federalists who charged that Republicanism is "disgraced" because Adams, "who used to boast that he could live on a turnip," has "set up his carriage."[35]

As for Fobes's warning that wealth led to moral decay, Adams suggested that he was not at risk, even with his inheritance from his son's death. Speaking to the legislature on January 27, 1797, Adams said that he had served Massachusetts during war and peace, "in various stations to the best of my ability, and I hope with general approbation; and I can say with truth, that I have not enriched myself in her service."[36] It was true; on stepping down from the governorship, Adams even returned the horses and carriage he had been given when he assumed the office from Hancock.[37]

# Chapter 10

# Passing of the Patriarch
## *1797 to the present*

*"I often asked myself, is this exactly in the spirit of the patriarch of liberty, Samuel Adams? Is it as he would express it? Will he approve of it?"*

—*Thomas Jefferson, 1801*

FTER RETIRING AS governor, Adams became less active. His writing hand was afflicted by a worsening of the palsy or essential tremor that had affected him even in the early 1770s. But his voice was apparently still strong. In 1789 he had formally transferred his membership from the Brattle Street Church to the Old South Church, where so many of the mass meetings during the run-up to the Revolution had taken place. A letter from the Brattle Street pastor, Peter Thacher, reported that Samuel Adams was "admitted to full communion with this church" in 1742 but had been congregating and communing for many years at the New South Church. "We do hereby recommend him," the letter said, "as he hath always (so far as is known to us) conducted agreeably to his covenant engagements." The church memory at Old South had it that Adams always walked to and from church with his family, but sat with the choir, singing, "often selecting the tune, and leading in that part of public worship."[1] He might have consulted *The New England Psalm-Singer* written by his neighbor and friend and sometimes musical collaborator William Billings, a one-eyed musical genius known for his capacious appetite for snuff.[2]

Adams lived in a yellow, three-story wood-framed house on Winter Street, next door to a bakery, spending many of his days in a ground-floor parlor before a fireplace edged with sky blue porcelain tiles.[3]

In the last issue of the *Boston Gazette*, September 17, 1798, Benjamin Edes mourned his going out of business and offered a valedictory for his newspaper in words that were in keeping with the career of his old columnist Samuel Adams. "Alas! The cause of Liberty is not always the channel of preferment or pecuniary reward," Edes wrote. He advised citizens to "trust to the Guardian Angel, which has conducted us through dangers, the most alarming and distressing." And he bid them farewell with an admonition to "Maintain your Virtue—Cherish your Liberties—and may The Almighty protect and defend you."[4]

Adams found other newspapers and newspapermen to fall in with. In 1798, Congress and President John Adams passed the Alien and Sedition Acts, a crackdown on the civil liberties of Republicans and on those sympathetic to the French. Massachusetts prosecuted the *Independent Chronicle* for criticizing the acts, and Samuel Adams responded by visiting the paper's bookkeeper in jail.[5]

Even in his fading years Adams posed a challenge to his opponents. The Federalist Fisher Ames wrote to Christopher Gore on November 10, 1799, expressing exasperation that "the captains of thousands" such as "old S. Adams," remained sympathetic to the French rather than the British, and skeptical of government and standing armies, even after the terror of the French Revolution and the passage of time since the American one had turned the general tone in Boston "decidedly anti-French."[6]

And even in Samuel Adams's fading years he was doing what he could to extend the legacy of the Puritan founders of Massachusetts Bay. On December 11, 1800, he wrote to Thomas Jefferson, then vice president of the United States, to introduce a twenty-two-year-old who "descended from that illustrious man Governor Winthrop, the leader of our first renowned ancestors, leaving what was called in those days a handsome fortune that he might plant the seeds of religious knowledge and liberty in this, as they then termed it, *outside of the world*. His descendants have sustained hitherto his principles and manners."[7]

Jefferson replied warmly: "A letter from you, my respectable friend, after three & twenty years of separation, has given me a pleasure I cannot express. It recalls to my mind the anxious days we then passed in struggling for the cause of mankind. Your principles have been tested in the crucible of time, & have come out pure. You have proved that it was monarchy, & not merely British monarchy, you opposed. A government by representatives, elected by the people at short periods, was our object; and our maxim at that day was, 'where annual election ends, tyranny begins.'" The letter concluded, "Adieu, my ever respected & venerable friend. May that kind & overruling providence which has so long spared you to our wishes, still foster your remaining years with whatever may make them comfortable to yourself & soothing to your friends. Accept the cordial salutations of your affectionate friends."[8]

On March 4, 1801, Jefferson gave his first inaugural address as president. It was a conciliatory speech to his political opponents: "Let us, then, fellow-citizens, unite with one heart and one mind. . . . We are all Republicans, we are all Federalists." It also seemed designed to reassure those who thought Jefferson, who had been vilified as an "atheist, deist, or devil" and who had edited his own version of the Christian Bible by emphasizing Jesus' moral teachings while deleting references to Jesus' divinity, was too much of a religious freethinker.[9] The inaugural address described Americans as "enlightened by a benign religion, professed, indeed, and practiced in various forms, yet all of them inculcating honesty, truth, temperance, gratitude, and the love of man; acknowledging and adoring an overruling Providence, which by all its dispensations proves that it delights in the happiness of man here and his greater happiness hereafter." He deemed "freedom of religion" and "freedom of the press" as among the "essential principles" of his government. And he concluded, "may that Infinite Power which rules the destinies of the universe lead our councils to what is best, and give them a favorable issue for your peace and prosperity."[10]

Shortly after that remarkable address, Jefferson sent Samuel Adams a remarkable letter:

I addressed a letter to you, my very dear & antient friend, on the 4th of March: not indeed to you by name, but through the medium of some of my fellow citizens, whom occasion called on me to address. In meditating the matter of that address, I often asked myself, is this exactly in the spirit of the patriarch of liberty, Samuel Adams? Is it as he would express it? Will he approve of it? I have felt a great deal for our country in the times we have seen. But individually for no one so much as yourself. When I have been told that you were avoided, insulted, frowned on, I could but ejaculate, "Father, forgive them, for they know not what they do." I confess I felt an indignation for you, which for myself I have been able, under every trial, to keep entirely passive. However, the storm is over, and we are in port. The ship was not rigged for the service she was put on. We will show the smoothness of her motions on her republican tack. I hope we shall once more see harmony restored among our citizens, & an entire oblivion of past feuds. Some of the leaders who have most committed themselves cannot come into this. But I hope the great body of our fellow citizens will do it. I will sacrifice everything but principle to procure it. . . . How much I lament that time has deprived me of your aid. It would have been a day of glory which should have called you to the first office of the administration. But give us your counsel my friend, and give us your blessing; and be assured that there exists not in the heart of man a more faithful esteem than mine to you, & that I shall ever bear you the most affectionate veneration and respect.[11]

Adams's last known piece of correspondence, which was widely reprinted in the press at the time, was a November 30, 1802, letter to an old friend from the Philadelphia days, Thomas Paine, whose *Common Sense* had helped awaken the colonists to the cause of independence. Adams pronounced himself "astonished" and "grieved" by the news that Paine planned to publish a pamphlet critical of faith. Asked Adams, "Do you think that your pen, or the pen of any other man, can unchristianize the mass of our citizens, or have you hopes of converting a few of them to assist you in so bad a cause?"[12] Paine issued a reply addressed to his "dear and venerable friend," but Adams never got a chance to respond.[13]

Samuel Adams died Sunday, October 2, 1803. The United States House of Representatives, meeting in Washington, resolved unanimously that its members would wear black crepe on their left sleeve for a month to mourn the man who "made an early and decided stand against British encroachment, while souls more timid were trembling and irresolute."[14] He was buried in the center of Boston at the Granary burial ground, where the graves of John Hancock and of the victims of the Boston Massacre lie nearby.

The occasion of the death found even Adams's detractors reflecting on his achievements. William Bentley, pastor of the East Church in Salem, had in 1794 described Adams in his diary as an "ungrateful wretch" who neglected John Hancock's widow after Hancock's death. Yet he traveled to Boston for Adams's funeral and wrote in his diary,

> No man contributed more towards our revolution, & no man left behind him less, distinctly to mark his resolutions, his peculiar genius & his communications. . . . He preserved the severity of Cato in his manners, & the dogmatism of a priest in his religious observances, for theology was not his study. Our New England Fathers was his theme, & he had their deportment, habits & customs. Often as I conversed with him, I saw always this part of his character zeal. He was a puritan in his manners always. . . . His

politics from two maxims, rulers should have little, the people much. The rank of rulers is from the good they do, and the difference among the people only from personal virtue. No entailments, not privileges. An open world for genius & industry.

Bentley's diary records both the funeral and the changed town that Adams left behind:

> The Flags were at half mast & minute guns were fired. All the bells tolled. The Cadets & Military Officers attended the procession, the Cadets under arms, did the funeral honours. The artillery were upon the Common & fired the minute guns. The Corpse was brought from the Mansion house in Winter street and was received by the procession. The Civil Officers went first & the Officers of the Town of Boston, then the Judicial Officers, then the Clergy, then the Military Officers & then the citizens. We passed by Frog lane, & Liberty Tree into the Main street, then down on the South side of the Old Town House into State Street, & upon the north side into Court street, & then into Tremont Street, & the Corpse was deposited in the Common ground.

After the burial, the Salem pastor visited "the New Catholic Church called the Church of the Holy Cross," complete with a painting of the Last Supper. The first Catholic Mass had been celebrated in Boston in 1788 to accommodate French Canadian immigrants, but now those Samuel Adams once called papists had practically a cathedral of their own.[15] Bentley also stopped at the Universal Church, which had a painting of the "Ascension," unlike the sparely elegant Congregationalist meeting houses but a sign of the direction in which many of them were headed. And Bentley, who remarked that in Boston "The value of real estate is increased greatly and increases constantly," also stopped at a new museum, featuring a wooden mammoth and "an old & a young alligator alive in his garden at this season, brought from the Southern continent of America."[16]

There was plenty of evidence that Boston's traditions and values were changing. But in the marking of Adams's death there were reminders, too, of the faith that sustained him. Rev. Thomas Thacher of Dedham published a tribute sermon that he had delivered the Lord's day after the funeral, in which Thacher praised the "sage and patriot—the important instrument of American sovereignty and independence," not only for his public acts, but for his daily morning and evening prayers, for his "reverence for the Christian Sabbath, and the altar of Jesus Christ, his compliance with every ritual derived from the authority of heaven." If Adams "preferred the mode of divine worship in which he was born" to other forms, it was not from prejudice, Thacher said, but "because he conceived our churches, when confined to their original design, were excellent schools of morality; that they were adapted to promote the future happiness of mankind; and because by experience he had known them a powerful auxiliary in defending the *civil* as well as *religious* privileges of America."[17]

And when the Suffolk County probate court considered Samuel Adams's will, they read his words: "Principally and first of all, I recommend my soul to that Almighty Being who gave it, and my body I commit to the dust, relying on the merits of Jesus Christ for a pardon of all my sins."[18]

On October 29, 1775, Adams, who was representing Massachusetts in Congress at Philadelphia, wrote to James Warren, then the speaker of the Massachusetts House of Representatives, "You must send your best Men here; therefore recall me from this Service. Men of moderate Abilities, especially when weakened with Age are not fit to be employd in *founding Empires*."[19]

It was a striking suggestion, because Adams, his hand shaking with palsy, proceeded to spend six more years serving in the Continental Congress in wartime, a period during which the Congress twice fled from Philadelphia, first a hundred miles to Baltimore, then a hundred miles to York. He helped draft the Massachusetts constitution and ratify the federal Constitution, which was in many ways modeled on it, and he served five years in the Massachusetts Senate, then four years as lieutenant governor, and then four years as governor. Not bad for a man of moderate abilities, weakened with age.

All these accomplishments came after Adams's role as the author of the 1764 "Instructions of the town of Boston," one of the earliest calls for protest against taxation without representation and for the colonies to join together. They came after all his articles in the *Boston Gazette*, after his role in publicizing the Boston Massacre and starting the Boston Tea Party, after creating the Committee of Correspondence of Boston, and after drafting the 1772 statement "Rights of the Colonists." They came after all those achievements that led historian George Bancroft to write that Samuel Adams's fellow signers of the Declaration of Independence considered Adams the man who had "the greatest part in the greatest revolution of the world."[20]

If Adams was so instrumental in achieving American independence and so influential even afterward, why then has his fame faded so badly with time? It is a long-standing problem. As early as the week of Samuel Adams's death his friends were warning of the risk that he would be "basely forgotten."[21] A few years later, in 1809, John Adams wrote to a friend that the portrait of Washington ought not to shove aside those of Samuel Adams and John Hancock in Fanueil Hall.[22] "Without the character of Samuel Adams, the true history of the American Revolution can never be written," John Adams insisted.[23]

One prominent nineteenth-century Massachusetts historian, Abner Cheney Goodell, Jr., spoke to the Massachusetts Historical Society in 1883 about "the cool presumption with which" Samuel Adams "has been stripped of his laurels to crown others."[24] Amid the resurgence of interest in America's founders in recent years, Samuel Adams has faded into the background, especially in comparison to his cousin John, so much so that contemporary writers often simply refer to "Adams," assuming that the reader will understand that the reference is to John, not Samuel.[25] Other founders have gained stature at Samuel Adams's expense.

This erosion of Samuel Adams's reputation can be overstated.

At that same 1883 meeting of the Massachusetts Historical Society, a judge in Boston who was chief of the Boston Public Library, Mellen Chamberlain, rose to defend Samuel Adams as "the greatest single personal force in bringing on and maintaining the struggle for independence."[26] Yale professor of history Edmund Morgan later echoed that contention, writing in 1953, "Probably no American did more than Samuel Adams to bring on the revolutionary crisis."[27] But Chamberlain and Morgan were exceptions rather than the rule.

Part of the explanation may be the relatively scant written record Samuel Adams left behind. George Washington's collected writings fill thirty-six volumes, thirty-eight if you include the two-volume index; Samuel Adams's a mere four.[28] John Adams recalls seeing his cousin in Philadelphia cutting up "with his scissors whole bundles of letters into atoms that could never be united, and throw them out of the window, to be scattered by the winds. This was in summer, when he had no fire. In winter he threw whole handfuls into the fire."[29] Samuel Adams urged his correspondents to exercise similar discretion, ending one wartime letter with the command: "Burn this."[30] One historian was so frustrated by what he termed an "exasperatingly meager" paper trail on Samuel Adams's early years that he turned hostile, diagnosing the patriot leader as a "neurotic" with an "inferiority complex."[31]

Another part of the explanation is that Adams never held national office as president or vice president or treasury secretary, as did other founding fathers such as Washington, John Adams, James Madison, Thomas Jefferson, and Alexander Hamilton. He never represented his country as an ambassador or as a minister to a foreign land, as Benjamin Franklin did. He was a Massachusetts man whose post-revolution service was to his home state rather than to the national government. But to see him strictly as a regional figure would be inaccurate. After all, he served seven years in Congress, most of it at Philadelphia, and through his relationships with fellow founders like Christopher Gadsden of South Carolina and Arthur and Richard Henry Lee of Virginia, as well as with Jefferson, John Adams, and

George Washington, he helped to join the colonies into the United States. His influence was felt as far away as London.

Another reason Adams's reputation has been tainted—without adequate justification—is his association with mob violence. In the popular imagination this linkage has extended well beyond the vandalism to the houses of Andrew Oliver and Thomas Hutchinson in August of 1765.[32] It is fair to say that Adams was no Gandhi, no adherent to nonviolence as a principle of opposition to the British as a colonial power. But neither was he a Robespierre, who enthusiastically drenched the French Revolution in the blood of counterrevolutionaries. There were three tar-and-featherings of customs informers during the revolutionary era in Boston, all of them spontaneous. As brutal and reprehensible as these actions were, there is no evidence that Adams or any of his prominent associates approved or participated in any of them.[33] The Town Meeting that Adams dominated publicly condemned the attack on Hutchinson's house. After the Revolution, Adams helped put down violent civil unrest in Western and Central Massachusetts. Adams came to understand that the use of military force would ultimately be necessary to win independence, and he did not flinch from that conclusion. But neither did he support wanton violence against civilians that would discredit the cause of liberty.

The negativity toward Adams has its origins, though, not only in the lack of documentation or the lack of national office or the association with mob violence. It has been motivated, too, by a feeling that the country has changed so thoroughly since his time that he has little to say to modern Americans. The changes in religion alone have been such that in Adams's home state of Massachusetts, once overwhelmingly Congregationalist, now about half the residents identify themselves as Catholic, and about 4 percent as Jewish.[34] The Massachusetts constitution Adams worked so hard to craft and shepherd to passage was amended in 1820 and 1821 so that top officeholders no longer had to declare they were Christians, and amended again in 1833 so that adherents of small religions were no longer taxed to support the Congregational Church.[35]

The Tories accused Adams of hiding behind a "religious mask," as Peter Oliver put it in his 1781 "Origin and Progress of the American Rebellion," written from exile in London.[36] Other critics acknowledge that his faith was genuine but fault him for his intolerance of disbelievers and those who did not share his Congregationalism. But one can differ with Adams's contempt for Catholics, object to his support for a ban on theater in Boston, and disagree with his approval of the taxation of non-Congregationalists to support the Congregational Church while at the same time finding much to respect and admire in Adams's religion. It was flexible enough to allow him to defend the deist patriot Thomas Young, to maintain a warm relationship with the relatively skeptical Thomas Jefferson, and to accommodate an alliance with the Catholic King of France. Yet it was firm enough to inspire Adams to engage and endure in the revolutionary cause, confident in his belief that God would protect Americans so long as they were virtuous, just as God had stood by the Israelites in their exodus from slavery so long as they were virtuous.[37] To dismiss Adams as the "last of the Puritans" would be to suggest that after him Americans ceased believing they were on a God-given mission to advance freedom. It would be a misinterpretation.

Yet another element in the explanation of the decline in Adams's reputation is the turn America took in the centuries after his death toward business and scientific innovation. In a country where inventors like Thomas Edison and Alexander Graham Bell were heroes, the inventor-founders such as Thomas Jefferson and Benjamin Franklin were bound to be beloved. In a country obsessed with amassing riches and building factories, the banker and advocate of industry Alexander Hamilton had a natural audience. Adams, who confessed he had little skill with business and was "wont to converse with poverty," who supported himself on a government salary and then on his dead son's military pension, seems an unlikely hero in a capitalist nation where many equate net worth with real worth. Even on this economic front, though, Adams's contributions are ample if underappreciated. While some may see Adams's aversion to extravagance and luxury as a vestige of Puritanism, others may see it as newly relevant in an age of unprecedented abundance and conspicuous consumption. And it was, after all, Adams's steadfast defense of property rights, the restraints he set on the powers of government, and his insistence that taxes be imposed by elected representatives of the people that have provided the conditions for American industry and commerce to prosper.

Finally distancing us from Adams is the puzzle of his personality. Edward Everett, a president of Harvard, governor of Massachusetts, and United States congressman, said in a speech at Lexington in 1835 marking the sixtieth anniversary of the battle there that "in all the excitement and turmoil of the anxious days that preceded the explosion," Adams was "of the few who never lost their balance," a fact Everett attributed to Adams's "religious tranquility."[38] What a wonderful phrase, "religious tranquility," and how paradoxical—a tranquil revolutionary. It was a characteristic Adams shared with his Puritan forefathers, of whom the Harvard historian Perry Miller has written that the characteristic of them that "remains the most difficult to evoke" was their "peculiar balance of zeal and enthusiasm with control and wariness."[39]

All of the founders are in some sense remote, separated from us by centuries and by the difficulty of evoking both the physical and political challenges they faced and the resolve with which they met them. Adams, because he was so influenced by a Puritanism that is no longer practiced, can seem one of the remotest of all. But he may not be as remote as had been thought. We can see Samuel Adams today when we see Americans for whom religion is central to their lives. We can see him when we encounter Americans who have higher values than material possessions. We can see him when we see what leaders and individuals around the world endure amid great risks in revolutions for freedom. These may not be qualities that correspond neatly to today's political factions, but they are aspects of the American spirit and, Samuel Adams would add, of the human one.

# Acknowledgments

THE ANSWER TO the question "How did you manage to write this book while also running a newspaper and taking care of two young children?" is that I have had a lot of wonderful help on all three fronts, some of it unavoidably interrelated.

This book and *The New York Sun* were born at about the same time, in early 2002. The ABC news anchorman Peter Jennings and his wife, Kayce Freed, were throwing a dinner party at their apartment in Manhattan, where an unlikely crowd had been assembled to celebrate the launch of *The New York Sun*. It was unlikely in that it included some of the most conservative journalists in the country—the editor of *The Wall Street Journal,* Robert Bartley, and of *The American Spectator,* R. Emmett Tyrrell, Jr.—and some of the most liberal, among them Frank Rich and Gail Collins of *The New York Times.* Conrad Black, who knew Jennings as a fellow native of Canada, and had helped to found the *Sun,* was there, as was my partner in the *Sun,* the paper's editor, Seth Lipsky, who it turned out had known Kayce Freed since their days as youths in the swimming holes of the Berkshires.

After dessert had been served one of the guests, Walter Isaacson, who was then running CNN, began to talk of his forthcoming biography of Benjamin Franklin. The conversation turned naturally to David McCullough's recent biography of John Adams. I piped in, "Well, the Adams *I* really like is *Sam.*" The crowd thought it was a reference to the beer and erupted in laughter, but after the laughter died down, Isaacson probed a bit, and when he realized that what I actually admired was the hard line Samuel Adams had taken with the British, he encouraged me to make a book of it. All of which is a long way of saying that Peter Jennings and Kayce Freed and Seth Lipsky should be thanked for sparking this project by bringing me within distance of Isaacson's encouragement.

It would have remained but an idea if not for the further encouragement and enthusiasm and intelligence and cheer and, not least, patience, of Sarah Chalfant at the Wylie Agency, who helped me craft the proposal that eventually was bought by Bruce Nichols at Free Press. Sarah was efficiently assisted by Edward Orloff. Bruce deserves thanks for seeing the potential of this project and, when he left Free Press, for placing it and me in the capable and equally enthusiastic hands of Martin Beiser, who improved the manuscript with his editing.

Jonathan Mahler and Josh Shenk offered me advice and encouragement and cautions early on in the craft of book writing, as did Amity Shlaes: "A book is just a collection of facts." Joshua Rosenthal and Andrew Sheivachman provided early research assistance. Mike Hill, who Jon Meacham was kind enough to connect me with, provided not only research assistance and his familiarity with the primary sources but valuable encouragement and wisdom on how to undertake such a project. Leon Neyfakh extracted Jeffrey Toobin's senior honors thesis on Samuel Adams for me from the depths of the Harvard library system. Hana Alberts provided research assistance in a pinch in the closing stretch. Also in the closing stretch, Jeremy Hockenstein and Joanna Samuels dispatched a private chef to cook a week's worth of meals, which I mention so that more friends of book authors will be inspired to intervene so constructively at critical junctures. Carl Darrow of the Greenleaf Press demonstrated a printing press for me, and, even better, allowed me to try demonstrating it for him, at Historic Deerfield in Deerfield, Massachusetts. James Koch, founder and chairman of the Boston Beer Company, shared with me during a beer tasting visit to *The New York Sun* his knowledge of a receipt for hops signed by Samuel Adams. Noah Phillips and K. C. Johnson provided helpful comments on a draft manuscript. Gary Shapiro helped with translations from Latin and Ancient Greek.

The historians upon whose work this book builds deserve a thank-you, too. Harry Alonzo Cushing's collection of Samuel Adams's works in four printed volumes made writing this one so much easier than it otherwise would have been, and William V. Wells's three-volume biography remains indispensable nearly 150 years after it was originally published. I have drawn on and enjoyed the works of David McCullough, David Hackett Fischer, Perry Miller, Edmund Morgan, Hiller Zobel, and the other scholars and writers whose works are cited, and Bernard Bailyn not only through his written works but through his Harvard College Core Course on the American Revolution.

I am grateful to all my partners at *The New York Sun* for giving me the freedom to complete this project while continuing to serve as the paper's vice president and managing editor. Seth Lipsky, Thomas Tisch, Roger Hertog, Bruce Kovner, Michael Steinhardt, and the rest of the merry band have created a newspaper that one does not want to take a book leave from. They, like Samuel Adams, understand the uses of newspapers in wars for freedom. My colleagues, including John Seeley, Martha Mercer, Robert Asahina, Nicholas Wapshott, Amity Shlaes, Pia Catton, David Lombino, and others too numerous to name, kept the place humming when I was away and always made me feel glad when I came back.

On the home front, Noah, Judith, and David Phillips, Liz Stoll, and David Schwartz helped care for Hannah and Naomi while I worked. My parents, Alan and Nina Stoll, did that, too, but long before that chose to settle in Massachusetts. They shared Samuel Adams's belief in the importance of "inculcating in the Minds of youth the fear, and Love of the Deity, and universal Phylanthropy; and in subordination to these great principles, the Love of their Country." In pursuit of this, my parents went so far as to start a new school for me, and to teach me in other ways that would ultimately attract me to the subject of this book. I am forever grateful to them; Samuel Adams would be proud to have them as citizens of his commonwealth.

Samuel Adams spent seven years of his life separated from his wife while in Philadelphia. He was starting a country; I was just writing a book. Still, I sometimes felt that his sentiment to his Elizabeth applied also to my Aliza: "I earnestly hope with you, my Dear, that our . . . Life is not always to live at this distance." What definitely applies is Amos Adams's praise of Elizabeth Adams for having "hold out with so much steadiness and calmness under tryals so grievous." My wife read the proposal and the manuscript and offered incisive comments, and she insisted that I give this book the time it needed. To her goes the biggest thank-you of them all.

# Notes

## Prelude

1. Robert Middlekauff, *The Glorious Cause: The American Revolution, 1763–1789* (New York: Oxford University Press, 1982 [1985]), 389.
2. to Charles Carroll, Sr., September 23, 1777, in *Letters of Delegates to Congress*: vol. 8, September 19, 1777–January 31, 1778, at http://memory.loc.gov/ammem/amlaw/lwdglink.html.
3. to Charles Carroll, Sr., September 25, 1777, in ibid.
4. Samuel Chase to Thomas Johnson, September 25, 1777, in ibid.
5. Charles Carroll to George Washington, September 27, 1777, in ibid.
6. Edmund G. Burnett, ed., *Letters of Members of the Continental Congress* (Washington: Carnegie Institution, 1921–1936) 2:497; *Journals of the Continental Congress, 1774–1789*, ed., Worthington C. Ford et al. (Washington, D.C., 1904–1937), Wednesday, September 17, 1777, at http://memory.loc.gov/ammem/amlaw/lwjclink.html.
7. The story of the bell's evacuation is told at the Liberty Bell Center in Philadelphia and in Charles Michael Boland, *Ring in the Jubilee: The Epic of America's Liberty Bell* (Riverside, Conn.: Chatham, 1973), 79–87.
8. James Lovell to Joseph Trumbull, September 23, 1777. "You will have heard before this reaches you that Congress left this City at 3 oClock in the morning of the 19th in Consequence of Advice by Express from Coll. A. Hamilton Gen. Washington's Aid de camp whose Horse was shot as he was passing the Schuylkill and one also of his Oarsmen was killed." In Burnett, *Letters of Members of the Continental Congress,* 2:500.
9. Thomas Burke to Richard Caswell, September 20, 1777, in *Letters of Delegates to Congress*.
10. James Lovell to Elbridge Gerry; September 20, 1777, in ibid.
11. John Adams diary, 28, February 6–November 21, 1777, *Adams Family Papers: An Electronic Archive*, Massachusetts Historical Society. http://www.masshist.org/digitaladams, entry for September 16, 1777.
12. Michael Novak, *On Two Wings: Humble Faith and Common Sense at the American Founding* (San Francisco: Encounter, 2002), 124. The beheading is also recounted

in Kenneth Silverman, *A Cultural History of the American Revolution* (New York: Columbia University Press, 1976 (1987), 279. John Cary, *Joseph Warren: Physician, Politician, Patriot* (Urbana: University of Illinois Press, 1961), 222, says that "some of the officers suggested cutting off the head, but one who was a mason put a stop to that indignity."

13. Mark Puls, *Samuel Adams: Father of the American Revolution* (New York: Palgrave Macmillan, 2006), 196.

14. William M. Fowler, Jr. *Samuel Adams: Radical Puritan* (New York: Longman, 1997), 146.

15. William V. Wells, *The Life and Public Services of Samuel Adams* (Boston: Little, Brown, 1866), 2:380.

16. On Adams's voice see ibid., 2:408–9.

17. Ibid., 2:491–93. The address also appears in Paul Lewis, *The Grand Incendiary* (New York: Dial, 1973), 303–4. Lewis says the address "was widely reprinted in the American press," though I have been unable to find any examples.

18. Middlekauff, *The Glorious Cause*, 384.

19. Burnett, *Letters of Members of the Continental Congress*, 2:544–45; Walter Isaacson, *Benjamin Franklin: An American Life* (New York: Simon & Schuster, 2003), 343: "the British surrender at Saratoga was a great turning point on the battlefield and—because Franklin knew that power on the battlefield correlated to power at the bargaining table—it was a great turning point for his diplomatic efforts."

20. *Journals of the Continental Congress*, Saturday, November 1, 1777.

# Introduction

1. Wells (*The Life and Public Services of Samuel Adams*) and Lewis (*The Grand Incendiary*) include it; Puls (*Samuel Adams*) includes it but edits out the religious references; Fowler (*Samuel Adams*) ignores it, as do James Hosmer, *Samuel Adams* (New York: Chelsea House, 1980; originally published 1898), Ralph Volney Harlow, *Samuel Adams: Promoter of the American Revolution* (New York: Henry Holt, 1923), John C. Miller, *Sam Adams: Pioneer in Propaganda* (Boston: Little, Brown, 1936), Stewart Beach, *Samuel Adams: The Fateful Years, 1764–1776* (New York: Dodd, Mead, 1965), and John K. Alexander, *Samuel Adams: America's Revolutionary Politician* (Lanham, Md.: Rowman & Littlefield, 2002). Part of the reluctance to include it may be a lack of clear documentation for the speech. Wells attributes the account to Perez Morton, a correspondent of Adams who became speaker of the Massachusetts House of Representatives and attorney general of Massachusetts. Parts of the speech are also quoted in Frank Moore, ed., *American Eloquence: A Collection of Speeches and Addresses by the Most Eminent Orators of America* (New York: D. Appleton, 1857), 1:322, a source noteworthy more for its early date than for its reliability.

2. Wells and Lewis include it; the other seven biographers leave it out. There is a controversy over who wrote the resolution. A footnote to the *Journals of Congress* for November 1, 1777, says, "This report, in the writing of Samuel Adams, is in the Papers of the Continental Congress, No. 24, folio 431." Wells says (2:493)

that the report "was from the pen of Richard Henry Lee," but that its language "reflects the fervor of religious sentiment animating each member of the committee." Mark A. Noll, in "The Contingencies of Christian Republicanism," in Thomas Engeman and Michael Zuckert, eds., *Protestantism and the American Founding* (Notre Dame: University of Notre Dame Press, 2004), 243, says the resolution was composed by Samuel Adams and credits Adams for "expertly" weaving together "Lockean, republican, and Christian themes into a single powerful statement." Noll also credits Samuel Adams for the resolution in his *America's God: From Jonathan Edwards to Abraham Lincoln* (New York: Oxford University Press, 2002 (2005), 84–85. James McClure, in *Nine Months in York Town* (York, Penn.: York Daily Record, 2001), 164, quotes the National Thanksgiving Foundation as saying that Adams "gave each of us the national thanksgiving tradition which every American has known since infancy. Thanksgiving could have died out a quaint New England custom, an accident of history, but Adams' determination started this—our most beautiful national tradition." There is no dispute that Samuel Adams was a member of the three-person committee that drafted the resolution. While the resolution's sentence is a long one for Adams's usually less windy style, and while the reference to the Holy Ghost is a somewhat unusual one, the references to "liberty, virtue and piety" and to education and religion are classic Samuel Adams.

3. *Continental Journal*, October 9, 1777.
4. *The Pennsylvania Ledger:* December 10, 1777, "From the rebel paper printed at Fish Kill, October the 16th, 1777."
5. *Journals of the Continental Congress*, Thursday September 11, 1777.
6. Ibid., Wednesday October 1, 1777.
7. Ibid., Monday, October 6, 1777.
8. Clifford K. Shipton, *Sibley's Harvard Graduates: Biographical Sketches of Those Who Attended Harvard College* (Boston: Massachusetts Historical Society, 1968), 14:638.
9. John Adams diary, 47, February 13, 1778–April 26, 1779, *Adams Family Papers: An Electronic Archive*, entry for February 11, 1779.
10. Gage's proclamation is reprinted in the *Essex Journal,* June 16, 1775, and at the Web site of the Gilder Lehrman Institute of American History.
11. John Adams diary, 11, December 18–29, 1765 *Adams Family Papers: An Electronic Archive,* entry for December 23, 1765.
12. Pauline Maier, "Coming to Terms with Samuel Adams," *American Historical Review* 81 no. 1 (February 1976): 36–37; Andrea Rich, *Rhetoric of Revolution: Samuel Adams, Emma Goldman, Malcolm X* (Durham, N.C.: Moore, 1970).
13. Wells, *The Life and Public Services of Samuel Adams,* 1:138; *The Writings of Samuel Adams,* 3:213, 4:351; Pauline Holmes, *A Tercentenary History of the Boston Latin School, 1635–1935* (Cambridge: Harvard University Press, 1935), 19–20.
14. Hosmer, *Samuel Adams,* 337; the sketch of Samuel Adams in Shipton, *Sibley's Harvard Graduates,* says, for example, "Among the New Englanders of his generation Sam Adams had preached and practiced hate to a degree without rival."
15. "It will be at once apparent to the reader that the writer feels that Israel, among the nations, should be regarded with reverence, even with awe, in times modern as well as ancient," wrote Hosmer in his *The Story of the Jews* (New York: G.P. Put-

nam's Sons, 1887), v. See Pauline Maier's introduction to the Chelsea House edition of Hosmer for more biographical information on Hosmer. Bernard Bailyn's *The Ordeal of Thomas Hutchinson* (Cambridge: Harvard University Press, 1974), 398–99, also discusses Hosmer, who wrote the only biography of Hutchinson that appeared before Bailyn's. The Hosmer quotes are from the Chelsea House edition, 337.

16. Wells, *The Life and Public Services of Samuel Adams*, 1:ix.

17. Hosmer, *Samuel Adams*, 336.


# 1 "Born a Rebel": *1722–1764*

1. http://www.bl.uk/treasures/magnacarta/translation.html.

2. Diarmaid MacCulloch, *The Reformation: A History* (New York: Viking, 2004), 499–503.

3. John Winthrop, "A Model of Christian Charity," in Paul F. Boller, Jr., and Ronald Story, eds., *A More Perfect Union, Documents in U.S. History*, 2nd ed. (Boston: Houghton Mifflin, 1988), 1:23.

4. Perry Miller and Thomas H. Johnson, eds, *The Puritans: A Sourcebook of Their Writings* (New York: Harper Torchbooks, 1963; originally published 1938), 1:208.

5. Harry S. Stout, *The New England Soul* (New York: Oxford University Press, 1986), 19; Miller and Johnson, eds., *The Puritans: A Sourcebook of Their Writings*, 1:213.

6. Stout, *The New England Soul*, 49.

7. G. B. Warden, *Boston, 1689–1776* (Boston: Little, Brown, 1970), 4–5.

8. Robert Middlekauff, *The Mathers: Three Generations of Puritan Intellectuals, 1596–1728* (Berkeley: University of California Press, 1999), 87.

9. "The Declaration of the Gentlemen, Merchants, and Inhabitants of Boston, and the Country Adjacent. April 18, 1689," in *An account of the Late Revolution in New England Together with the Declaration of the Gentlemen, Merchants, and Inhabitants of Boston and the Country adjacent April 18, 1689 Written by Mr. Nathanael Byfield, a merchant of Bristol in New-England, to his Friends in London. London 1689*, 11–18, in W. H. Whitmore, ed., *The Andros Tracts: Being a Collection of Pamphlets and Official Papers Issued During the Period Between the Overthrow of the Andros Government and the Establishment of the Second Charter of Massachusetts. Reprinted from the original editions and manuscripts. With notes and a memoir of Sir Edmund Andros* (Boston: Prince Society, 1868). *The Andros Tracts* attributes the authorship to Cotton Mather by citing Hutchinson's history of Massachusetts (1:381). Mary Lou Lustig, in *The Imperial Executive in America: Sir Edmund Andros, 1637–1714* (Madison, N.J.: Fairleigh Dickinson University Press, 2002), 195, says the declaration was "probably written during the course of the day by Mather and the other ministers in the Town House."

10. Byfield, in *The Andros Tracts*, 8. Lustig describes this as "possibly true," noting that the account was denied by an Anglican minister, but that immediately after the alleged escape attempt security on Andros was stepped up.

11. Lustig, *The Imperial Executive in America Sir Edmund Andros,* 203, 211, 214.

12. Fowler, *Samuel Adams*, 4.

13. http://home.earthlink.net/~anderson207/MatherIndex.html.

14. Andrew N. Adams, ed., *A Genealogical History of Henry Adams of Braintree, Mass., and His Descendants*, (Rutland Vt.: The Tuttle Company, Printers, 1898; reprint: Newburyport, Mass.: Parker River Researchers, 1984).

15. Wells, *The Life and Public Services of Samuel Adams*, 1:3.

16. The founder and chairman of the Boston Beer Company, parent of today's Samuel Adams beer, James Koch, told me in an interview that he was once offered for sale a receipt for hops signed by the patriot Samuel Adams, proving that Samuel Adams was a brewer and not just a maltster.

17. Wells, *The Life and Public Services of Samuel Adams*, 1:2–9; Miller, *Sam Adams*, 7–15. On the founding of New South, see Hamilton A. Hill, *History of the Old South Church* (Boston: Houghton Mifflin, 1890) 1:376–77.

18. *The New England Primer* (Boston: Printed by S. Kneeland & T. Green, 1727), facsimile reproduced in Paul Leicester Ford, ed., *The New England Primer A History of Its Origin and Development* (New York: Dodd, Mead, 1897; reprint: New York: Teachers College, Columbia University, 1962). The Bible passage is 1 Chronicles 28:9.

19. Samuel Eliot Morison, *The Intellectual Life of Colonial New England*, 4th ed. (New York: New York University Press, 1956), 80. The Zaccheus reference is to a character in the book of Luke, chapter 19, who "sought to see who Jesus was, but could not, on account of the crowd, because he was small of stature. So he ran on ahead and climbed up into a sycamore tree to see him, for he was to pass that way."

20. See also the work at the University of Virginia Library's Electronic Text Center, http://etext.lib.virginia.edu/toc/modeng/public/AesFabl.html, viewed August 14, 2006. Holmes, *A Tercentenary History of the Boston Public Latin School,* 258–59. The other four Boston Latin students who signed the Declaration are John Hancock, Benjamin Franklin, Robert Treat Paine, and William Hooper.

21. The full record of the Boston Latin School curriculum of 1712 is in ibid., 258–60. The curriculum makes reference to Cicero's "Epistles" and his "Offices."

22. *Letters of Marcus Tullius Cicero with His Treatises on Friendship and Old Age*, translated by E. S. Shuckburgh (New York: P. F. Collier & Son, 1909), 83–84.

23. Ibid., 98.

24. *Ethical Writings of Cicero: De Officiis (On Moral Duties); De Senectute (On Old Age); De Amicitia (On Friendship), and Scipio's Dream*, translated by Andrew P. Peabody (Boston: Little, Brown, 1887), http://oll.libertyfund.org/EBooks/Cicero 0265.pdf, 22.

25. Morison, *The Intellectual Life of Colonial New England*, 106; see also Holmes, *A Tercentenary History of the Boston Public Latin School*, 260.

26. http://bls.org/cfml/13tmpl_history.cfm.

27. James Grant, *John Adams: Party of One* (New York: Farrar, Straus & Giroux, 2005), 186.

28. Wells, *The Life and Public Services of Samuel Adams,* 1:5.

29. John C. Miller, *Sam Adams*, 5.

30. Shipton, *Sibley's Harvard Graduates*, 10.

31. Samuel Eliot Morison, *Three Centuries of Harvard* (Cambridge: Harvard University Press, 1936), 77–84.
32. Hill, *History of the Old South Church,* 1:505–7.
33. George Whitefield, *A Continuation of the Reverend Mr. Whitefield's Journal From Savannah, June 25, 1740, to his arrival at Rhode-Island, his travels in other Governments of New England, to his departure from Stanford for New-York* (Boston: Printed by G. Rogers, for J. Edwards and S. Eliot on Cornhill, 1741), 52.
34. Hill, *History of the Old South Church,* 1:507.
35. Whitefield, *A Continuation of the Reverend Mr. Whitefield's Journal,* 53–54.
36. Ibid., 56.
37. Ibid., 57, 71.
38. Thomas Prince, *Account of the Revival of Religion in Boston, in the Years 1740–1–2–3* (Boston: Republished by Samuel T. Armstrong, 1823), 9.
39. Whitefield, *A Continuation of the Reverend Mr. Whitefield's Journal,* 74.
40. Hill, *History of the Old South Church,* 1:509–12.
41. Ibid., 2:247–48.
42. Charles W. Akers, *The Divine Politician: Samuel Cooper and the American Revolution in Boston* (Boston: Northeastern University Press, 1982), 119.
43. Hill, *History of the Old South Church,* 2:247–50. See also page 254.
44. *The Writings of Samuel Adams,* 4:237.
45. Prince, *Account of the Revival of Religion in Boston,* 47.
46. Cole as quoted in Harry S. Stout, "Religion, Communications, and the Ideological Origins of the American Revolution," *William & Mary Quarterly*, 3rd Series, vol. no.4 (October 1977): 519, and in David L. Holmes, *The Faiths of the Founding Fathers* (New York: Oxford University Press, 2006), 27. Both Holmes and Stout cite Michael J. Crawford, ed., "The Spiritual Travels of Nathan Cole," *William and Mary Quarterly,* 3rd Series, 33 (1976).
47. Letter from John Adams to Abigail Adams, 26, January 1794, *Adams Family Papers: An Electronic Archive.*
48. *Salem Gazette,* June 30, 1815, 3.
49. The year has been converted to modern style; before 1752, the new year began on March 25, so Adams's family Bible contemporaneously records the date of the death of Samuel Adams the Elder as March 8, 1747.
50. Shipton, *Sibley's Harvard Graduates,* 6:74–7; see also Hill, *History of the Old South Church*, 1:396.
51. Wells, *The Life and Public Services of Samuel Adams*, 1:25.
52. Ibid., 3:428–29.
53. Isaiah Thomas, *The History of Printing in America*, ed. Marcus A. McCorison from the 2nd ed. (Barre, Mass.: Imprint Society, 1970), 255.
54. Wells, *The Life and Public Services of Samuel Adams,* 1:16–23, excerpts both essays.
55. Charles Chauncy, "Civil Magistrates Must Be Just, Ruling in the Fear of God," in Ellis Sandoz, ed., *Political Sermons of the American Founding Era, 1730–1805,* 2nd ed. (Indianapolis: Liberty Fund, 1998), 1:157
56. Warden, *Boston, 1689–1776,* 128, 136.
57. *The Boston Gazette,* October 27, 1755.
58. Ibid., March 20, 1753.

59. *Boston Evening Post,* March 15, 1756.

60. *Ethical Writings of Cicero,* http://oll.libertyfund.org/Home3/HTML.php?record ID=0265, viewed August 24, 2006.

61. A. C. Goodell, Jr. "Charges Against Samuel Adams," *Proceedings of the Massachusetts Historical Society* (1883): 218. Alexander, *Samuel Adams,* 9, puts the number at 5 percent. Samuel Adams himself, in his March 13, 1769, "Petition To the Freeholders of the Town of Boston," characterized the premium as "three & three quarters p Cent only," which is less than the 5 percent Alexander says, and at the low end of the range cited by Goodell, who was president of the New England Historic Genealogical Society.

62. Warden, *Boston, 1689–1776,* 115, 358.

63. Miller, *Sam Adams,* 59.

64. Alexander, *Samuel Adams,* 27, 53–54.

65. *The Boston Gazette,* April 9, 1754.

66. *The Boston Gazette, or Weekly Journal* October 22, 1755.

67. A list of the towns is in the *Journals of the House of Representatives of Massachusetts, 1768–1769* (Boston: Massachusetts Historical Society, 1976).

68. Captain John Bonner's map is reproduced handsomely in Samuel Adams Drake, *Old Boston Taverns and Tavern Clubs* (Boston: W. A. Butterfield, 1917); see also Warden, *Boston, 1689–1776,* 68, 96.

69. Mayhew's election sermon is reprinted in A. W. Plumstead, ed., *The Wall and the Garden: Selected Massachusetts Election Sermons, 1670–1775* (Minneapolis: University of Minnesota Press, 1968), 288–319.

70. Samuel Checkley, *A Day of Darkness* (Boston: John Draper, 1755).

71. Amos Adams, *The Expediency And Utility of War* (Boston: Fowle & Draper, 1759).

72. Dunbar sermon is in Sandoz, ed., *Political Sermons of the American Founding Era,* 1:208–30.

73. On Connecticut, see Alice Baldwin, *The New England Clergy and the American Revolution* (New York: Frederick Ungar, 1928; reprinted 1965), 86–87. The Virginia sermon, by Samuel Davies, is in Sandoz, ed., *Political Sermons of the American Founding Era,* 1:180–206.

74. John Brooke, *King George III* (New York: McGraw-Hill, 1972), 79.

75. Ibid., 83–85.

76. On Cooper's salary, see Akers, *The Divine Politician,* 60. On John Adams's house, see Grant, *John Adams,* 107. On size of Hancock fortune, see Miller, *Sam Adams,* 99.

77. *Boston Evening Post,* February 15, 1762.

78. Ibid., February 22, 1762.

79. Christopher Hibbert, *George III* (New York: Basic Books, 1998), 51.

80. Brooke, *King George III,* 63, 65.

81. Middlekauff, *The Glorious Cause,* 57; Edmund S. Morgan and Helen M. Morgan, *The Stamp Act Crisis: Prologue to Revolution* (New York: Collier, originally published 1953), 36; Robert W. Tucker and David C. Hendrickson, *The Fall of the First British Empire: Origins of the War of American Independence* (Baltimore: Johns Hopkins University Press, 1982), 87.

82. Arthur H. Cash, *John Wilkes: The Scandalous Father of Civil Liberty* (New Haven: Yale University Press, 2006), 78, 100–16.
83. Morgan and Morgan, *The Stamp Act Crisis*, 38.
84. Ibid., 39–43; Middlekauff, *The Glorious Cause*, 60–62. The Yale effort is mentioned in Warden, *Boston, 1689–1776*, 161.
85. *The Writings of Samuel Adams*, 1:1–6.
86. On the Albany Plan of Union, see Gordon Wood, *The Americanization of Benjamin Franklin* (New York: Penguin, 2004), 72–78, and Isaacson, *Benjamin Franklin*, 158–62. For an example of an exaggerated claim of the importance of the instructions, see Wells, *The Life and Public Services of Samuel Adams*, 1:48–49, which describes them as "containing the first public denial of the right of the British Parliament to tax the Colonists without their consent; and the first suggestion of a union of the Colonies for redress of grievances."
87. Wells, *The Life and Public Services of Samuel Adams*, 1:53–54. The text of Wells has her as age twenty-four at the wedding, though Wells 3:429 gives her date of birth as January 26, 1735/6, which would make her twenty-eight.
88. Beach, *Samuel Adams*, xii.

## 2 "Zealous in the Cause": *1765–1769*

1. House of Commons Information fact sheet, G11.
2. Morgan and Morgan, *The Stamp Act Crisis*, 97.
3. Ibid., 92–96; Middlekauff, *The Glorious Cause*, 74–76.
4. Miller, *Sam Adams*, 52–53; *Boston Gazette*, August 19, 1765.
5. Francis S. Drake, *Tea Leaves: Being a Collection of Letters and Documents Relating to the Shipment of Tea to the American Colonies in the Year 1773, by the East India Tea Company* (Boston: A. O. Crane, 1884; reprint: Kessinger Publishing), xxiv–xxv.
6. *Boston News-Letter*, May 22, 1766; Hill, *History of the Old South Church*, 1:461.
7. Ad from John Gore, Jr., in *Boston Post Boy*, October 6, 1766.
8. *Boston Gazette*, March 30, 1767; Arthur M. Schlesinger, "The Liberty Tree: A Genealogy," *New England Quarterly* 25, no. 4 (December 1952); 435–58; Alfred F. Young, *Liberty Tree: Ordinary People and the American Revolution* (New York: New York University Press, 2006), 347, 363.
9. Miller, *Sam Adams*, 52–53; *Boston Gazette*, August 19, 1765; Morgan and Morgan, *The Stamp Act Crisis*, 160–69.
10. Warden, *Boston, 1689–1776*, 166.
11. Bailyn, *The Ordeal of Thomas Hutchinson*, 35.
12. Middlekauff, *Glorious Cause*, 93; Abram English Brown, *Faneuil Hall and Faneuil Hall Market* (Boston: Lee & Shepard, 1901), 152–54.
13. Miller, *Sam Adams*, 53, 66–67; William M. Fowler, Jr., *Samuel Adams: Radical Puritan*, 66.
14. Alexander, *Samuel Adams*, 29.
15. Warden, *Boston, 1689–1776*, 168.

16. John Adams diary, 12, December 30, 1765–January 20, 1766, *Adams Family Papers: An Electronic Archive*; entry for January 16, 1766.

17. *The Writings of Samuel Adams*, 2:201.

18. The Bass letter, Henry Bass to Samuel Savage, December 19, 1765, is at http://boston1775.blogspot.com/search/label/Henry%20Bass, and at *Massachusetts Historical Society Proceedings* 44 (June 1911): 688.

19. *The Writings of Samuel Adams*, 1:60, 7–12.

20. Wells, *The Life and Public Services of Samuel Adams*, 1:70.

21. *The Writings of Samuel Adams*, 1:13–23.

22. Ibid., 1:23–26.

23. Ibid., 1:35.

24. Ibid., 1:27.

25. Ibid., 1:38.

26. Harry Stout, *The Divine Dramatist: George Whitefield and the Rise of Modern Evangelism* (Grand Rapids: William B. Eerdmans, 1991), 254, 262–65; John Gillies, ed., *Memoirs of George Whitefield* (New Haven: Whitmore & Buckingham and H. Mansfield, 1834), 181.

27. *The Writings of Samuel Adams*, 1:53, 55.

28. John Adams diary, 11, December 18–29, 1765, *Adams Family Papers: An Electronic Archive*, entry for December 23, 1765.

29. Middlekauff, *The Glorious Cause*, 117.

30. Gillies, ed., *Memoirs of George Whitefield*, 184.

31. Brooke, *King George III*, 171.

32. *Boston Post Boy*, April 21, 1766.

33. *The Boston News-Letter and New-England Chronicle*, May 22, 1766.

34. *Boston Post Boy*, May 12, 1766.

35. Anne Rowe Cunningham, ed., *Letters and Diary of John Rowe, Boston Merchant* (Boston: W. B. Clarke, 1903), 97.

36. Alexander, *Samuel Adams*, 40.

37. *Boston Evening Post*, June 2, 1766.

38. *The Writings of Samuel Adams*, 1:74–77.

39. Ibid., 1:86.

40. Ibid., 1:109.

41. Alexander, *Samuel Adams*, 46; Wells, *The Life and Public Services of Samuel Adams*, 1:138.

42. Wells, *The Life and Public Services of Samuel Adams*, 1:138.

43. David McCullough, *John Adams* (New York: Simon & Schuster, 2005), 15.

44. Arthur M. Schlesinger, *Prelude to Independence: The Newspaper War on Britain, 1764–1776* (New York: Vintage, 1965; originally published 1957), vii.

45. Wells, *The Life and Public Services of Samuel Adams*, 1:202–3.

46. Schlesinger, *Prelude to Independence*, 104.

47. Rollo G. Silver, "Benjamin Edes, Trumpeter of Sedition," *Papers of the Bibliographical Society of America* 47 (1953): 259.

48. Thomas, *The History of Printing in America*, 258–59.

49. Silver, "Benjamin Edes, Trumpeter of Sedition," 257.

50. Ibid., 258.

51. Schlesinger, *Prelude to Independence*, 92.
52. Richard Buel, Jr., "Freedom of the Press in Revolutionary America: The Evolution of Libertarianism, 1760–1820," in Bernard Bailyn and John B. Hench, eds., *The Press and the American Revolution* (Boston: Northeastern University Press, 1981), 59.
53. Schlesinger, *Prelude to Independence*, 97–98.
54. G. Thomas Tanselle, "Some Statistics on American Printing, 1764–1783," in Bailyn and Hench, eds., *The Press and the American Revolution*, 315–63.
55. Lockridge as cited by Robert M. Weir, "The Role of the Newspaper Press in the Southern Colonies on the Eve of the Revolution: An Interpretation," in Bailyn and Hench, eds., *The Press and the American Revolution*, 135–36.
56. Silver, "Benjamin Edes, Trumpeter of Sedition," 265.
57. Douglass Adair, *Fame and the Founding Fathers* (Indianapolis: Liberty Fund/ W. W. Norton, 1974), 386.
58. *The Writings of Samuel Adams*, 1:71–73.
59. Alan Dershowitz, *America Declares Independence* (Hoboken: John Wiley & Sons, 2003), 15.
60. *The Writings of Samuel Adams*, 1:153.
61. Ibid., 1:201–2.
62. Ibid., 1:135–51.
63. Ibid., 1:156.
64. Ibid., 1:175.
65. Ibid., 1:269.
66. Ibid., 1:277.
67. Ibid., 1:309.
68. *Boston Under Military Rule, 1768–1769 as revealed in A Journal of the Times*, compiled by Oliver Morton Dickerson (Boston: Chapman & Grimes, 1936; reprint: New York: Da Capo, 1970), 19, 39–40, 93, 106.
69. Ibid., x; Eric Burns, *Infamous Scribblers: The Founding Fathers and the Rowdy Beginnings of American Journalism* (New York: PublicAffairs, 2006), 148, 169.
70. *The Writings of Samuel Adams*, 1:145–49.
71. Patricia Bonomi, *Under the Cope of Heaven: Religion, Society, and Politics in Colonial America* (New York: Oxford University Press, 2003), 203.
72. *The Writings of Samuel Adams*, 1:203, 207.
73. Ibid., 1:212.
74. Ibid., 1:154.
75. Ibid., 1:202.
76. Beach, *Samuel Adams*, 147.
77. Akers, *The Divine Politician*, 35.
78. Cotton Mather, *Ratio Disciplina Fratrum Nov Anglorum* (Boston: 1726), 2, 66.
79. Jonathan Sarna, Ellen Smith, and Scott-Martin Kosofsky, eds, *The Jews of Boston* (New Haven: Yale University Press, 2005) 28–31; Nitza Rosovsky, *The Jewish Experience at Harvard and Radcliffe* (Cambridge: Harvard University Press, 1986).
80. *The Writings of Samuel Adams*, 1:135.
81. Ibid., 1:157.

82. Ibid., 1:271.
83. Edmund S. Morgan, "The Puritan Ethic and the American Revolution," *William and Mary Quarterly*, 3rd Series, vol. 24, no. 1 (January 1967), 13.
84. *Journals of the House of Representatives of Massachusetts, 1768–1769*, vii.
85. The text of the circular letter is in *The Writings of Samuel Adams*, 1:184–88.
86. *Journals of the House of Representatives of Massachusetts, 1768–1769*, 68–69.
87. *The Writings of Samuel Adams*, 1:228.
88. Ibid., 1:236.
89. Cunningham, ed., *Letters and Diary of John Rowe*, 171. Rowe's diary also reports the bowl weighs forty-five ounces and holds forty-five gills.
90. The Museum of Fine Arts in Boston's online catalogue page for this object.
91. The bowl is on display at the Museum of Fine Arts in Boston.
92. *The Boston Gazette*, August 22, 1768.
93. Douglass Adair and John Schutz, eds., *Peter Oliver's Origin & Progress of the American Rebellion* (Stanford: Stanford University Press, 1967), 41.
94. *Boston Evening-Post*, August 22, 1768.
95. *Boston Evening-Post*, September 19, 1768; also, *The Boston Gazette,* September 19, 1768.
96. Middlekauff, *The Glorious Cause*, 172.
97. *Boston Evening Post*, September 19, 1768.
98. *Boston Post Boy*, October 3, 1768; *The Boston Gazette*, October 10, 1768.
99. Shipton, *Sibley's Harvard Graduates*, 13:178–83.
100. *Boston Evening Post*, October 10, 1768.
101. Ms Sparks 10, vol. 3, p. 12, Houghton Library, Harvard University.
102. Beach, *Samuel Adams*, 172–73, makes a strong case for disbelieving it, writing, "the bombastic tone of the alleged statements is unlike Adams."
103. *The Writings of Samuel Adams*, 1:249.
104. Ibid., 1:250.
105. Bailyn, *The Ordeal of Thomas Hutchinson*, 71, 137.
106. *The Writings of Samuel Adams*, 1:319–22.
107. *The Boston Chronicle*, May 8, 1769.
108. *Journals of the House of Representatives of Massachusetts, 1768–1769*, 196, 113, 117.
109. *The Writings of Samuel Adams*, 1:424.
110. Ibid., 1:427.
111. Ibid., 1:349–54.
112. Warden, *Boston, 1689–1776*, 225.
113. John Adams diary, 24, September 15, 1775–January 3, 1776, *Adams Family Papers: An Electronic Archive,* entry for September 21, 1775.
114. *The Boston Gazette*, August 21, 1769.
115. John Adams diary, 15, January 30, 1768, August 10, 1769–August 22, 1770, *Adams Family Papers: An Electronic Archive*, entry for August 14, 1769.
116. The list is at http://www.masshist.org/cabinet/august2001/sonsoflibertyfull.htm.
117. *The Boston Gazette*, September 4, 1769.
118. Ibid., September 11, 1769.
119. *Boston Post Boy*, September 11, 1769.
120. *The Writings of Samuel Adams*, 1:380.

121. On the effect of the blow on Otis's mind, see, for example, Bailyn, *The Ordeal of Thomas Hutchinson*, 137, and Warden, *Boston, 1689–1776*, 223.

122. *The Writings of Samuel Adams*, 1:396, 420, 445.

123. Ibid., 1:428, 445.

124. Ibid., 1:392. On the St. George's Fields Massacre, see Cash, *John Wilkes*, 223.

125. *The Writings of Samuel Adams*, 1:447.

# 3 Massacre: *1769–1773*

1. The inventory, dated March 2, 1770, is in the Samuel Checkley Papers file at the American Antiquarian Society.

2. *Boston Evening-Post*, and *Boston Post Boy*, December 11, 1769.

3. *Mr. Bowen's Sermon on the Death of the Reverend Mr. Samuel Checkley* (Boston: Edes & Gill, 1770).

4. Hiller B. Zobel, *The Boston Massacre* (New York: W. W. Norton, 1970), 170–71. Zobel judges Adams's reply "a perfect example of the unctuous insolence Sam Adams sometimes affected when dealing from a position of strength." Others may not find it unctuous.

5. Memorandum on Boston Town Meeting, October 4, 1769, in Sparks New England Papers, Houghton Library, Harvard, cited by Matthew Seccombe, "From Revolution to Republic: Samuel Adams, 1774–1803" diss.; New Haven: Yale University, 1978), 53.

6. Zobel, *The Boston Massacre*, 173–177; Cary, *Joseph Warren*, 36, 92.

7. *The Boston Gazette, and Country Journal*, March 5, 1770.

8. Zobel, *The Boston Massacre*, 182–83.

9. Ibid., 184–87, 190.

10. *The Writings of Samuel Adams*, 2:100, 124.

11. Zobel, *The Boston Massacre*, 190, 194.

12. Testimony of massacre witnesses is in L. Kinvin Wroth and Hiller B. Zobel, eds, *Legal Papers of John Adams* (New York: Atheneum, 1968; originally published by Harvard University Press), 50–80.

13. Zobel, *The Boston Massacre*, 198–200.

14. Wroth and Zobel, eds, *Legal Papers of John Adams*, 3:1.

15. Letter from John Adams to Judge Tudor, *Salem Gazette*, May 19, 1818.

16. *Legal Papers of John Adams*, 2:401–10; the description of Preston is at Zobel, *The Boston Massacre*, 184.

17. *Legal Papers of John Adams*, 3:3.

18. Ibid., 3:7.

19. Ibid., 3:46.

20. *The Boston Gazette,* March 12, 1770.

21. *The Writings of Samuel Adams*, 2:10.

22. Ibid., 2:33.

23. *Legal Papers of John Adams*, 3:24.

24. *The Writings of Samuel Adams*, 2:141.

25. Ibid., 2:117.

26. Ibid., 2:83.
27. Ibid., 2:94.
28. Ibid., 2:143.
29. Zobel, *The Boston Massacre*, 214–15.
30. Seccombe, "From Revolution to Republic," 57, accused Adams of having "rejected the testimony of a black man upon racial grounds." And Shipton, *Sibley's Harvard Graduates*, 437, has Adams dismissing deathbed testimony of Carr "on the ground that since he was probably a Roman Catholic his testimony was worthless."
31. *The Writings of Samuel Adams*, 2:132, 2:146.
32. Stephen T. Riley and Edward W. Hanson, eds., *The Papers of Robert Treat Paine* (Boston: Massachusetts Historical Society, 1992, 2005), 2:480–81.
33. Hibbert, *George III*, 141.
34. *The Writings of Samuel Adams*, 2:9.
35. Akers, *The Divine Politician*, 118.
36. David Hackett Fischer, *Paul Revere's Ride* (New York: Oxford University Press, 1994), 23–25.
37. *The Writings of Samuel Adams*, 2:296–97.
38. Jules David Prown, *John Singleton Copley* (Cambridge: Published for the National Gallery of Art, Washington, by Harvard University Press, 1966) 1:83–84.
39. *The Writings of Samuel Adams*, 2:41.
40. Ibid., 2:182.
41. Ibid., 2:180, 184.
42. James Curtis Ballagh, ed., *The Letters of Richard Henry Lee* (New York: Macmillan, 1911), 2:198.
43. Richard Henry Lee, *Life of Arthur Lee* (Boston: Wells & Lilly, 1829), 1:12–15.
44. Ibid., 1:216–17.
45. *The Writings of Samuel Adams*, 2:231.
46. Ibid., 2:345.
47. Ibid., 2:231.
48. Ibid., 2:236.
49. Warden, *Boston, 1689–1776*, 246, describes Adams as "paranoid."
50. Beach, *Samuel Adams*, 139.
51. Carl Bridenbaugh, *Mitre and Sceptre: Transatlantic Faiths, Ideas, Personalities, and Politics, 1689–1775* (New York: Oxford University Press, 1962), 269–70. See also Bernard Bailyn, *The Ideological Origins of the American Revolution* (Cambridge: Harvard University Press, 1967), 95–99.
52. *Pennsylvania Chronicle and Universal Advertiser*, September 18, 1769.
53. Adair and Schutz, eds., *Peter Oliver's Origin & Progress of the American Rebellion*, 42.
54. Bailyn, *The Ordeal of Thomas Hutchinson*, 138.
55. Ibid., 21–23.
56. *The Writings of Samuel Adams,* 2:174–75; see also Baldwin, *The New England Clergy and the American Revolution,* 116–17.
57. *The Writings of Samuel Adams*, 2:192.
58. Ibid., 2:196.
59. Ibid., 2:248.
60. Ibid., 2:273.
61. Ibid., 2:275.

62. Stout, *The New England Soul*, 276.
63. Akers, *The Divine Politician*, 133; *The Writings of Samuel Adams*, 2:376–77.
64. Wells, *The Life and Public Services of Samuel Adams*, 1:378, 379.
65. Hutchinson to John Pownall, secretary to the Board of Trade, October 17, 1771, in George Bancroft, *History of the American Revolution* (London: Richard Bentley, 1854), 3:449.
66. Wells, *The Life and Public Services of Samuel Adams*, 1:389.
67. John Adams diary, 17, April 16,–June 14, 1771, *Adams Family Papers: An Electronic Archive*, entry for June 2, 1771; see also Wells, *The Life and Public Services of Samuel Adams*, 1:395–96.
68. Wells, *The Life and Public Services of Samuel Adams*, 1:399.
69. *Journals of the House of Representatives of Massachusetts, 1770–1771*, 16; McCullough, *John Adams*, 69.
70. Grant, *John Adams*, 108; John Adams diary, 16, January 10, 1771–November 28 [i.e. 27], 1772, *Adams Family Papers: An Electronic Archive*, entry for November 21, 1772.
71. Wells, *The Life and Public Services of Samuel Adams*, 1:389.
72. *The Writings of Samuel Adams*, 2:255.
73. Ibid., 2:336.
74. Ibid., 2:381.
75. *Warren–Adams Letters: Being Chiefly a Correspondence Among John Adams, Samuel Adams, and James Warren* (Boston: Massachusetts Historical Society, 1917, 1925), 1:11.
76. *The Writings of Samuel Adams*, 2:338
77. SA to James Warren, July 16, 1772, Gilder Lehrman Collection, GLC01215.
78. Richard D. Brown, *Revolutionary Politics in Massachusetts: The Boston Committee of Correspondence and the Towns, 1772–1774* (Cambridge: Harvard University Press, 1970), 56–57; Wells, *The Life and Public Services of Samuel Adams*, 1:496–97.
79. Brown, *Revolutionary Politics in Massachusetts: The Boston Committee of Correspondence and the Towns, 1772–1774*, 60–61.
80. *The Writings of Samuel Adams*, 2:349.
81. Brown, *Revolutionary Politics in Massachusetts: The Boston Committee of Correspondence and the Towns, 1772–1774*, 64.
82. *The Writings of Samuel Adams*, 2:352–53.
83. Ibid., 2:355.
84. Ibid., 2:355.
85. Ibid., 2:367–68.
86. Ibid., 2:372.
87. *The Pennsylvania Packet; and the General Advertiser,* March 1, 1773.
88. *The Writings of Samuel Adams*, 2:393.
89. Ibid., 2:394.
90. *Warren–Adams Letters*, 1:245.
91. *The Writings of Samuel Adams*, 2:293.
92. Ibid., 2:382, 386.
93. Ibid., 3:3, 12.
94. Ibid., 2:210.
95. *The Works of John Locke in Nine Volumes*, 12th ed. (London: Rivington, 1824),

4:390. Facsimile pdf edition downloaded from Online Library of Liberty, http://oll.libertyfund.org/Intros/Locke.php.

96. *The Writings of Samuel Adams*, 2:300. The quotation appears in *The Works of John Locke in Nine Volumes*, 4:422.

97. *The Writings of Samuel Adams*, 2:354–55.

98. Ibid., 2:385.

99. Brown, *Revolutionary Politics in Massachusetts: The Boston Committee of Correspondence and the Towns, 1772–1774*, 88; Peter Orlando Hutchinson, ed., *The Diary and Letters of His Excellency Thomas Hutchinson Esq* (New York: Burt Franklin, 1971; originally published, 1884–86), 1:15.

100. *The Writings of Samuel Adams*, 2: 422–23.

101. Ibid., 3:5.

102. Ibid., 3:34.

103. Ibid., 3:35.

104. Ibid., 3:33.

# 4 Tea Party: *1773–1774*

1. *The Writings of Samuel Adams*, 3:23–24.

2. *Massachusetts Spy*, May 6, 1773.

3. Benjamin Woods Labaree, *The Boston Tea Party* (London: Oxford University Press, 1966, 62–71.

4. Charles Turner, *A Sermon Preached Before His Excellency Thomas Hutchinson* (Boston: Richard Draper, 1773).

5. *Journals of the Massachusetts House of Representatives, 1773–1774*, x; *The Writings of Samuel Adams*, 3:44–45.

6. The text of the Virginia resolution is at http://www.yale.edu/lawweb/avalon/amerrev/amerdocs/va_res_corres_1773.htm, viewed August 27, 2007.

7. *Journals of the Massachusetts House of Representatives, 1773–1774*, 11–14.

8. Ibid., 26.

9. Bailyn, *The Ordeal of Thomas Hutchinson*, 227.

10. *Journals of the Massachusetts House of Representatives, 1773–1774*, 27.

11. Ibid., 26–29, 41, 44.

12. Wood, *The Americanization of Benjamin Franklin*, 144.

13. *Journals of the Massachusetts House of Representatives, 1773–1774*, 57–61.

14. *The Writings of Samuel Adams*, 3:46–48.

15. *Journals of the Massachusetts House of Representatives, 1773–1774*, 75.

16. Ibid., 74.

17. *The Writings of Samuel Adams*, 3:44.

18. Ibid., 3:59.

19. Labaree, *The Boston Tea Party*, 83.

20. Bailyn, *The Ordeal of Thomas Hutchinson*, 326.

21. The familial relationship between North and Dartmouth is given in Middlekauff, *The Glorious Cause*, 229, and in Labaree, *The Boston Tea Party*, 83.

22. *The Writings of Samuel Adams*, 3:62.

23. The text of the letter is in Wells, *The Life and Public Services of Samuel Adams*, 2:99–102, the quote is on page 100.

24. Labaree, *The Boston Tea Party*, 104.

25. *The Writings of Samuel Adams*, 3:62–67.

26. Warden, *Boston, 1689–1776* 277–79.

27. *The Writings of Samuel Adams*, 3:67–69.

28. Drake, *Tea Leaves*, 301.

29. *The Massachusetts Spy,* November 26, 1773. The Baghdad reference is cited in Labaree, *The Boston Tea Party*, 116.

30. Alexander, *Samuel Adams*, 79.

31. Labaree, *The Boston Tea Party*, 118–20.

32. Drake, *Tea Leaves*, xliv.

33. Labaree, *The Boston Tea Party*, 127 (quoting Hutchinson on the instructions to the captain).

34. L F S. Upton, "Proceedings of Ye Body Respecting the Tea," *William and Mary Quarterly*, 3rd Series, vol. 22, no. 2 (April 1965): 287–300; Alexander, *Samuel Adams*, 124.

35. Labaree, *The Boston Tea Party*, 133.

36. Drake, *Tea Leaves*, 355.

37. Ibid., lv.

38. Labaree, *The Boston Tea Party*, 137–41.

39. Wells, *The Life and Public Services of Samuel Adams*, 2:122–23.

40. Ibid.

41. Silver, "Benjamin Edes, Trumpeter of Sedition," 260. A letter by Benjamin Edes's son Peter recounting the events of the night is given in Drake, *Tea Leaves*, lxxviii.

42. *The Writings of Samuel Adams*, 3:72.

43. Ibid., 3:74.

44. *Journals of the House of Representatives of Massachusetts, 1773–1774*, 85.

45. *The Writings of Samuel Adams*, 3:78.

46. *Journals of the House of Representatives of Massachusetts, 1773–1774*, 104.

47. George H. Moore, *Notes on the History of Slavery in Massachusetts* (New York: D. Appleton, 1866), 137–38.

48. Petition for freedom to Massachusetts Governor Thomas Gage, His Majesty's Council, and the House of Representatives, 25 May 1774, From the Jeremy Belknap Papers, http://www.masshist.org/database/query3.cfm?queryID=589, viewed September 8, 2007.

49. Wells, *The Life and Public Services of Samuel Adams*, 2:138–39. William M. Fowler, Jr., in *The Baron of Beacon Hill: A Biography of John Hancock* (Boston: Houghton Mifflin, 1980), 165, says Adams probably collaborated on the speech.

50. *The Writings of Samuel Adams*, 3:104; Adams to Arthur Lee, April———, 1774.

51. The oration text is at http://www.law.umkc.edu/faculty/projects/ftrials/boston massacre/hancockoration.html and in Peter Edes, ed., *Orations Delivered at the Request of the Inhabitants of the Town of Boston, To Commemorate the Evening of the Fifth of March, 1770* (Boston: Peter Edes, 1785), 43–56.

52. Fowler, *Baron of Beacon Hill*, 166, says the speech "went through four local editions" and was "reprinted in several other American towns, making it one of the best-known polemics of the pre-Revolutionary period."

53. Labaree, *The Boston Tea Party*, 178; Brooke, *King George III*, 174.
54. R. C. Simmons and P. D. G. Thomas, eds. *Proceedings and Debates of the British Parliaments Respecting North America, 1754–1783,* Volume 4, January to May 1774 (White Plains, N. Y.: Kraus International Publications, 1982).
55. Seccombe, "From Revolution to Republic," 79.
56. *The Writings of Samuel Adams*, 3:93.
57. Ibid., 3:99.
58. Labaree, *The Boston Tea Party*, 195–96; Middlekauff, *The Glorious Cause*, 230–31.
59. *The Writings of Samuel Adams*, 3:102.
60. *Boston Post Boy*, May 9, 1774.
61. *The Writings of Samuel Adams*, 3:115.
62. Ibid., 3:128.
63. Bailyn, *The Ordeal of Thomas Hutchinson*, 264, 271, 273.
64. Hutchinson, ed., *The Diary and Letters of His Excellency Thomas Hutchinson Esq*, 1:152–83.
65. Bailyn, *The Ordeal of Thomas Hutchinson*, 284–85.
66. A text of the Quebec Act is at http://www.solon.org/Constitutions/Canada/English/PreConfederation/qa_1774.html, viewed September 9, 2007.
67. *Boston Post Boy*, May 23, 1774.
68. Gad Hitchcock election sermon 1774 in Charles Hyneman and Donald Lutz, eds., *American Political Writing During the Founding Era* (Indianapolis: Liberty Press, 1983), 1:295, 298, 303–4.
69. *Journals of the House of Representatives of Massachusetts, 1773–1774*, 264–65.
70. Labaree, *The Boston Tea Party*, 236–37; Wells, *The Life and Public Services of Samuel Adams*, 2:174–75.
71. Wells, *The Life and Public Services of Samuel Adams*, 2:177.
72. *Journals of the House of Representatives of Massachusetts, 1773–1774*, 288.
73. Gage quoted in Fischer, *Paul Revere's Ride*, 42.
74. *Journals of the House of Representatives of Massachusetts, 1773–1774*, 289–91.
75. Warden, *Boston, 1689–1776*, 296; Wells, *The Life and Public Services of Samuel Adams*, 2:182–86.
76. Wells, *The Life and Public Services of Samuel Adams*, 2:193.
77. *The Writings of Samuel Adams*, 3:153.
78. Wells, *The Life and Public Services of Samuel Adams*, 2:208–9.
79. Ibid., 2:21.
80. Ibid., 2:214–215; Grant, *John Adams*, 132.
81. John Adams autobiography, part 1, "John Adams," through 1776, sheet 16 of 53, *Adams Family Papers: An Electronic Archive*.

## 5 Congressman: *1774–1775*

1. John Adams diary, 21, August 15–September 3, 1774, *Adams Family Papers: An Electronic Archive*, entry for August 16, 1774.
2. *The Writings of Samuel Adams*, 3:158.
3. Isaacson, *Benjamin Franklin*, 282, 285.

4. Ron Chernow, *Alexander Hamilton* (New York: Penguin, 2004), 51–56.
5. Washington to Captain Robert Mackenzie, October 9, 1774, available at http://etext.virginia.edu/washington/fitzpatrick/.
6. Silas Deane to Mrs. Deane, September 7, 1774, in Burnett, *Letters of Members of the Continental Congress*, 1:18.
7. Burnett, *Letters of Members of the Continental Congress,* 1:65, citing Drayton's Memoirs, 1:165.
8. Galloway, Statement, September 28, 1774, in Burnett, *Letters of Members of the Continental Congress*, 1:55
9. Silas Deane to Mrs. Deane, September 5–6, 1774, in Burnett, *Letters of Members of the Continental Congress*, 1:11.
10. Ballagh, ed., *The Letters of Richard Henry Lee*, 1:111.
11. Letter from John Adams to Abigail Adams, September 16, 1774, *Adams Family Papers: An Electronic Archive*. The letter is also in Burnett, *Letters of Members of the Continental Congress*, 1:32–33.
12. *Boston Gazette*, September 26, 1774.
13. Burnett, *Letters of Members of the Continental Congress*, 1:xli–lxvi.
14. *The Writings of Samuel Adams*, 3:155.
15. Fischer, *Paul Revere's Ride*, 26.
16. The text of the resolves is in *Journals of the Continental Congress*, Saturday, September 17, 1774.
17. Ibid.
18. *The Writings of Samuel Adams*, 3:155–56.
19. September 25, 1774; *The Writings of Samuel Adams*, 3:157–59.
20. *Massachusetts Spy*, September 22, 1774.
21. Ibid., September 1, 1774.
22. *Journals of the Continental Congress*, October 6, 1774.
23. *The Writings of Samuel Adams*, 3:162–63; Wells, *The Life and Public Services of Samuel Adams*, 2:237–39.
24. *Journals of the Continental Congress*, Friday, October 7, 1774, and Monday, October 10, 1774.
25. *Journals of the Continental Congress*, Friday, October 14, 1774.
26. Ibid., Thursday, October 20, 1774.
27. Ibid., Friday, October 21, 1774.
28. Josiah Quincy, Jr., quoted in Beach, *Samuel Adams*, 313.
29. *Journals of the Continental Congress*, Wednesday, October 26, 1774.
30. Ibid.
31. J. Moss Ives, *The Ark and the Dove: The Beginning of Civil and Religious Liberties in America* (New York: Cooper Square, 1969), 323.
32. McCullough, *John Adams*, 83.
33. John Adams diary, 22, September 4, November –9, 1774, *Adams Family Papers: An Electronic Archive*, entry for October 9, 1774.
34. Ibid.
35. *Journals of the House of Representatives of Massachusetts, 1773–1774*, 282.
36. Sandoz, ed., *Political Sermons of the Founding Era, 1730–1805*, 1:328. On the life of Backus, the introduction in William G. McLoughlin, ed., *Diary of Isaac Backus* (Providence: Brown University Press, 1979), is a clear and concise guide.

37. Sandoz, ed., *Political Sermons of the Founding Era, 1730–1805*, 1:363.
38. Ibid., 1:344.
39. Ibid., 1:356–57.
40. Backus as quoted in *The Founders' Constitution*, vol. 5, Amendment I (Religion), Document 21, The University of Chicago Press. Stokes, Anton Phelps, ed. Church and State in the United States. 3 vols. (New York: Harper & Bros., 1950) available at http://press-pubs.uchicago.edu/founders/documents/amendI_religions21.html.
41. Ibid. The account is also in McLoughlin, ed., *Diary of Isaac Backus*, 916–17. John Adams's diary provides some additional detail, including the site and ending time of the meeting. John Adams diary, 22, September 4–November 9, 1774, *Adams Family Papers: An Electronic Archive*, entry for October 14, 1774.
42. *The Writings of Samuel Adams*, 3:159.
43. For date and weather of departure, John Adams diary, 22 September 4,–November 9, 1774, *Adams Family Papers: An Electronic Archive*, entry for October 28, 1774. There is also an account of Backus's meeting with Adams in Philadelphia in Mark A. Noll, *The Old Religion in a New World* (Grand Rapids: William B. Eerdmans, 2002), 78–79.
44. John Adams diary, 22, September 4–November 9, 1774, *Adams Family Papers: An Electronic Archive;* entry for November 3, 1774.
45. John Adams diary for November 8, 1774, ibid.,
46. *Massachusetts Spy,* November 3, 1774.
47. Wells, *The Life and Public Services of Samuel Adams,* 2:247.
48. Introduction to *Journals of the House of Representatives of Massachusetts, Vol. 50, Part 1, 1775,* ix.
49. Wells, *The Life and Public Services of Samuel Adams,* 2:261; *The Journals of Each Provincial Congress of Massachusetts in 1774 and 1775 and of the Committee of Safety, With an Appendix, Containing The Proceedings of the County Conventions, Narratives of the Events of the Nineteenth of April, 1775, Papers Relating to Ticonderoga and Crown Point, and Other Documents, Illustrative of the Early History of the Revolution* (Boston: Dutton and Wentworth, Printers to the State, 1838), 55, 57.
50. *The Journals of Each Provincial Congress of Massachusetts,* 86.
51. Wells, *The Life and Public Services of Samuel Adams,* 2:253.
52. *The Boston News-Letter,* November 24, 1774.
53. December 19, 1774, *Warren–Adams Letters,* 1:34–35.
54. Fischer, *Paul Revere's Ride,* 54–56.
55. *The Writings of Samuel Adams*, 3:170–71.
56. Fischer, *Paul Revere's Ride*, 51.
57. R T. Paine to Stephen Collins, January 14, 1775, in Hanson, ed., *The Papers of Robert Treat Paine,* 3:31–32.
58. *The Writings of Samuel Adams,* 3:173.
59. Fischer, *Paul Revere's Ride,* 62–63.
60. Ibid., 32, 67, 70, 72–74.
61. Ballagh, ed., *The Letters of Richard Henry Lee,* 1:127–28.
62. *The Writings of Samuel Adams,* 3:196–97.
63. Ibid., 3:197.
64. Ibid., 3:206.

65. Wells, *The Life and Public Services of Samuel Adams*, 2:278. The significance of the toga, and of the address, is discussed further by Eran Shalev in "Dr. Warren's Ciceronian Toga: Performing Rebellion in Revolutionary Boston," www. common-place.org, vol.7, no. 2, January 2007.
66. The text of the oration is at http://ahp.gatech.edu/boston_mass_orat_1775.html, viewed September 18, 2007, and in Edes, ed., *Orations Delivered at the Request of the Inhabitants of the Town of Boston, To Commemorate the Evening of the Fifth of March, 1770*, 57–72.
67. Warden, *Boston, 1689–1776*, 206–7.
68. *The Writings of Samuel Adams*, 3:207.
69. Ibid., 3:199–200.
70. Ibid., 3:199.

# 6 Lexington and Concord: *1775*

1. Fischer, *Paul Revere's Ride*, 310. "Appendix G, "The Royal Navy in America, January 1, 1775—Admiral Samuel Graves's 'List of the North American Squadron, on the 1st of January 1775,'" attributed to Graves Papers, Gay Transcripts, Massachusetts Historical Society.
2. "To Jonathan Augustine Washington," March 21, 1775, *The Writings of Samuel Adams*, 3:211.
3. *The Journals of Each Provincial Congress*, 109–10.
4. *The Writings of Samuel Adams*, 3:213.
5. *Journals of the House of Representatives of Massachusetts, Vol. 51, Part 1, 1775*, 148–49.
6. Wells, *The Life and Public Services of Samuel Adams*, 2:285; *The Journals of Each Provincial Congress*, 135.
7. *The Journals of Each Provincial Congress*, 136–37.
8. Ibid., 144–64.
9. Warden, *Boston, 1689–1776*, 314–15.
10. Fischer, *Paul Revere's Ride*, 76.
11. Warden, *Boston, 1689–1776*, 305, 314–15.
12. Fischer, *Paul Revere's Ride*, 88–91.
13. Ibid., 95, 97.
14. Ibid., 105–9.
15. Ibid., 110–11, 132–34.
16. Ibid., 151, 159.
17. Ibid., 80.
18. Wells, *The Life and Public Services of Samuel Adams*, 2:292.
19. Fischer, *Paul Revere's Ride*, 320–21.
20. Ibid., 273, 205.
21. Ibid., 176–83; Wells, *The Life and Public Services of Samuel Adams*, 2:294.
22. John Adams autobiography, part 1, "John Adams," through 1776, sheet 18 of 53, *Adams Family Papers: An Electronic Archive*.

23. Wells, *The Life and Public Services of Samuel Adams*, 2:296–98; *Journals of Each Provincial Congress*, 170.

24. Peter Force, ed., *American Archives*, 4th series, 2:428–29, "To the Inhabitants of New York," April 28, 1775.

25. John Adams autobiography, part 1, "John Adams," through 1776, sheet 18 of 53, *Adams Family Papers: An Electronic Archive*.

26. Andrew Oliver, ed., *The Journal of Samuel Curwen, Loyalist* (Cambridge: Harvard University Press, 1972), 1:8, entry for Wednesday, May 10, 1775.

27. *The Writings of Samuel Adams*, 3:355–56.

28. Ibid., 3:214–17.

29. Silver, "Benjamin Edes, Trumpeter of Sedition," 262.

30. *The Journals of Each Provincial Congress of Massachusetts*, 683.

31. Helen R. Pinkney, *Christopher Gore, Federalist of Massachusetts* (Waltham, Mass.: Gore Place Society, 1969), 11.

32. Force, *American Archives*, 4th series, 2:386, "Extract of a Letter from London to a Gentleman in Massachusetts, Dated April 25, 1775."

33. *The Writings of Samuel Adams*, 3:214–15.

## 7 Congressman, II: *1775–1779*

1. *Journals of the Continental Congress*, May 10, 1775, May 13, 1775, May 18, 1775.

2. Langdon's sermon is reprinted in John Wingate Thornton, *The Pulpit of the American Revolution* (Boston: D. Lothrop & Co., 1876). The quotes are from pp. 237, 239. The sermon and the concept of the "Jewish Republic" are also covered in Stout, *The New England Soul*, 293–95.

3. *Journals of the Continental Congress*, May 11, 1775.

4. Ibid., May 15, 1775.

5. Ibid., May 26, 1775.

6. Ibid., May 27, 1775.

7. Ibid., May 29, 1775.

8. Ibid., May 29, 1775.

9. Ibid., May 25, 1775.

10. Burnett, ed., *Letters of Members of the Continental Congress*, 1:136.

11. *Journals of the Continental Congress*, May 27, 1775.

12. Ibid., June 21, 1775.

13. A letter from Dr. John Morgan of New York, June 25, 1776, was addressed to Samuel Adams, "Member of the Medical Committee of Congress," and described Washington's decision not to inoculate his troops against smallpox but instead to quarantine those who fell ill with the disease in a special "small-pox Hospital." Force, *American Archives*, 4th Series, 6: 1069–70. Another letter, from Samuel Chase to General Gates, August 9, 1776, reports, "Mr. S. Adams showed me your letter to him from Tyonderoga, of the 17th of July, wherein you write, 'I desire, if Chase is returned to Congress, he may know how much I have been *deceived* and *disappointed* in being removed from a place where I might have done the public

service, and fixed in a situation where it is exceedingly doubtful if it will be in my power to be more than the wretched spectator of a ruined army.'" Force, *American Archives*, 5th series, 1:864. Richard Smith's diary of March 26, 1776, reports Samuel Adams on a committee to attend to funeral arrangements for Governor Samuel Ward of Rhode Island, a delegate to Congress who had died of smallpox. Burnett, ed., *Letters of Members of the Continental Congress*, 1:409.

14. Force, *American Archives*, 5th Series, 3:1583–84.
15. *Warren–Adams Letters*, 1:54–55
16. *Journals of the Continental Congress,* June 12, 1775.
17. Wells, *The Life and Public Services of Samuel Adams*, 2:318.
18. Burnett, ed., *Letters of Members of the Continental Congress*, 1:145.
19. *The Writings of Samuel Adams*, 3:220.
20. A March 18, 1777, letter on the subject from SA to Miss Mercy Scollay is at http://www.masshist.org/objects/2006june.cfm, discussing whether to keep the children together or to send one of the boys off to Dummers Academy, a Massachusetts boarding school that had been founded in 1763 and remains in existence today as the Governor's Academy. A copy of another letter from SA to Mercy Scollay on the topic, dated February 27, 1779, is at Harvard's Houghton Library Ms Sparks 49, p. 164. In that letter, Adams urges Scollay to "instill into their young minds the principles of piety and virtue, and thereby lay a foundation for their being hereafter useful and happy."
21. Gage's proclamation is reprinted in the *Essex Journal*, June 16, 1775, and at the Web site of the Gilder Lehrman Institute of American History.
22. *The Writings of Samuel Adams*, 3:220–21.
23. McCullough, *John Adams*, 83; *The Writings of Samuel Adams*, 3:223.
24. John Adams diary, 22B, April 30–December 1775, January–February 1777, *Adams Family Papers: An Electronic Archive*, entries for August 28, 1775, and December 9, 1775.
25. John Adams autobiography, part 1, "John Adams," through 1776, sheets 20 and 21 of 53, *Adams Family Papers: An Electronic Archive*.
26. R. T. Paine to Joseph Hawley, January 1, 1776, in Hanson, ed., *The Papers of Robert Treat Paine*, 123–25.
27. Akers, *The Divine Politician*, 316.
28. Burnett, ed., *Letters of Members of the Continental Congress*, 1:394.
29. *Journals of the Continental Congress*, Wednesday, June 21, 1775.
30. *The Writings of Samuel Adams*, 3:218–19.
31. *Journals of the Continental Congress*, Tuesday, July 25, 1775.
32. *Massachusetts Spy*, August 16, 1775.
33. *Journals of the Continental Congress*, Tuesday, August 1, 1775.
34. Wells, *The Life and Public Services of Samuel Adams*, 2:320.
35. *The Writings of Samuel Adams*, 3:227.
36. George Washington, November 5, 1775, General Orders, George Washington Papers at the Library of Congress, 1741–1799, Series 3g, Varick Transcripts, Letterbook 1, Image 108 of 419, accessible online via http://memory.loc.gov/ammem/gwhtml/gwhome.html. The letter is also mentioned in Ives, *The Ark and the Dove*, 317–18.
37. *Journals of the House of Representatives of Massachusetts, 1775*, 3–7.
38. Ibid., 81.

39. *The Writings of Samuel Adams*, 3:226.
40. Ibid., 3:217.
41. Amos Adams to SA, July 18, 1775, Samuel Adams Papers, Manuscripts and Archives Division, New York Public Library Astor, Lenox and Tilden Foundations.
42. *The Writings of Samuel Adams*, 3:227, 229.
43. Ibid., 3:228.
44. Ibid., 3:239–40.
45. Tara Dirst and Allan Kulikoff, "Was Benjamin Church a Traitor?," www.common-place.org, vol. 6, no. 1, October 2005.
46. *The Writings of Samuel Adams*, 3:236–37.
47. Cash, *John Wilkes*, 322.
48. Simmons and Thomas, eds. *Proceedings and Debates of the British Parliaments Respecting North America, 1754–1783,* Vol. 4, April 1775 to May 1776, 291.
49. Cash, *John Wilkes*, 316–24.
50. *Proceedings and Debates of the British Parliaments Respecting North America 1754–1783*, Vol. 6, April 1775 to May 1776, 295–96.
51. Ibid., 371.
52. *The Writings of Samuel Adams*, 3:234.
53. *Journals of the Continental Congress*, Monday, December 11, 1775.
54. *The Writings of Samuel Adams*, 3:244.
55. William Duane, ed., *Extracts from the Diary of Christopher Marshall, 1774–1781* (New York: New York Times & Arno Press, 1969), 43.
56. Ibid., 49.
57. Ibid., 51–53.
58. *The Writings of Samuel Adams*, 3:247.
59. Craig Nelson, *Thomas Paine: Enlightenment, Revolution, and the Birth of Modern Nations* (New York: Viking, 2006), 38–45.
60. Rush memoir quoted in ibid., 79.
61. Nelson, *Thomas Paine*, 176.
62. William Checkley to SA, February 26, 1776, Samuel Adams Papers, New York Public Library.
63. Warren to SA, February 14, 1776, *Warren–Adams Letters*, 434.
64. Bailyn, *The Ideological Origins of the American Revolution*, 18.
65. Nelson, *Thomas Paine*, 92.
66. *The Writings of Samuel Adams*, 3:261.
67. Ibid., 3:264.
68. Ibid., 3:265–66.
69. The text of the letter is available at http://etext.virginia.edu/washington/fitzpatrick/.
70. *Journals of the Continental Congress*, January 15 and 16, 1776; Wells, *The Life and Public Services of Samuel Adams*, 2:344.
71. *Journals of the Continental Congress*, June 2, 1778.
72. Duane, ed., *Extracts from the Diary of Christopher Marshall*, 61.
73. Washington to Samuel Adams, March 22, 1776, text is online at http://etext.virginia.edu/toc/modeng/public/WasFi04.html.
74. *The Writings of Samuel Adams*, 3:281.
75. Ibid., 3:273.

76. SA to Warren, April 16, 1776, in *Warren–Adams Letters*, 1:224.
77. *The Writings of Samuel Adams*, 3:286.
78. Cushing renders the name as "Moulton."
79. *The Writings of Samuel Adams*, 3:293.
80. Wells, *The Life and Public Services of Samuel Adams*, 2:380.
81. Justin Winsor, *The Memorial History of Boston* (Boston: Ticknor, 1880–1881), 3:159.
82. *The Writings of Samuel Adams*, 3:276.
83. *Journals of the Continental Congress*, June 7, 1776.
84. Garry Wills, *Inventing America: Jefferson's Declaration of Independence* (New York: Doubleday, 1978), 19.
85. *The Writings of Samuel Adams*, 3:295.
86. General Orders, Head Quarters, New York, July 9, 1776, at http://etext.virginia .edu/toc/modeng/public/WasFi05.html; see also Novak, *On Two Wings*, 19–20.
87. http://www.newenglandancestors.org/online_exhibits_3474.asp.
88. Elizabeth Adams to SA, February 12, 1776, Samuel Adams Papers, New York Public Library.
89. James Warren to SA, August 15, 1776, *Warren–Adams Letters*, 2:438–39.
90. *The Writings of Samuel Adams*, 3:313.
91. Ibid., 3:305.
92. Amos Adams, *A Concise, historical view of the perils, hardships, difficulties and discouragements which have attended the planting and progressive improvements of New-England, Sermon preached at Roxbury April 6, 1769* (Boston: Kneeland & Adams, 1769).
93. http://boston1775.blogspot.com/2006/08/samuel-adams-what-did-sam-publican. html.
94. SA to Savage, July 23, 1776, in *Massachusetts Historical Society Proceedings*, February 1910, 43:328.
95. Force, *American Archives*, 5th Series, vol 1: 1172.
96. Wells, *The Life and Public Services of Samuel Adams*, 2:442.
97. Edward H. Tatum, Jr., ed., *The American Journal of Ambrose Serle Secretary to Lord Howe, 1776–1778* (San Marino: Huntington Library, 1940), 66.
98. *The Writings of Samuel Adams*, 3:320–21.
99. Ibid., 3:325–26.
100. Ibid., 3:328–29.
101. David McCullough, *1776* (New York: Simon & Schuster, 2005), 243.
102. The text is published in, among other places, Moncure Daniel Conway, ed., *The Writings of Thomas Paine* (New York: G P. Putnam's Sons, 1894), vol. 1.
103. *The Writings of Samuel Adams*, 3:334.
104. McCullough, *1776*, 281, 290.
105. *Journals of the Continental Congress*, December 26 and 27, 1776.
106. Burnett, *Letters of Members of the Continental Congress*, 2:202.
107. Force, *American Archives*, 5th Series, 3: 1505–6.
108. Tatum, ed., *The American Journal of Ambrose Serle Secretary to Lord Howe, 1776–1778*, 167.
109. *The Writings of Samuel Adams*, 3:349–50.
110. Ibid., 3:353.
111. Ibid., 3:355–56.

112. *Warren–Adams Letters*, 1:324.
113. Samuel Adams to Samuel Cooper, April 23, 1777, Burnett, ed., *Letters of Members of the Continental Congress*, 2:339.
114. *Journals of the Continental Congress*, January 13, 14, 18, 22, 31, 1777.
115. Wells, *The Life and Public Services of Samuel Adams*, 2:465.
116. *Journals of the Continental Congress* January 24, 1777.
117. McCullough, *John Adams*, 162; *Journals of the Continental Congress*, February 4, 1777.
118. John Adams diary, 28, February 6–November 21, 1777, *Adams Family Papers: An Electronic Archive*, entry for February 16, 1777.
119. *Journals of the Continental Congress*, March 18, 1777.
120. *The Writings of Samuel Adams*, 3:403.
121. Ibid., 3:409.
122. Ibid., 3:412.
123. Letters of Delegates to Congress: Volume 8 September 19, 1777 - January 31, 1778. "Marine Committee to Charles Alexander, September 26, 1777." Available at http://memory.loc.gov/ammem/amlaw/lwdglink.html. William M. Fowler, Jr., *Rebels Under Sail* (New York: Charles Scribner's Sons, 1976), 215, appears to place the loss of the *Delaware* somewhat later, "two months" after September.
124. http://memory.loc.gov/learn/features/timeline/amrev/homefrnt/duche.html, Duché to Washington, October 8, 1777.
125. Kevin Dellape, "Jacob Duché: Whig-Loyalist?", *Pennsylvania History* 62, no. 3 (1995): 293–305.
126. SA to Samuel Phillips Savage, October 26, 1777, in *Massachusetts Historical Society Proceedings* 43 (February 1910): 31.
127. John Adams diary, 28, February 6,–November 21, 1777, *Adams Family Papers: An Electronic Archive,* entry for November 18, 1777.
128. *The Writings of Samuel Adams*, 3:416–17. Cushing names the recipient of the letter, almost certainly erroneously, as John Adams; Burnett repeats the error in his 2:537 but rectifies it in 3:2.
129. *Boston Gazette*, December 8, 1777.
130. Franklin Bowditch Dexter, ed., *The Literary Diary of Ezra Stiles, D.D., LL.D. President of Yale College*, Vol. 2 (New York: Charles Scribner's Sons, 1901), 262.
131. *The Writings of Samuel Adams*, 4:246–47.
132. Burnett, ed., *Letters of Members of the Continental Congress*, 3:458.
133. *Continental Journal*, January 28, 1778.
134. See the instructions of the town of Boston to its representatives, May 26, 1777, in Oscar Handlin and Mary Handlin, eds., *The Popular Sources of Political Authority: Documents on the Massachusetts Constitution of 1780* (Cambridge: Belknap Press, 1966), 176.
135. Grant, *John Adams*, 194–97.
136. *The Writings of Samuel Adams,* 4:16–17.
137. *A Report of the Record Commissioners of the City of Boston, Containing the Boston Town Records, 1778 to 1783* (Boston: Rockwell and Churchill, 1895), 15.
138. *The Writings of Samuel Adams,* 4:22–25.
139. Burnett, ed., *Letters of Members of the Continental Congress*, 3:264.
140. *Warren–Adams Letters* 1:9.

141. *Journals of the Continental Congress*, May 21, 23, 1778.
142. Ibid., May 26, 27, 29, 1778.
143. Ibid., June 6, 1778.
144. Ibid., June 16, 1778.
145. *The Writings of Samuel Adams*, 4:34–38. Puls, *Samuel Adams*, 15, contends, plausibly but without detail, that this piece is "erroneously attributed" to Samuel Adams. Burnett, ed., *Letters of Members of the Continental Congress,* 3:315–16, carries a letter from Gouverneur Morris to John Jay in which Morris appears to claim authorship.
146. Middlekauff, *The Glorious Cause*, 407.
147. *Journals of the Continental Congress*, June 24, 1778.
148. Wells, *The Life and Public Services of Samuel Adams*, 4:27.
149. *Journals of the Continental Congress*, July 14, 1778.
150. Ibid., July 20, 1778.
151. Ibid., July 30, 1778.
152. Wells, *The Life and Public Services of Samuel Adams*, 4:32.
153. *Journals of the Continental Congress*, August 6, 1778.
154. Ibid., August 5, 1778.
155. Ibid., August 6, 1778.
156. Francis D. Cogliano, *No King, No Popery: Anti-Catholicism in Revolutionary New England* (Westport, Conn.: Greenwood, 1995), 81–82; [Rivington's New York] *Royal Gazette*, March 1, 1780.
157. *The Writings of Samuel Adams*, 4:51.
158. Ibid., 4:49.
159. Ibid., 4:57.
160. Ibid., 4:65.
161. *Journals of the Continental Congress*, October 12, 1778.
162. *The Writings of Samuel Adams*, 4:74.
163. *Journals of the Continental Congress*, October 16, 1778.
164. Ibid., October 22, 1778.
165. *The Writings of Samuel Adams*, 4:85–86. Burnett, on the evidence of an August 17, 1778, letter of Gouverneur Morris, plausibly attributes the Manifesto to Morris.
166. *The Writings of Samuel Adams*, 4:91–92.
167. Ibid., 4:104.
168. Ibid., 4:123–24.
169. Ibid., 4:67–68.
170. Ibid., 4:76.
171. SA to Samuel Phillips Savage, July 3, 1778, in *Massachusetts Historical Society Proceedings*, 43 (February 1910) 332–33.
172. Ibid.
173. *The Writings of Samuel Adams*, 4:94.
174. Ibid., February 10, 1779, 4:122–23.
175. Ibid., 4:137–39.
176. Ibid., 4:139.
177. *Boston Town Records*, 62.
178. *Journals of the Continental Congress*, June 4, 7, 8, 9, 15, 1779.

## 8 Back to Massachusetts: *1779–1793*

1. Samuel the Elder was born May 6, 1689, and died March 8, 1747; see Wells, *The Life and Public Services of Samuel Adams*, 3:427–28.
2. *Independent Ledger*, July 12, 1779.
3. *Continental Journal*, August 19, 1779.
4. Handlin and Handlin, *The Popular Sources of Political Authority*, 5.
5. *Journal of the Convention for Framing a Constitution of Government for the State of Massachusetts Bay, From the Commencement of their First Session, September 1, 1779, to the close of their last session, June 16 1780, including a list of the members* (Boston: Dutton & Wentworth, Printers to the State, 1832), 23.
6. Ibid., 8–19.
7. Ibid., 8.
8. Ibid., 30.
9. SA to Richard Henry Lee, September 30, 1779, University of Virginia, Richard Henry Lee Papers.
10. See William D. Williamson, *The History of the State of Maine* (Hallowell, Maine: Glazier, Masters, 1832), 2:483; Charles Francis Adams, ed., *The Works of John Adams* (Boston: Little, Brown, 1865), 4:215–16, 221; McCullough, *John Adams*, 220–25; Grant, *John Adams*, 222–26.
11. *Journal of the Convention*, 38–40.
12. Charles Francis Adams, ed., *The Works of John Adams*, 4:215.
13. *Journal of the Convention*, 51–52.
14. Ibid., 77.
15. Ibid., 90–91, 97; Handlin and Handlin, *The Popular Sources of Political Authority*, 467–68.
16. *Journal of the Convention*, 92, 136.
17. Ibid., 93.
18. Ibid., 130.
19. Ibid., 155, 163.
20. Handlin and Handlin, *The Popular Sources of Political Authority*, 440, 752–53.
21. The text of the constitution is in ibid., 441–72.
22. Middlekauff, *The Glorious Cause*, 608, 618.
23. The return of Suffolk County, which includes Boston, and records of the Boston Town Meeting are in Handlin and Handlin, *The Popular Sources of Political Authority*, 749–64.
24. *Journal of the Convention*, 170, 184–85.
25. *The Writings of Samuel Adams*, 4:199.
26. McCullough, *John Adams*, 225.
27. The gay marriage case was *Goodridge v. Department of Public Health*, SJC-08860. The slavery cases, *Brom & Bett v. John Ashley, Esq.* and the *Quock Walker* cases, are described at http://www.masshist.org/endofslavery/.
28. Burnett, ed., *Letters of Members of the Continental Congress*, 4:54.
29. *The Writings of Samuel Adams*, 4:181.
30. Ibid., 4:188–89.
31. Ibid., 4:256.

32. *Boston Town Records*, 137.
33. Wells, *The Life and Public Services of Samuel Adams*, 3:102; Journals of the Continental Congress, June 29, 1780.
34. *Journals of the Continental Congress*, July 1, 1780.
35. Ibid., July 3, 1780.
36. Ibid., July 21, 1780.
37. Ibid., August 2, 1780.
38. *The Writings of Samuel Adams*, 4:210.
39. Ibid., 4:204–5.
40. Ibid., 4:228.
41. Elan D. Louis, MD, "Samuel Adams' Tremor," *Neurology* 56 (2001): 1201–5. See also http://www.webmd.com/brain/understanding-essential-tremor-making-diagnosis.
42. Elan D. Louis and Patricia Kavanagh, "John Adams' Essential Tremor," *Movement Disorders* 20, no.12 (December 2005):1537–42.
43. Burnett, ed., *Letters of Members of the Continental Congress*, 5:580.
44. *The Writings of Samuel Adams*, 4:208.
45. Ibid., 4:212.
46. Samuel Phillips Savage to SA, October 1778, in *Massachusetts Historical Society Proceedings* 43 (February 1910): 334–35.
47. *Massachusetts Spy*, November 9, 1780.
48. *The Writings of Samuel Adams*, 4:236–38.
49. Ibid., 4:201.
50. Ibid., 4:225.
51. Ibid., 4:230.
52. Ibid., 4:232.
53. Wells, *The Life and Public Services of Samuel Adams*, 3:119–21.
54. *The Writings of Samuel Adams*, 4:227.
55. Wells, *The Life and Public Services of Samuel Adams*, 3:135.
56. *Boston Town Records*, 200.
57. *The Writings of Samuel Adams*, 4:265.
58. *Journals of the Continental Congress*, Tuesday, August 20, 1782.
59. Leonard L. Richards, *Shays's Rebellion: The American Revolution's Final Battle* (Philadelphia: University of Pennsylvania Press, 2002), 60; Robert E. Moody, "Samuel Ely: Forerunner of Shays," *New England Quarterly* 5, no. 1 (January 1932): 105–13.
60. Moody, "Samuel Ely: Forerunner of Shays," 115–16; Seccombe, "From Revolution to Republic," 195–96; Wells, *The Life and Public Services of Samuel Adams*, 3:161–63; Richards, *Shays's Rebellion*, 60.
61. Wells, *The Life and Public Services of Samuel Adams*, 3:223; George Richards Minot, *The History of the Insurrections in Massachusetts in the Year 1786 and the Rebellion Consequent Thereon* (Worcester: Isaiah Thomas, 1788), 35.
62. Minot, *The History of the Insurrections*, 35–37.
63. Richards, *Shays's Rebellion*, 10–13.
64. Wells, *The Life and Public Services of Samuel Adams*, 3:v–vi.
65. Ibid., 3:116; Shipton, *Sibley's Harvard Graduates*, 459.
66. William Pencak, "Samuel Adams and Shays's Rebellion," *New England Quarterly* 62, no. 1 (March 1989): 64.

67. *American Herald*, September 11, 1786. Identical reports appear in the *Independent Ledger* of the same date, the *Massachusetts Gazette* of September 12, and the *Essex Journal* of September 13.

68. The text of the circular letter is reproduced in the *Massachusetts Gazette*, September 12, 1786.

69. *Massachusetts Gazette*, February 6, 1787; Pencak, "Samuel Adams and Shays's Rebellion," 64, 72.

70. Wells, *The Life and Public Services of Samuel Adams*, 3:246.

71. W. B. Allen, ed., *Works of Fisher Ames as Published by Seth Ames* (Indianapolis: Liberty Classics, 1983), 301.

72. *Warren–Adams Letters*, 2:293, letter of May 18, 1787, cited also in Seccombe, "From Revolution to Republic," 231.

73. *Journals of the Continental Congress*, September 25, 1783.

74. August 8, 1780, in Richard K. Showman, ed., *The Papers of General Nathanael Greene* (Chapel Hill: University of North Carolina Press, 1976–2005), 6:193.

75. *Boston Town Records*, 314.

76. *The Writings of Samuel Adams*, 4:298.

77. J. J. Boudinot, ed., *The Life, Public Services, Addresses, and Letters of Elias Boudinot* (Boston: Houghton Mifflin, 1896), 2:356–58; also in Noll, "The Contingencies of Christian Republicanism," in Engeman and Zuckert, eds., *Protestantism and the American Founding*, 239.

78. *The Writings of Samuel Adams*, 4:311.

79. Ibid., 4:314–15.

80. Gilder Lehrman Collection, Document 4009.

81. *The Writings of Samuel Adams*, 4:315–16.

82. Charles Warren, "Samuel Adams and the Sans Souci Club," *Massachusetts Historical Society Proceedings* 60 (1927).

83. Richards, *Shays's Rebellion*, 118.

84. Charles L. Mee, Jr., *The Genius of the People* (New York: Harper Perennial, 1988), 39–40; Richards, *Shays's Rebellion*, 128–34.

85. Thomas H. O'Connor and Alan Rogers, *This Momentous Affair: Massachusetts and the Ratification of the Constitution of the United States* (Boston: Trustees of the Public Library of the City of Boston, 1987), 11.

86. Gore to King, December 30, 1787, in Charles R. King, ed., *Life and Correspondence of Rufus King* (New York: G. P. Putnam's Sons, 1894) 1:266–67.

87. Gore to King, January 6, 1788, in ibid., 1:311–12.

88. *Debates and Proceedings in the Convention of the Commonwealth of Massachusetts, Held in the Year 1788 and Which Finally Ratified the Constitution of the United States* (Boston: William White, Printer to the Commonwealth, 1856), 44.

89. *Massachusetts Centinel*, January 16, 1788.

90. *Debates and Proceedings in the Convention*, 62.

91. Wells, *The Life and Public Services of Samuel Adams*, 3:255.

92. *Debates and Proceedings in the Convention*, 196.

93. Henry Knox to Egbert Benson, January 20, 1788, Gilder Lehrman Collection, GLC02437.03766.

94. *Debates and Proceedings in the Convention*, 203.

95. *Massachusetts Centinel*, January 19, 1788. On Ames, see Allen, ed., *Works of Fisher Ames, as Published by Seth Ames*, 1:xix–xxii.

96. *Debates and Proceedings in the Convention*, 209.

97. Wells, *The Life and Public Services of Samuel Adams*, 3:259–61.

98. Pinkney, *Christopher Gore, Federalist of Massachusetts*, 24.

99. O'Connor and Rogers, *This Momentous Affair*, 55–57.

100. *Debates and Proceedings in the Convention*, 225–26.

101. King to Madison, February 3, 1788, in King, ed., *Life and Correspondence of Rufus King*, 1:318.

102. *Debates and Proceedings in the Convention*, 86; Wells, *The Life and Public Services of Samuel Adams*, 3:267.

103. O'Connor and Rogers, *This Momentous Affair*, 64.

104. Dexter, ed., *The Literary Diary of Ezra Stiles, D.D., LL.D. President of Yale College*, 3:90.

105. J. P. Brissot de Warville, *New Travels in the United States of America, 1788* (Dublin: Printed by W. Corbet, for P. Byrne, A. Grueber, W. McKenzie, J. Moore, W. Jones, R. M'Allister, and J. Rice, 1792), 66; Alexander, *Samuel Adams*, 209.

106. *The Writings of Samuel Adams*, 4:287.

107. These are on display at the Old State House in Boston, which is maintained by the Bostonian Society.

108. Wood, *The Americanization of Benjamin Franklin*, 57.

109. Hill, *History of the Old South Church*, 2:205.

110. Akers, *The Divine Politician*, 279.

111. *The Writings of Samuel Adams*, 4:226.

112. Checkley, *A Day of Darkness*, 9.

113. Zabdiel Adams election sermon, 1782, in Hyneman and Lutz, eds., *American Political Writing During the Founding Era, 1760–1805*, 1:550–51.

114. Wells, *The Life and Public Services of Samuel Adams*, 3:332–33.

115. For the decline in Hancock's fortune, see Fowler, *The Baron of Beacon Hill*, 223–24, 251–52, 281.

116. *The Writings of Samuel Adams*, 4:328–29.

117. Ibid., 4:339.

118. *Boston Gazette*, October 26, 1789.

119. Letter from John Adams to Abigail Adams, November 8, 1789, *Adams Family Papers: An Electronic Archive*.

120. *The Writings of Samuel Adams*, 4:342–43.

121. Ibid., 4:351.

122. Holmes, *A Tercentenary History of the Boston Latin School, 1635–1935*, 19–20.

123. Mercy Otis Warren to SA, February 26, 1786, Mercy Otis Warren letterbook, Massachusetts Historical Society, 475. The finding aid to this and the microfilm version of the Mercy Otis Warren papers mistakenly places the letter on page 745.

124. Holmes, *A Tercentenary History of the Boston Latin School, 1635–1935*, 19–20.

125. Zabdiel Adams election sermon, 1782, in Hyneman and Lutz, eds., *American Political Writing During the Founding Era, 1760–1805*, 1:556–57.

126. Cogliano, *No King, No Popery*, 146–47.

127. Pinkney, *Christopher Gore, Federalist of Massachusetts*, 53–54.

## 9 Governor: *1793–1797*

1. Wells, *The Life and Public Services of Samuel Adams*, 3:331–32.
2. *The Writings of Samuel Adams*, 4:356.
3. Ibid., 4:359.
4. Peres Fobes, *A Sermon Preached Before His Excellency Samuel Adams, May 27, 1795* (Boston: Printed at the Mercury Press, by Young & Minns, 1795), 38.
5. *The Writings of Samuel Adams*, 4:361–62.
6. Ibid., 4:364.
7. Ibid., 4:377–78.
8. Ibid., 4:377.
9. SA to Arthur Fenner, governor of Rhode Island, December 6, 1794, Samuel Adams Papers, New York Public Library.
10. *The Writings of Samuel Adams*, 4:383–85.
11. Ibid., 4:393–96.
12. Ibid., 4:390–91.
13. The text of the treaty is available at http://www.yale.edu/lawweb/avalon/diplomacy/britain/jay.htm.
14. http://www.loc.gov/rr/program/bib/ourdocs/jay.html.
15. Gore to King, January 21, 1796, in Charles King, ed., *Life and Correspondence of Rufus King*, 2:55; Pinkney, *Christopher Gore, Federalist of Massachusetts*, 62.
16. A text of the speech is at http://www.ourdocuments.gov/.
17. Wells, *The Life and Public Services of Samuel Adams*, 3:361.
18. Letter from John Adams to Abigail Adams, December 12, 1796, *Adams Family Papers: An Electronic Archive*.
19. Grant, *John Adams*, 380–81.
20. *The Writings of Samuel Adams*, 4:399–401.
21. Seccombe, "From Revolution to Republic," 347.
22. *The Writings of Samuel Adams*, 4:405–7.
23. Pinkney, *Christopher Gore, Federalist of Massachusetts*, 67.
24. Seccombe, "From Revolution to Republic," 341.
25. Ibid., 315.
26. Wells, *The Life and Public Services of Samuel Adams*, 3:291.
27. Samuel Eliot Morison, "Two 'Signers' on Salaries and the Stage, 1789," *Proceedings of the Massachusetts Historical Society* 62 (1928–29).
28. Certificate of Freedom, August 23, 1794, Society Collection, Historical Society of Pennsylvania.
29. Samuel Deane, *A Sermon, Preached before His Honour Samuel Adams* (Boston: Adams & Larkin, 1794).
30. Fobes, *A Sermon, Preached Before His Excellency Samuel Adams*, in Hyneman and Lutz, eds., *American Political Writing During the Founding Era, 1760–1805*, 2:991–1013.
31. Jonathan French, *A Sermon Preached Before His Excellency Samuel Adams* (Boston: Printed at the State Press, by Adams & Larkin, 1796).
32. Deane, *A Sermon, Preached before His Honour Samuel Adams*, 24–25.
33. Fobes, *A Sermon, Preached Before His Excellency Samuel Adams*, 24–25.

34. *The Writings of Samuel Adams*, 4:379.
35. Seccombe, "From Revolution to Republic," 317.
36. *The Writings of Samuel Adams*, 4:404.
37. Wells, *The Life and Public Services of Samuel Adams*, 3:332.

## 10 Passing of the Patriarch: *1797 to the Present*

1. Hill, *History of the Old South Church*, 2:247–50.
2. Silverman, *A Cultural History of the American Revolution*, 198–99.
3. Wells, *The Life and Public Services of Samuel Adams*, 3:332–34.
4. Silver, "Benjamin Edes, Trumpeter of Sedition," 266.
5. Seccombe, "From Revolution to Republic," 351.
6. Allen, ed., *Works of Fisher Ames, as Published by Seth Ames*, 1327.
7. The Thomas Jefferson Papers, Series 1, General Correspondence, 1651–1827, Samuel Adams to Thomas Jefferson, December 11, 1800, in http://memory.loc. gov/ammem/collections/jefferson_papers/index.html.
8. Thomas Jefferson to Samuel Adams, February 26, 1800, in ibid.
9. Charles B. Sanford, *The Religious Life of Thomas Jefferson* (Charlottesville: University Press of Virginia, 1987), 6, 104.
10. http://www.yale.edu/lawweb/avalon/presiden/inaug/jefinau1.htm, viewed on November 30, 2007.
11. The Thomas Jefferson Papers, Series 1. General Correspondence, 1651–1827, Thomas Jefferson to Samuel Adams, March 29, 1801.
12. *The Writings of Samuel Adams*, 4:412.
13. Nelson, *Thomas Paine*, 270.
14. Wells, *The Life and Public Services of Samuel Adams*, 2:101, 3:378.
15. Warden, *Boston, 1689–1776*, 334.
16. *The Diary of William Bentley, D.D. Pastor of the East Church Salem, Massachusetts* (Salem: Essex Institute, 1907–1911), 2:101, 3:54–52.
17. The full text of the Thacher discourse is in Wells, *The Life and Public Services of Samuel Adams*, 3:383–98. The quoted portions are at 396–97.
18. Wells, *The Life and Public Services of Samuel Adams*, 3:379.
19. *The Writings of Samuel Adams*, 3:235.
20. Puls, *Samuel Adams*, 188. George Bancroft, *History of the United States from the Discovery of the American Continent* (Boston: Little, Brown, 1866), 9:59.
21. Thacher funeral oration in Wells, *The Life and Public Services of Samuel Adams*, 3:398.
22. *Correspondence Between the Hon. John Adams, late president of the United States, and the late Wm. Cunningham Esq.* (Boston: E. M. Cunningham, 1823), 215.
23. Seccombe, "From Revolution to Republic," 357.
24. Goodell, "Charges Against Samuel Adams," 213–26.
25. One example is George F. Will, writing in the *New York Times Book Review* of Sunday, October 22, 2006, describing an author's thesis "that the six most important founders—Franklin, Washington, Adams, Jefferson, Madison and Hamilton—subscribed, in different ways, to the watery and undemanding enlightenment

faith called deism." A late-life drift by "Adams" toward Unitarianism is described, making clear the reference is to John, not Samuel, but the first name of neither Adams appears in the article. Another example, also from the *Times Book Review*, is Barry Gewen's August 8, 2004, article on a Benjamin Franklin book describing Franklin as likable compared to "Adams," who was "too difficult, a royal pain." No first name for Adams was given.

26. Goodell, "Charges Against Samuel Adams," 25.

27. Morgan and Morgan, The Stamp Act Crisis, 368. Others who recognized Adams's stature included Governor Thomas Hutchinson, who called Samuel Adams the "Grand Incendiary of the Province" and said of him, "The whole Continent is ensnared by that Matchiavel of Chaos" (Schlesinger, Prelude to Independence, 149, 204), and Isaiah Thomas, the *Massachusetts Spy* editor who knew Samuel Adams firsthand and wrote in 1827, "No man, I believe, devoted more time to the service of his country, or did more in bringing forward the Revolution" (Isaiah Thomas to Samuel Adams Wells. Worcester, Mass., July 25, 1827, Isaiah Thomas papers at American Antiquarian Society).

28. http://etext.virginia.edu/washington/fitzpatrick/, *The Writings of George Washington from the Original Manuscript Sources, 1745–1799,* ed. John C. Fitzpatrick, 1931–1944.

29. John Adams to William Tudor, June 5, 1817, in Wills, *Inventing America*, 22.

30. To————, January 10, 1778, *The Writings of Samuel Adams*, 4:8

31. Harlow, *Samuel Adams*, 2, 38.

32. Esther Forbes's 1943 historical novel *Johnny Tremain*: "Look at Sam Adams. If he looks as pleased as an old dog fox with a fat pullet in his mouth, we'll know they've agreed to violence if everything else fails." HBO's 2008 miniseries *John Adams* portrays Samuel Adams looking on during a tar-and-feathering. "God, Sam, that's barbarism," John cries to his cousin, who stands silent. "Do you approve of this? Answer me Sam, can you?"

33. Young, *Liberty Tree*, 155–56.

34. http://www.adherents.com/adhloc/Wh_200.html.

35. http://www.mass.gov/legis/const.htm.

36. Adair and Schutz, eds., *Peter Oliver's Origin & Progress of the American Rebellion*, 41.

37. The role of religion in the Revolution has been the subject of an extensive literature in its own right. Increasing numbers of scholars and writers have come to the conclusion that religion was indeed an important factor in the American Revolution. Michael Novak, the holder of the Jewett Chair in Religion and Public Policy at the American Enterprise Institute and the winner of the $1 million Templeton Prize for Progress in Religion, wrote in his 2002 book *On Two Wings* that the American founding depended on religion like an eagle on one of its wings. Novak reports a study of writings of the founders that shows the Bible was quoted far more than Locke or Montesquieu. He notes that Jefferson himself suggested, as a design for the Great Seal of the United States, that same image invoked by Samuel Adams at that gloomy moment in September of 1777, the Children of Israel in the wilderness, led by a cloud by day and a pillar of fire by night. (Novak, *On Two Wings*, 6, 8). The Harvard government professor Samuel Huntington, in his 2004 book *Who Are We?*, wrote, "Eighteenth-century Americans and their leaders saw their Revolution in religious and largely biblical terms. . . . The Revo-

lution reflected their 'covenant with God' and was a war between 'God's elect' and the British 'Antichrist'" (Samuel Huntington, *Who Are We? The Challenges to America's National Identity* [New York: Simon & Schuster, 2004], 83). David Gelernter wrote an article in the January 2005 issue of the neoconservative journal *Commentary* arguing that Puritanism became Americanism, a kind of "American version of biblical Zionism" that featured "a promised land, a chosen people, and a universal, divinely ordained mission."

Nathan Hatch, a historian who took over in 2005 as president of Wake Forest University after spending nearly a decade as the provost of Notre Dame, wrote in his 1977 book *The Sacred Cause of Liberty* of "the religious patriotism that animated the revolution." (Nathan O. Hatch, *The Sacred Cause of Liberty: Republican Thought and the Millennium in Revolutionary New England* [New Haven: Yale University Press, 1977]). A professor of history and religion at Brown University, William G. McLoughlin, wrote in 1978 that the American Revolution was "the secular fulfillment of the religious ideals of the First Great Awakening" (William G. McLoughlin, *Revivals, Awakenings, and Reform* [Chicago: University of Chicago Press, 1978], 97). Robert Middlekauff, a University of California historian who wrote a book about the Mathers, also wrote a history of the American Revolution that was published in 1982 as part of the *Oxford History of the United States*. He said that the revolutionary cause was understood by Americans as a "providential struggle of good against evil," expressed in language "imbued with traditional religious meanings" (Middlekauff, *The Glorious Cause*, 581). The Jonathan Edwards Professor of American Christianity at Yale University, Harry Stout, argued in his 1986 book *The New England Soul* that eighteenth-century New Englanders had a "self-image as a divinely assisted people of war." Stout writes that "Israel remained as crucial to New England's self-identity in 1760 as it had been a century earlier," and that "New England audiences were taught to understand that the ultimate issue in the Revolution was not forms of government but the preservation of God's pure churches and their own piety." He describes the American Revolution in New England as "nothing less than America's sermon to the world" (Stout, *The New England Soul*, 236, 252, 310–11). A history professor at New York University, Patricia Bonomi, wrote in 1986 that "religious doctrine and rhetoric" contributed "in a fundamental way to the coming of the American Revolution and to its final success," in part by "turning colonial resistance into a righteous cause" (Bonomi, *Under the Cope of Heaven*, 216). More recently, Mark Noll, a history professor at Notre Dame, has written approvingly of "the general opening up of early American ideological history to the possibility that religious belief played an active role" (Noll, "The Contingencies of Christian Republicanism," in Engeman and Zuckert, eds., *Protestantism and the American Founding*, 230).

The scholars have gone beyond merely asserting that religion is important in the Revolution. They have described some of the mechanics of how it was so. Alice Baldwin, a history professor at Duke and the daughter and granddaughter of Congregational ministers, argued that there was a connection between Congregationalist "democracy in church government" and "democracy in the state" (Baldwin, *The New England Clergy and the American Revolution*, 29). Harvard historian Bernard Bailyn wrote in his Pulitzer Prize–winning *The Ideological Origins of the American Revolution* that Puritanism and "the epidemic evangelism of the mid-eighteenth century had created challenges to the traditional notions of social stratification by generating the conviction that the ultimate quality of men was to be found elsewhere than in their external condition, and that a cosmic achievement lay within each man's grasp" (Bailyn, *The Ideological Origins of the American Revolution*, 303). The Great Awakening "crossed class and geographic boundaries," arousing "the sense of American destiny under God and "contributing to an emerging feeling of American unity," wrote Conrad Cherry, a distinguished professor at Indiana University (Conrad Cherry, *God's New Israel: Religious Interpretations of American Destiny* [Englewood Cliffs, N.J.: Prentice Hall, 1971], 29–30). Other sources for the influence of religion on the founding include Alan Heimert, *Religion and the American Mind: From the Great Awakening to the Revolution* (Cambridge: Harvard University Press, 1966); Page Smith, *Religious Origins of the American Revolution* (Missoula, Mont.: Scholars Press, 1976), and Dale S. Kuehne, *Massachusetts Congregationalist Political Thought, 1760–1790* (Columbia: University of Missouri Press, 1996). At an even more basic level, a religion that stressed Bible reading and interpretation made for a literate population receptive to newspapers like the *Boston Gazette*.

These observations are all true so far as they go, and important for understanding the Revolution. The theory that the American Revolution was driven largely by Puritanism would tend to be supported by the idea that Catholic Canada did not join the revolution against Britain. And it is true that heavily Anglican New York, particularly Columbia University, which was known until the Revolution as King's College, had more Tory leanings than Harvard or Congregationalist Massachusetts, where the American Revolution began with the Boston Massacre, the Boston Tea Party, and Lexington and Concord. Acknowledging the role that religion played in the Revolution is a necessary corrective to those who would deny it or have forgotten it.

But there are serious obstacles to understanding the American Revolution entirely as a religious movement. After all, nominally Catholic France had a violent, anti-religious revolution against its king in 1789. And as Michael Novak points out, of the fifty-six signers of the Declaration of Independence, thirty-four were Anglican, while only thirteen were Congregationalist, the religious descendants of the Puritans. The signers also included a Catholic, Charles Carroll of Carrollton, Maryland, who wrote, "To obtain religious, as well as civil liberty, I entered zealously into the Revolution" (Novak, *On Two Wings*, 129, 67).

Bernard Bailyn gets the balance about right, as he so often does. He has acknowledged "the force of religious ideas in the process by which political arguments became a revolutionary creed," and asserted that "religious ideas in general and the views of specific denominational groups in particular provided significant reinforcement to the revolutionary movement." But he has cautioned, "it is a gross simplification to believe that religion as such, or any of its doctrinaire elements, had a unique political role in the Revolutionary movement. The effective determinants of revolution were political." (Bernard Bailyn, "Religion and Revolution: Three Biographical Studies," *Perspectives in American History* 4 [1970]).

38. Edward Everett, *Orations and Speeches on Various Occasions, 8th ed.* (Boston: Little, Brown, 1870), 1:546–47.

39. Miller and Johnson, eds., *The Puritans*, 60.

# Bibliography

## Samuel Adams's Writings

The writings of Samuel Adams, primarily those in the Samuel Adams Papers given by George Bancroft to the Lenox Library, which became the New York Public Library, are collected in four volumes edited by a professor at Columbia University:

Cushing, Harry Alonzo, ed. *The Writings of Samuel Adams.* New York: G. P. Putnam's Sons, 1904–1908.

Two volumes of correspondence include many letters not included in Cushing's collection:

*Warren–Adams Letters: Being Chiefly a Correspondence Among John Adams, Samuel Adams, and James Warren.* Boston: Massachusetts Historical Society, 1917, 1925.

And some other Samuel Adams letters not included in Cushing or the Warren–Adams letters were published in the *Massachusetts Historical Society Proceedings*, February 1910, vol. 43.

## Archives and Manuscript Collections

Other Samuel Adams writings and documents bearing on his life that have been used for this work are at:

American Antiquarian Society, Worcester, Massachusetts.

Gilder Lehrman Collection, New-York Historical Society, New York, New York.

Historical Society of Pennsylvania, Philadelphia, Pennsylvania.

Houghton Library, Harvard University, Cambridge, Massachusetts.

Massachusetts Historical Society, Boston, Massachusetts.

New York Public Library Rare Books and Manuscripts Division, New York, New York.

Albert and Shirley Small Special Collections Library, University of Virginia, Charlottesville, Virginia.

## Books

Adair, Douglass. *Fame and the Founding Fathers*. Indianapolis: Liberty Fund/W. W. Norton, 1974.

Adair, Douglass, and John Schutz, eds. *Peter Oliver's Origin & Progress of the American Rebellion*. Stanford: Stanford: Stanford University Press, 1967.

Adams, Amos. *A Concise, historical view of the perils, hardships, difficulties and discouragements which have attended the planting and progressive improvements of New-England, Sermon preached at Roxbury April 6, 1769*. Boston: Kneeland & Adams, 1769.

———. *The Expediency and Utility of War*. Boston: Fowle & Draper, 1759.

Adams, Andrew N., ed. *A Genealogical History of Henry Adams of Braintree, Mass., and His Descendants*. Rutland, Vt.: Tuttle Company, Printers, 1898. Reprint: Newburyport, Mass.: Parker River Researchers, 1984.

Adams, Charles Francis, ed. *The Works of John Adams*. Boston: Little, Brown, 1865.

Adams, John. *Correspondence Between the Hon. John Adams, late president of the United States, and the late Wm. Cunningham Esq*. Boston: E. M. Cunningham, 1823.

Akers, Charles W. *The Divine Politician: Samuel Cooper and the American Revolution in Boston*. Boston: Northeastern University Press, 1982.

Alexander, John K. *Samuel Adams: America's Revolutionary Politician*. Lanham, Md.: Rowman & Littlefield, 2002.

Allen, W. B., ed., *Works of Fisher Ames as Published by Seth Ames*. Indianapolis: Liberty Classics, 1983.

Bailyn, Bernard. *The Ideological Origins of the American Revolution*. Cambridge: Harvard University Press, 1967.

————.*The Ordeal of Thomas Hutchinson*. Cambridge: Harvard University Press, 1974.

Bailyn, Bernard, and John B. Hench, eds. *The Press and the American Revolution*. Boston: Northeastern University Press, 1981.

Baldwin, Alice. *The New England Clergy and the American Revolution*. New York: Frederick Ungar, 1928, 1965.

Ballagh, James Curtis, ed. *The Letters of Richard Henry Lee*. New York: Macmillan, 1911.

Bancroft, George. *History of the American Revolution*. London: Richard Bentley, 1854.

————. *History of the United States from the Discovery of the American Continent*. Boston: Little, Brown, 1866.

Beach, Stewart. *Samuel Adams: The Fateful Years, 1764–1776*. New York: Dodd, Mead, 1965.

Bentley, William. *The Diary of William Bentley, D.D. Pastor of the East Church Salem, Massachusetts*. Salem: Essex Institute, 1907–1911.

Boland, Charles Michael. *Ring in the Jubilee: The Epic of America's Liberty Bell*. Riverside, Conn.: Chatham, 1973.

Boller, Paul F., Jr., and Ronald Story, eds. *A More Perfect Union, Documents in U.S. History*, 2nd ed. Boston: Houghton Mifflin, 1988.

Bonomi, Patricia. *Under the Cope of Heaven: Religion, Society, and Politics in Colonial America*. New York, Oxford University Press, 2003.

Boudinot, J. J., ed. *The Life, Public Services, Addresses, and Letters of Elias Boudinot*. Boston: Houghton Mifflin, 1896.

Bowen, Penuel. *Sermon on the Death of the Reverend Mr. Samuel Checkley*. Boston: Edes & Gill, 1770.

Bridenbaugh, Carl. *Mitre and Sceptre: Transatlantic Faiths, Ideas, Personalities, and Politics, 1689–1775*. New York: Oxford University Press, 1962.

Brooke, John. *King George III*. New York: McGraw-Hill, 1972.

Brown, Abram English. *Faneuil Hall and Faneuil Hall Market*. Boston: Lee & Shepard, 1901.

Brown, Richard D. *Revolutionary Politics in Massachusetts: The Boston Committee of Correspondence and the Towns, 1772–1774*. Cambridge: Harvard University Press, 1970.

Burnett, Edmund G., ed. *Letters of Members of the Continental Congress*. 8 volumes. Washington: Carnegie Institution, 1921–1936.

Burns, Eric. *Infamous Scribblers: The Founding Fathers and the Rowdy Beginnings of American Journalism*. New York: Public Affairs, 2006.

Cary, John. *Joseph Warren: Physician, Politician, Patriot*. Urbana: University of Illinois Press, 1961.

Cash, Arthur H. *John Wilkes: The Scandalous Father of Civil Liberty*. New Haven: Yale University Press, 2006.

Checkley, Samuel. *A Day of Darkness*. Boston: John Draper, 1755.

Chernow, Ron. *Alexander Hamilton*. New York: Penguin, 2004.

Cherry, Conrad. *God's New Israel: Religious Interpretations of American Destiny*. Englewood Cliffs, N.J.: Prentice Hall, 1971.

Cicero, Marcus Tullius. *Ethical Writings of Cicero: De Officiis (On Moral Duties); De Senectute (On Old Age); De Amicitia (On Friendship), and Scipio's Dream*. Translated by Andrew P. Peabody. Boston: Little, Brown, 1887.

————. *Letters of Marcus Tullius Cicero with His Treatises on Friendship and Old Age*. Translated by E. S. Shuckburgh. New York: P. F. Collier & Son, 1909.

Cogliano, Francis D. *No King, No Popery: Anti-Catholicism in Revolutionary New England*. Westport, Conn.: Greenwood, 1995.

Conway, Moncure Daniel, ed. *The Writings of Thomas Paine*. New York: G. P. Putnam's Sons, 1894.

Cunningham, Anne Rowe, ed., *Letters and Diary of John Rowe, Boston Merchant*. Boston: W. B. Clarke, 1903.

Deane, Samuel. *A Sermon, Preached before His Honour Samuel Adams*. Boston: Adams & Larkin, 1794.

Dershowitz, Alan. *America Declares Independence*. Hoboken: John Wiley & Sons, 2003.

Dexter, Franklin Bowditch, ed. *The Literary Diary of Ezra Stiles, D.D., LL.D. President of Yale College*. New York: Charles Scribner's Sons, 1901.

de Chastellux, Marquis. *Travels in North America in the Years 1780–81–82*. New York: White, Gallaher & White, 1827.

de Warville, J. P. Brissot. *New Travels in the United States of America, 1788*. Dublin: Printed by W. Corbet, for P. Byrne, A. Grueber, W. McKenzie, J. Moore, W. Jones, R. M'Allister, and J. Rice, 1792.

Dickerson, Oliver Morton. ed. *Boston Under Military Rule, 1768–1769 as revealed in A Journal of the Times*. Boston: Chapman & Grimes, 1936. Reprint: New York: Da Capo, 1970.

Drake, Francis S. *Tea Leaves: Being a Collection of Letters and Documents Relating to the Shipment of Tea to the American Colonies in the Year 1773, by the East India Tea Company*. Boston: A. O. Crane, 1884. Reprint: Kessinger Publishing.

Drake, Samuel Adams. *Old Boston Taverns and Tavern Clubs*. Boston: W. A. Butterfield, 1917.

Duane, William, ed. *Extracts from the Diary of Christopher Marshall, 1774–1781*. New York: New York Times and Arno Press, 1969.

Edes, Peter, ed. *Orations Delivered at the Request of the Inhabitants of the Town of Boston, To Commemorate the Evening of the Fifth of March, 1770*. Boston: Peter Edes, 1785.

Engeman, Thomas, and Michael Zuckert, eds. *Protestantism and the American Founding*. Notre Dame: University of Notre Dame Press, 2004.

Everett, Edward. *Orations and Speeches on Various Occasions, 8th ed.* Boston: Little, Brown, 1870.

Fischer, David Hackett. *Paul Revere's Ride*. New York: Oxford University Press, 1994.

Fobes, Peres. *A Sermon Preached Before His Excellency Samuel Adams, May 27, 1795*. Boston: Printed at the Mercury Press, by Young & Minns, 1795.

Force, Peter, ed. *American Archives*. Washington: 1837–1853. Also online at http://dig.lib.niu.edu/amarch/.

Ford, Paul Leicester, ed. *The New England Primer: A History of Its Origin and Development*. New York: Dodd, Mead, 1897, Reprint: New York: Teachers College, Columbia University, 1962.

Fowler, William M., Jr. *The Baron of Beacon Hill: A Biography of John Hancock*. Boston: Houghton Mifflin, 1980.

———. *Rebels Under Sail*. New York: Charles Scribner's Sons, 1976.

———. *Samuel Adams: Radical Puritan*. New York: Longman, 1997.

French, Jonathan. *A sermon preached before His Excellency Samuel Adams*. Boston: Printed at the State Press, by Adams & Larkin, 1796.

Gillies, John, ed. *Memoirs of George Whitefield*. New Haven: Whitmore & Buckingham and H. Mansfield, 1834.

Grant, James. *John Adams: Party of One*. New York: Farrar, Straus & Giroux, 2005.

Handlin, Oscar, and Mary Handlin, eds. *The Popular Sources of Political Authority: Documents on the Massachusetts Constitution of 1780*. Cambridge: Belknap Press, 1966.

Harlow, Ralph Volney. *Samuel Adams: Promoter of the American Revolution*. New York: Henry Holt, 1923.

Hatch, Nathan O. *The Sacred Cause of Liberty: Republican Thought and the Millennium in Revolutionary New England*. New Haven: Yale University Press, 1977.

Heimert, Alan. *Religion and the American Mind: From the Great Awakening to the Revolution*. Cambridge: Harvard University Press, 1966.

Hibbert, Christopher. *George III*. New York: Basic Books, 1998.

Hill, Hamilton A. *History of the Old South Church*. Boston: Houghton Mifflin, 1890.

Holmes, David L. *The Faiths of the Founding Fathers*. New York, Oxford University Press, 2006.

Holmes, Pauline. *A Tercentenary History of the Boston Latin School, 1635–1935*. Cambridge: Harvard University Press, 1935.

Hosmer, James. *Samuel Adams*. New York: Chelsea House, 1980. Reprint of 1898 edition.

———. *The Story of the Jews*. New York: G. P. Putnam's Sons, 1887.

Huntington, Samuel. *Who Are We? The Challenges to America's National Identity*. New York: Simon & Schuster, 2004.

Hutchinson, Peter Orlando, ed. *The Diary and Letters of His Excellency Thomas Hutchinson Esq*. New York: Burt Franklin, 1971. Originally published, 1884–1886.

Hyneman, Charles, and Donald Lutz, eds, *American Political Writing During the Founding Era*. Indianapolis: Liberty Press, 1983.

Isaacson, Walter. *Benjamin Franklin: An American Life*. New York: Simon & Schuster, 2003.

Ives, J. Moss. *The Ark and the Dove: The Beginning of Civil and Religious Liberties in America*. New York: Cooper Square, 1969.

King, Charles R., ed., *Life and Correspondence of Rufus King*. New York: G. P. Putnam's Sons, 1894.

Kuehne, Dale S. *Massachusetts Cangregationalist Political Thought, 1760–1790*. Columbia: University of Missouri Press, 1996.

Labaree, Benjamin Woods. *The Boston Tea Party*. London: Oxford University Press, 1996.

Lecky, William Edward Hartpole. *The American Revolution*. New York: D. Appleton, 1921.

Lee, Richard Henry. *Life of Arthur Lee*. Boston: Wells & Lilly, 1829.

Lewis, Paul. *The Grand Incendiary*. New York: Dial, 1973.

Locke, John. *The Works of John Locke in Nine Volumes,* 12th ed. London: Rivington, 1824.

Lustig, Mary Lou. *The Imperial Executive in America: Sir Edmund Andros, 1637–1714*. Madison, N.J.: Fairleigh Dickinson University Press, 2002.

MacCulloch, Diarmaid. *The Reformation: A History*. New York: Viking, 2004.

Maier, Pauline. *The Old Revolutionaries: Political Lives in the Age of Samuel Adams.* New York: Vintage, 1980.

Mather, Cotton. *Ratio Disciplina Fratrum Nov Anglorum.* Boston, 1726.

McClure, James. *Nine Months in York Town.* York, Penn.: York Daily Record, 2001.

McCullough, David. *1776.* New York: Simon & Schuster, 2005.

——. *John Adams.* New York: Simon & Schuster, 2001.

McLoughlin, William G., ed. *Diary of Isaac Backus.* 3 volumes. Providence: Brown University Press, 1979.

——. *Revivals, Awakenings, and Reform.* Chicago: University of Chicago Press, 1978.

Mee, Charles L., Jr. *The Genius of the People.* New York: Harper Perennial, 1988.

Middlekauff, Robert. *The Glorious Cause: The American Revolution, 1763–1789.* New York: Oxford University Press, 1982.

——. *The Mathers: Three Generations of Puritan Intellectuals, 1596–1728.* Berkeley: University of California Press, 1999.

Miller, John C. *Sam Adams: Pioneer in Propaganda.* Boston: Little, Brown, 1936.

Miller, Perry, and Thomas H. Johnson, eds, *The Puritans: A Sourcebook of Their Writings.* New York: Harper Torchbooks, 1963. Originally published, 1938.

Minot, George Richards. *The History of the Insurrections in Massachusetts in the Year 1786 and the Rebellion Consequent Thereon.* Worcester: Isaiah Thomas, 1788.

Moore, Frank, ed. *American Eloquence: A Collection of Speeches and Addresses by the Most Eminent Orators of America.* New York: D. Appleton, 1857.

Moore, George H. *Notes on the History of Slavery in Massachusetts.* New York: D. Appleton, 1866.

Morgan, Edmund S., and Helen M. Morgan. *The Stamp Act Crisis: Prologue to Revolution.* New York: Collier, 1963: originally published, 1953.

Morison, Samuel Eliot. *The Intellectual Life of Colonial New England*, 4th ed. New York: New York University Press, 1956.

———. *Three Centuries of Harvard*. Cambridge: Harvard University Press, 1936.

Nelson, Craig. *Thomas Paine: Enlightenment, Revolution, and the Birth of Modern Nations*. New York: Viking, 2006.

Noll, Mark A. *America's God: From Jonathan Edwards to Abraham Lincoln*. New York: Oxford University Press, 2002.

———. *The Old Religion in A New World*. Grand Rapids: William B. Eerdmans, 2002.

Novak, Michael. *On Two Wings: Humble Faith and Common Sense at the American Founding*. San Francisco: Encounter Books, 2002.

O'Connor, Thomas H., and Alan Rogers. *This Momentous Affair: Massachusetts and the Ratification of the Constitution of the United States*. Boston: Trustees of the Public Library of the City of Boston, 1987.

Oliver, Andrew, ed. *The Journal of Samuel Curwen, Loyalist*. Cambridge: Harvard University Press, 1972.

Pinkney, Helen R. *Christopher Gore, Federalist of Massachusetts*. Waltham, Mass.: Gore Place Society, 1969.

Plumstead, A. W., ed. *The Wall and the Garden: Selected Massachusetts Election Sermons, 1670–1775*. Minneapolis: University of Minnesota Press, 1968.

Prince, Thomas. *Account of the Revival of Religion in Boston, in the Years 1740–1–2–3*. Boston: Republished by Samuel T. Armstrong, 1823.

Prown, Jules David. *John Singleton Copley*. Cambridge: Published for the National Gallery of Art, Washington, by Harvard University Press, 1966.

Puls, Mark. *Samuel Adams: Father of the American Revolution*. New York: Palgrave Macmillan, 2006.

Rich, Andrea. *Rhetoric of Revolution: Samuel Adams, Emma Goldman, Malcolm X*. Durham, N.C.: Moore, 1970.

Richards, Leonard L. *Shays's Rebellion: The American Revolution's Final Battle*. Philadelphia: University of Pennsylvania Press, 2002.

Riley, Stephen T., and Edward W. Hanson, eds. *The Papers of Robert Treat Paine*. 3 volumes. Boston: Massachusetts Historical Society, 1992, 2005.

Rosovsky, Nitza. *The Jewish Experience at Harvard and Radcliffe*. Cambridge: Harvard University Press, 1986.

Sandoz, Ellis, ed. *Political Sermons of the American Founding Era, 1730–1805*, 2nd ed. Indianapolis: Liberty Fund, 1998.

Sanford, Charles B. *The Religious Life of Thomas Jefferson*. Charlottesville: University Press of Virginia, 1987.

Sarna, Jonathan, Ellen Smith, and Scott-Martin Kosofsky, eds. *The Jews of Boston*. New Haven: Yale University Press, 2005.

Schlesinger, Arthur M. *Prelude to Independence: The Newspaper War on Britain, 1764–1776*. New York: Vintage, 1965; originally published, 1957.

Shipton, Clifford K. *Sibley's Harvard Graduates: Biographical Sketches of Those Who Attended Harvard College*. Boston: Massachusetts Historical Society, 1968.

Showman, Richard K., ed. *The Papers of General Nathanael Greene*. Chapel Hill: University of North Carolina Press, 1976–2005.

Silverman, Kenneth. *A Cultural History of the American Revolution*. New York: Columbia University Press, 1987; originally published, 1976.

Smith, Page. *Religious Origins of the American Revolution*. Missoula, Mont.: Scholars Press, 1976.

Stout, Harry S. *The Divine Dramatist: George Whitefield and the Rise of Modern Evangelism*. Grand Rapids: William B. Eerdmans, 1991.

———. *The New England Soul*. New York: Oxford University Press, 1988.

Tatum, Edward H. Jr., ed., *The American Journal of Ambrose Serle Secretary to Lord Howe, 1776–1778*. San Marino: Huntington Library, 1940.

Thomas, Isaiah. *The History of Printing in America*. Edited by Marcus A. McCorison from the 2nd ed. Barre, Mass.: Imprint Society, 1970.

Thornton, John Wingate. *The Pulpit of the American Revolution*. Boston: D. Lothrop & Co., 1876.

Tucker, Robert W., and David C. Hendrickson. *The Fall of the First British Empire: Origins of the War of American Independence.* Baltimore: Johns Hopkins University Press, 1982.

Turner, Charles. *A Sermon Preached Before His Excellency Thomas Hutchinson.* Boston: Richard Draper, 1773.

Warden, G. B. *Boston, 1689–1776.* Boston: Little, Brown, 1970.

Warren, Mercy Otis. *History of the Rise, Progress, and Termination of the American Revolution.* Indianapolis: Liberty Fund, 1994, originally published: 1805.

Wells, William V. *The Life and Public Services of Samuel Adams.* Boston: Little, Brown, 1866. (This three-volume work by Samuel Adams's great-grandson includes copies and transcripts of many original documents.)

Whitefield, George. *A Continuation of the Reverend Mr. Whitefield's Journal From Savannah, June 25, 1740, to his arrival at Rhode-Island, his travels in other Governments of New England, to his departure from Stanford for New-York.* Boston: Printed by G. Rogers, for J. Edwards and S. Eliot on Cornhill, 1741.

Whitmore, W. H., ed. *The Andros Tracts: Being a Collection of Pamphlets and Official Papers Issued During the Period Between the Overthrow of the Andros Government and the Establishment of the Second Charter of Massachusetts. Reprinted from the original editions and manuscripts. With notes and a memoir of Sir Edmund Andros.* Boston: Prince Society, 1868.

Williamson, William D. *The History of the State of Maine.* Hallowell, Maine: Glazier, Masters, 1832.

Wills, Garry. *Inventing America: Jefferson's Declaration of Independence.* New York: Doubleday, 1978.

Winsor, Justin. *The Memorial History of Boston.* Boston: Ticknor, 1880–1881.

Wood, Gordon. *The Americanization of Benjamin Franklin.* New York: Penguin, 2004.

Wroth, L. Kinvin, and Hiller B. Zobel, eds. *Legal Papers of John Adams.* New York: Atheneum, 1968. Originally published by Harvard University Press.

*Bibliography*

Young, Alfred F. *Liberty Tree: Ordinary People and the American Revolution*. New York: New York University Press, 2006.

Zobel, Hiller B. *The Boston Massacre*. New York: W. W. Norton, 1970.

## Articles

Bailyn, Bernard. "Religion and Revolution: Three Biographical Studies." *Perspectives in American History* 4 (1970).

Dellape, Kevin. "Jacob Duché: Whig-Loyalist?" *Pennsylvania History* 62 no. 3 (1995): 293–305.

Dirst, Tara, and Allan Kulikoff, "Was Benjamin Church a Traitor?" www.common-place.org, vol. 6, no. 1 (October 2005).

Gelernter, David. "Americanism—And Its Enemies." *Commentary*, January 2005.

Goodell, A. C., Jr. "Charges Against Samuel Adams." *Proceedings of the Massachusetts Historical Society* 20 (1883).

Louis, Elan D., MD. "Samuel Adams' Tremor." *Neurology* 56 (2000) 1201–5.

Louis, Elan D., and Patricia Kavanagh. "John Adams' Essential Tremor." *Movement Disorders* 20, no. 12 (December 2005): 1537–42.

Maier, Pauline. "Coming to Terms with Samuel Adams." *American Historical Review* 81, no. 1 (February 1976).

Miller, Perry. "From the Covenant to the Revival." In James Ward Smith and A. Leland Jamison, eds., *The Shaping of American Religion*. Princeton: Princeton University Press, 1961.

Moody, Robert E. "Samuel Ely: Forerunner of Shays." *New England Quarterly* 5, no. 1 (January 1932): 105–13.

Morgan, Edmund S. "The Puritan Ethic and the American Revolution," *William and Mary Quarterly*, 3rd Series, vol. 24, no. 1 (January 1967): 3–43.

Morison, Samuel Eliot. "Two 'Signers' on Salaries and the Stage, 1789." *Proceedings of the Massachusetts Historical Society* 62 (1928–1929).

Pencak, William. "Samuel Adams and Shays's Rebellion." *New England Quarterly* 62, no. 1 (March 1989).

Schlesinger, Arthur M. "The Liberty Tree: A Genealogy." *New England Quarterly* 25, no. 4 (December 1952): 435–58.

Shalev, Eran. "Dr. Warren's Ciceronian Toga: Performing Rebellion in Revolutionary Boston." www.common-place.org, vol. 7, no. 2 (January 2007).

Silver, Rollo G. "Benjamin Edes, Trumpeter of Sedition." *Papers of the Bibliographical Society of America* 47 (1953): 259.

Stout, Harry S. "Religion, Communications, and the Ideological Origins of the American Revolution." *William and Mary Quarterly*, 3rd Series, vol. 34, no. 4, (October 1977): 519–541.

Upton, L. F. S. "Proceedings of Ye Body Respecting the Tea." *William and Mary Quarterly*, 3rd Series, vol. 22, no. 2 (April 1965): 287–300.

Warren, Charles. "Samuel Adams and the Sans Souci Club." *Proceedings of the Massachusetts Historical Society* 60 (1927).

## Doctoral Dissertation

Seccombe, Matthew "From Revolution to Republic: Samuel Adams, 1774–1803." Ph.D. diss., Yale University, 1978.

## Newspapers

*American Herald*
*The Boston Chronicle*
*Boston Evening-Post*
*The Boston Gazette*
*The Boston News-Letter*
*Boston Post Boy*
*Continental Journal*
*Essex Journal*
*Independent Ledger*
*Massachusetts Centinel*
*Massachusetts Gazette*

*Massachusetts Spy*
*Pennsylvania Chronicle and Universal Advertiser*
*The Pennsylvania Ledger*
*The Pennsylvania Packet; and the General Advertiser*
[Rivington's New York] *Royal Gazette*
*Salem Gazette*

## Government Records

*A Report of the Record Commissioners of the City of Boston, Containing the Boston Town Records, 1778 to 1783.* Boston: Rockwell & Churchill, 1895.

*A Volume of Records Relating to the Early History of Boston, Containing Boston Town Records, 1784 to 1796.* Boston: Municipal Printing Office, 1903. These offer minutes of the Boston Town Meeting. I have referred to both these volumes in the end notes simply as Boston Town Records.

*Debates and Proceedings in the Convention of the Commonwealth of Massachusetts, Held in the Year 1788 and Which Finally Ratified the Constitution of the United States.* Boston: William White, Printer to the Commonwealth, 1856.

*Journal of the Convention for Framing a Constitution of Government for the State of Massachusetts Bay, From the Commencement of their First Session, September 1, 1779, to the close of their last session, June 16 1780, including a list of the members.* Boston: Dutton & Wentworth, Printers to the State, 1832.

*Journals of the House of Representatives of Massachusetts, Vol. 45–51.* Boston: Massachusetts Historical Society, 1976–1982. These volumes, with lucid and perceptive introductions by Malcolm Freiberg, contain the official records of the Massachusetts House of Representatives for the years 1768 to 1776.

*The Journals of Each Provincial Congress of Massachusetts in 1774 and 1775 and of the Committee of Safety, With an Appendix, Containing The Proceedings of the County Conventions, Narratives of the Events of the Nineteenth of April, 1775, Papers Relating to Ticonderoga and Crown Point, and Other Documents, Illustrative of the Early History of the Revolution.* Boston: Dutton & Wentworth, Printers to the State, 1838.

R. C. Simmons and P. D. G. Thomas, eds. *Proceedings and Debates of the British Parliaments Respecting North America, 1754–1783.* Vol. 4, January to May 1774; Volume 6, April 1775 to May 1776. White Plains, N.Y.: Kraus International Publications, 1982.

The Supreme Judicial Court of Massachusetts's decision in the same sex marriage case is *Goodridge v. Department of Public Health,* SJC-08860.

The Massachusetts Constitution as amended, with explanatory notes on the amendments, is online at http://www.mass.gov/legis/const.htm.

## Internet Resources

The past decade has seen an explosion of historical resources on the Internet, making it easier than ever to access the primary sources. Among the most useful are:

Gilder Lehrman Institute of American History. Displays images, transcripts, and summaries of dozens of documents by or bearing on Samuel Adams from the Gilder Lehrman Collection, which is on deposit at the New-York Historical Society. Accessible at http://www .gilderlehrman.org/collection/index.html.

Liberty Fund Online Library of Liberty. This site, at http://oll.libertyfund .org/, includes electronic copies of works by Cicero, John Locke, Thomas Paine, Mercy Otis Warren.

Library of Congress. The online edition of the *Journals of the Continental Congress, 1774–1789*, ed., Worthington C. Ford et al. Washington, D.C.: 1904–1937, http://memory.loc.gov/ammem/amlaw/lwjclink.html, is the one I used. Unless otherwise specified, my references to *Letters of Delegates to Congress* are to the online edition at the Library of Congress Web site: Paul H. Smith, ed., *Letters of Delegates to Congress, 1774–1789.* Washington: Library of Congress, 1976–2000, http://memory.loc.gov/ammem/amlaw/lwdglink.html. The Library of Congress Web site also hosts the papers of George Washington at http://memory.loc.gov/ammem/gwhtml/gwhome.html, and the papers of Thomas Jefferson at http://memory.loc.gov/ammem/collections/jeffersonpapers/index.html.

Massachusetts Historical Society. This hosts *Adams Family Papers: An Electronic Archive*, http://www.masshist.org/digitaladams/. It also hosts a fine online exhibit on the abolition of slavery in Massachusetts, http://www.masshist.org/endofslavery/.

New England Historic Genealogical Society. This site, http://www.new englandancestors.org/, allows members access to a database of early American newspapers. It also sometimes features interesting documents from the society's collections.

University of Virginia. The university library's etext center maintains online copies of the thirty-eight-volume *Writings of George Washington from the Original Manuscript Sources, 1745–1799*, ed., John C. Fitzpatrick, and published 1931–1944, at http://etext.virginia.edu/washington/fitzpatrick/. It also maintains an online copy of Aesop's *Fables*, http://etext.lib.virginia.edu/toc/modeng/public/AesFabl.html.

Yale University. The Avalon Project of the Lillian Goldman Law Library at Yale Law School collects and posts historical documents, including the text of Jay's Treaty between America and Great Britain, http://www.yale.edu/lawweb/avalon/diplomacy/britain/jay.htm, and of Jefferson's inaugural address, http://www.yale.edu/lawweb/avalon/presiden/inaug/jefinau1.htm.

Also deserving of mention is bookfinder.com, which, by aggregating the inventories of used bookstores, allowed me to collect many of the out-of-print works I consulted. Finally, the historian J. L. Bell writes an entertaining and lively Web log at http://www.boston1775.blogspot.com/, which he describes as "History, analysis, and unabashed gossip about the start of the American Revolution in Massachusetts." It was useful in pointing me to, among other things, the medical journal articles on the tremors of the Adamses. Other Web sites used are cited within the end notes.

# Index

# About the Author

IRA STOLL is vice president and managing editor of *The New York Sun*, which he helped to found. A graduate of Harvard, where he was president of *The Harvard Crimson,* Stoll has been a consultant to the editorial page of *The Wall Street Journal*, managing editor and Washington correspondent for the *Forward*, and a reporter for the *Los Angeles Times*. He lives in New York City.